Three Sons

AGM STUDIES

AVANT-GARDE & MODERNISM

Three Sons

Franz Kafka and the Fiction
of J. M. Coetzee, Philip Roth,
and W. G. Sebald

DANIEL L. MEDIN

Northwestern

University Press

Evanston

Illinois

Northwestern University Press
www.nupress.northwestern.edu

"Secretaries" and "Ars Poetica" from Czesław Miłosz, *The Collected Poems 1931–1987,* copyright © 1998 by Czesław Miłosz Royalties, Inc. Reprinted by permission of HarperCollins Publishers.

Printed in the United States of America

10 9 8 7 6 5 4 3 2 1

Library of Congress Cataloging-in-Publication Data
Medin, Daniel L.
    Three sons : Franz Kafka and the fiction of J.M. Coetzee, Philip Roth, and W.G. Sebald / Daniel L. Medin.
        p. cm. — (AGM studies)
    Includes bibliographical references and index.
    ISBN 978-0-8101-2567-4 (cloth : alk. paper)—ISBN 978-0-8101-2568-1 (pbk. : alk. paper) 1. Kafka, Franz, 1883–1924—Influence. 2. Coetzee, J. M., 1940- —Criticism and interpretation. 3. Sebald, Winfried Georg, 1944–2001—Criticism and interpretation. 4. Roth, Philip—Criticism and interpretation. 5. Fiction—20th century—History and criticism. I. Title. II. Series: Avant-garde and modernism studies.
    PT2621.A26Z7733 2010
    809.304—dc22

                                            2009028434

For my parents

Often I have felt like calling him back and asking him how things were going, why he cut himself off so from his father, and what he was basically after, but by now he is so remote and so much time has passed, now things had better just stay as they are.

—Franz Kafka, "Eleven Sons"

Contents

Acknowledgments

Many persons and institutions have supported this project since its inception. First and foremost I wish to thank my *Doktorvater*, Mike Lützeler. It is hard to imagine a more committed scholar, instructor, or supervisor. I feel fortunate to count myself among his academic progeny.

I offer my warm personal thanks to the following for sharing their knowledge (and in many cases, providing critical feedback about my own ideas): Mark Anderson, David Auerbach, Miriam Bailin, Bernard Banoun, Jillian Barber, Delphine Bechtel, Russell Berman, Susan Bernofsky, Harold Bloom, Michale Boganim, Frank Brunner, Stanley Corngold, Alec Dill, Márton Dornbach, Margo Drakos, Jon Eastwood, Bernhard Echte, Dan Edelstein, Amir Eshel, John Felstiner, Jessie Ferguson, Wayne Fields, Xavier Galmiche, Katja Garloff, William Gass, Mark Gelber, Sander Gilman, Laura Greengold, María Guðmundsdóttir, Dan Gunn, Mark Harman, Robert Harrison, Robert Hegel, Michael Hulse, Dalia Inbal, Gerald Izenberg, Paul Kerschen, Hillel Kieval, Marshall Klimasewiski, Hans-Gerd Koch, Lutz Koepnick, Joshua Landy, Naomi Lebowitz, Stefanie Leuenberger, Cornelius Ludwig, Marina MacKay, Karen Medin, Leemore Medin, Winfried Menninghaus, David Pan, Ruth Pawel, Delphine Regnauld, Derek Parker Royal, Eric Santner, Galili Shahar, Maria Snyder, Roberta Vassallo, Klaus Wagenbach, Hannah Wirth-Nesher, James Wood, and Nicole Zdeb. I have benefited, too, from the contributions of students who attended my seminars at Washington University in St. Louis and at Stanford University.

This book was researched, written, and revised with the generous assistance of the DAAD (German Academic Exchange Service), the Graduate School of Arts and Sciences at Washington University, the Alexander von Humboldt Foundation, and a Mellon Foundation research leave (supported by the Introduction to the Humanities program at Stanford University). I am indebted to my hosts at the Technical University of Berlin, Norbert Miller and Hans Dieter Zimmermann, as well as to Johannes Birkenmeier, Teresa Künle, and Susan Neiman for helping to facilitate my stays abroad. I wish to thank Heather Antti, Henry Carrigan Jr., Jenny Gavacs, Paul Mendelson, Rainer Rumold, and others at Northwestern University Press for their careful appraisals of the manuscript. Earlier versions of "Lovely Lies?" and "Almost Grounded in Fact" appeared, respectively, in *Comparative Literature Studies* 44, no. 1–2 (2007) and *Über*

Gegenwartsliteratur: Interpretationen und Interventionen, edited by Mark W. Rectanus (Bielefeld, Ger.: Aisthesis Verlag, 2008). The Houghton Library at Harvard University kindly gave its permission to publish excerpts of material from the Winfried Georg Sebald papers.

I am particularly grateful to my anonymous readers for their judicious critiques of the manuscript, and to Jenny Blair, who provided invaluable comments and suggestions for improvement.

Patrice Gullaud accompanied this book from its beginnings, and enriched it with his own attentive readings: *C'est là ce que nous avons eu de meilleur.*

Three Sons

Introduction

The Postwar Legacy of Franz Kafka

In 1947 Edmund Wilson published an article called "A Dissenting Opinion on Kafka" in the *New Yorker*. His purpose was to rebut W. H. Auden's claim, published some six years before and popular with New York and Paris intellectuals, that the war had elevated Franz Kafka's status to that of "the artist who comes nearest to bearing the same kind of relation to our age that Dante, Shakespeare, and Goethe bore to theirs."[1]

For at least a decade after Berlin's capitulation in 1945, Kafka was the rage. A mania for his fiction spread like wildfire across the European and American continents. His posthumously published novels[2] and collected tales[3] became objects of fascination to the era's most prominent minds, among them Albert Camus and Jean-Paul Sartre. The fact that so many of these figures were affiliated—in name if not in spirit—with another fashion of the age, French existentialism, helped to further disseminate the already widespread interest in Kafka's work.

Wilson acknowledges that the zeitgeist he himself identifies with, the view of history as unmitigated progress that dominated the nineteenth century, has probably passed. What he contests is not Kafka's relevance to the spirit of the time but his rapid election to the canon on the basis of a few unfinished manuscripts. "To compare Kafka . . . with Joyce and Proust and even with Dante," he objects, "great naturalists of personality, great organizers of human experience, is obviously quite absurd."[4]

3

In Wilson's view, Kafka's fragments—though noteworthy for their portrayals of "the manias of neurotic states" in luminous detail—have no place alongside masterworks whose legacies to future generations of readers offer, at the very least, a higher bar of formal perfection. Compared to *Ulysses* and *In Search of Lost Time,* Wilson suggests, *The Trial* and *The Castle* come across as "ragged performances" sorely lacking the "consistent progression" maintained by other major works of modernism. Wilson is also irritated by Kafka's unrelenting skepticism, and especially by the admiration of contemporaries for the religious tone of his work, one that he fails to detect. "What today's readers stand to inherit from Kafka," he concludes, "is the half-expressed gasp of a self-doubting soul trampled under. I do not see how one can possibly take him for either a great artist or a moral guide."[5]

That Kafka's work survived this challenge is a testament to the way in which classics surmount controversy, according to J. M. Coetzee in a 1991 essay. (Though to deem "A Dissenting Opinion on Kafka" a *challenge* may be generous, since Wilson's complaint left hardly a crease in the idolatrous trend of reception common at the time. The battle over Kafka's canonization was fiercer by far in German-speaking countries.) The paradox of criticism, Coetzee writes, is that "the classic defines itself by surviving. Therefore the interrogation of the classic, no matter how hostile, is part of the history of the classic, inevitable and even to be welcomed. For as long as the classic needs to be protected from attack, it can never prove itself classic."[6]

In the next half-century, the harshest denunciations of Kafka were launched not by critics fatigued by his modishness, but by authorities in the Eastern bloc who branded his fiction decadent—a desecration of the principles of socialist realism (where people do not turn into insects) and an example of bourgeois malaise.[7] Yet his popularity in those countries grew. Although public thinkers like Theodor W. Adorno and Hannah Arendt were quick to deflect orthodox socialists' charges, Kafka's most effective advocates were those who truly, to paraphrase Coetzee, *could not afford* to let him go. He became, for example, the unlikely hero of Czech writers during the Soviet occupation who, as Philip Roth noted, blithely misrepresented his work in order to mine it for comic, symbolic, and spiritual inspiration.[8]

To recapitulate the history of Kafka's reception in the West since Auden and Wilson is beyond the scope of this book. What I wish to stress here is the *international* aspect of this postwar breakthrough.[9] When Kafka's readership began to expand during the mid- to late 1940s, it did so predominantly through translations from the German. In other words, fictions like "The Metamorphosis" and *The Trial* were, from the start, inheritances of *Weltliteratur,* gifts to posterity that had to circumnavigate the globe before finding a broader audience in Germany and Austria. In a paragraph contributed to an article on Samuel Beckett's importance for contemporary writers, Don DeLillo suggests why these works have had such a lasting effect on such a broad audience:

> Beckett is a master of language. He is all language. Out of the words come the people instead of the other way around. He is the last writer whose work extends into the world so that (as with Kafka before him) we can see or hear something and identify it as an expression of Beckett beyond the book or stage.[10]

Hence the widespread currency of that unwieldy modifier, "Kafkaesque," and its frequent application to phenomena (e.g., filing a legal petition, receiving false directions, being arrested without warrant or explanation) that, on the surface at least, have nothing whatsoever to do with literature.

Another token of Kafka's classic status—his "universalism," as Harold Bloom puts it, "in and for our century"—is that he inspired many other authors of consequence.[11] He has emerged over the past half-century as the unlikely father to successive generations of literary disciples, a line whose range extends far beyond the German-speaking world. Many of these sons and daughters—from Borges and Schulz to Ishiguro and Kundera—have become prominent within their own national literary traditions. This, as with Sartre and Camus after the war, only helped to magnify Kafka's influence.[12]

In the winter of 2003, the German monthly *Literaturen* devoted a special issue to the topic of Kafka's literary paternity. Entitled "Kafka and His Children," it featured interviews with and articles by contemporary writers on the subject of his "fatherhood." Though the mode of admiration for some is identification—Hans-Ulrich Treichel speaks incessantly of "my Kafka," while Ilse Aichinger superimposes passages from *The Man Who Disappeared* (*Amerika*) against a personal history of Austrian relatives murdered, "like Kafka's three sisters," during the Holocaust—other authors temper their enthusiasm with signs of mild ambivalence. Imre Kertész came to Kafka late because the latter's books were unavailable in Hungary while he was growing up. He suggests that this circumstance of history might well have been fortunate for his writing: "My primary literary experiences were Camus and Mann. Had I read Kafka from the beginning, I do not know whether I would have been able to write, whether he would have endangered my writing from the start. Kafka can paralyze a writer."[13]

Evidence of a widespread paralysis of the sort Kertész depicts is actually scant. On the contrary, the proliferation of writings by writers about Kafka has scarcely let up over the past five decades. But ambivalence recurs in these articles frequently enough. To consider a recent example: the American novelist Jonathan Lethem remembers—or misremembers (see note 14 below)—his own reservations about *The Castle* in a review of Robert Calasso's *K.* published May 1, 2005, in the *New York Times Book Review*. His critique distinctly resembles Edmund Wilson's point of contention in "A Dissenting Opinion": "I couldn't accept," Lethem recalls,

> that Kafka's novel *The Castle* had no ending. Nobody warned me—I wasn't reading Kafka for a class, but had taken him from the school library, driven by the same erratic booklust that had driven me that same year through volumes of Priestley, Camus and Allen Drury—and when I got to the last page, which ends midsentence, I felt betrayed. This was meant to be one of the century's greatest writers' greatest novels, and he couldn't even finish it?[14]

In any case, Lethem continues, a first reading of Kafka is likely to beget a lifetime of rereading. Fragmentary though they may be, his fictions, letters, and diaries compel countless attentive returns. Thomas Bernhard renders this aspect of the work finely in his novel *Extinction,* when the protagonist Franz-Josef Murau observes his increased enthusiasm for *The Trial* upon reading it a second time: "There are writers," Murau tells his pupil Gambetti,

> who fascinate the reader, when he reads them for a second time, to an extent far greater than the first, this always happens to me with Kafka. I remember Kafka as a great writer . . . but while reading him again I was completely convinced of reading an even greater one. Not many writers become more important, more magnificent upon a second reading, we read most a second time and feel ashamed for having read them once, and so it goes with us for hundreds of writers, but not for Kafka.[15]

The three "sons" examined in the following pages, Philip Roth, W. G. Sebald, and J. M. Coetzee, have all revisited Kafka in this fashion, that is, *regularly,* over a period of at least thirty years. In my separate studies of their fiction, I try to demonstrate the incarnation of his influence—and other signs of Kafka's literary paternity—in novels I deem representative of their encounter with his legacy: Roth's *Zuckerman Bound* (1979–85); Sebald's *Schwindel. Gefühle/ Vertigo* (1991/2000); and Coetzee's *Elizabeth Costello* (2003). Before discussing my approach in closer detail, however, a few words on the "anxiety of influence" and its founding theorist will be in order.

Harold Bloom and the Poetics of Influence

The Anxiety of Influence was published in 1973 and reprinted seventeen times before being replaced by a second edition twenty-four years later. At the time of its appearance Bloom had already established himself as a seminal thinker in the field of English Romanticism; *Anxiety* elevated the author's visibility and exposed him to a larger and less specialized audience. More significantly, it determined the trajectory his scholarship would take over the decades to come. "When *A Map of Misreading* appeared in 1975," Bloom confesses in a recent preface, "I hoped it was a final statement of my concerns with the enigma of poetic influence and its anxieties. But I have been thinking through this intricate matter ever since, and doubtless I will end before my meditation does."[16]

While Bloom has revised certain aspects of his poetics from volume to volume, his core premise has changed little since that opening salvo. James Wood, perhaps the most influential Anglophone critic at the moment (and in this respect, heir to a position long held by Bloom), encapsulates it smartly in his review of Bloom's *Shakespeare: The Invention of the Human:*

> In Bloom's battle of the generations, the younger poet must struggle with the poetic ancestor who most influences him or her. The struggle must not be immediately apparent—and, indeed, must be acknowledged or even resisted. But the repressed must always return, and the traces of the struggle can be detected, in part because the strong precursor has always modified—has always imprinted—the younger heir. All poets, says Bloom, "misread" (that is, read selfishly, anxiously, and for their own purposes) their predecessors; sometimes they "strongly" misread them and throw them over (as Shakespeare threw over Marlowe); sometimes they only "weakly" misread them and palely mimic them (as

Arnold failed to oust Wordsworth). In either case, strong or weak, the younger writer is modified powerfully by the older, whether he knows it or not.[17]

Strong readings take precedence in Bloom's corpus, as does the process by which post-Enlightenment poets take arms against the priority of their forebears, sometimes denying them (as in Wallace Stevens's disavowal of Walt Whitman) but inevitably to some extent distorting and misrepresenting them.

The Anxiety of Influence is not a theory in the systematic sense of the word, despite its "six revisionary ratios" and its proposal of ideas developed further in *A Map of Misreading, Kabbalah and Criticism,* and other works. The book is heuristic and declamatory, and does not shy away from confessing its highly autobiographical project. Bloom insists all the while that he is working toward what he calls "a practical criticism"; hence his 1976 assertion that the "systematic . . . mapping of the poet's defences" in *The Anxiety of Influence* and beyond could be put to use as a "machine for criticism."[18]

And yet these "maps of misprision" have found scant application in subsequent critical literature, in all likelihood because they, like the Law in Kafka's parable, are meant for Bloom alone. In part this must be due to their highly figurative nature. Bloom's remark about a particular Kierkegaardian conceit helps illlustrate this: "I haven't ever encountered a useful discursive summary of Kierkegaard's notion, and I myself won't try to provide one, because Kierkegaard's idea of repetition is more trope than concept, and tends to defeat discursiveness."[19]

Bloom concedes just as much in an essay about two poems by John Ashbery ("Wet Casements" and "Tapestry") published the same year (1982), announcing that he will "read *Tapestry* rather strictly on the High Romantic crisis-poem model of six revisionary ratios, that is to say, by a kind of criticism overtly canonical and antithetical, a poor thing doubtless but my own."[20]

The Anxiety of Influence stresses a particular kind of agonistic relation between poets and their forebears, one that draws heavily on the language of psychoanalysis. No attentive reader, then, could have been surprised that within a few years of its publication Bloom would identify the "Oedipal interpretation of poetic history . . . the usual misunderstanding that my own work provokes."[21] In a new preface composed on the occasion of *Anxiety*'s reprinting, Bloom explains:

I never meant by "the anxiety of influence" a Freudian Oedipal rivalry, despite a rhetorical flourish or two in this book. . . . Influence anxiety does not so much concern the forerunner but rather is an anxiety achieved in and by the story, novel, play, poem, or essay. The anxiety may or may not be internalized by the later writer, depending upon temperament and circumstances, yet that hardly matters: the strong poem is the achieved anxiety. "Influence" is a metaphor, one that implicates a matrix of relationships—imagistic, temporal, spiritual, psychological— all of them ultimately defensive in their nature.[22]

I cannot read this passage without recalling Freud's essay on negation, another intricate evasion of fallibility whose model Bloom invokes with relish several times in his critical writings. A quick review of these "rhetorical flourishes" in *The Anxiety of Influence* and a few later works will no doubt clarify the general inclination to view his interpretations as Oedipally inclined.

The greatest challenge faced by every modern poet, according to *Anxiety*, is that of his own belatedness as an author. This condition engenders ambivalent feelings toward prior models; hence the agonistic stance of the aspiring successor, who, oblivious to the absurdity of the task, challenges the anteriority of his forerunner: "Every major aesthetic consciousness," writes Bloom, "seems peculiarly more gifted at denying obligation as the hungry generations go on treading one another down."[23] The decisively competitive nature of this rivalry and the later writer's denials of his own indebtedness are rife with *Freudian* Freudian (as opposed to *Francophone* Freudian) implications—a relation the author fails to discourage when he asserts, for example, that "in this book . . . I center upon intra-poetic relationships as parallels of family romance."[24] The encounter between precursor and successor, he affirms, is nothing less than a "battle between strong equals, father and son as mighty opposites, Laius and Oedipus at the crossroads; only this is my subject here, though some of the fathers, as will be seen, are composite figures."[25]

When poets appropriate, Bloom argues, it is never a painless act. To mark himself off from those who came before, the aspiring "ephebe" relies on defensive psychic maneuvers to repress and scramble evidence of indebtedness to a forebear. "Poetry when it aspires to strength," Bloom asserts, "is necessarily a competitive mode, indeed an obsessive mode, because poetic strength involves self-representation that is reached *only through trespass,* through crossing a daemonic threshold" (my italics).[26]

This violation can best be witnessed through the ephebe's misreadings—his "misprision"—of prior texts. There is no place in "strong poetry," according to Bloom, for benign misprision; the work in question and the subsequent representation of the precursor undergo "a violent narcissistic metamorphosis" in the resulting product.[27] In his Charles Eliot Norton lectures of 1987–88, Bloom poses the question of whether such aggressive recourse to one's antecedents is truly unavoidable:

> Can you "correct" a precursor poet without savagely caricaturing him? Is there really a sense in which one strong poem can fulfill or complete a poem of the same eminence by another poet who comes earlier? All strong poets . . . must ruin the sacred truths to fable and old song, precisely because the essential condition for poetic strength is that the new song, one's own, always must be a song of one's self. . . . Every sacred truth not one's own becomes a fable, an old song that requires corrective vision.[28]

And yet any close examination of authorial ambivalence that encompasses the history of canonical Western literature will inevitably reveal a variety of manifestations. Bloom's insistence that "revisionism . . . unfolds itself *only in fighting*" exaggerates the nature of ambivalence rather reductively. Ambivalence is a state where antithetical inclinations, favorable and unfavorable, coexist in infinite combinations of proportion and are constantly in flux.[29] The antithetical inclinations are not necessarily symptoms of anxiety generated by priority alone. Though Bloom denies the association, the rivalry depicted in *The Anxiety of Influence* and later writings *is* Oedipal. And while the tensions he depicts are certainly present in many confrontations—this study alone will offer numerous instances of verification—Bloom's fixation upon rivalry and competition fails to account for subtler, even reverent, effects of influence.

Notes on Methodology, or Questions of Travel

In "*Apophrades* or The Return of the Dead," Bloom's chapter on the last of his six "revisionary ratios," the author declares that "strong poets keep returning from the dead, and only through the quasi-willing mediumship of other strong poets. *How* they return is the decisive matter."[30] This study takes as its goal the close analysis of precisely how they return—the manner in which three contemporary "sons," all of them writers of eminence emerging from different national literatures, invoke and evoke Kafka's life and work in their own. I am particularly interested in exploring Kafka's influence on their stylistic development and choice of symbolic imagery. I will also probe modifications in their approach to Kafka (or, when applicable, their resistance to change) over a span of three decades, speculating on the significance of such adjustments for their oeuvre.

Above all I am curious about modes and aspects of appropriation, formal as well as ethical—the strains of ambivalence, as it were. I strongly contest Bloom's postulation that "there is no difference between the act of quoting with a favorable or with an unfavorable intention."[31] As such, I have endeavored to distinguish between what I take to be two opposing methods of appropriation: those bent, Bloom-like, on usurpation through imitative violence and those that pursue misreadings with greater reverence, aspiring to stand alongside or in the company of an antecedent rather than above him.

In literature as in life, a moral parameter marks the lies we tell—the stories we invent for, and then assign to, others. An example of the first method would be Dante's treatment of Brunetto Latini in the *Inferno*— his inexplicable placement of a former teacher and eminent scholar in the circle of hell reserved for sodomists. (No evidence beyond the *Commedia* exists to substantiate this claim.) All fictionalization requires, of course, some degree of invention. But surely we ought to distinguish between the aggressive, even destructive redefinition of another on the one hand as in the above instance, and Robert Walser's affectionate fantasies of Kleist in Thun or Goethe in Rome or Verlaine in Paris, all examples of the second model.

The American romancer Philip Roth gained an international reputation with *Portnoy's Complaint,* a novel he later claimed was indebted to Kafka for its comic obsession with guilt. His misprisions of Kafka during the late 1960s and early 1970s teem with manic humor and cling unabashedly to sexual themes. In works like "I Always Wanted You to Admire My Fasting," a distinct self-portrait emerges from an ostensible analysis of Kafka. Over the course of a decade, however, Roth's methods and his understanding of this author underwent a marked change. His annual sojourns to Prague gave him a deeper understanding of the conflict faced by Kafka's generation of secular, German-speaking Jews. *Zuckerman Bound,* Roth's trilogy and epilogue, expresses this complex historical understanding. The arc of his relation to Kafka from *Portnoy* to the present matches the stages of limitation, substitution, and *re*presentation stressed by Bloom more closely than any of the writers discussed in this study.

Similarly, W. G. Sebald's critical essays and his first novel, *Schwindel. Gefühle* (revised and translated as *Vertigo* a decade later), adopt a pose of genuine admiration while working aggressively to redefine—and in this respect, undermine—Kafka's fiction and biography through misrepresentation. The result of these projections is a "Franz Kafka" who, in his melancholy paralysis and moribund fixation with death, comes much closer to resembling "W. G. Sebald," protagonist and first-person narrator of *The Emigrants* and other longer fictions. Sebald's mode of rewriting belongs to the first category mentioned above, that of aggressive displacement. His approach to Kafka and other literary antecedents like Walser, Stendhal, and Shakespeare remained much the same from the time of his critical writings in the early 1970s through *Austerlitz* and the more overtly autobiographical essays posthumously gathered in *Campo Santo*.[32]

Kafka's impress can be detected throughout J. M. Coetzee's corpus, though always accompanied by a restraint absent from the appropriations of Sebald and the young Roth. Born in South Africa in 1940, Coetzee began writing fiction at age twenty-nine, a year after completing his dissertation on Samuel Beckett and receiving his Ph.D. from the University of Texas at Austin. His novels integrate what could be called Kafka's interpretive elusiveness. They also mimic his overlapping senses of time and his fondness for parabolic interpolations. His 2003 fiction *Elizabeth Costello* uses Kafka's stories "A Report to an Academy" and "Before the Law" to plumb topics that have engaged him since the beginning of his career: the mechanics of power, the creatureliness of humans, and late twentieth-century poetic belatedness.

My readings of these three disciples detect extraordinarily diverse attitudes toward Kafka's influence. I have made it a point to distinguish between the different grades of competitive jousting—between instances of forceful usurpation on the one hand and those that fall under the rubric of what Robert Walser calls, in a turn-of-the-century feuilleton inspired by the life of the Romantic poet Clemens Brentano, "lovely lies." The most effective method for revealing these qualities is that of juxtaposition. For this reason I have found W. J. Dodd's remarks on the subject, cited below from his study of Dostoevsky's impact on Kafka, extraordinarily helpful. "I take it as axiomatic," Dodd writes,

that influence is a variant of coincidence, occurring when there is a fruitful meeting of minds, and that influence presupposes affinity of some
kind. . . . There are occasions when the more tentative vocabulary of
"affinity" is appropriate. It is also important to remember that minds
do not always meet in agreement, and that influence can take extremely
productive antagonistic forms, even when there is also a strong vein of
sympathy and admiration. . . . If . . . Kafka borrowed images, scenarios, even much of the ground-plan of a novel from Dostoyevsky, then
merely pointing out the parallels . . . misses the point that *where borrow-
ing is discernible, it is the differences within the parallels that are particularly interesting.* [My italics][33]

I have also found Harold Bloom's concept of *clinamen*—the first of six
"revisionary ratios" proposed in *The Anxiety of Influence*—useful for understanding the transformative dynamic that governs every reading experience. I reproduce his definition more or less in full:

Clinamen . . . is poetic misreading or misprision proper; I take the word
from Lucretius, where it means a "swerve" of the atoms so as to make
change possible in the universe. A poet swerves away from his precursor,
by so reading his precursor's poem as to execute a *clinamen* in relation
to it. This appears as a corrective movement in his own poem, which
implies that the precursor poem went accurately up to a certain point,
but then should have swerved, precisely in the direction that the new
poem moves.[34]

It is this movement *away* from the original that I locate at the center of
my analyses.

In the sections that follow I attempt to chart the distance between what
Kafka wrote and what his "three sons" in their fictions and in their essays
imply, suggest, and claim that he wrote. The difference, I argue, lies in the
difference—that is, by subtracting the original passage from the successor's representation of it and scrutinizing what remains. As such, I have
purposely chosen to focus on primary literary sources and to devote particular attention to the reading histories of each of my authors. Fathers and
sons share, after all, a common lineage—what Kafka refers to, in a letter to
Felice, as a *Blutverwandtschaft*, or "blood relation."[35] A critic unacquainted
with this material will invariably miss its atavistic returns to the subject's
fiction.

A recent full-length study of J. M. Coetzee's body of work cites twenty-two texts by Jacques Derrida and one each by Dostoevsky and Kafka in its bibliography. This would be no cause for alarm were this ratio not so discouragingly typical of current scholarship on Coetzee and Sebald (and to a lesser extent, Roth)—authors for whom immersion in others' fiction has always been crucial to the creation of their own. To write literature is, in Kafka's words, to be made of it; it surely merits our critical attention no less than, say, Lacan has for Coetzee or trauma theory for Sebald.

In my readings of these three contemporary authors, I have made every attempt to follow the instruction offered by Goethe in a section devoted to the "better understanding" of his *West-Eastern Divan:*

> If you want to understand the writing of poems,
> You must go to the land of poetry;
> If you want to understand the poet,
> You must go to the poet's land.[36]

Goethe's epigraph represents this quest both literally and figuratively. The voyage to the poet's country may entail a physical journey, as is implied by J. M. Coetzee's use of the motto for the second volume of his memoirs. *Youth* recounts an aspiring writer's arrival in London—the city its protagonist associates with authors after whom he wishes to shape his own future oeuvre (T. S. Eliot, Ezra Pound, and Ford Madox Ford).

"And yet it is precisely the laconic quality of this saying," observe the editors of the Munich edition of Goethe's *Divan,* "that preserves its ambiguity":

> The assertion *If you want to understand the writing of poems, / You must go to the land of poetry* implies a conscious turning away from the reality of practical life and entrance into a realm in which only the power of the imagination and the laws of literary tradition hold sway.[37]

To study the effects of Kafka's authority on later generations of authors (his literary paternity), I have privileged this convergence of literary landscapes with the imagination.

Therefore all my published works are but fragments of one great confession, which this little book is a bold attempt to complete.

—Goethe, *Poetry and Truth*

1. Kafka's Hovering Trope

Between January and February 1920, Franz Kafka composed a cycle of meditative aphorisms in his journal. Max Brod, arranging them for publication many years later, titled the sequence "He," after the pronoun that begins several of these unusually autobiographical entries. Kafka's use of a third-person pronoun for an expressly first-person narrative recalls the pronoun-shifting that marked the making of his best-known works. (While writing the execution scene in *The Trial*, Kafka accidentally substituted an "I" for "Josef K."; he started *The Castle* as a narrative in the first person but switched to the third after the narrator's sexual encounter with Frieda—and then went back to replace every previous "I" with a "K.") This maneuver, however, was not exclusive to the longer fictions. It recurs often in his diaries and, surprisingly, even in his letters—particularly those addressed to Felice Bauer during the years of their engagement.[1]

Hartmut Binder has identified "He" as the author's attempt to grapple with the turmoil of a life in crisis.[2] Only a few months before, Kafka had abandoned his second attempt to start a family by breaking off his engagement to Julie Wohryzek. Like his monumental and carefully designed *Letter to His Father*, these autobiographical entries constitute an attempt to take stock. Some of the aphorisms dating from this period constitute self-analysis; others are more inventive. Narrative voices overlap in a manner strikingly similar to Philip Roth's use of free indirect speech in *Sabbath's Theater*, described here by Ross Posnock:

Often the narrative voice when inside Sabbath's mind shifts almost seamlessly from "he" to "I" (whereas conventional free indirect discourse retains a third-person narrator who mimes first-person thoughts and feelings). The relation of third and first person could be described as collaborative, a not inappropriate word given that Sabbath describes his lovers as collaborators.[3]

In similar fashion, the "he" of Kafka's entries, as Klaus Wagenbach observes, "is clearly developed from an *I* in certain passages, or blended into one."[4]

Kafka never fulfilled his "desire to write an autobiography" in a conventional way, but his lifelong defiance of traditional generic perimeters meant that much of his work can be read that way.[5] "Kafka's radical inversion of the writing process," Mark Anderson has noted of the author's imbrication of forms, "calls into question the distinction between life and work."[6] Every volume of the critical edition of his whole oeuvre is replete with "fragments of a great confession"—pieces, in Robert Walser's marvelous formulation, from a "cut up or disjointed book of the self."[7]

Kafka lays out his strategy for fusing poetry and truth in an early, first-person entry from "He":

> It is a question of the following: One day many years ago I was sitting, sorrowfully enough to be sure, on the slopes of the Laurenziberg. I was examining the wishes that I had for my life. What emerged as the most important or the most attractive was the wish to gain a view of life (and—this is certainly a necessary part of it—to be able to convince others of it in writing), in which life, while still retaining its natural, full-bodied rise and fall, would simultaneously be recognized no less clearly as a nothing, as a dream, as a hovering. A beautiful wish, perhaps, if I had wished it rightly. If it had been, say, like the wish to hammer a table together with painfully accurate craftsmanship, and simultaneously to do nothing, and moreover not so that people could say: "Hammering is nothing to him," but rather "Hammering is to him a real hammering, and at the same time it is nothing," whereby indeed the hammering would have become bolder, still more determined, still more real, and, if you will, more insane.[8]

The paragraph continues by performing a third-person "hovering":

But he could not wish in this fashion, for his wish was no wish, it was merely a defense, a domestication of nothingness, a touch of animation that he wanted to give to nothingness, to that empty space in which he had by then scarcely taken his first conscious steps, but which he already felt as his element. It was at that time a sort of farewell that he took from the illusory world of youth; although youth had never directly deceived him, but only caused him to be deceived by the speeches of all the authorities around him. Thus had the necessity of his "wish" arisen.

Kafka deems this a defining moment in his life, not only because he views it as "[a] sort of farewell . . . from the illusory world of youth," but because it articulates the effect he wishes to accomplish through his prose.[9]

The lucid but evasive quality of Kafka's writing—its dreamlike precision—has long intrigued critics and subsequent authors. The conceit of *Schweben* (hovering) featured in this excerpt is a particularly apt image of a writer whose work has come to mean so many different things to different readers. Kafka deploys the figure to render states of indeterminacy or vacillation between opposing poles—between tradition and modernity; the autonomous individual and his community; the psychic and somatic; German national identity and Czech; Western and Eastern Jewishness; and so on. In each case, he apprehends, like the aphorisms' speaker, "two antagonists; the first presses him from behind, from his origins, the second bars his road ahead. He struggles with both."[10] The tension cannot be resolved. Kafka's protagonists—the man from the country seeking entry to the law, the messenger bearing news from a dead emperor, the land surveyor K. with his vague, undisclosed mission—never reach their respective destinations. Each hovers perpetually at a threshold, his goal just out of reach.

The Impossibility of Writing in German

My life consists, and basically always has consisted, of attempts at writing, mostly unsuccessful. But when I didn't write, I was at once flat on the floor [*dann lag ich auch schon auf dem Boden*], fit for the dustbin.
—Franz Kafka, letter to Felice Bauer, November 1, 1912

Shortly after completing "He," Kafka, recuperating in Meran from a bout of tuberculosis, told his friends an anecdote of a "completely German-Christian" general installed at the same sanatorium. The officer cannot place Kafka's accent, though he concedes its Austrian color. One thing is certain, however: this tubercular Jew is no German. Upon learning of Kafka's Prague origins, the general asks whether he is Czech—then replies to his own question at once, in the negative. "So now explain," Kafka writes in his epistolary restaging of the event, "to those true German military eyes what you really are."[11]

Introducing a volume of essays on Kafka and Judaism, Hans Dieter Zimmermann long ago asserted that those unfamiliar with Jewish traditions and literature would necessarily miss its presence in his work.[12] The same holds true for Kafka's historical quandary; *The Trial* and "In the Penal Colony" owe a great deal, after all, to the First World War, which helped engender them. And while such connections may appear oblique in his fiction, Kafka's journals and letters confront the turbulent era headlong. They confirm his absorption of then-current anti-Semitic discourse, and document his readiness to exploit that language to launch rhetorical assaults against himself. For these and other reasons, it is important to consider the environment that shaped him.

Approximately 450,000 people lived in Prague in 1900, the majority (415,000, or 90 percent) of them Czech. At 34,000 souls, Germans constituted the second-largest population (5–6 percent). Croatians, Hungarians, and Jews filled in the remaining 3–4 percent. "The Jews of Prague were a small group," notes Ritchie Robertson:

> Though some had Czech as their native language, the majority spoke German and probably formed between a third and a half of the city's German-speaking community. Official statistics indicate that the number of German speakers dwindled from 38,591 in 1880 to 32,332 in 1910, so that they represented an ever-decreasing fraction of the city's total population.[13]

The census reporting this data was a concession to Czechs, aimed to enlist their support for the Austro-Hungarian *Ausgleich's* (Compromise's) decennial renewal. As national consciousness spread throughout Bohemia, hostility between militant Czechs and Germans increased, erupting time and again into violence. As a common enemy of those two ethnic groups, the Jewish community in Prague was especially vulnerable. Mark Twain reported from the scene in late November 1897 after witnessing the removal by force of a group of obstreperous parliamentarians from the House in Vienna. (They had been protesting the passing of the Falkenhayn ordinances, which provided linguistic concessions to Czechs in order to ensure the Compromise's survival—a maneuver that outraged German nationalists and socialists alike.)

The Badeni government came down with a crash; there was a popular outbreak or two in Vienna; there were three or four days of furious rioting in Prague, followed by the establishing there of martial law; the Jews and Germans were harried and plundered, and their houses destroyed; in other Bohemian towns there was rioting—in some cases the Germans being the rioters, in others the Czechs—and in all cases the Jew had to roast, no matter which side he was on.[14]

"If I had time to run around and talk," wrote Twain to Joe Twichell a few months earlier,

I would do it; for there is much politics agoing, and it would be interesting if a body could get the hang of it. It is Christian and Jew by the horns—the advantage with the superior man, as usual—the superior man being the Jew every time and in all countries. Land, Joe, what chance would the Christians have in a country where there were 3 Jews to 10 Christians! Oh, not the shade of a shadow of a chance. The difference between the brain of the average Christian and that of the average Jew—certainly in Europe—is about the difference between a tadpole's and an Archbishop's. It's a marvelous race—by long odds the most marvelous that the world has produced, I suppose. And there's more politics—the clash between the Czechs and the Austrian. I wish I could understand these quarrels, but of course I can't.[15]

The prominent Zionist Theodor Herzl published "Vanished Times" that same year, in 1897. The essay included a joke that evokes the very scenario depicted by Twain:

In this anecdote two coachmen meet on a narrow path. Neither will make way for the other, and in each coach sits a Jew. The first coachman snaps his whip at the other man's passenger: "[If] you beat my Jew, I'll beat yours!" But in Bohemia they would also add: "and my own too!" So the Bohemian Jews receive two beatings for a single ride. Granted, they were the ones attempting to pass through a national conflict as stowaways.[16]

Unlike the Galician refugees who streamed into central Europe after the outbreak of war in 1914, Prague Jews did not on the whole define themselves by their religious culture. On the contrary, middle-class families like Kafka's were mainly secular, their primary loyalty being to German language and *Kultur.*

And yet complete integration was nearly impossible, for even those who converted. Successful Jews continued to encounter resistance at the threshold of public approbation. Pointing to Sigmund Freud's deferred promotion to professor in Vienna, Peter Gay avers that "the anti-Semitism of the 1890s was more virulent, more open than the anti-Semitism of the 1870s."[17] Robert Musil captured this trend in *The Man Without Qualities* when he described Klementine Fischel's experience of intermarriage:

> As matters stood then, she almost felt there was something particularly refined in rising above the crude anti-Semitic prejudice of the common people. Later the poor woman was destined to see a nationalist spirit welling up all over Europe, and with it a surge of Jew-baiting [*Judenangriffe*], transforming her husband in her very arms, as it were, from a respected free spirit into a corrosive spawn of an alien race [*in den Ätzgeist eines bodenfremden Abstämmlings*].[18]

Prejudices active in the Austrian capital were of course shared by its satellites, among them Prague.

True fluency was denied of German-speaking Jews like Klementine's husband or Kafka's contemporaries. Their command of the language was perceived as imitative, inorganic, even corrupted (which helps explain why Max Brod detected an allegory of assimilation in "A Report to an Academy," Kafka's story of an ape who by mimicry and sheer force of will acquires the same level of cultivation as the average European). A new verb, *mauscheln,* was coined by linguistic anti-Semites to describe this "organic compound of bookish German and pantomime."[19] In his study *Jewish Self-Hatred: Anti-Semitism and the Hidden Language of the Jews,* Sander Gilman defines *mauscheln* as "the use of altered syntax and bits of Hebrew vocabulary and a specific pattern of gestures to represent the spoken language of the Jews."[20] Accordingly, to *mauscheln* was to betray one's primal Jewishness. Kafka thus came to think of his own German as "impure," not just because "the Jew writing in German was misappropriating and misusing another people's heritage," but because he was highly sensitive to Jewish turns of phrase, gesticulations, and hyperbole—mannerisms that surfaced occasionally in his own speech and prose (as hinted at in the Meran anec-dote above).[21]

Questions of authenticity led to some odd public debates in Kafka's Austria-Hungary, the crowning example of which may have been Karl Kraus's 1921 assault on the "Jewish prose" of Franz Werfel's play *The Mirror Man*. Kraus—a convert to Christianity who had been born into an afflu-ent Jewish family—had already authored a series of articles reviling Hein-rich Heine for his journalistic contamination of the German language. In *Literature, or We'll See About That* (*Literatur oder Man wird doch da sehn*), he restages Werfel's expressionist father-son conflict, turning it into a Jew-ish farce that ultimately accuses Werfel—another Jewish-born convert—of having "corrupted the German language, . . . polluted it with jargon, Yid-dishisms, [and] elements of Jewish thought . . . in even the seemingly most accomplished German prose."[22]

Kafka's response to *Literature* is preserved in a letter to Max Brod. He begins by noting amusedly that Kraus's own writing shares the very quali-ties he wishes to excise from the language—and is, in fact, emblematic of them: "The joke is mainly the *mauscheln,* no one can *mauscheln* like Kraus."[23] Kraus's play skewered the mediocre poetry that had been passing for high art, and Kafka reveled in its insight and wit. Yet the implications of Kraus's satire *for his own writing* beget a concern that culminates, by the end of this letter, in a profound paradox:

> They existed among three impossibilities, which I just happen to call linguistic impossibilities. It is simplest to call them that. But they might also be called something entirely different. These are: the impossibility of not writing, the impossibility of writing German, the impossibility of writing differently. One might also add a fourth impossibility, the impossibility of writing.[24]

"Firm ground" is an expression that Kafka reserved for those who pos-sessed a stable, unambiguous national, cultural, and linguistic identity. Thus Kafka depicts his youngest sister's fiancée, a decidedly nationalistic Czech, as one who

> lives among his own people, is cheerful and healthy, essentially (the inci-dentals do not matter) is rightly content with himself, content with his large circle, rightly (there is no other word for it, *just the way a tree rightly stands upon the ground*) and in quite specific ways discontented with the

others—I don't know, but in a sense it is almost the "estate" which you have wished for yourself for so long, *the firm ground* [*der feste Boden*], the ancient holding, the clear air, freedom. [My italics][25]

For many German-speaking Jews, the Hasidim of eastern Europe and even the Zionists were perceived as having profited from a collective experience. Although he followed with avidity the activities and literature of both, Kafka's secular skepticism prevented him from identifying fully with either. Invited to assume an editorial position at Martin Buber's *Der Jude,* he firmly declined, citing this distance in his defense:

> As far as I am concerned, it is unfortunately only in joke or in a semicomatose moment that my name should come up in connection with the vacant editorship at *Der Jude.* How could I think of such a thing, with my boundless ignorance of affairs, my complete lack of connection with people, the absence of any firm Jewish ground beneath my feet? No, no.[26]

In an interview published by the *Süddeutsche Zeitung* to mark the 125th anniversary of Kafka's birth, Alice Herz-Sommer recalls his astonished response to a group of Galician Jews encountered during an afternoon stroll: "*I* belong to *them?*"[27] It comes as little surprise, then, that Kafka, an assimilated German Jew excluded from *Deutschtum* by his Jewishness and from so-called authentic Judaism by his secularity, would find the image of *Boden* so apropos.

Threatened by Threats: Blood-Libel Trials and Pogroms

In one of her earliest letters to Kafka, Milena Jesenská, who was then translating "The Stoker" into Czech, posed a question: *Are you a Jew?* In reply, Kafka ventures an account of Jewish anxiety:

> Their insecure position, insecure within themselves, insecure among people, would above all explain why Jews believe they possess only whatever they hold in their hands or grip between their teeth, that furthermore only tangible possessions give them a right to live, and that finally they will never again acquire what they once have lost—which swims happily away from them, gone forever. Jews are threatened by dangers

from the most improbable sides or, to be more precise, let's leave the dangers aside and say: "They are threatened by threats."[28]

The passivity of this last formulation hints at the dangerous isolation experienced by secular, partially integrated Jews like Kafka who were incapable of finding refuge by reaching for the "hem of the Jewish prayer shawl . . . as the Zionists have."[29]

The "threats" they faced were real. Between 1881 and 1900, no fewer than fifteen blood-libel cases occurred on the Continent. Three had a profound, and documented, impact on Kafka. The first occurred in the small Hungarian town of Tiszaeszlár in 1883 after the supposed assault and murder of an eighteen-year-old girl. The young son of a synagogue caretaker was accused of the crime. August Rohling, professor of Semitic languages at the University of Prague, claimed that the Talmud endorsed such killings.[30] Although the case was weak and could not hold up in court—"not only did the body never turn up, but the supposed victim was reportedly seen very much alive by several later witnesses"—anti-Semitic journalists and local politicians used the affair to perpetuate a myth of Jewish parasitism.[31]

The virulent hatred expressed during these episodes justified the fear that haunted Czech Jews. Outbreaks of violence and boycotts of Jewish businesses confirmed it. This was the milieu into which Kafka was born, and it improved little between the years of his childhood and those of his correspondence with Jesenská. He was direct witness to two such outbreaks during his lifetime: first, the street pogroms of 1897 (the "December storm" Twain had covered in "Stirring Times in Vienna" and "Concerning the Jews"), then the riots of November 16–19, 1920, which Kafka actually watched from his window. In 1916 he read *Ritual Murder in Hungary*, Arnold Zweig's literary adaptation of the Tiszaeszlár trial. The story, which incorporated actual court documents from the case, moved him to tears.[32]

Austria-Hungary's most infamous trial occurred in 1899, when Kafka was sixteen. On April 1 (Easter Sunday), nineteen-year-old Anežka Hrůsová was found on the side of a road near Polna with a gash in her throat. Jaromír Hušek, the anti-Semitic editor of a Czech newspaper who had already written inflammatory articles about previous blood-libel cases, charged Jewish shoemaker Leopold Hilsner with her murder. That the evidence against Hilsner was scanty at best did little to prevent parliamentarians in Vienna from entering the affair. "From this point forth," writes Christoph Stölzl, "a connection was made between localized and centralized anti-Semitic movements in Austria and the affair's proceedings developed into a massive psychological trial against the Jews that could only conclude, from the very start, with a guilty verdict."[33] The state's prosecuting attorney and later mayor of Prague, Karl Baxa, promptly obtained a death sentence for Hilsner. Tomáš Garrigue Masaryk, then still a professor of sociology, pressed for a retrial but to little avail.[34] In 1901 the emperor's pardon ameliorated the sentence to life in prison. Hilsner served seventeen years before being released by the Austrian government—even then, against the will of a Czech court. ("The historian Wilma Iggers," writes Peter Demetz, "reminds us that a Czech newspaper, on May 4, 1968, reported that Anežka Hrůzová's brother on his deathbed in 1961 confessed that *he* had killed his sister: he had not wanted her to have the dowry she asked for.")[35] It was 1916, the year Kafka read Arnold Zweig's play about the affair.[36] By this time, Hilsner's trial had embedded itself firmly in the collective memory of Prague's Gentiles and Jews—among the former as further evidence of a "Jewish problem," amid the latter as yet another reminder that anti-Semitism was a far from exclusively German phenomenon.

Kafka subscribed to *Selbstwehr,* the Prague-based Zionist paper edited by his friend Felix Weltsch. He in all likelihood followed the Kiev blood-libel trial of Mendel Beiliss in its pages between 1911 and 1913 (the years of his heightened interest in Yiddish theater and, more generally, in eastern European Jewish culture). Years later he reportedly wrote a story inspired by the case; the manuscript was probably destroyed, at his request, by Dora Diamant during the period of their cohabitation in Berlin. Beiliss's trial set off a wave of pogroms across Russia.

Although the fate of Prague's Jews in 1912 was by no means as terrible as that of those settled further east—the worst of the Czech riots never approached the brutality recounted by Isaac Babel in his *Red Cavalry* tales—the emperor's army was hardly equipped to safeguard its Jewish citizens from a libelous press, local boycotts, and isolated attacks. Hillel Kieval notes that the three days of "December Storm" riots

> produced a measurable trauma within the ranks of the Czech-Jewish movement, to say nothing of the Bohemian Jewish community. The carefully constructed plans and cherished hopes of countless Czech-speaking Jews lay strewn along the sidewalks of Prague and tens of smaller communities together with the shards of glass and broken furniture of Jewish homes and shops.[37]

The Jews of Prague understood their situation as precarious. They knew themselves to be "threatened by threats" that might materialize at any instant. Kafka was profoundly aware of the provisional nature of his family's security, and alluded to this vulnerability as a lack of *fester Boden*.

A Nothing, A Dream, A Hovering

Some of the alienation expressed in Kafka's writings can be traced to historical conditions such as those described above. Yet his application of anti-Semitic language was often opportunistic. It appears most visibly in his letters to Milena Jesenská, an extraordinary journalist who defied her father (a prominent Czech patriot) by marrying a Jewish man of letters.[38] These documents teem, as do the diaries and notebooks, with fantasies of punishment. I am convinced that the self-critical hangman that speaks through them would have thrived well enough without an anti-Semitic discourse to assimilate. "Jewish self-hatred" scarcely surfaces in his missives to Jewish friends; the deprecatory impulse manifests itself in other guises. Kafka enlisted his hovering trope to depict a lack of firm ground within, and not just without—to illustrate the abysses of self, as a writer and as a son. The imagery marshaled in his letter to Jesenská concerning the endangered position of Jews who "believe they possess only whatever they hold in their hands or grip between their teeth" thus reappears in the letter to his father, where his failure to break free from Hermann Kafka's sphere of power is depicted in similar terms: "I was so unsure of everything that, in fact, I possessed only what I actually had in my hands or in my mouth or what was at least on the way there."[39]

For much of his life, the compulsion to write was thwarted by his responsibilities as a lawyer for the Workmen's Accident Insurance Institute for the kingdom of Bohemia in Prague. Kafka served the company devotedly from 1908 until 1922. Testimonials by coworkers and friends affirm that he was well-liked and respected at the office.[40] The quality of his work was exemplary; superiors declared him indispensable during the First World War, a status that sheltered him from the draft. At the time of his hiring, Kafka was one of the company's few Jews. When the Czech state was established a decade later, most of the company's German speakers were dismissed; despite frequent leaves of absence for illness, Kafka was again an exception.[41]

Before joining the institute, Kafka had been employed by the Prague branch of a Trieste-based insurance firm. The company's policies, according to Ernst Pawel, "remained obdurately medieval, a relic of Austrian feudalism at its sanctimonious worst."[42] After a few months of struggling through a ten-hour workday, six days a week—plus overtime—Kafka quit. Seven years later he described in his diary the consequences of an incident with the department head:

> Humiliation at Eisner's. . . . How lightly I bore the humiliation, how easily I forgot it, how little impression even his indifference made on me. I could have floated [*hätte ich unberührt schweben können*] unperturbed down a thousand corridors, through a thousand offices, past a thousand former friends now grown indifferent, without lowering my eyes. Imperturbable but also unawakeable.[43]

This passage, set in the subjunctive—a case Kafka thoroughly mastered—performs the very hovering depicted in the Laurenziberg episode of "He" by capsizing the banality of the workplace into "a nothing, . . . a dream, . . . a hovering."[44] The figure also surfaces in references to his writing life. After five months of scant production in 1910, Kafka began keeping a diary. In an early entry, he depicts the consequences of not writing:

> My condition is not unhappiness, but it is also not happiness, not indifference, not weakness, not fatigue, not another interest—so what is it then? That I do not know this is probably connected with my inability to write. And without knowing the reason for it [*ohne ihre Grund zu kennen*], I believe I understand the latter.[45]

The inability to write begets an account which belies that very failure. Here too we see the literary hovering outlined in "He." Every clause qualifies, if not cancels, an assertion made in the preceding one.

As the entry continues, Kafka disparages his own writing:

> But every day at least one line should be trained on me, as they now train telescopes on comets. And if then I should appear before that sentence once, lured by that sentence, just as, for instance, I was last Christmas, when I was really so far gone that I was barely able to control myself and when I seemed really on the last rung of my ladder, which, however, rested quietly on the ground and against the wall. But what a ground, what a wall![46]

This passage follows the blueprint laid out in his Laurenziberg epiphany, where the writing craft is substituted for hammering and the inability to write is so entirely inverted that the description of failure becomes, paradoxically, its very subject and culmination.

Literature and Loathing

An avid reader of biographies, autobiographies, memoirs, diaries, and letters, Kafka recognized himself in other writers who were compelled to sacrifice family happiness for their work. Equally revealing was his intimidation by the prodigiousness of Balzac and Goethe, titans of an earlier generation.[47] Their demonic productivity never ceased to astonish him. He often contrasted their perpetual renewal of creative energy with his own tedious waiting for inspiration. Max Brod, whose creative fecundity impressed Kafka much more than the fruits it produced, cites an interesting example in this excerpt from his biography: "Kafka once said: "Balzac carried a stick with the slogan, 'I crush every obstacle'—mine would rather be, 'Every obstacle crushes me.'"[48]

"Every obstacle crushes me"—if this was the motto Kafka chose for himself, a self "made of literature," then Goethe's preeminence in German letters was as much an impediment as it was an inspiration. In 1911 Kafka anticipated Harold Bloom when he voiced his concern that Goethe's successors had to choose between imitating their antecedent and writing against him. Even today, no German writer of ambition can entirely evade the shadow of Goethe's influence, if only because the many aspects of the very language these writers use remains, to an astonishing extent, his creation. Kafka comments upon this indebtedness in another diary entry dated from the same year: "The isolated momentary observation, 'Castanet rhythms of the children in wooden shoes' [excerpted from *Wilhelm Meister's Years of Apprenticeship*], made such an impression, is so universally accepted, that it is unthinkable that anyone, even if he had never read this remark, could feel this observation as an original idea."[49]

Kafka wrote less during periods of intensive engagement with Goethe's diaries, letters, and the multivolume autobiographical project *From My Life*. Reflections like those cited above appear *after* the reading phase has concluded. Often, they are juxtaposed against Kafka's own autobiographical reflections. (A detailed exposition of his Hebrew name and family history follows the remark on Goethe's retarding effect on the development of German language.)[50]

The reversal of Balzac's inscription is a good example of Kafka's wit, a wit ever trained against its master. "In the Penal Colony" depicts a more hideous inscription, and bears witness to Kafka's imaginative brilliance as an inventor of punishments. In a September 1920 letter to Jesenská, Kafka includes a sketch of a man torn in two, his four limbs attached to poles and pulled apart so his body splits down the middle. To the right of the scene, the designer—clearly, Kafka acknowledges himself not only the victim of this outrageous torture, but its vain creator as well—looks on nonchalantly, one arm folded over the other while leaning back against a column "as if the whole thing were his original invention, whereas all he really did was watch the butcher in front of his shop, drawing out a disemboweled pig."[51]

This image of butchery recalls another fantastic punishment of Kafka's, here recorded in a letter to Max Brod: "My mind is daily prey to fantasies, for example that I lie stretched out on the floor [*daß ich ausgestreckt auf dem Boden liege*], sliced up like a roast, and with my hand I am slowly pushing a slice of meat toward a dog in the corner."[52] It is an interesting variation of a similar passage transcribed into his diary on May 4, 1913: "Always the image of a pork butcher's broad knife that quickly and with mechanical regularity chops into me from the side and cuts off very thin slices which fly off almost like shavings because of the speed of the motion."[53]

Determining the extent to which Kafka's repeated allusions to butchery stem from contemporary ritual murder accusations is impossible. Nevertheless, I suspect that his slaughterhouse imagery serves mainly as a means to a descriptive end, and is in this way analogous to the anti-Semitic language present throughout the *Letters to Milena*. Kafka's masochistic imagination favors the metaphor that will most effectively render his (often autobiographical) subject's suffering. In light of this, Sander Gilman's hypothesis that "the victim, the torturer, the butcher, and the butcher's knife . . . refer back to the discourse about the uncleanness of pork, or illness, of the imagined torture of Kafka's body, of the nature of the Jew's body, as well as to the idea of inheritance" seems misleadingly reductive. (Although Gilman is definitely right to link the above to Kafka's family history.)[54]

Jakob Kafka, Franz's paternal grandfather, was the butcher of the small Czech Jewish community of Wossek (today Osek), a village that numbered approximately a hundred residents in 1850. Kafka once accounted him responsible for his own vegetarianism, an imputation that indirectly implicates Hermann Kafka for further "imposing" the inheritance. The remark appears in a letter to Milena Jesenská dated June 25, 1920:

Unmusicality is not as clearly a misfortune as you say—in the first place it isn't for me; I inherited it from my predecessors (my paternal grandfather was a butcher in a village near Strakonitz; I have to not eat as much meat as he butchered) and it gives me something to hold on to; being related means a lot to me. But it is definitely a general human misfortune, similar or equal to being unable to cry or sleep.[55]

The passage expresses, if facetiously, Kafka's ambivalence about the burdens of patrimony. For Kafka and his later disciple Philip Roth, inheritance is blessing and curse alike to the son who must forge his own identity to write. Kafka here exposes the myth of self-begottenness. Even the most apparently autonomous of his decisions (for example, the refusal to eat meat) derives, in fact, from *opposition* to an authoritative rival (in this case, Jakob Kafka). Georg Christoph Lichtenberg summed this up in a characteristically insightful apothegm: "To do just the opposite of something is also a form of imitation, namely an imitation of its opposite."[56]

Clayton Koelb has observed that "Franz . . . sees himself as a combination [of his mother and father], but unlike Goethe and unlike even his sister Ottla, the parts fail to fuse into a successful whole."[57] Though closer to Ottla than to any of his other siblings, Kafka on occasion expressed his inability to understand her, in part because he associated her willingness to confront their father directly with the strong father himself: "Nowhere, then, do I accept an alien element so readily as I accept it in my sister. Here I can submit. I can also submit to my father lying outstretched on the ground. (I would gladly do so when he is standing erect, but that is not permitted.)"[58] The conventional standards of upwardly striving middle-class families were destined to alienate someone who could assert that "everything that is not literature bores me and I hate it, for it disturbs me or delays me, if only because I think it does."[59] The consequences of such a position—as an author and as a son—are clearly laid out in the *Letter to His Father.*

The Advocate's Tricks

On the continuum of texts about the generational battle between fathers and their sons, Kafka's "The Judgment" lies somewhere between the unreflective expressionism of Walter Hasenclever's 1916 *The Son* and Karl Kraus's *Literature, or We'll See About That,* his 1921 satire of middle-class Jewish families. (Tellingly, the fulcrum of Kafka's tale is not poetry, as in

Hasenclever or Kraus, but a letter.) The sons in all these works seek to move beyond paternal authority.

Kafka stresses this need repeatedly in the *Letter to His Father*. Literature provided an ostensible *Ausweg*—a way out—from the bourgeois pursuits of career and family that Kafka found so inimical to his calling as a writer. It offered a sphere of autonomy, however short-lived, that was critical for his sense of self-determination: "Here I had, in fact," he asserts, "got some distance away from you by my own efforts, even if it was slightly reminiscent of the worm that, when a foot treads on its tail end, breaks loose with its front part and drags itself aside."[60]

Unable to fulfill his father's career-oriented expectations, the narrator gains his independence through literature, but at the cost of internalizing the former's disapproval. Several of Kafka's characters inherit this "guilty innocence." "The Judgment's" Georg Bendemann is a particularly salient example. "An innocent child, yes, that you were, truly," Herr Bendemann triumphantly booms, moments before condemning him to death, "but still more truly have you been a devilish human being!"[61] Innocence and guilt are combined in a single sentence. Georg succumbs to his father's authority in the story, a sign that he acknowledges its validity at some level. His final words, uttered while hanging from a bridge's railing, confess love for his parents while attesting to the immense ambivalence of a struggle for self-determination undermined by this very affection.

Josef K.'s behavior in *The Trial* also demonstrates the workings of a guilt that has become internalized. When first arrested, K. refuses to consider even the possibility of his own culpability, attempting to repel the charge by any means necessary (e.g., through the use of rhetorical sophistication, calculation, role-playing, seduction, threats). By the end of the novel, his resistance to the court has weakened so much that he actually helps his executioners evade a policeman whose curiosity is aroused by their strange appearance.

Kafka's letter depicts the terrible paradox that arises from this struggle. Only by writing can he break away from his father's influence, just as others stake out their independence by grounding a family, or founding a business. And yet his efforts produce a portrait of imprisonment, since everything he composes turns out to be about his father: "My writing was all about you; all I did there, after all, was to bemoan what I could not bemoan on your breast. It was an intentionally long and drawn-out leave-taking from you, yet, although it was enforced by you, it did take its course in the direction determined by me."[62] Writing to escape Hermann Kafka's shadow, Franz comes to dwell in it.

These similarities between the dilemmas of "Franz Kafka" and his characters Georg Bendemann and Josef K. stress again the symbiotic relation between direct experience and the written life. Despite its genuine complaint, the *Letter to His Father* remains above all indebted to its literary construction; Kafka conceded as much in his missives to Milena Jesenská. To advance his case, he reuses figures developed in his novels and stories. Consider, for example, the language in the following excerpt, as Kafka asserts that his secretive conferences with his sister Ottla were not conspiratorial, as they had appeared to their father, but rather were

> in order to discuss—with all our might and main, jokingly and seriously, in affection, defiance, anger, revulsion, submission, consciousness of guilt, with all the resources of our heads and hearts—this terrible trial that is pending between us and you [*diesen schrecklichen Proceß, der zwischen uns und Dir schwebt*], to examine it in all its details, from all sides, on all occasions, from far and near—a trial in which you keep on claiming to be the judge [*diesen Proceß, in dem Du immerfort Richter zu sein behauptest*], whereas, at least in the main (here I leave a margin for all the mistakes I may naturally make) you are a party too, just as weak and deluded as we are.[63]

Kafka calls this maelstrom of guilt, love, resistance, and concession—emotions characteristic of countless generational conflicts—"a terrible trial," a *Proceß* that the family must endure. "Hermann Kafka," like Herr Bendemann, retains his authority far beyond its natural term. In contrast, Kafka's authority is circumscribed within a literature that takes this struggle as its subject. Perhaps this is why he alludes to it shortly thereafter, citing in his defense an authority whose origins are fictional: "I had lost my self-confidence where you were concerned, and in its place had developed a boundless sense of guilt. (In recollection of this boundlessness I once wrote of someone, accurately: 'He is afraid the shame will outlive him.')"[64] This "someone" is none other than Josef K.; Kafka's quotation stems from the concluding lines of *The Trial*.

The letter contains numerous references to his fiction. When, for example, he designates his father's hypocritical stance toward Judaism a *Komödie* (comedy, act), he mimics Georg Bendemann's feeble affront in "The Judgment," *Komödiant* (comedian, actor).[65] Furthermore, the admonishments Kafka expresses through the voice of his father reproduce the language he had used years before to depict Gregor Samsa's overnight transformation into an *ungeheuren Ungeziefer* (monstrous vermin) in "The Metamorphosis." Commandeering the voice of "Hermann K," he likens their struggle to "the combat of vermin [*den Kampf des Ungeziefers*], which not only sting but, on top of it, suck your blood in order to sustain their own life." "You are unfit for life," the father continues; "to make life comfortable for yourself, without worries and without self-reproaches, you prove that I have taken your fitness for life away from you and put it in my own pocket."[66] This verdict, in turn, poaches from Herr Bendemann's declaration in "The Judgment": "I am still much the stronger. All by myself I might have had to give in, but your mother has given me her strength, I have established a fine connection with your friend, and I have your customers in my pocket!"[67]

The built-in rebuttals of Kafka's letter are easy to overlook, especially when read as a guileless confession. Its author has suggested as much, warning Milena Jesenská not to be taken in by the text's deliberative rhetoric: "The only thing I do fear," he wrote her on June 23, 1920, "is this inner conspiracy against myself (which the letter to my father will help you understand better, although not entirely, since the letter is too much focused on its purpose)."[68] The *Letter to His Father* does tally incidents and expectations that have contributed to the breach between the two, but it also documents the son's "inner conspiracy" against himself, recalling Kafka's call to arms of nearly a decade earlier to every day train a line against himself.[69] The letter bristles, he insists to Jesenská, with *advokatorischen Kniffen* (a lawyer's tricks), and therefore should not be taken at face value.[70]

Ultimately, Kafka sent it to Jesenská, not his father. Hans Dieter Zimmermann's observation about "The Judgment" seems relevant here as well: "It had little to do with reality, but offered relief for the writer."[71] Like that earlier fiction, the *Letter to His Father* circles their relationship, one degree removed. The *Nichts von Judentum* (Nothing of Judaism) he accuses his father of foisting upon him anticipates the hovering *Nichts* portrayed a year later in "He": "It was a mere Nothing, a joke—not even a joke."[72]

Kafka extends this critique of the father's ambivalent stance toward Judaism in a 1921 missive to Max Brod—the same letter that addresses Kraus's critique of Werfel. In the passage below, he offers a Kafkan, rather than Freudian, conjecture concerning the wellsprings of inspiration for Jewish writers of his milieu:

Psychoanalysis lays stress on the father complex, and many find the concept intellectually fruitful. In this case I prefer another version, where the issue revolves not around the innocent father but around the father's Jewishness. Most young Jews who began to write in German wanted to leave Jewishness behind them, and their fathers approved of this, but vaguely (this vagueness was what was outrageous to them). But with their posterior legs they were still glued to their father's Jewishness and with their waving anterior legs they found no new ground. The ensuing despair became their inspiration.[73]

German Jewish writers like Kafka thus found themselves suspended between warring adversaries in an increasingly perilous environment. Trapped like the vermin depicted above, Kafka re-creates its fate and its despair. In the process, the distinction between traditional genres, and between poetry and truth, dissolves. Like the floating dogs from *The Investigations of a Dog*, he hovers above, apart from and yet invariably tethered to, his family, culture, and age.[74]

Coda: A Circus Rider on Two Horses

> Of course the writer in me will die right away, since such a figure has no base [*hat keinen Boden*], no substance, is less than dust. He is only barely possible in the broil of earthly life, is only a construct of sensuality. That is your writer for you.
>
> —Franz Kafka, letter to Max Brod, July 5, 1922

Perhaps because the performative aspect of such suspension was not lost on Kafka, he set many of his stories at the circus. Theatrical works such as "Up in the Gallery," "A Report to an Academy," "First Sorrow," "A Hunger Artist," "Josephine the Singer," and the Nature Theater of Oklahoma fragment in his *America* novel all thematize delicate acts of balance. Kafka portrays each of his protagonists—be it a trapeze artist, intellectual ape, or equestrienne—in a state of precarious suspension.[75] He perceived his own writing in similar terms, as an activity full of risk, the grounded equivalent of aerial acrobatics. A third-person entry in the diary phrases it thus:

> But forgetting is not the right word here. The memory of this man has suffered as little as his imagination. . . . He has only as much ground as his two feet take up [*soviel Boden als seine zwei Füße brauchen*], only as

much of a hold as his two hands encompass, so much the less, therefore, than the trapeze artist in a variety show, who still has a safety net hung up for him below.[76]

The history of Kafka's critical reception has entailed, and will continue to entail, systematic readings by commentators that are founded on one or several of the surfaces offered by the author's "immutable" texts.[77] My ensuing chapters will show how *creative* approaches to his work have been equally rich and varied. Kafka was of course fully cognizant of the endless suggestiveness of his words. In a 1916 letter to Felice Bauer, Kafka bemusedly comments on two ostensibly antithetical reviews of "The Metamorphosis":

> And incidentally, won't you tell me what I really am: in the latest *Neue Rundschau, Metamorphosis* is mentioned and rejected on sensible grounds, and then says the writer: "There is something fundamentally German about K's narrative art." In Max's article on the other hand: "K's stories are among the most typically Jewish documents of our time." A difficult case. Am I a circus rider on 2 horses? Alas, I am no rider, but lie prostrate on the ground [*Leider bin ich kein Reiter, sondern liege am Boden*].[78]

Kafka's story is neither exclusively Jewish nor *Urdeutsch*. It wavers between the two, balanced precariously between opposing poles and drawing its inspiration from the consequent despair. Understanding Kafka's body of work as an aesthetic of hovering illuminates his fiction no less than it does his letters or diaries. To overlook this aspect amounts to placing oneself on *too firm* an interpretive ground—reducing the author, so to speak, to a single horse.

To me it seems as though [Bruno] Schulz could not keep his imagination
away from anything, including the work of other writers, and particularly
the work of someone like Kafka, with whom he does seem to have had
important affinities of background and temperament. Just as in *The Street
of Crocodiles* he reimagines his hometown of Drohobycz into a more terrifying and wonderful place than it actually was . . . so, in a way, he reimagines
bits and pieces of Kafka for his own purposes.
  —Philip Roth, interview with I. B. Singer

H.L.: One of the fault lines in the novel is between generations. The passion
that strikes Zuckerman strikes across a generation gap—just as Zuckerman's
long-ago meeting with Lonoff was a crossing between generations. How central to this novel do you think are the impossibilities and grotesqueries—and
the possible benefits—of such generational crossings?
P.R.: Absolutely central.
  —Philip Roth, *New Yorker* interview with Hermione Lee, October 1,
  2007

2. Philip Roth: *Zuckerman Bound*

Kafka has been instrumental in the self-discovery of countless authors
across Europe and the United States. His "genes" can be detected in much
of today's fiction via the physiognomy of literary allusion, thematic variation, and allegorical imitation. For Roth as for Sebald and Coetzee, reading
Kafka raises a mirror to the narrating self and leads to important discov-
eries. Like Bruno Schulz in the example above, they discover in his work
strategies, models, and themes that prove fruitful for their own. For the
first two authors at least, this engagement involves literal looking as well. In
"'I Always Wanted You to Admire My Fasting'; or, Looking at Kafka," an
examination of Kafka's Berlin portrait leads Roth to contrast his fate with
those of the European Jews who *didn't* get away.[1] When Sebald examines a
photograph of the young Franz Kafka in his essays "Thanatos" and "The
Undiscover'd Country," he perceives an implacable melancholic. Looking
at pictures of Kafka, each author expresses something essential about his
own worldview.

Kafka is given priority in both Roth's and Sebald's oeuvres. The effect of
this priority, however, varies distinctly between the two. Although he consistently refined his execution, Sebald's method of literary appropriation

remained essentially unchanged from the earliest essays to the final works. He forcefully bent the voices of Kafka, Walser, Conrad, and others toward that of his own narrator, divesting them of their original spirit to reinforce his own thematic emphases. His repeated likening of textual allusion to a friendly tipping of the hat belied the aggression inherent in his approach.

At first, Roth's fiction treated Kafka similarly. *Portnoy's Complaint* (1969), *The Breast* (1972), and "Looking at Kafka" (1973) are all symptomatic of what Bloom calls the anxiety of influence: in these works, Roth usurps Kafka by flagrantly misrepresenting him. He marshals comic hyperbole for his misprisions, which he then deploys (as Freud knew jokes could) "in service of aggression."[2] (The first part of this chapter will deal with some explicit examples.) Roth's aggressive treatment of Kafka began to wane around the mid-1970s—not long after the author's run of annual visits to communist Prague. David Kepesh's hysterical surrealism in *The Breast* is superseded by his namesake's more nuanced characterization in *The Professor of Desire* (1977). In *The Ghost Writer* (1979), the first install-ment of Roth's trilogy plus epilogue *Zuckerman Bound,* Nathan Zuck-erman finally steps forward to take the narrative reins of Roth's middle years. By now Roth's apprenticeship has come to a close. His fictions are no longer marked by agonistic ambivalence. The urgent compulsion to out-Kafka Kafka recedes, even as the Prague author remains a defin-ing antecedent and, as I shall shortly show, *Zuckerman Bound*'s resident specter.[3]

I have already cited Kafka's seminal 1921 letter to Max Brod, wherein he argued that the inspiration of contemporary Jewish writers in German was rooted in their inability to escape the Judaism of their fathers. The latter group's wavering approval of assimilation, he adds, was precisely what the sons found so maddening: "This vagueness was what was outrageous to them."[4] After six years of visiting Prague regularly and nearly a decade of extensive engagement with Kafka's texts, Philip Roth identified an ana-logue that bound the dilemma of his precursor's generation to that of his own. *Zuckerman Bound* depicts the conflict between a "first generation American father possessed by the Jewish demons" and his "second genera-tion American son possessed by their exorcism."[5] Having located the uni-versal (filial ambivalence) in the particular (Kafka's relation to his father, his writing, and his time), Roth builds on Kafka's model without any need to distort it.

His protagonist exorcises these demons, but at a cost. Zuckerman is star-tled to discover that paternal authority transcends time and even the grave, as the conclusion of *Zuckerman Unbound* makes clear—that the "Jewish son who grows up to be the novelist is 'in possession' of his material, but he is also 'unbound, dispossessed, no longer any man's son.'"[6] *The Anatomy Lesson* unravels his subsequent guilt and provides a paradigm of punishment further informed by its subtle allusions to *The Trial,* "In the Penal Colony," and Kafka's letters to Felice Bauer and Milena Jesenská. Roth continues to "reimagine bits and pieces of Kafka for his own purposes," but now, unlike "Looking at Kafka" and other early appropriations, he does so without reductively misreading his antecedent.[7] His use of Kafka is no longer a forced refitting; on the contrary, it provides a broadened perspective of a shared dilemma.

In this chapter's four sections I trace the arc of Philip Roth's filial relation to Kafka, from his first rebellious projections to his mature renewal of the Kafkan dilemma of Jewish fathers and Jewish sons in *Zuckerman Bound.* I start with his "Looking at Kafka," a hybrid of essay, story, and memoir produced in 1972 while the novelist taught at the University of Pennsylvania. "Higher Education" will examine *The Ghost Writer* as an extended prologue on the quandary of literary paternity, while "Art with a Trial" addresses correspondences between *Zuckerman Unbound*'s climactic ending and Kafka's "The Judgment." Lastly, "A Corpus Bound" homes in on Nathan Zuckerman's self-destruction in *The Anatomy Lesson,* the trilogy's final novel.[8]

Lovely Lies? Philip Roth's "Looking at Kafka"

> Had one to name the artist who comes nearest to bearing the same kind of relation to our age that Dante, Shakespeare, and Goethe bore to theirs, Kafka is the first one would think of.
>
> —W. H. Auden, "The Wandering Jew"

In 1941, Auden's bold assertion went largely unnoticed; Kafka was still a buzz in the ears of those in the know, an insider's tip. Within a decade, however, the poet's statement had been validated. J. M. Coetzee has defined the test of a classic as one of survival: despite any and all criticism, the classic endures because "generations of people cannot afford to let go of it and therefore hold on to it at all costs."[9] This is a precise depiction of the fate of Kafka's fiction, whose audience over the past century has proven immense. *The Trial, The Castle,* and "The Metamorphosis" have not lost their contemporaneity for their readers around the world.

An author's power can be gauged by the degree to which his influence exerts itself upon the preeminent writers of later generations. In 1911 Goethe was still enough of a towering figure in German letters for Kafka to lament in his diary that the sheer strength of his precursor's corpus "probably retards the development of the German language."[10] But influence need not be disabling, nor must it confine itself to the province of a single language. "Literary influence," Jeffrey Eugenides has noted, "is like genetics":

> Rushdie got some of his fireworks from Günter Grass and Gabriel García Márquez. García Márquez got things from Kafka and Faulkner. . . . Influence isn't just a matter of copying someone or learning his or her tricks. You get influenced by writers whose work gives you hints about your own abilities and inclinations. Being influenced is largely a process of self-discovery.[11]

Philip Roth has been one of the most self-consciously *literary* writers of the past three decades. "I know of no other novelist," Martin Green has written, "who makes the discussion of books such a valuable part of his story's action."[12] Roth's novels conflate life and art—the "written and unwritten worlds"—in a manner that not only upsets the modern dichotomy represented so obsessively in the early works of Thomas Mann, but, at considerable risk of irrelevance, boldly navigates Cervantes's terrain, where fictions pen the lives of their authors. While Mann, Dostoevsky, Flaubert, and Henry James have all featured prominently in Roth's work, Kafka alone has surfaced with obstinate regularity since the publication of *Portnoy's Complaint* in 1969. He even dominates Roth's nonfiction: *Shop Talk,* a collection of his interviews with and essays on other writers from 1976 to 2000, could well have been titled "Responses to Kafka." Of the ten authors considered, only two—an exchange of letters with Mary McCarthy (regarding her response to Roth's representation of Christianity in *The Counterlife*) and a conversation with the Irish author Edna O'Brien—fail to allude to him.

Roth has made repeated efforts to express his filial relationship to Kafka in print. He has always declared his indebtedness openly, crediting, for example, his reading of the latter's "tales of spiritual disorientation and obstructed energies" with enabling his composition of *Portnoy:* "The ways in which Kafka allowed an obsession to fill every corner of every paragraph," he wrote in 1976, "and the strange grave comedy he was able to make of the tedious enervating rituals of accusation and defense, furnished me with any number of clues as to how to give my imaginative expression to preoccupations of my own."[13]

"'I Always Wanted You to Admire My Fasting'; or, Looking at Kafka" (1973) demonstrates the author's schooling in Kafka better than any of his other works from this period. Here Roth aggressively rewrites the life and work of his forebear through a blend of descriptive biography and unrestrained fictionalization. His distortions signal a deep ambivalence— a competitive underside to the enthusiastic tributes that recur in his fictions, interviews, and other writings from 1969 until 1979. Not until his later *Zuckerman Bound* trilogy and epilogue (1979–85) would Roth begin to break away from this model.

The story's opening sentence, "I am looking, as I write of Kafka, at the photograph taken of him at the age of forty (my age)," begins Roth's meditation and suggests, via the parenthetical, that he identifies with Kafka.[14] (Joyce Carol Oates reports that a reproduction of Kafka's Berlin portrait from the winter of 1923–24 occupied a prominent space on the wall of Roth's study at the time he wrote this essay.) "His face is sharp and skeletal," he continues:

> A burrower's face: pronounced cheekbones and even more conspicuous by the absence of sideburns; the ears shaped and angled on his head like angel wings; an intense, creaturely gaze of startled composure—enormous fears, enormous control; a black towel of Levantine hair pulled close around the skull the only sensuous feature; there is a familiar Jewish flare in the bridge of the nose, the nose itself is long and weighted slightly at the tip—the nose of half the Jewish boys who were my friends in high school. Skulls chiseled like this one were shoveled by the thousands from the ovens; had he lived, he would have been among them, along with the skulls of his three younger sisters.[15]

Thus does the causal chain of associations lead directly, by way of Kafka's nose, from Roth's study in Manhattan to Weequahic High School in Newark. He lingers in the late 1940s briefly before springing over the Atlantic (and half a decade) and into the furnaces of Auschwitz. Roth's Kafka— and can this come as a surprise for an American Jew born in 1933?—is an adamantly postwar Kafka, a Kafka read in the wake of atrocities that, the author cannot help but realize, might have been inflicted on the Prague Jew (as they indeed were on his three sisters) had he only lived long enough.

But Roth's task as an author is, as he has remarked elsewhere, "to transform meager facts into compelling fiction." So the narrator imagines alternative lives for Kafka; for example, one who might have found a way out of Europe by taking up a position at an American university.[16] These impossible scenarios are then retracted in favor of another, albeit less unlikely, impossible scenario, one in which Kafka, a Berlin-based pensioner with a suitcase full of manuscripts (including, writes Roth, *six* unfinished novels), becomes a "Jewish refugee arriving in America in 1938 . . . a frail and bookish fifty-five-year-old bachelor, . . . an author, yes, but of a few eccentric stories, mostly about animals, stories no one in America had heard of and only a handful in Europe had read."[17]

Roth's "compelling fiction" also drives the remainder of the story's first part, a biographical overview of the last year of Kafka's life, particularly the time spent with Dora Diamant in Berlin. This narrative is interrupted periodically by passages drawn from the Prague author's stories, novels, and letters. Their inclusion serves to gloss Roth's own, frequently questionable, interpretations of these tragic final months.

Roth's projections resemble the particular form of "misreading" discussed in an interview conducted for the publication of *Reading Philip Roth* in 1988. Asked whether or not he himself expects to be misread (as misreading is "more or less the fate of most good writing"), he acknowledges in turn that

> the only reading resembling the ideal reading that a writer sometimes yearns for is the writer's reading of himself. Every other reading is something of a surprise—to use your word, a "misreading," if what's meant isn't reading that's shallow and stupid but that's fixed in its course by the reader's background, ideology, sensibility, etc.[18]

Roth had already established this view eight years earlier in an article for the *New York Times* when he related how his preoccupation with Kafka first brought him to Prague. There he experienced "fixed readings" in an entirely new guise—censorship:

> In a way all novels are read (as they are written) from essentially personal points of view, and generally, the only way to prevent books from meaning different things to different people is to prevent them from being read. Or else to try to do away with the differences in the people who read them.[19]

This theme was later developed in *The Prague Orgy*, Roth's coda to the *Zuckerman* trilogy.

Many of the "misreadings" in "Looking at Kafka" emerge from the narrator's tendency to mistake K., Josef K., Gregor Samsa, and Georg Bendemann for *Franz Kafka:* the Gerer Rebbe who turns down Kafka's petition for Dora Diamant's hand is Klamm; his one-syllable response, "No," is embodied by the voice of Bendemann's father sweeping aside his son's other women; Kafka's abandonment of Berlin and with it his attempt to find (like Josef K.) a "mode of living completely out of jurisdiction of the court" is represented by the cage cleared out after the hunger artist's death to make room for a vital panther.[20] While Peter Demetz is right to assert that few other American authors have read or studied Kafka as well as Roth has, the latter's apparent reliance on Max Brod's biography—not to mention his own thematic preoccupations—frequently leads to dubious conclusions about Kafka's motives. One of the most telling examples occurs toward the end of the first section. *"As Franz Kafka awoke one morning from uneasy dreams,"* writes the narrator, *"he found himself transformed in his bed into a father, a writer, and a Jew."*[21] I will respond to the first third of this playful assertion—the narrator's assessment of Kafka's relationship with Dora Diamant—momentarily. For now, I would like to focus on the last two points, both of which strike me as problematic.

The writer Kafka's aversion to publication is well known. "Years earlier, in Prague," Roth writes, "he had directed Max Brod to destroy all his papers . . . upon his death; now, in Berlin, when Brod introduces him to a German publisher interested in his work, Kafka consents"—here the narrator quotes directly from Brod's biography—"'without much need of long arguments to persuade him.'" Philip Roth, for whom Kafka's obsessive identification with literature applies no less, knows that authorship is no overnight achievement. His narrator nevertheless disregards what Malcolm Pasley has elsewhere referred to as Kafka's sense of *Beruf* (calling) as well as the material circumstances under which he suffered during the difficult, inflation-troubled winter of 1923–24.[22] "Brod's intimation of a 'principal change' in Kafka's attitude toward the publication of his work," writes Joachim Unseld,

is, upon closer observation however, quite questionable. For in his justification for "poorly executing the will as written," Brod makes no mention of his friend's continuing urgent need, which was in the end the basis for his decision to publish again.[23]

Nor is Kafka's view of his own Judaism so uncomplicated. The only evidence the narrator provides for this "metamorphosis" is Kafka's diary entry from 1914: "What have I in common with Jews? I have hardly anything in common with myself and should stand very quietly in the corner, content that I can breathe."[24] Against this outcry, the narrator contrasts Kafka's attendance of Talmud lectures as well as his renewed study of Hebrew in Berlin.

But the latter's engagement with Judaism began years earlier and developed gradually through his interactions with Yiddish language and literature, his proximity to the Zionist movement, and his initial study of Hebrew. Kafka's interest was neither weaker nor more pervasive in 1911 than in 1923; it was always defined by a particular context. The idea that Kafka might have been transformed magically in Berlin, whether into a writer or a Jew, is a projection on the part of Roth's narrator. It arises less from Kafka's biography than from Roth's imagination.

The most flagrant misreading in the first part of "Looking at Kafka" occurs on the following page. It qualifies as an approach equally "bizarre" to those Roth attributed to Freud in a 1988 interview, in Roth's view "the all-time influential misreader of imaginative literature."[25] Interspersing quotations from "The Burrow" over the last three pages of the first section, the narrator associates Kafka's composition of that "endlessly suggestive story, this story of life in a hole," with Dora Diamant's genitalia.

Certainly a dreamer like Kafka need never have entered the young girl's body for her tender presence to kindle in him a fantasy of a hidden orifice that promises "satisfied desire," "achieved ambition," and "profound slumber," but that once penetrated and in one's possession, arouses the most terrifying and heartbreaking fears of retribution and loss.[26]

No further justification for implying that Dora's "hidden orifice" was the inspiration for this story follows. The narrator switches tracks and quotes other, unrelated passages from the tale before concluding with two brief sentences that recount the author's death on June 3 and his partner's inconsolable mourning.[27] His imagination untethered, Roth performs radical interpretations of Kafka and offers them to his reader in the form of a biographical lecture. Such adventurous readings may well have liberated Roth as a storyteller, but invariably at the cost of distorting Kafka's own life and work. Hermione Lee's probing study of Roth's fiction summarizes "what Roth's novels do with literary influence" in a way that is succinctly relevant to this story's many misappropriations: they "batten on to it, consume it, use and abuse it, and finally break free of it to find their own voice and style."[28]

The first part of "Looking at Kafka" disguises itself as a professor's lecture. The second is fictional autobiography, a tribute to the milieu of Roth's Newark. In *The Ghost Writer* (1979), mention of the Broadway production of *The Diary of Anne Frank* triggers in Zuckerman a wish-fulfilling fantasy that eventually produces Frank's fictional resurrection in the next chapter. Here, Roth's literal *looking at Kafka* produces similar outlandish results. It is 1942, one year after Auden's review for the *New Republic*. The narrator is nine, and Franz Kafka is the Hebrew-school teacher he and his Jewish classmates resent for "having to learn an ancient calligraphy at the very hour we should be out screaming our heads off on the ball field."[29] A precocious "little borscht-belt comic," the narrator retaliates by amusing his friends with his imitations of their awkward and frail instructor, for whom he invents the sobriquet *Dr. Kishka*—Yiddish for "guts" or "intestines."

Remorseful for providing entertainment at the Doctor's expense and burdened by a sense of helpless guilt for the "Jews in Europe," he tells his parents that his Hebrew teacher lives in one of the poorest sections of Newark.[30] Their sympathy exceeds his expectations: Doctor Kafka will be invited to a Friday night dinner with the family. The narrator's father perceives a further possibility of marrying off his wife's younger sister, Aunt Rhoda (who is forty years old). To the boy's surprise, the strange European with "Old World ways" accepts.[31] At dinner, his father makes feverish pitches in favor of "familial bliss." Dr. Kafka, the target of these addresses, listens politely and finally responds affirmatively to the arguments in favor of family life: "Softly he says, 'I agree,' and inspects again the pages of our family book. 'Alone,' says my father, in conclusion, 'alone, Dr. Kafka, is a stone.' Dr. Kafka, setting the book gently down upon my mother's gleaming coffee table, allows with a nod that it is so."[32]

The Doctor unexpectedly calls and invites Aunt Rhoda to a movie. "I am astonished," writes the narrator, "both that he calls and that she goes; it seems there is more desperation in life than I have come across yet in my fish tank."[33] They begin to see one another more frequently, and after attending a play together, Aunt Rhoda regains her long-forgotten interest in acting. Kafka visits her at her workplace. He recites one of Chekhov's plays to her from beginning to end.[34] They even converse in Yiddish about gardening. But during a weekend trip to Atlantic City, something happens, something, the narrator says, "I am not allowed to know about."[35]

Puzzled by the inconsolable aunt and the secret discussions in the kitchen, he asks his brother what could have possibly undone "everything good . . . in a moment": "My brother, the Boy Scout, smiles leeringly and, with a fierce hiss that is no answer and enough answer, addresses my bewilderment: 'Sex!'"[36]

The next paragraph skips to the narrator's junior year of college (ca. 1953), the day he receives a clipping from his mother containing Dr. Kafka's obituary. The now twenty-year-old author is living in the house of an English professor and his wife, writing stories. He cannot go home again; his demand for independence has led to a family crisis of drastic proportions. Roth here inverts the Kafka father-son dynamic, while preserving its distress:

> "Keep him away from me!" I scream at my mother. "But darling," she asks me, "what is going on? What is this all about?" . . . "He *loves* you," she explains. But that, of all things, seems to me precisely what is blocking my way. Others are crushed by parental criticism—I find myself oppressed by his high opinion of me! Can it possibly be true (and can I possibly admit) that I am coming to hate him for loving me so? Praising me so? But that makes no sense—the ingratitude! the stupidity! the contrariness![37]

This cameo appearance of a topic Roth recognized in Kafka but, with little exception, left unmentioned in his essays and stories of the 1970s—the alienating and inexplicable generational conflict that tears apart even the most loving families—is successfully incorporated in *Zuckerman Bound,* the compendium undertaken with *The Ghost Writer* some five years later (approximately the time Roth's visa to Czechoslovakia was revoked).[38] Here, however, little more is added but a note from the narrator's mother, who attempts to keep the peace in the upset household: "Remember poor Kafka," he reads, "Aunt Rhoda's beau?"[39]

The story ends with the symbolic clearing out of the hunger artist's cage. Roth's "fictional" Kafka dies without leaving any of his writing for posterity. "Thus," concludes the narrator,

> all trace of Dr. Kafka disappears. Destiny being destiny, how could it be otherwise? Does the Land Surveyor reach the Castle? Does K. escape the judgment of the court, or Georg Bendemann the judgment of his father? . . . No, it is simply not in the cards for Kafka ever to become *the*

Kafka—why, that would be stranger even than a man turning into an insect. No one would believe it, Kafka least of all.[40]

> Who would want to tell a true story about a poet? And who would dare
> to palm off on a poet a merely true story? I, for example, since I'm also a
> poet, would like my eulogy one day to contain nothing but lies. As long as
> they're lovely lies.
>
> —Robert Walser, "Brentano: A Phantasy"

Among Roth's American interpreters, surprisingly few have ventured to express critical resistance to "Looking at Kafka." Sanford Pinsker calls it "intriguing," attributing the text's weaknesses to historical currents of the time; Harold Bloom refers to it as Roth's "best and most revealing critical performance"; Bernard Rodgers counts it among "his best work" and even ascertains that it is "certainly one of his most mature."[41] Astute European observers also seem in accord: Peter Demetz declares the work "magnificent," while Hermione Lee asserts that Roth always writes of Kafka "brilliantly" and lauds the text's "penetrating, sympathetic exactness."[42] Such sympathy and penetration, however, apply more to Lee's view of Roth than to Roth's of Kafka.

Although it is difficult to recognize any sign of Walser's "lovely lies" in "Looking at Kafka," Roth's mature fictions from *The Ghost Writer* on begin to build on, rather than usurp, the themes in Kafka's fiction that so resemble his own. Seen by themselves, these early fictions represent Roth's attempt to overthrow Kafka's influence and to assert his own manner. The legacy advances from burden of inspiration to rich patrimony, contributing significantly to the ambitious scope of *Zuckerman Bound* and many of the novels that followed. Walser's epithet is thus most relevant when Roth's entire corpus is taken into consideration. (Considered alone, *The Breast* and "Looking at Kafka" are anything but *lieblich* in their treatment.)

Roth admits in an interview about *The Great American Novel* (1973) that he wanted to see what would happen if he muffled his internal censor and bypassed the superego of literary discretion. The quality of most of the other works published at this time (many of which allude to Kafka) suffers for their lack of restraint. The reason for this may very well be that "Portnoy wasn't a character for me, *he was an explosion* [my italics], and I wasn't finished exploding after *Portnoy's Complaint*."[43]

For all of their brilliant moments of comic outrageousness and keen social observation, the post-*Portnoy* fictions protest too much. Not that implacable complaint need diminish the work: Nathan Zuckerman's unrelenting flood of yammering in *The Anatomy Lesson* is an outstanding portrait of the Jew as an unstoppable mouth, one of the great tragicomic inventions of postwar American literature. "It's a kind of *sensibility*," Roth writes,

> that makes, say, *The Anatomy Lesson* Jewish, if anything does: the nervousness, the excitability, the arguing, the dramatizing, the indignation, the obsessiveness, the touchiness, the playacting—above all the *talking.* The talking and the shouting. Jews will go on, you know. It isn't what it's talking *about* that makes a book Jewish—it's that the book won't shut up. The book won't leave you alone. Won't let up. Gets too close. "Listen, listen—that's only the half of it!" I knew what I was doing when I broke Zuckerman's jaw. For a Jew a broken jaw is a terrible tragedy. It was to avoid this that so many of us went into teaching rather than prizefighting.[44]

It is rather the conspicuous absence of a self-critical, Erasmian countervoice—or better yet, *countervoices*—that downgrades "Looking at Kafka" and many of his other writings from the early 1970s to experiments in form.[45]

Kafka is a "sit-down" comic for Roth: the recognition that a "morbid preoccupation with punishment and guilt" could be "hideous but funny" is, as he has mentioned elsewhere, what led him to discover a method of writing that resulted in *Portnoy's Complaint.*[46] In "Looking at Kafka," Roth fuses "Sheer Playfulness" with "Deadly Seriousness" in a fictional tribute to this most seriously playful of authors.[47] Yet Sheer Playfulness and Playful Playfulness fall short here, for "Looking at Kafka" is finally a misreading according to Roth's own definition: "skillful, cultivated, highly imaginative, [and] widely read," but ultimately "quite bizarre" and "fixed in its course by the reader's background, ideology, sensibility, etc."[48]

"Looking at Kafka" and *The Breast* are admittedly fictions; reading Kafka is not the objective of these stories, but rather is their point of departure. Roth's is a calculating, even disingenuous approach, since in these works "he looks at Kafka," as Harold Bloom has observed, "and, in that mirror, beholds much of himself."[49] *The Professor of Desire* (1977), a major transitional work in Roth's corpus, also contains outrageous inventions drawn from the author's extensive readings (the most prominent of which is surely "Kafka's whore"). But this later novel draws analogical parallels with Kafka's paradoxes to invoke more expansive themes of authority and desire, while the earlier texts read like "explosions," opportunistic acts of self-fashioning.

Higher Education in *The Ghost Writer*

> One doesn't defend one's god: one's god is in himself a defense.
>
> —Henry James, "The Aspern Papers"

When art comes between Nathan Zuckerman and his father, it is not because "Doctor" Zuckerman lacks conviction regarding his son's talent or from fear of the vocation's fiscal vicissitudes. Grounds like these accounted for differences between *Vater* and *Sohn* in Kraus's *Literature, or We'll See About That,* as they had in innumerable middle-class households a century before and after—Gentile no less than Jewish. "Our trouble had begun," explains Zuckerman, "when I gave my father the manuscript of a story based on an old family feud in which he had played the peacemaker for nearly two years before the opponents ended up shouting in court."[50]

Nathan launches his story from this episode. The result, titled "Higher Education," is fifty pages long and his "most ambitious" work to date. Roth's synopsis suggests that its strength and originality are rooted in muscular dialogue and vivid portrayals of character: the hard-working Meema Chaya, who diligently saves her earnings as a seamstress for her grandchildren's "higher education"; daughter Essie, now widowed, who tries to use the trust to send her sons to medical school; and—most memorably—her profligate younger brother Sidney, impatient to purchase a parking lot with his allocated share. Sidney wins the case (determined, to the family's chagrin, by a *goyisher* judge) and is awarded the legacy. "Iron-willed" Essie earns their tuition by peddling shingles and siding over the course of a decade.[51]

Zuckerman's startling conclusion recalls the moral seriousness and pathos of work by Jewish and American writers weaned on Russian literature, then (the mid- to late 1950s) in ascent in American fiction.[52] On a hot August workday, Essie pauses for a rest in an air-conditioned movie theater. The man seated beside her places his hand on her knee. "He must have been a very lonely fellow," considers Zuckerman; "it was a very stout knee; nonetheless, she broke the hand for him, at the wrist, with the hammer carried with her in her purse all these years to protect herself and the future of two fatherless sons. My story . . . concluded with Essie taking aim." Nathan's father is unimpressed by the narrator's artful omission of the final strike. On the contrary, his first response takes careful aim itself: "Well, you certainly didn't leave anything out, did you?"[53]

Until this moment, the relationship between Zuckerman father and son, though marked by occasional conflict, has been on the whole affectionate and unproblematic: "We had emerged from our fifty scenes of domestic schism much the same close family bound by the same strong feelings."[54] *The Ghost Writer*'s opening sentence implies that we are reading Zuckerman's bildungsroman—a novel about his education, inspired by the form developed by Karl Philip Moritz and Goethe and modernized by Proust, Mann, and Joyce (hence the title for the chapter in which this rupture occurs, "Nathan Dedalus") at the beginning of the twentieth century. Roth's first-person narrator looks back on events that have taken place twenty years ago, a position from which he can better discern his failure to acknowledge the shock caused by "Higher Education." Despite all of the knowledge and "experience" he has gathered from his studious forays in literature, Zuckerman cannot begin to conceive that his art might have detrimental consequences, least of all for his most immediate relations:

> Whether or not I wholly knew just how extensive the addiction, I was much in need of their love for me, of which I assumed there was an inexhaustible supply. That I couldn't—wouldn't?—assume otherwise goes a long way toward explaining why I was naïve enough to expect nothing more than the usual encouragement for a story that borrowed from our family history instances of what my exemplary father took to be the most shameful and disreputable transgressions of family decency and trust.[55]

Victor Zuckerman (his first name surely no coincidence) scorns the content of his son's tale for its merciless exposure of greed and petty behavior within the clan. He is alarmed that Nathan underplays the rectitude of relatives like Meema Chaya to focus instead on the conflict between Sidney and Essie, lavishing attention on what Judge Leopold Wapter calls "warped human behavior in general."[56] But the elder Zuckerman's concern extends beyond the humiliation he feels upon seeing the family's dirty laundry aired for a wider audience. "Do you fully understand," he asks, "what a story like this story, when it's published, will mean to people who don't know us?"[57]

Graver than the local offense is its likely reception by the general public. "People don't read art," he continues, "they read about *people*."[58] Roth's italics are key, for when Doctor Zuckerman speaks of "*people*" he alludes not only to the Newark Jews of Nathan's childhood but invokes the Jewish people at large: "Nathan, your story, as far as gentiles are concerned, is about one thing and one thing only. . . . It is about kikes. Kikes and their love of money. That is all our good Christian friends will see, I guarantee you."[59] Conflicting perceptions of American anti-Semitism aggravate the dissent between father and son. Only a decade has passed since the liquidation of the camps, and while it goes without saying that the Holocaust affects *both* generations of postwar Jewish Diaspora consciousness, this scene makes clear that Nathan understands the local threat of anti-Semitism differently than his father. This difference, thrust now into the spotlight by Nathan's story, leads to a profound break between the two Zuckermans.

In her study of Roth's oeuvre, Debra Shostak notes that "the context within which Nathan struggles is at once personal and world history. Not only does he need to face the essential history of modern Jews from which, by the accident of birth, he feels himself estranged, but he also must face his family's sense that he has betrayed them *as* Jews."[60] Aharon Appelfeld depicted this estrangement (that is, of the secular Jew) perspicaciously when asked by Roth in a 1988 interview about Kafka's pertinence to his writing: "Another discovery showed me that behind the mask of placelessness and homelessness in his work stood a Jewish man, like me, from a half-assimilated family, whose Jewish values had lost their content and whose inner state was barren and haunted."[61] Implicit in Appelfeld's response is the notion that this hauntedness may serve the writer well, and the young Zuckerman's example seems to prove it. But Nathan's transgression is perceived by his father as nothing less than a betrayal of his family and, furthermore, of a people "of which, only some five thousand days past, there had been millions more."[62]

Zuckerman boards a bus bound for Manhattan. From there he will depart for Quahsay (a writer's colony). The argument with his father is left unresolved. Looking back, Zuckerman is overcome by a wave of elegiac feeling:

And what I saw, when I went to wave goodbye for the winter, was my smallish, smartly dressed father—turned out for my visit in a new "fingertip" car coat that matched the coffee-toned slacks and the checkered peaked cap, and wearing, of course, the same silver-rimmed spectacles, the same trim little mustache that I had grabbed at from the crib; what I saw was my bewildered father, alone on the darkening street-corner by the park that used to be our paradise, thinking himself and all of Jewry gratuitously disgraced and jeopardized by my inexplicable betrayal.[63]

Victor Zuckerman, unable to "talk sense" into Nathan, looks here as helpless as those ostensibly impotent fathers of Kafka's "sons," Herr Bendemann (senescent, needs to be carried to bed) and Herr Samsa (has not worked for five years). (At the beginning of "The Judgment" and "The Metamorphosis," Kafka's protagonists have already surpassed the authority of their fathers: Georg Bendemann has taken over the family business, and Gregor Samsa is the Samsa breadwinner. This dynamic is of course overturned as each story takes its course.) Nathan's bus returns him to his writing and removes him irrevocably from an Edenic past. Although his stance is uncompromising in the above scene, Zuckerman appears by no means unaware of the perpetual threat of anti-Semitism or the rationale behind his father's concern.

Their disagreement can partly be explained by his parents' closer (generational) proximity to Europe and the Holocaust. Their fear of anti-Semitism in the United States—or anywhere, for that matter—is exceedingly, and understandably, visceral. Nathan's perspective is comparatively sober. In a telling exchange, he chides Judge Leopold Wapter, a prominent Newark Jew his father has approached with "Higher Education," for asking whether "there is anything in your story that would not warm the heart of a Julius Streicher or a Joseph Goebbels?"[64] "The Big Three, Mama!" Zuckerman cries to his mother, who is struggling valiantly but ineffectively to mend the rift between husband and son:

> "Streicher, Goebbels, and your son! What about the *judge's* humility? Where's *his* modesty?"
> "He only meant that what happened to the Jews—"
> "In Europe—not in Newark! We are not the wretched of Belsen! We were not the victims of that crime!"
> "But we *could* be—in their place we *would* be. Nathan, violence is nothing new to the Jews, you *know* that!"[65]

In *The Plot Against America* (2004) Roth would take up this premise in all seriousness. Still soaring "Nathan Dedalus," however, counters by claiming that nose jobs are the principal source of Jewish bloodletting in Essex County—a hint of the outrageous hyperbole that will mark his breakthrough novel of a decade later, *Carnovsky.*[66]

But the historical fears of post-Holocaust American Jews cannot alone account for this schism. Roth raises questions that have less to do with ethnic and national identity than with Zuckerman's calling—his responsibility not to family, but to literature. More significantly, they are *brought to light by the fictions themselves.* Victor Zuckerman's bewilderment before "Higher Education" reveals the contrast between Nathan's life as a son (loyal, obedient) and his emerging work as an artist (uncompromising, oppositional), a critical split between filial loyalty and fidelity to the dictations of the muse, or rather, *daimon.* Nathan will no longer be defined by his father, mother, or community; their insistence that he is *not* what he writes is precisely what stokes his fury: "This story isn't us," his father protests by the bus stop, "and what is worse, it isn't even *you*":

> "You are a loving boy. I watched you like a hawk all day. I've watched you all your life. You are a good and kind and considerate young man. You are not somebody who writes this kind of story and then pretends it's the truth."
>
> "But I *did* write it." The light changed, the New York bus started toward us across the intersection—and he threw his arms onto my shoulders. Making me all the more belligerent. "I *am* the kind of person who writes this kind of story!"
>
> "You're not," he pleaded, shaking me just a little.[67]

Judge Wapter's letter and his "TEN QUESTIONS FOR NATHAN ZUCKERMAN" convey the same ethos, namely that the author so recklessly dismissive of "Jewish values" in "Higher Education" betrays his "obligation to those who have stood behind [him] in the early days."[68] Enraged by the patronizing missive on the one hand and his father's concordance with the judge on the other, Nathan refuses his mother's request to call Victor, who has been waiting impatiently for a response. "Darling, phone him at his office," she pleads. "Phone him now. For me." "No." "I beg of you." "No." "Oh, I can't believe this is you." "It *is* me!" "But—what about your father's love?" "I am on my own!"[69]

Nathan's visit to E. I. Lonoff is one of particular symbolic consequence for the young artist; having forsaken paternal love ("I am on my own!") for his fiction, he arrives at the austere farmhouse in the Berkshires looking for nothing less than a paternal surrogate: "I was off and away," the narrator asserts, "seeking patriarchal validation elsewhere."[70] And though the discipleship he seeks is aesthetic, the boundary between his desire for artistic recognition and filial affection is repeatedly blurred: "For I had come, you see, to submit myself for candidacy as nothing less than E. I. Lonoff's spiritual son, to petition for his moral sponsorship and to win, if I could, the magical protection of his advocacy and his love." No terrible surprise in a discipline where the border between life (blood kinship) and vocation (literary paternity) is so porous.[71]

Lonoff's handling of Jewish characters in his stories (Roth's compact summary of their content salutes Bernard Malamud's short fictions of the 1950s) inspires in the young Zuckerman "feelings of kinship" that affect him deeply.[72] It awakens him to how profoundly his Jewish upbringing has shaped his sensibility. Thus the two artists between whom Zuckerman "selects" his ersatz father are American writers who are also secular Jews.

In the two-plus decades since *The Ghost Writer*'s publication, readers have identified correspondences between E. I. Lonoff and Felix Abravanel, the pair in Roth's novel, and their contemporary (Malamud and Singer on the Lonovian side; Bellow and to a lesser extent Mailer on Abravanel's) and antecedent (Kafka and James; above all Babel) models.[73] Both are surely composites. What interests me most, however, are Roth's portrayal of literary kinship in this novel, his troping of biological patrimony, and the emerging parallels between Nathan Zuckerman's dilemma and the one discussed by Kafka in a letter to Max Brod so many years before.[74]

For those immersed in literature, the claims of an imaginary world generate an unnatural kinship. Authors and their disciples share an affinity so strong it is like consanguinity. Hence Kafka's September 1913 letter to Felice, in which he claims (to the diminishment of his own family) Grillparzer, Dostoevsky, Kleist, and Flaubert as his "true blood relations."[75] Discussing Kafka with Lonoff forty-three years later across the Atlantic, Zuckerman proposes a similar "alternative paternity" in his hypothesis that Isaac Babel, the Jewish writer from Odessa renowned for his stories about marauding Cossacks, constitutes what he calls "the missing link" between Lonoff and Abravanel. "Those stories are what connects you," Zuckerman explains, "if you don't mind my mentioning your work—"

He crossed his hands on his belly and rested them there, movement enough to make me say, "I'm sorry."

"Go ahead. Connected to Babel. How?"

"Well, 'connected' of course isn't the right word. Neither is 'influence.' *It's family resemblance that I'm talking about.* It's as though, as I see it, you are Babel's American cousin—and Felix Abravanel is the other." [My italics][76]

Zuckerman's association of Lonoff's parables of failure—tales that feature bachelors, widowers, orphans, foundlings, and reluctant fiancés as their protagonists—with Babel's hardened fiction seems at first glance absurd. Nathan cites a story from Babel's *Red Cavalry* cycle and his "Sin of Jesus," a pair of fictions conspicuously dissimilar to the corpus attributed to Lonoff in the opening pages of *The Ghost Writer.* Lonoff's ephebe, however, detects a resemblance through his precursor's "ironic dreaming," "blunt reporting," "the writing itself."[77]

He then locates the vital roots of Felix Abravanel's work in the Jewish gangster tales of Babel—"Benya Krik and the Odessa mob." He also credits the need to escape the dutiful obedience that Babel expressed in his 1931 story "The Awakening." But Lonoff sees through Zuckerman. The key line from "The Awakening" is not, as Roth's abridged paraphrase goes, "In my childhood I led the life of a sage, when I grew up I started climbing trees," but old Mr. Trottyburn's repeated assertion about his brother's consummate craftsmanship (he carves pipes): "You have to make your children with your own hands."[78]

"And what about you?" queries the old master: "Aren't you a New World cousin in this Babel clan too? What is Zuckerman in all this?" "Why—nothing," answers Nathan:

"I've only published the four stories I sent you. My relationship is nonexistent. I think I'm still at the point where my relationship to my *own* work is practically nonexistent."[79]

So I said, and quickly reached for my glass so as to duck my disingenuous face and take a bitter drop of brandy on my tongue. But Lonoff had read my designing mind, all right; for when I came upon Babel's description of the Jewish writer as a man with autumn in his heart and spectacles on his nose, I had been inspired to add, "and blood in his penis," and had then recorded the words like a challenge—a flaming Dedalian formula to ignite *my* soul's smithy.[80]

Zuckerman wants to fuse the sensitive Jew (with spectacles on his nose and autumn in his heart) with the virile male ("a tiger, . . . a lion, . . . a cat" of a man) in his writings. *You have to make your children with your own hands* is another way of noting that apprenticeship is but a springboard to originality. If we subtract what is known of Lonoff and Abravanel from Zuckerman's attributions, the remaining qualities are no one's but Nathan's own.

Zuckerman's interpretation of Lonoff's work *and life*—"I see you as the Jew who got away"—is in this respect especially revealing.[81] It starts with psychological biography and ends in paradox, in the very contradiction lodged at the heart of Roth's trilogy. Lonoff, according to Nathan, has *gotten away* from the Russian pogroms, the Soviet purges, the Zionist solution, the ideological vice of Jewish intellectuals, even "from Brookline and the relatives" by emigrating to the United States and resettling in the recesses of rural New England. "But where's the secret, Nathan?" Lonoff asks. "What's the puzzle?"

> "Away from all the Jews, and a story by you without a Jew in it is unthinkable. The deer, the farmers, the game warden—"
> "And don't forget Hope. And my fair-headed children."
> "And still all you write about are Jews."
> "Proving what?"
> "That," I said cautiously, "is what I'd like to ask you."[82]

The eminent ironist counters with a punch line: "It proves why the young rabbi in Pittsfield can't live with the idea I won't be 'active.'" Zuckerman waits for more, but nothing follows. This answer (or lack of one), however, is of less consequence to *The Ghost Writer* than the "puzzle" posed by Nathan and its relevance to his own writing.

By calling him "a wonderful new writer" with "the most compelling voice I've encountered in years," E. I. Lonoff extends to Nathan the very approval withheld by Zuckerman's biological father.[83] Roth invariably expresses the protagonist's feelings through tropes of kinship. "I loved him!" exclaims his narrator after fielding yet another deadpan retort a few pages later: "Yes, all Lonoff had to say was that he did not even have the horse to talk to and somehow that did it, released in me a son's girlish love for the man of splendid virtue and high achievement who understands life, and who understands the son, and who approves."[84] Both fathers, literary and genetic, merge in this outpouring of gratitude. After Lonoff retires (having invited Zuckerman to stay the night), the young writer proceeds to pursue his discipleship like the diligent student so recently the pride of his parents and teachers in Newark.

Too stimulated to sleep, he examines every centimeter of Lonoff's study (where a daybed has been prepared): the portable typewriter, photographs of children, a framed postcard. He removes a lined pad from his "bulging *Bildungsroman* briefcase" and begins, shelf by shelf, to "methodically . . . list everything . . . I had not read."[85] On a bulletin board by the desk he finds two annotated note cards, one with Schumann's likening of a Chopin scherzo to a poem by Byron and the other with a quotation excerpted from Henry James's "The Middle Years": "We work in the dark—we do what we can—we give what we have. Our doubt is our passion and our passion is our task. The rest is the madness of art."[86] Nathan Zuckerman, twenty-three years old and simmering with promise, fails to grasp the passage's import ("The art what was sane, no? Or was I missing something?"), even after his repeated reading of the tale before night's end. For now he is spared intimate familiarity with *the madness of art*—Roth postpones this discovery until his chronicle of the next stage of Nathan's education, *Zuckerman Unbound.*

Zuckerman's elation ebbs as the night progresses. He gradually realizes that his need for paternal approval has not receded after all, and he struggles in one failed draft after another to "explain to my father—the foot-doctor father, *the first of my fathers*—the 'voice' that, according to no less a vocalist than E. I. Lonoff, started back of my knees and reached above my head" (my italics).[87] Yet these attempts only reinforce his original conviction—namely, that he doesn't owe anyone an explanation for his writing. The conflict is intractable. Zuckerman's complaint resembles that made by Roth's narrator in "Looking at Kafka," who laments that his parents, who once "together cleared all obstructions from my path," are "now to be my final obstruction!"[88] Zuckerman is blocked, from within and from without. But the insolubility of his dilemma begets an outrageous, wish-fulfilling fiction worthy of the Babel-inspired revisionary task he has set for himself.

The subject of this fiction is Amy Bellette, a former student of Lonoff's at the nearby women's college. Bellette, who now lives in Cambridge, is visiting Lonoff to sort through the drafts of his manuscripts. She works for the library at Harvard, from whence she has been dispatched in hope of acquiring his papers for their special collection. Zuckerman's sight of her amid these materials on the living room floor stimulates a fantasy that incarnates his literary kinship to the old master: presuming her to be his daughter, Nathan imagines marrying the girl. His deduction shortly thereafter that she cannot be of direct relation does not impair his imagination, but excites it more. "*I must see you again,*" he thinks when Lonoff leaves the room for a moment, while concurrently striving to "dispel . . . [his] insidious daydreams and wait . . . like a thoughtful man of letters."[89]

Zuckerman's awe is compounded when he is told, later that afternoon, that Bellette also writes. "She has a remarkable prose style," Lonoff remarks. "The best student writing I've ever read. Wonderful clarity. Wonderful comedy. Tremendous intelligence. She wrote stories about the college which capture the place in a sentence. Everything she sees, she takes hold of."[90] She too has been taken under Lonoff's wing, but more than just figuratively; we learn at the dinner table that his generous response to a letter she had written him years earlier in England (where she had been displaced, presumably by the war) ultimately brought her across the Atlantic to Athena College. Her promising talent, intriguing accent, and easy familiarity with Lonoff inspire an erotic charge in the aspiring acolyte with "blood in his penis." Zuckerman awaits her return "just to be awake and unclothed in one bed while she was awake and nearly unclothed in another."[91] This stimulation culminates in Nathan's masturbation on the daybed, a transgression he tries to amend by taking "to the high road," that is, by reading Henry James.

His study of "The Middle Years" is arrested when he hears the voices of Bellette and Lonoff through the ceiling. Zuckerman's curiosity exceeds his will to decorum. In a farcical act of symbolic usurpation, Roth's protagonist stands atop the edition of James's tales to eavesdrop on the colloquy above.[92] What he learns leads him to wonder at "the thinness of my imagination"; "Oh, if only I could imagine the scene I'd overheard!" he thinks. "If only I could invent as presumptuously as real life!"—an echo of Roth's famous postulation that American reality "is continually outdoing our talents," that "the culture tosses up figures almost daily that are the envy of almost any novelist."[93] Roth reproduces the exchange between the two in dialogue form. In it, Lonoff thwarts a desperate attempt by Bellette to seduce him, deploying the same "mad, heroic restraint" we have already learned is characteristic of his fiction.[94]

Bellette's childishness (she calls Lonoff "Dad-da," sits in his lap, and asks him to tell her a story or sing her a song) invokes on the one hand Freud's 1909 essay about "The Neurotic's Family Romance." More relevant to Zuckerman's writing, however, is an axiom set forth in Freud's "Creative Writers and Daydreaming," a text published one year earlier: "You will see from such an example how the wish employs some event in the present to plan a future on the pattern of the past."[95] The line from the past that boomerangs back, impelled by Zuckerman's onanism and then his eavesdropping, comes from the postscript of Judge Wapter's letter: "P.S. If you have not yet seen the Broadway production of *The Diary of Anne Frank*, I strongly advise that you do so. Mrs. Wapter and I were in the audience on opening night; we wish that Nathan Zuckerman could have been with us to benefit from that extraordinary experience." A few pages later, Nathan's mother mentions the play too in her attempt to reconcile father and son.[96]

Cynthia Ozick's "Who Owns Anne Frank?" challenges the "shamelessness of appropriation" these middle-class Newark Jews so enthusiastically enact. The 1955 Broadway production was the first staging to have immorally (she argues) "bowdlerized, distorted, transmuted, traduced, reduced, . . . infantilized, Americanized, homogenized, sentimentalized . . . falsified, kitschified, and, in fact, blatantly and arrogantly denied" Frank's diary. In "Femme Fatale," *The Ghost Writer's* third chapter, Zuckerman contributes his own "distortion" to the Frank myth: a wish-fulfilling fiction inspired by his undiminished yearning for his parents' approval.[97]

He invents a history for Amy Bellette *as the real Anne Frank*—another Jew who got away. Having escaped from the camps, Frank changes her name to Bellette, not, like Coleman Silk in Roth's *The Human Stain,* "to disguise her identity" but rather "to forget her life."[98] She emigrates to England and then the United States for much the same reason, learning of her father's survival years later when she comes across a feature story in *Life* magazine about her diary's discovery and publication. Yet her authorial ambition has strengthened since 1944, the year when the real Anne Frank exclaimed in her diary, "I want to go on living even after my death!" and she concludes that "if she was going to be thought exceptional, it would not be because of Auschwitz and Belsen but because of what she had made of herself since"—a motive analogous to Silk's for passing as white in the later novel.[99] Furthermore, Zuckerman's Frank realizes that the work's impact is contingent upon her having been murdered, which adds a historical dimension (and urgency) to Doctor Hugh's definition of the novelist's glory, directed at the expiring and still skeptical Dencombe at the end of "The Middle Years": "The thing is to have made somebody care."[100]

In order to retain her power as a writer, she must renounce any future reunion with her father. Roth quotes a passage from Frank's diary where she expresses her failure to connect with immediate family (sentiments, as we have seen, that Kafka shared): "*Before we came here,*" she writes, "*I used at times to have the feeling that I didn't belong to Mansa, Pim, and Margot, and that I would always be a bit of an outsider. Sometimes I used to pretend I was an orphan.*"[101] Having chosen her fate, "fatherless and all on her own," she adopts Lonoff as Pim's literary replacement—and in yet another twist on the family romance, falls in love with the man. Bellette then invents this biography (Zuckerman concludes) to win over the solitary writer, compel his imagination, and draw him from his wife.[102]

Debra Shostak and Sander Gilman stress the historical components of Zuckerman's fantasy, above all its expression of the "devastations of diasporic history" and its "roots in the linkage between language, Jewish identity, and the sexual etiology of self-hatred."[103] By understating the prominence of literary ambition, however, both miss a critical point. Roth alludes to it overtly in his citations of Frank, and when Zuckerman depicts Lonoff's reaction to the girl's "confession," he refers to Bellette as "his former student and quasi daughter, a young woman of twenty-six, who had disclosed to him that of all the Jewish writers, from Franz Kafka to E. I. Lonoff, she was the most famous."[104] In Zuckerman's portrayal of Kafka and Frank as secret sharers we *can* detect his recognition of history's unforeseeable role in shaping the fame of both writers: "I was thinking," Zuckerman tells Bellette in the novel's closing pages, "she's like some impassioned little sister of Kafka's, his lost little daughter—a kinship is even there in the face. I think."

Kafka's garrets and closets, the hidden attics where they hand down the indictments, the camouflaged doors—everything he dreamed in Prague was, to her, real Amsterdam life. What he invented, she suffered. Do you remember the first sentence of *The Trial*? We were talking about it last night, Mr. Lonoff and myself. "Someone must have falsely traduced Anne F., because one morning without having done anything wrong, she was placed under arrest."[105]

But we also sense his yearning for their accomplishment. And furthermore, his identification with their ambivalence to Judaism, their election of literary fathers over real ones, and the curious yet persistent resurfacing of these issues in their writings.

Zuckerman's literature, Lonoff rightly suggests, thrives on this opposition. Roth's second novel of the series, *Zuckerman Unbound,* begins to delve into the consequences of his protagonist's break for artistic freedom.

Zuckerman Unbound: Art with a Trial

> Unless painting proves its right to exist by being critical and self-judging, it
> has no reason to exist at all—or is not even possible. The canvas is a court
> where the artist is prosecutor, defendant, jury, and judge. Art without a
> trial disappears at a glance: it is too primitive or hopeful, or mere notions,
> or simply startling, or just another means to make life bearable.
>
> —Philip Guston, "Faith, Hope and Impossibility"

Kafka initially intended to title his second collection of short prose pieces *Verantwortung*—"Responsibility" in English.[106] The book appeared in 1920 as *A Country Doctor: Little Stories* after a three-year war-related delay. In the tales gathered in this volume, Kafka moves beyond the themes that led him to group some of his 1912–14 stories under rubrics like *The Sons* and *Punishments*. His stress on one character's ambivalent relation to family or work persists, but now enlarged and modified in scope to encompass his civilization and culture—indeed, his age.[107] All of Kafka's fictions during these years share an emphasis on *Verantwortung,* on conscience and culpability.

To every action or thought, unspoken or professed, its consequences: this axiom prevails even when Kafka (as in *The Trial*) never makes the original transgression explicit. As "The Judgment" approaches its climax, the death wishes Georg Bendemann harbors against his father race through his mind faster than he can register them; his best defense amounts to a few hyperbolic exclamations, wielded so clumsily that they instead reinforce his opponent's indictment. Georg is held accountable for being a "devilish person," though the "nevertheless" of his last words—"Dear parents, I have always loved you, all the same"—hints at an identification with his father's verdict that is less than complete.[108]

A similar reflex governs *Zuckerman Unbound.*[109] *Die Schuld ist immer zweifellos,* goes the motto of Kafka's penal colony: Guilt is never to be doubted.[110] But while that prisoner's culpability seems dubious indeed, *The Ghost Writer*'s Nathan Zuckerman feels too offended by his father's provincial reservations to experience anything beyond prideful rage for his own "transgressions": "I will not prate in platitudes to please the adults!" cries Roth's young Prometheus in refusing his mother's request to call his father and account for his refusal to answer Judge Wapter's letter.[111]

Roth's second installment of the Zuckerman saga is set thirteen years later. The wound opened by "Higher Education" has only partially healed. Despite the backing given by father to son in public—"As Daddy always says," Selma explains, "what is a family if they don't stick together?"—Victor Zuckerman can no better comprehend his son's motives now than he can relinquish his moral authority.[112] When Nathan boards the bus to New York in 1956, he abandons a confounded father trying to reconcile the polite boy he had raised with the freewheeling author unafraid to mine his own family, community, and people for interesting material. The son's path has veered away for good. So far as writing is concerned, he is finally "on his own."

Thanks to a timely stroke, Victor is hospitalized before *Carnovsky*'s sensational publication thirteen years later.[113] But "when a writer is born in the family," Czesław Miłosz once observed—Roth quotes him in Roly Keating's BBC documentary—"the family is finished." And the likelihood of unanticipated repercussions (referred to elsewhere by Roth as the "Law of 26") lingers still.[114] Doctor Zuckerman's sons have inherited his prioritization of family bonds when the novel begins. Though they live dispersed, the Zuckerman clan remains closely knit. *Zuckerman Unbound,* however, relates more than just "the unreckoned consequences of a life in art" discussed below. Roth's novel grapples relentlessly with questions of paternity and guilt, responsibility and restraint, captivity and liberation—and nowhere with such concentrated intensity as in its climactic chapter, "Look Homeward, Angel."[115]

Of the three novels in the series, *Zuckerman Unbound* sends up the fewest number of direct allusions to Kafka.[116] Yet the latter's presence is more profound in the absence of all the declarations and hectic semaphoring typical of Roth's prior work. For the first time Roth integrates Kafka without reducing him or his fiction to parody (compare, for example, *The Breast* or "Looking at Kafka") by "domesticating and deflating what is awesome in its own context."[117] Roth references "A Report to an Academy" and especially "The Judgment" at length in ways that illuminate Zuckerman's central dilemma while preserving the integrity of those earlier texts.

Kafka's "Report," a 1916 tale about a captured ape's accelerated evolution into "an average European," is itself a kind of bildungsroman in miniature. Using the script for an address as his framing device, Kafka has his protagonist, Red Peter, relate the history of his development from the time of his capture to his acquisition of human speech. His report focuses mainly on "the line an erstwhile ape has had to follow in entering and establishing himself in the world of men."[118] Pivotal to this transformation, Red Peter insists, was the panic unleashed by his placement in a narrow cage upon the Hagenbeck steamship:

Until then I had had so many ways out of everything, and now I had none. I was pinned down. Had I been nailed down, my right to free movement would not have been lessened. . . . I had no way out but I had to devise one, for without it I could not live. All the time facing that locker—I should certainly have perished. Yet as far as Hagenbeck was concerned, the place for apes was in front of a locker—well then, I had to stop being an ape. A fine, clear train of thought, which I must have constructed somehow with my belly, since apes think with their bellies. [119]

Red Peter's parable about entrapment, freedom, and most of all, the urgency of finding a way out resonates at numerous levels with Roth's trilogy. Zuckerman's best material thrives on resistance: "His work has turbulence," Lonoff tells his wife early in *The Ghost Writer;* "he oughtn't to stifle what is clearly his gift." [120] To nourish this talent, Zuckerman *needs* the pressure of opposing forces. He distances himself from his family so he can write "freely," but then finds his subject staked to this very tension.

In the wake of *Carnovsky's* resounding success, Zuckerman is repeatedly mistaken for the protagonist of his novel. He becomes, in effect, entrapped by the very fiction he'd engendered: "Zuckerman is chained and bound," Edward Rothstein observes, "—by his readers—to the book itself." [121] At a time of already heightened national paranoia (intensified by the escalating war in Vietnam and the recent assassinations of Robert Kennedy and Martin Luther King, Jr.), Nathan, transformed overnight into a public celebrity by his notorious bestseller, finds himself a magnet for hate mail and ominous threats from anti-Semites, offended Jews, and maniacs of every conviction. He is accosted by strangers who mistake him for *Carnovsky's* sex-addled protagonist—intimations at last of James's "madness of art," though not at all in the decorous guise he had anticipated. Zuckerman bucks desperately against the irreversibility of the book's effect, but his attempts to continue living as if nothing had changed (riding the bus instead of taking a taxi, eating at greasy delicatessens) cannot turn back the clock.

"To fight the way your life is going," his agent André Schevitz commiserates, "to be unable to accept what has happened to you, this I . . . understand":

"Especially a boy with your background. What with Papa telling you to be good, and Mama telling you to be nice, and the University of Chicago training you four years in Advanced Humanistic Decisions, well, what chance did you ever have to lead a decent life? To take you away to that place at sixteen! It's like stealing a wild little baby baboon from the branches of the trees, feeding him in the kitchen, letting him sleep in your bed and play with the light switch and wear little shirts and pants with pockets, and then, when he is big and hairy and full of himself, giving him his degree in Western Civilization and sending him back to the bush. I can just imagine what an enchanting baboon you were at the University of Chicago. Pounding the seminar table, writing English on the blackboard, screaming at the class they had it all wrong—you must have been all over the place. Rather like in this abrasive little book."[122]

The "little baby baboon" Schevitz speaks of is the creature of appetency and ambition already identified by Lonoff in *The Ghost Writer*. It invokes Red Peter but also Zuckerman's vision of himself as a fusion of Babel and Kafka (or, to restate the fictional coordinates of that earlier novel, Abravanel and Lonoff)—a canonical Jewish writer with autumn in his heart, spectacles on his nose, *and blood in his penis*.[123] *Carnovsky* is the offspring of this crossbreed. But now that Zuckerman has finally changed his life, finding a "way out" from the stultifications of "proper, responsible" novels and "dreary virtuousness," he is dismayed to discover there's no going back: metamorphosis is, as Schevitz asserts, "a cruel, irreversible process." As with the seminar baboon, so with Zuckerman's family ties.[124]

"My son," commands the eighth and ninth verses of Proverbs 1, "hear the instruction of thy father, and forsake not the law of thy mother; for they *shall be* an ornament of grace unto thy head, and chains about thy neck." The young and impetuous Zuckerman forsakes law and instruction alike in order to retain the "freedom" his vocation demands. In "Look Homeward, Angel," the irreversible trajectory from deed to consequence takes its course, reaching its acme in a deathbed scene that refers directly to "The Judgment."

When Victor suffers a coronary, the core of the Zuckerman family—Nathan, his mother Selma, brother Henry, Cousin Essie and her husband, Mr. Metz—gathers around the patriarch as his condition deteriorates. The once-mighty father is, like Herr Bendemann in Kafka's story, "tucked way down into the bedsheets."[125] His chin quivers, and his unintelligible attempts to speak resemble "the squeals of a mouse." A day and a half into the vigil, Essie grasps his hand and, looking into his "gray, imploring eyes," lovingly recalls his father's winepress, his mother's *mandel* bread, and the "family character" Uncle Markish.[126]

Nathan's farewell address, which follows Essie's nostalgic reminiscence, summarizes a contemporary theory about the Big Bang—a subject as abstract as his cousin's had been tangible. Although his intent is to console—"It wasn't just a father who was dying," he reasons, "or a son, or a cousin, or a husband: it was the whole creation, whatever comfort that gave"—Zuckerman's lecture inappropriately foregoes a show of affection, asserting and imparting his own authority instead. "Proceed, Nathan," he reprimands himself, "to father the father. Last chance to tell the man what he still doesn't know. Last chance ever to make him see it all another way. You'll change him yet." His narrative, as his mother rightly indicates ("Talk to *him*, Nathan"), is more soliloquy than direct address.[127] Upon its conclusion Nathan imagines death as a leveling reconciler: "Enough for now of what is and isn't so," he thinks. "Enough science, enough art, enough of fathers and sons"—presumptions vastly incongruous with his father's impeded fury:

> Though Dr. Zuckerman didn't officially expire until the next morning, it was here that he uttered his last words. Word. Barely audible, but painstakingly pronounced. "Bastard," he said. Meaning who? . . . When he spoke his last, it wasn't to his correspondence folders that he was looking, or upward at the face of an invisible God, but into the eyes of the apostate son.[128]

The son who had once sought surrogate paternity in literature finally achieves his authorial aspirations, but in accordance with Emily Dickinson's awful implacable dictum: *All—is the price of all.*[129] *Carnovsky* seals Zuckerman's reputation as a writer at the cost of eliciting an irreversible condemnation from his dying father. Although Roth relays the repudiation unambiguously, his protagonist initially fails to register its import or subconsciously refuses to do so. Despite all evidence to the contrary, Nathan "wonders" whether he has misheard the "painstakingly pronounced" verdict: perhaps it was "faster," he thinks, or "vaster" or even "better."[130] Unlikely possibilities, but to Zuckerman the alternative seems more implausible: such a deathbed rebuke would be, as Elizabeth Costello complains in Coetzee's "Before the Gate," *too literary.*[131] Doctor Zuckerman's judgment is thus suspended for the time being, at least in Nathan's conscience.

The "strain of feeling no grief" Nathan experiences at the funeral broadens into a "heady feeling of untrammeled freedom" when he and his brother board the plane in Miami for home—a moral equivalent to the boundlessness elaborated by Red Peter as "the spacious feeling of freedom on all sides."[132] All of the opposition stemming from Doctor Zuckerman's prohibitions and disapproval seems to have died with the man. Feeling released, Nathan reels in a "tide of elation" generated by his newfound independence: "He had become himself again—though with something unknowable added: he was no longer any man's son. Forget fathers, he told himself. Plural."[133]

Having "fathered the father" a couple of days before, Zuckerman now offers guidance to his conflicted younger brother as they fly northward. Henry Zuckerman is Nathan's dutiful counter-self, the obedient son par excellence—a model of ascetic self-restraint like E. I. Lonoff but devoted to family instead of Art.[134] Unhappy in his marriage and stricken with guilt for his affairs, Henry (as shaken by Victor's death as Nathan is composed) confesses to his brother the terrible repercussions of loyalty to their father's governing principles of responsibility, devotion, and self-sacrifice. Though desperate for an *Ausweg*—his life at home, he says, is "murder"—resignation prevails because of the misery that flight would confer upon his wife and children. Nathan responds by invoking yet another literary father: "Do you know what Chekhov said as a grown man about his youth? He said he'd had to squeeze the serf out of himself drop by drop. Maybe what you ought to start squeezing out of yourself is the obedient son."[135]

Despite the elder sibling's goodwill, his advice cannot help but condescend. And as in "The Judgment," the power dynamic between the two turns decisively in a single stroke. Before parting at the airport, Nathan offers his apartment as a refuge if needed—implying or even encouraging Henry's readiness to flee from his family. This elicits a passionate outburst in which the younger Zuckerman stands in for their father, broadcasting the earlier judgment conclusively:

"He did say 'Bastard,' Nathan. He called you a bastard."
"What?"
Suddenly Henry was furious—and weeping. "You *are* a bastard. A heartless conscienceless bastard. What does loyalty mean to you? What does responsibility mean to you? What does self-denial mean, *restraint*—anything at all? To you everything is disposable! Everything is *ex*posable! Jewish morality, Jewish endurance, Jewish wisdom, Jewish families—everything is grist for your fun-machine. Even your shiksas go down the drain when they don't tickle your fancy any more. Love, mar-

riage, children, what the hell do you care? To you it's all fun and games. *But that isn't the way it is to the rest of us.* And the worst is how we protect you from knowing what you really are! And what you've done! You killed him, Nathan. Nobody will tell you—they're too frightened of you to say it. They think you're too famous to criticize—that you're far beyond the reach now of ordinary human beings. But you killed him, Nathan. With that book. *Of course* he said 'Bastard.' He'd seen it! He'd seen what you had done to him and Mother in that book!"[136]

Unbeknownst to Nathan, his father had demanded that Essie's kind but aloof husband bring over a copy of *Carnovsky* and read from it aloud. "Zuckerman thought he had beaten the risk," writes Roth, "and beaten the rap. He hadn't."[137] The excessive literariness of the situation makes it no less tragic: Victor dies in "misery" and "the most terrible disappointment," his coronary equivalent to a broken heart. Nathan, of course, *had* been able to imagine his father reading the book as he wrote it, had anticipated the risk of its discovery. "But he'd written it anyway." And then published it. This knowledge now compounds his culpability.

For all of his fury, Henry, like the father at the end of Kafka's tale, is radiant with insight. Nathan's egoism, particularly as a writer, lies at the heart of his accusation: "It's one thing, God damn you, to entrust your imagination to your instincts," he says, "it's another, Nathan, to entrust your *own family!*" In an essay on Richard Wagner, Thomas Mann had disingenuously declared that "innocent may be the last adjective to apply to art; but the artist he is innocent."[138] *Carnovsky* is anything but innocent, but according to this formula Zuckerman is guiltless. As an author he answers to literature's standards, not those of his family or milieu.

But Mann's rationalization, this author knows—as did his late friend Philip Guston, to whom this novel is dedicated—belies the ethical dubiousness of misrepresentation and the fiction-making enterprise as a whole. Zuckerman's characters follow a Proustian model: they are composites of various individuals, imagined and real.[139] However distinctly the *representation* of Gilbert Carnovsky's parents veers away from the *actual* Victor and Selma Zuckerman, their relation is clear to all involved. Nathan's, and by extension Roth's, exaggerations are harmful because his fictions expose their subjects, often in an unflattering light, to a larger audience in guises *undetermined by themselves.* "Art is, in fact, 'playing king,'" James Wood asserts; "it is guilty innocence, innocent guilt." Zuckerman is innocent insofar as his writing follows the dictates of talent, temperament, and truth; he harbors no intention to harm his family. But his craft is derivative and therefore rooted in theft.[140]

Thoroughly acquainted with the experience of guilt, Nathan Zuckerman has until now inclined to self-exculpation *for being an artist*—as if a writer and his corpus were exclusively discrete entities. Had Roth failed to represent the validity of Henry's (i.e., Victor's) charge, his novel would have been tantamount to what Guston disparagingly called "art without a trial."[141] The final chapter of *Zuckerman Unbound* holds him accountable for what his work has wrought. Like Georg Bendemann, young Zuckerman's ambitions are innocent enough. It is the *context* through which they are achieved that makes such innocence devilish.

Georg's marriage proposal and his takeover of the family business are in themselves "natural" transitions into adulthood, advances that will elevate him to the role of paterfamilias. But this ascension necessarily unseats his precursor, and usurpation never lacks a value charge—especially for the usurped. ("You can't have a pair of scales with both sides rising at the same time," Kafka had written to Grete Bloch on February 1, 1914.)[142] Tucking in one's father, whether in southern Florida at the end of the twentieth century or central Europe some seventy years before, remains a figurative way of burying him.

Henry's verdict banishes Nathan. Death now undoes the bonds so persistently preserved by Victor Zuckerman during his lifetime. After the funeral Nathan had been overcome by a sense of "untrammeled freedom"; Roth transposes this elation into a minor key as Zuckerman directs his armed driver around the Weequahic neighborhood of his youth. "Over," he thinks as he looks out the window at the slums once the site of his happy childhood: "Over. Over. Over. Over. Over. I've served my time."[143] The prison of Zuckerman's past is irretrievable, the resistance of paternal authority silenced. He guides the driver to his old house, immersed in memory and loss.

"Across the street from the boys' back bedroom," Roth writes, "on the other side of a high wire fence, was a Catholic orphanage with a small truck farm where the orphans worked when they weren't taught."[144] As a boy, Zuckerman had wondered about life on the other side of the fence. It inspired one of his first stories (titled "Orphans"); twenty years later he acknowledges that the fence "had been his first subject"—his "first momentous encounter with caste and chance, with the mystery of a destiny."[145] Disowned by his father and dismissed by his brother, the orphaned author is greeted by the harsh poverty of release—a lesson Red Peter imparts in

"Report" when he notes, "In passing: all too often men are betrayed by the word freedom. And as freedom is counted among the most sublime feelings, so is the corresponding disappointment."[146] Stopped before the garage where a superintendent's daughter had once drawn him in and made him repeat phrases he'd been too young to understand, Nathan is confronted by a young black man who steps out of the house and asks who he is. "No one," he answers, mimicking not Odysseus—Zuckerman's reply is no ruse—but the abandoned Nobodies of Kafka's "Excursion in the Mountains" and "The Hunter Gracchus."

Zuckerman is truly on his own. In her trenchant analysis of the novel (all the more admirable given that *Philip Roth* was published in 1981, years before the scope of Roth's trilogy and epilogue became clear), Hermione Lee notes that *Zuckerman Unbound*, like *The Ghost Writer*, grapples with "the son's need to revolt from the community in order to master it as material." "The Jewish son who grows up to be the novelist," she affirms, "is 'in possession' of his material, but he is also 'unbound, dispossessed, no longer any man's son.'"[147] In order to be a writer Nathan must cease to be a son. Conversely, the "freedom" of being unfettered from this past necessitates yet additional unforeseen consequences for the writer. *The Anatomy Lesson* explores this aftermath.

A Corpus Bound

The Anatomy Lesson is set in December 1973, four years after Victor Zuckerman's death. Beset by chronic pain in his neck and shoulders, Nathan Zuckerman turns to his anthology of seventeenth-century verse, searching for spiritual alleviation. He directs his attention to "The Collar," hoping George Herbert's poem will somehow "help him wear his own."[148] In it, a rebellious speaker resists the constraints invoked by the metaphorical title. "No more," he cries in the opening stanza, "I will abroad." Herbert's choleric persona gives vent to his yearning to escape a presumably self-imposed bondage: "What? shall I ever sigh and pine? / My lines and life are free; free as the road, / Loose as the wind, as large as store." This speaker's urgent wish to "forsake [his] cage" recalls the bristling will to freedom expressed by Roth's young protagonist in *The Ghost Writer* and *Zuckerman Unbound*.[149]

Nearly two decades have passed since Zuckerman first asserted his writerly independence from the suffocating moral obligations of his father's (American-born, Jewish, lower middle-class) generation. When the novel opens, he has long since overcome the need for external appraisal; his parents are dead, his brother still estranged, his marriage record a litany of failure. In effect, he is not responsible to anyone but himself—that is, to his own work. Yet this victory brings with it little satisfaction: Nathan has not written anything substantial since *Carnovsky* was published in 1969. He *cannot* write, figuratively or literally. An incessant pain of mysterious origin prevents him from so much as pushing a pen. And "with nothing to write," Zuckerman has "no reason to be."[150] Like Kafka's lecture-hall ape, he has simply altered the conditions of his imprisonment.[151] "For every avenue liberation opens," Saul Bellow reminds us, "two are closed."[152]

The sublimating conclusion of "The Collar" (reproduced by Roth in the text) compels an ailing Nathan to launch his volume across the room in rage—ostensibly because the hallowing transformation Herbert records mocks his own indecorous suffering. Zuckerman's complaint, however, evades an aspect of the poem's diction that surely elicits some of the hostility in his response. After thirty-two lines of railing steadily against an unnamed suppressive force, an alien yet *paternal* voice rises from *within the speaker's own*. With a single utterance this doubling persona asserts his authority, to which the subject immediately submits: "But as I rav'd and grew more fierce and wild / at every word, / Me thoughts I heard one calling, *Childe:* / And I reply'd, *My Lord.*"[153] Zuckerman refuses to succumb to such compliant resolutions, but shares with his author an adamant "resistance to plaintive metaphor and poeticized analogy."[154]

Nathan's inexplicable ague resembles an ailment suffered by an earlier Roth protagonist. A mysterious pain strikes the lower back of the eponymous hero in "Novotny's Pain" (a story published in 1962 and revised for *A Philip Roth Reader* eighteen years later) shortly after the U.S. Army drafts him at the onset of the Korean War. Its origin is also obscure: "He told the doctor that all he knew was that he had a pain. He tried to explain that taping it up didn't work; the pain wasn't on the surface but deep inside his back. The doctor said it was deep inside his head." Novotny's superiors imply that his lumbago is a psychosomatic stratagem designed to evade combat, a coward's recourse. Against this diagnosis Roth contrasts the recalcitrant insistence of the soldier's "invented" illness: "That all the doctors were unable to give a satisfactory diagnosis did not make his pain any less real."[155]

Novotny's motives, though scrutinized thoroughly, are not so central to the story as the life-altering puissance of fantasy and its indisputably "real" consequences.[156] Roth's repeated emphasis on the imagination's transformative power over four decades of writing places him in the line of distinguished Cervantists whose fictions have thematized one's becoming what one reads, a realization Roth enacts in the highest and most bathetic registers. When Novotny consults a medical encyclopedia to compare his condition to that of someone with a slipped disc, he corroborates his pain while learning more about his ailment. He awakens the next morning suffering from the symptoms he had studied the day before. The mind, like the hideous device featured in Kafka's "Penal Colony," is a "remarkable apparatus," capable of inscribing terrible sentences upon the body.[157]

Zuckerman, of course, spurns any thought that his affliction might arise from guilt—that it could be a self-inflicted concession to his father's condemnation. Disconsolate after enduring eight days of traction (an unpleasantness Novotny shares that evokes the "Bed" of Kafka's *Apparat*),[158] he visits an analyst who tells him that "the Zuckerman . . . getting paid off [i.e., psychically] wasn't the self he perceived as himself but the ineradicable infant, the atoning penitent, the guilty pariah—perhaps it was the remorseful son of the dead parents, the author of *Carnovsky*":

> It had taken three weeks for the doctor to say this out loud. It might be months before he broke the news of the hysterical conversion symptom. "Expiation through suffering?" Zuckerman said. "The pain being my judgment on myself and that book?" "Is it?" the analyst asked. "No," Zuckerman replied, and three weeks after it had begun, he terminated the therapy by walking out.[159]

As during the penultimate scene of the preceding novel, Zuckerman is offended by the reductive symbolism of this presumptuous, hyper-literary reading of his own life. He can recognize its compatibility with the conversion theory Freud had delineated in *Studies on Hysteria* (as demonstrated by his hostile understatement), but not with the blunt, unrelenting ache in his neck.[160]

And yet he continues to entertain the possibility, however skeptically, since no convincing explanation—certainly no medical one—comes to the fore. Besides, he has long been accustomed to seeing this pattern reproduced in literature, from the great nineteenth-century Russians down to the Bible.[161] According to this theory of self-infliction (to which most of his friends and colleagues, referred to by Zuckerman as "comforters," subscribe),[162]

Zuckerman was taking "pain" back to its root in *poena,* the Latin word for punishment: poena for the family portrait the whole country had assumed to be his, for the tastelessness that had affronted millions and the shamelessness that had enraged his tribe. The crippling of his upper torso was, transparently, the punishment called forth by his crime: mutilation as primitive justice. If the writing arm offend thee, cut it off and cast it from thee.[163]

The father's judgment survives death by grafting itself into the conscience of his apostate son. Victor becomes the ultimate ghostwriter, and Nathan, like the prisoner in the penal colony, is condemned to feel "the commandment he has disobeyed . . . written upon his body."[164]

Kafka, of course, mined a similar conceit in his writing, and even asserted an inner unity between his stories about transgression and correction. When it became clear that the one-volume gathering of tales he had hoped to publish as *The Sons* was no longer feasible, he suggested an alternative combination of "The Judgment," "The Metamorphosis," and "In the Penal Colony." These three fictions would appear together under the apposite title *Punishments.*[165] The protagonist of each yields to putative measures pronounced by an authoritarian figure in decline—Georg Bendemann and Gregor Samsa to their aging fathers, the penal colony officer to the code of an old Commandant. All three stories share a similar climactic moment, namely, the instant the hero identifies with his superior's verdict.

Several parallels can also be drawn between the pain Nathan Zuckerman suffers in *The Anatomy Lesson* and Josef K.'s guilt in *The Trial.* Nathan's pain, more than that of any other figure in Roth's fiction, complements the evasiveness of meaning in Kafka—what I referred to earlier as his "hovering trope." Zuckerman's pain appeals to interpretation (i.e., diagnosis) while defying it. Its origin remains obscure for the duration of the novel; occasional flashes of insight occur, but only hypothetically, by way of metaphor (e.g., pain as punishment). Josef K.'s guilt is similarly opaque and fleeting. He never learns why he has been arrested, under whose orders, or according to what law. To this extent *The Trial* reads like a modern novel of education. Josef K. develops as the book progresses, but negatively; he is shaped by what he cannot assimilate. The same can be said for Nathan in *Zuckerman Bound.*[166]

In a celebrated chapter of *The Trial,* a prison chaplain censures K.'s reckless course of defense. He singles out K.'s tendency to enlist women associated with the court to help him influence his case: "'You seek too much outside help,' the priest said disapprovingly, 'particularly from women. Haven't you noticed that it isn't true help.'"[167]

The chaplain's insight stuns K., and rightfully so; from the moment of his arrest, K. incessantly pursues the attention, assistance, and attraction of the opposite sex, always to the detriment of his cause. His reenactment before Fräulein Bürstner of an interrogation by a court-appointed inspector precedes his falling upon her early in the book. He is then drawn to a washerwoman by her proximity to an examining magistrate, who keeps her like a concubine.[168] Later, K. carelessly offends his "true helpers" by abandoning his uncle, lawyer, and the chief clerk of the court in order to flirt with Leni, the advocate's maid and mistress. In an unfinished section of the novel titled "To Elsa," Kafka explicitly demonstrates how his protagonist's sexual diversions damage his standing with the court. K. is summoned, and sternly advised to eschew further truancy: "Today's summons was a final attempt. He could do as he wished, but he should bear in mind that the high court could not permit itself to be mocked." K. disregards the order and visits his girlfriend.[169]

Zuckerman is also beset with irresponsible diversions. Lying supine on a red play mat—a curious variation on Beckett's Malone and Macmann, with an erect penis—he maintains a seraglio of four women.[170] "They were all the vibrant life he had," Roth writes:

secretary-confidante-cook-housekeeper-companion—aside from the doses of Nixon's suffering, they were the entertainment. On his back he felt like their whore, paying in sex for someone to bring him the milk and the paper. They told him their troubles and took off their clothes and lowered the orifices for Zuckerman to fill. Without a taxing vocation or a hopeful prognosis, he was theirs to do with as they wished; the more conspicuous his helplessness, the more forthright their desire.[171]

Josef K. convinces himself that he can harness the agency of women to influence his case; despite his ironic qualifications, Zuckerman on the whole accedes to the self-deluding conviction that his relationships will have a salutary effect. "Maybe he'd learn something and maybe he wouldn't," he reasons, "but at least they [i.e., his four women] would help to distract him, and according to the rheumatologist at NYU, distraction, pursued by the patient with real persistence, could reduce even the worst pain to tolerable levels."[172] In their pursuit of immediate gratification and the quick fix,

Nathan and Josef perilously divert their energy from mounting a proper defense, one that would introspectively examine their guilt in earnest.

Both characters are dimly aware of this deleterious effect. K. concedes that the chaplain is generally right, while Nathan in one of his monologues makes the following curious association: "They all [i.e., the women], with their benevolence, with their indulgence, with their compliance to my need, make off with what I most need to climb out of this pit. Diana is smarter, Jenny's the artist, and Jaga *really* suffers. And with Gloria I mostly feel like Gregor Samsa waiting on the floor beneath the cupboard for his sister to bring him his bowl of slops."[173]

Both characters also possess a similar intransigence and instinctual resistance to authority. K.'s refusal to recognize the court's emissaries as equals (much less as figures in whose hands his destiny might lie) leads to confrontational hearings that then accelerate the process against him. "You're too stubborn, the way I hear it," Leni admonishes. "Don't be so stubborn; you can't defend yourself against this court, all you can do is confess."[174] Convinced that he is innocent—at least until the end of the trial, when his conscience begins to assimilate the guilty verdict—Josef K. rebuffs this call for confession and assails the court instead, acting as though he can rewrite the system's laws to suit himself.[175]

Kafka never tells us whether K. is *truly* culpable: his innocence, as the novel's first sentence discloses, is merely subjunctive. Roth is equally ambiguous about whether Zuckerman's pain is a penance for transgressions committed against father and family. He does, however, expose us to his protagonist's aversion to this conclusion; Nathan's opposition is no less reflexive than Josef K.'s to the unknown law that tries him. Zuckerman parries every consideration of complicity encountered from the moment he tosses his edition of metaphysical poetry across the room in the novel's opening pages: "Absolutely not!" goes his retort to "The Collar."[176] Nathan's demurral scarcely lessens as the book proceeds. "No," he replies when his analyst asks if his pain is self-inflicted; "Zuckerman wasn't buying it," Roth tells us of his obstinate hero's later reevaluation of the same.[177]

In a 1984 interview with Roth for the *London Sunday Times,* Ian Hamilton observes that "because the pain isn't diagnosed, because it's a mystery pain, we tend to view it as a symbolic pain."[178] Many of his readers have seconded this vision. "The displaced father gets his savage revenge," writes Debra Shostak of *The Anatomy Lesson,* and not without justification—it was Roth, after all, who a decade earlier spoke of his fascination for the following passage from Kafka's cathedral chapter regarding the phenomenon of "characterological enslavement":[179]

> If the man would only quit his pulpit, it was not impossible that K. could obtain decisive and acceptable counsel from him which might, for instance, point the way, not toward some influential manipulation of his case, but toward a circumvention of it, a breaking away from it altogether, a mode of living completely outside the jurisdiction of the Court. This possibility must exist, K. had of late given much thought to it.[180]

"Enter irony," Roth adds, "when the man in the pulpit turns out to be oneself. If only one *could* quit one's pulpit, one might well obtain decisive and acceptable counsel. How to devise a mode of living completely outside the jurisdiction of the Court when the Court is of one's own devising?" If this is indeed the case, then Zuckerman's denial of any relation between his affliction and his father's death is not to be so easily dismissed.

Roth's "man in the pulpit," a self divided and sitting in judgment upon itself, reenacts what Philip Guston calls "art with a trial," the phenomenon that led Kafka to believe himself at his most critically acute while reciting his prose to his father.[181] That this figure usually appears in a paternal guise is no coincidence. The first two novels of *Zuckerman Bound* chronicle Nathan's flight from Victor, his search for a figurative replacement, and the price of the independence he finally attains. Milton Appel, the Jewish American doyen of canonical literature who synthesizes salient qualities of fatherhood for Zuckerman, occupies a central position in *The Anatomy Lesson*. Not because he is, as Robert Kiely and others have observed, a "mirror image or echo of [Zuckerman] himself," and certainly not corollary to the obvious correspondences between Appel's critique of *Carnovsky* and Irving Howe's scalding 1972 article, "Philip Roth Reconsidered."[182] Zuckerman's agonized obsession with Appel's "reconsidered judgment" reinforces the themes of paternity, authority, and rebellion Roth has been developing throughout the trilogy. The despair released as a natural by-product of generational friction between fathers and sons serves in turn as the inescapable subject of the sons' work—a paradox of freedom and entrapment Kafka identified as the inspiration, however negative, of his generation of writers German and Jewish.

What makes Nathan particularly vulnerable to the attack is the fact that Appel had been a "leading wunderkind of the Jewish generation preceding his own."[183] If E. I. Lonoff and Felix Abravanel were the immediate *literary* precursors Nathan chose for himself as an aspiring novice in *The Ghost Writer,* Appel was the renegade *critical* father who paved the way for not only Zuckerman alone, but his contemporaries as well:

> One of Appel's own *Partisan [Review]* essays, written when he was just back from World War II, had been cherished reading among Zuckerman's friends at the University of Chicago circa 1950. No one, as far as they knew, had ever written so unapologetically about the gulf between the coarse-grained Jewish fathers whose values had developed in an embattled American immigrant milieu and their bookish, nervous American sons.[184]

In this key autobiographical work, the intellectual son of an "impoverished immigrant household" chronicles the unhappy history of a crossbreed caught, like so many other second-generation American children, between two worlds and belonging to neither.[185] Appel's essay, Mark Shechner notes, trenchantly expresses "the perplexities of second-generation Jewish boys too thoroughly Americanized to rest easily in their parents' Jewish world but too Jewish, too inward, too painfully intellectual to embrace confidently a rude, jostling America.[186] "*Alienated, rootless, anguished, bewildered, brooding, tortured, powerless*"—these are the dire modifiers Appel deployed to depict his struggle against a man of modest means unable to speak a language fluently besides Yiddish, much less appreciate the profundities of Tolstoy, Faulkner, and Proust. "When," Roth resumes, "in his twenties, the time came for the son to break away . . . and take a room of his own for himself and his books, the father couldn't begin to understand where he was going or why. They shouted, they screamed, they wept, the table was struck, the door was slammed, and only then did young Milton leave home."

For young Zuckerman, the possibilities of self-invention implicit in this critic's story consoled as they inspired. They offered a perspective to contrast with and against his own skirmishes at home. Moreover, he found in Milton Appel an exemplary model of the rebellious (Jewish, literate) son and perpetual agonist. This becomes evident when Roth imparts Nathan's enthusiasm for an anthology of Yiddish fiction edited by Appel:

> Far from signaling anything so comforting and inauthentic as a prodigal son's return to the fold, it seemed, in fact, a stand *against:* to Zuck-

erman, if to no one else, . . . an exhilarating stand against the snobbish condescension of those famous departments of English literature from whose impeccable Christian ranks the literary Jew . . . had until just yesterday been pointedly excluded. To Appel's restless, half-formed young admirer, there was the dynamic feel of a rebellious act in the resurrection of those Yiddish writers, a rebellion all the more savory for undercutting the anthologist's own early rebellion. The Jew set free, an animal so ravished and agitated by his inexhaustible new hunger that he rears up suddenly and bites his tail, relishing the intriguing taste of himself even while screaming anguished sentences about the agonies inflicted by his teeth.[187]

Zuckerman relishes the twofold nature of his precursor's strike; Appel's anthology lashes out against a hostile environment as well as against an earlier self (i.e., the angry youth portrayed in the *Partisan* essay who does all he can to flee his father's stultifying world). Again we find ourselves confronted with the bind Roth has been revisiting, with ever-keener discernment, since Zuckerman applauded Lonoff for being "the Jew who got away" at the beginning of *The Ghost Writer.*

Seventeen years later, Nathan is "shocked and outraged and hurt" by the reappraisal of this other literary father, all the more because of their overlapping family resemblances. Zuckerman shares Appel's limitless ambition, inclination to contentiousness, and fanatical devotion to literature. At the time of the novel's narration (late 1973) both are physically ailing. And as if these parallels weren't conspicuous enough, Roth gives Zuckerman's foe his own—middle—name: Milton. He also lends Appel the powerful priority exhibited by fathers featured in Kafka's writing, one that manifests itself in the son's ineradicable need for approbation and his sensitivity to disapproval. Nathan tries to brush aside the verdict—he "had heard most of this before"—but cannot.[188] *Appel's condemnation matters,* however exacerbated it may be by Zuckerman's pain. It carries weight that far exceeds reasonable expectations, as do the disapprovals of Herr Bendemann and Herr Samsa.

Kafka and Roth add a nuanced distinction to the struggle depicted in their work that sets them apart from their predecessors. For all of his identification with Appel, young Nathan nevertheless recognizes an essential difference between their "cases." Appel stages the battle between father and son as a "conflict of integrities" or "tragic necessity." "Zuckerman at twenty," however, "didn't feel tortured *plus* powerless *plus* anguished— he really just wanted his father to lay off."[189] Where Appel's clash draws associations with Freud's Oedipal catastrophes, Nathan perceives a well-spring of misunderstanding brimming with comic potential *because even the misunderstanding is incomplete:*

> Zuckerman's problem was that his father *half* understood. They shouted and screamed, but in addition they sat down to reason together, and to that there is no end. Talk about torture. For the son to butcher the father with a carving knife, then step across his guts and out the door, may be a more merciful solution all around than to sit down religiously to reason together when there is nothing to reason about.[190]

In a seminal letter to Max Brod from June 1921, Kafka pinpoints this partial understanding as the origin of so much frustration and rage. Here the Jewish father nourishes, even encourages, his son's secularity by extolling a set of standardized middle-class values. To allay his upward striving, he has had him educated in German and aided him in the pursuit of a respectable career. But the father's vague but lingering relation to Judaism—or wish to sustain that relation—persists, and results in a contradictory upbringing whose ambivalence becomes the unwilling subject of the next generation of writer sons.[191] Although he belongs to an era of German Jewish sons rebelling against fathers whose thoughts and sensibilities extend back deep into the nineteenth century, Kafka stands apart from his contemporaries by deflecting the blame from the father's person to his confused "half-understanding" of his Jewishness.

This uneasy wavering between tradition and modernity engenders the entrapment depicted by Kafka, that of an insect whose posterior legs remain attached to the father's Jewishness while its anterior legs flail in search of new ground. In *Zuckerman Bound,* we witness its return: a Jewish son wrests his freedom from the imposing injunctions of his father—*his father's Judaism*—through writing, only to rediscover them again and again in his own work. "Get up off the floor," challenges Diana, Nathan's shrewd amanuensis (and combative comforter),

> and write a book that isn't *about* the Jews. *And then the Jews won't bug you.* Oh, what a pity you can't shake free. That you should still be aroused and hurt by this! Are you *always* fighting your father? I know it may sound like a cliché, probably it would be with someone else, but in your case I happen to think that it's true. I look through these books

on your shelves . . . and every single line about a father is underlined.[192] Yet when you describe your father to me, he doesn't sound like a creature of any stature at all.[193]

Diana draws attention to the discrepancy between Zuckerman's mythopoetic representations of his father and Victor's contrasting "lack of stature." Roth adds to Kafka's vision the insight that a son's experience of paternal tyranny is by no means restricted to the traditional model of domineering father and sensitive son evinced, say, in the *Letter to His Father* or Henry Roth's *Call It Sleep*.

On the contrary: the ostensibly "weaker" fathers in *Portnoy's Complaint* and *Zuckerman Bound* marshal an influence as pervasive as that exercised by the doddering yet deadly patriarchs in Kafka's fiction. "The weight of paternal power in its traditional oppressive or restraining guises," Roth maintained in a 1974 interview, "was something I had hardly to contend with in adolescence."

My father had little aside from peccadilloes to quarrel with me about, and if anything weighed upon me, it was not dogmatism, unswervingness, or the like, but his limitless pride in me. When I tried not to disappoint him, or my mother, it was never out of fear of the mailed fist or the punitive decree, but of the broken heart; even in post-adolescence, when I began to find reasons to oppose them, it never occurred to me that as a consequence I might lose their love.[194]

Roth briefly hinted at this toward the end of "'I Always Wanted You to Admire My Fasting'; or, Looking at Kafka," published only two years before. "Keep him away from me!" the young narrator yells at his mother:

"But darling," she asks me, "what is going on? What is this all about? . . . He *loves* you," she explains. But that, of all things, seems to me precisely what is blocking my way. Others are crushed by parental criticism—I find myself oppressed by his high opinion of me! Can it possibly be true (and can I possibly admit) that I am coming to hate him for loving me so? Praising me so? But that makes no sense—the ingratitude! the stupidity! the contrariness! . . . All that we have constructed together over the course of two century-long decades, and look how I must bring it down—in the name of this tyrannical need that I call my "independence."[195]

In *Zuckerman Unbound,* Nathan acquires the "tyrannical freedom" to write without fear of offending his sensitive father after the latter's fatal heart attack. But Victor's dying imprecation, brother Henry's subsequent estrangement, and his mother's death a year later leave him what Kafka calls "in sober truth a disinherited son" in relation to his family and— much to his astonishment and dismay—his writing.[196] Elsewhere in the *Letter to His Father,* Kafka proclaims that all of his writing has been about his father; correspondingly, all of Zuckerman's *not writing* seems determined by his.[197]

In "Looking at Kafka," Roth's removal to Newark of his Prague precursor had been overdetermined and forced: it revealed the thematic kernel embedded in much of his future fiction but had little to do with Kafka. This was an act of usurpation driven by, as Roth himself once conceded, "the search for credentials."[198] But what Martin Green discerned of other antecedents annexed by Roth's later writing also stands true for Kafka:

> When, in *The Ghost Writer,* we are aware of Henry James, and in *The Professor of Desire,* of Chekhov, it is part of the subject matter. As "influences"—as rivals the author must measure up to, face up to—they have been successfully distanced, just by being incorporated. The reader feels no anxiety of influence."[199]

His integration of these authors expands upon and enriches; their place is no longer confined to parody. With similar success, *The Anatomy Lesson* transposes the dilemma illustrated in Kafka's letters into a postwar American setting.[200]

Nowhere do Kafka's recurring themes of freedom as escape and generational misunderstanding so plainly converge with Roth's subject as the scene in which Zuckerman acknowledges Appel's influence on his own perception of Jewish American identity:

> Reading the quarterlies for the essays and fiction of Appel and his generation—Jewish sons born into immigrant families a decade or more after his own father—only corroborated what he'd first sensed as a teenage undergraduate at Chicago: to be raised as a post-immigrant Jew in America was to be given a ticket out of the ghetto into a wholly unconstrained world of thought. Without an Old Country link and a strangling church like the Italians, or the Poles, without generations of American forbearers to bind you to American life, or blind you by

your loyalty to its deformities, you could read whatever you wanted and however you pleased. Alienated? Just another way to say "Set free!" A Jew set free from even Jews—yet only by steadily maintaining self-consciousness as a Jew. That was the thrillingly paradoxical kicker.[201]

For Zuckerman, a "Jew who got away," this paradox generates the despair to which his inspiration is bound. His experience in *The Anatomy Lesson* enacts Tolstoy's remarks to Maxim Gorky on the pitfalls of freedom: "Only think seriously for a moment and you will see, you will feel, that in the ultimate sense of the word freedom is a void, a vacuum, mere formless space. . . . Freedom . . . would mean that everything and everyone agreed with me, but then I would no longer exist, for we are only conscious of ourselves in conflict and opposition."[202] In Kafka (*The Sons, Punishments, Letter to His Father*) as in Roth, impressions of paternal opposition are fixed, in childhood, for an entire lifetime. This novel, the third volume of Zuckerman's bildungsroman, features Nathan's confrontation with the past's unyielding grip on his "posterior legs."

Eight years later, in the closing paragraphs of *Patrimony* (a biographical account of his father's struggle against terminal cancer), Roth expressed this power unforgettably in a passage as relevant to Kafka's generation of fathers and sons as to his or our own:

Then, one night . . . at around 4:00 A.M., he came in a hooded white shroud to reproach me. He said, "I should have been dressed in a suit. You did the wrong thing." I awakened screaming. All that peered out from the shroud was the displeasure in his dead face. And his only words were a rebuke: I had dressed him for eternity in the wrong clothes. In the morning I realized that he had been alluding to this book, which, in keeping with the unseemliness of my profession, I had been writing all the while he was ill and dying. The dream was telling me that, if not in my books or in my life, at least in my dreams I would live perennially as his little son, with the conscience of a little son, just as he would remain alive there not only as my father but as *the* father, sitting in judgment on whatever I do.[203]

And yet, how consistent even an abnormal mental state is if it is normally present. People are always shouting that a melancholic should fall in love, and then his melancholy would all vanish. If he actually is melancholy, how would it be possible for his soul not to become melancholically absorbed in what has come to be the most important of all to him?

—Søren Kierkegaard, *Repetition*

3. W. G. Sebald: *Vertigo*

"It now sometimes horrifies me," remarked Sebald in a 1998 interview, "when I think of how many books I have read. At the same time, the number of writers I cannot do without keeps shrinking. I can gather hardly more than a patrol of seven."[1] If literary influence can be measured by mimesis as well as by the degree of intensity with which an author's work resists the impress of a particular forerunner, it is sensible to guess that Franz Kafka is at the fore of this little troop.

Sebald referenced no other writer as frequently. Between 1972 and 1997 he published five critical essays on Kafka, translating two of them into (slightly revised) English-language versions. In the early 1970s, he printed a short poem named after the hero of Kafka's *Castle*. His fiction teems with allusions to the work and life of his precursor from Prague, and his debut as a novelist, *Vertigo* (1990), assigns one of the novel's central roles to none other than "Dr. K." himself.

Harold Bloom's studies on literary influence stress the interpretive cost of authorial indebtedness. "Nothing is got for nothing": these are the terms of his repeatedly declared "Emersonian law of compensation." It states that the ambitious poet at the start of his career must find a way to distance himself from his most influential antecedent—whatever the cost—if he is to develop his own strong voice.[2] Although many of the details Sebald ascribes to Dr. K. resemble those of Franz Kafka's biography, the characters represented in the fictions remain projections of the author. And like all projections, Sebald's inevitably distorts. According to Bloom, this distortion is essential to the poet's development, for "the strong imagination comes to its painful birth through savagery and misrepresentation."[3]

The site of primal origin for Sebald preceded *Vertigo* by nearly two decades; his distinctive narrative voice can be traced back to "The Undiscover'd Country: The Death Motif in Kafka's *Castle*" (1972) and its later revision, "Das unentdeckte Land: Zur Motivstruktur in Kafkas *Schloß*" (1985).[4] In both, Sebald's approach to *The Castle* swerves defiantly from Kafka's novel. His emphasis on the death motif skews rather than clarifies the work.

Such misprisions helped Sebald forge the narrative voice of his later fiction. His invocation of Gracchus at the study's conclusion prefigures his debut novel, where various narrators merge into the persona of Kafka's wandering huntsman. Sebald's early critical essays can help today's reader navigate *Vertigo*'s densely symbolic terrain. Only a handful of critics—all of them German or Swiss—noted this from the outset. In his 1990 review of the novel for *Die Zeit*, Andreas Isenschmid referred to Kafka's Gracchus fragment as the "secret motor" of the novel.[5]

Marcel Atze concurred a few years later in an extensive analysis of intertextuality in Sebald. Atze additionally possessed the foresight to recognize, at a time when the only novels Sebald had published were *Vertigo* and *The Emigrants,* that "both collections of . . . essays constitute a true gold mine in respect to his stories. One might even go so far as to designate them a quarry of themes and motifs for his literary work."[6] "The Undiscover'd Country," then, yields greater insights when considered as a workshop for Sebald's later prose fictions.

In the pages that follow, I address Sebald's willful *misrepresentations* of Kafka in that analysis, demonstrating incongruities between his reading of *The Castle* and the actual text. I also consider, when relevant, how some of his alterations to the essay for its 1985 publication in *Die Beschreibung des Unglücks* (*Describing Misfortune*) reveal significant interpretive predispositions. The bulk of this chapter examines *Vertigo* section by section, pointing out reappearances of the death motif *as defined by his earlier essay(s).* Throughout I will devote attention to Sebald's approach to literary precursors other than Kafka (e.g., Stendhal or Robert Walser), and how the effect of their influence manifests itself through like patterns of projection and appropriation.

Discovering a Narrator in "The Undiscover'd Country"

> The thing is to darken, or even indeed to blot out, the picture in this one
> life of ours through our actions.
> —Kafka, *Aphorisms*

W. G. Sebald begins "The Undiscover'd Country" with a curious examination of the very portrait Walter Benjamin depicted in his tribute to Franz Kafka nearly four decades earlier.[7] Kafka's interpreters, Sebald charges, have "failed to come to terms" with the child's somber gaze, in which he himself detects "the yearning, fearful images of death which pervade [the] work and which impart that melancholy whose onset was as early as it was persistent."[8] The reluctance of other critics to acknowledge this melancholy has contributed to a collective striving "to wrest some positive meaning from Kafka's work." Sebald concludes that the gloomy countenance of the child symbolizes why "the smooth surface of his work . . . has remained an enigma . . . against the advances of criticism." This opening was omitted from Sebald's later version, perhaps in recognition of the fact that affirmative readings had long since begun to ebb, especially by 1972.[9]

A more significant justification for this revision emerges when we contrast Kafka's childhood portrait with Sebald's account of it. A comparison of the two reveals a slight discrepancy more manipulative than might appear at first glance, and yields an instance of Bloom's "creative revisionism."[10] The author draws attention to the "shiny black walking stick and . . . straw hat" held by the young boy in order to invoke Charon the boatsman with his round hat and punt-pole—a direct allusion to Death and its figurative history in literature.[11] (One recalls, for example, the appearance of a Charon-figure in front of a Munich mortuary, hat in hand, early in Thomas Mann's *Death in Venice*—a text whose presence also adumbrates *Vertigo*.) A closer look reveals, however, that the child's hat is not made of straw; except for its circular crown, it scarcely resembles one. Sebald's alteration, negligible in itself, hints at the revisionary approach that his entire essay will practice. His reading of the young boy's apparel establishes continuities irrelevant to Kafka's novel and helps to reinforce his own fictionalized vision of the author.

Eventually, Sebald would exploit similar appearances to infer parallels between characters in his own novels and the figure of Death-as-wanderer. The walking stick, rucksack, and hat are conspicuous trademarks of Sebald's future protagonists for precisely this reason; he seals the two roles together associatively, affixing to his character a heavy sadness. Sebald's likening of Kafka's sorrowful glance to an equally sorrowful corpus reveals a tendency to conflate the historical Franz Kafka with the fictional "K." and vice versa. One thus observes a process by which Sebald projects his own fictive persona onto both the historical Kafka and onto Kafka's creative writings.[12]

Sebald jettisoned this initial opening from "Das unentdeckte Land," his version of the same essay in German. Instead of focusing on the portrait, he asserts that K. (whose declared profession of land surveyor seems equivocal) is "merely a wanderer" who arrives in the village possessing little other than a rucksack and walking stick—an identification that can be readily verified by the text.[13] His next sentence, however, steers away to add that "psycho-analysis designates the image of a journey or a hike as a symbol of death."[14] Instead of explaining this relation and why it might lend validity to its implied correlation between K., the wanderer, and death, Sebald expands his network of references by diverting attention to Theodor W. Adorno's essay on Franz Schubert's *Winter Journey*, whose nameless protagonist is unhappily trapped in a timeless state that resembles death yet withholds its consolations.

Likening Schubert's circular landscape to the environs of *The Castle*, Sebald surprisingly concludes that their topographies resemble *Kafka's* (as opposed to the character K.'s) own yearning for death: "There can seldom have been a more apposite description," he claims, "of the way in which the avowedly unmusical Kafka circles about the geometric location than in these lines of Adorno's on the structure of Schubert's work." Sebald weaves together an intertextual argument, "saturated with reference," where sundry citations reinforce similar images and impose them collectively upon *The Castle*, leading the reader through a blend of biography, fiction, and text.[15]

The Castle's topography may be circular, but this feature taken alone fails to substantiate Sebald's attribution to Kafka of a negatively charged fixation with death (as implied by his allusion to Adorno's essay on Schubert). *Fixation* is the key word here, since the presence of a death motif in Kafka's novel is all but indisputable; the question is one of degree. And Sebald seems determined, in this study, to accentuate the bleakness of K.'s environment: the entirety of the area surrounding the Castle, he insists, "is like a mockery of the sense and end of our own existence, an eternally recurring nightmare."[16] These negative intensifications (*Hohn, Alptraum*) disclose his own perspective on the novel. More importantly, they express his vision or worldview *beyond* it. Bleak though Kafka's worlds may be, they rarely insist upon their darkness in such unequivocal terms. When Josef K. posits, in the penultimate chapter of *The Trial,* that "lies are made into a universal system," the narrator is quick to qualify: "K. said that with finality, but it wasn't his final judgment."[17] As a rule, Sebald systematically omits nuances like this in his interpretations.

In fact, the most convincing textual evidence marshaled by Sebald to support this position comes not from Kafka's novel, but from the fourth volume of the *Handwörterbuch des deutschen Aberglaubens* (*Concise Dictionary of German Superstition*)—the external work cited most frequently in both the English and German versions of his essay. Yet here too Sebald amends the original context so the extracted passage will conform to his purposes. It is a pattern that recurs frequently, whatever the source. Consider, for example, this lengthy excerpt from Kierkegaard's *Repetition,* quoted to sound once again the theme of endless circularity in a land of the dead:

> He is not only able to walk, but he is able to *come walking.* To come walking is something very distinctive, and by means of this genius he also improvises the whole scenic setting. He is able not only to portray an itinerant craftsman; he is also able to come walking like one and in such a way that one experiences everything, surveys the smiling hamlet from the dusty highway, hears its quiet noise, sees the footpath that goes down by the village pond when one turns off there by the blacksmith's— where one sees B. walking along with his little bundle on his back, his stick in his hand, untroubled and undaunted. He can come walking onto the stage followed by street urchins one cannot even see.[18]

Sebald claims that this is a humorous instance of "a progression directed against its own teleology." The passage thus renders a circling intended to parallel the one already affixed to Kafka, one whose end can only be the grave.[19]

But Kierkegaard's recollection of Friedrich Beckmann (leading actor of the Königstädter Theater in Berlin during the mid-nineteenth century) does not, as Sebald suggests, express the futility of forward motion—on the contrary, it is a dithyrambic bristling with aperçus on the art of comic performance. Kierkegaard's purpose was to rank Beckmann above a contemporary actress whom a leading Danish critic had praised for her ability to rush on stage "with a rustic scene in tow." Beckmann is so good, writes Kierkegaard, he doesn't even have to rush: he *walks,* and the rural scenery tumbles in after him.[20] The passage, then, has little to do with the Becket-tian inertia.[21] In all likelihood, Sebald reproduces it because of several dis-crete details: its village, bundle, and stick.

K. inhabits a *"paysage mort"* from the moment he crosses the bridge and enters the Castle's jurisdiction. In this realm, all development is para-doxically annulled, "for at the point where," Sebald writes, "he crosses the wooden bridge over the stream and invades the territory of the Castle, he is like 'those wretched souls who travel hither and thither but have no history.'" Like the unburied souls who populate the underworld of the *Aeneid,* Kafka's villagers can never truly rest. And to drive this comparison home, Sebald insists that distinguishing between life and death in *The Castle* would prove to be no more than an act of irrelevant sophistry.[22] He then proceeds to link the novels' characters with other literary variations of the undead. His recourse to swamp creatures, mummies, and vampires sug-gests that he is not interested in discerning a neutral suspension between the two spheres.

In *Beyond the Pleasure Principle,* Freud postulated that the compulsion to repeat—the famous *Wiederholungszwang*—originates in the organism's drive to return to its former inorganic state: in short, "the aim of all life is death."[23] The world of Sebald's *Castle* shares this directive, but with two crucial revisions. Freud pits the death drive against the pleasure principle: "[a] vision," writes Peter Gay, "of two elemental pugnacious forces in the mind, Eros and Thanatos, locked in eternal battle."[24] Sebald's original title for his Kafka essay, "Thanatos," speaks worlds about the outcome of this (not quite eternal) battle—certainly insofar as *Vertigo* is concerned, where love and the pursuit of pleasure are likened to madness and find their end in the longing for death.

Sebald literalizes the kinship between living and dead by expressing it at the most superficial level—that is, through the physical appearance of *The Castle's* characters. In "The Undiscover'd Country," the village's in-habitants no longer resemble living beings. Sebald places special emphasis on physiognomy to reinforce their affiliation with the dead. In a passage excised from a later version, he refers to Olga's rendering of Sortini, the Castle functionary who has a peculiar way of wrinkling his forehead. The mannerism, Sebald concludes, proves that Sortini is "a harbinger of death," since it "reminds one readily of a mummy distorted by a shrinking pro-cess."[25] Revising the essay more than a decade later, Sebald turns him into a different breed of undying monster: "The manner in which Olga describes Sortini's physiognomy, with its features drawn into the center of the face, perhaps identifies him sufficiently as an agent of that Transylvanian line, which has as its master the lord of the castle."[26] Perhaps. But there is little in Kafka's text to substantiate this tie, and the substitution of a vampire for a mummy appears to confirm this author's willful effort to recast *The Castle* in his own image.

As a matter of fact, Sortini acts rather lively for an "envoy of death," springing over the shaft of a fire engine in order to approach Amalia.[27] Sebald attempts to account for this leap by noting that the "haggard" Sortini's legs are "stiffened by his sedentary occupation." This rigidness is another interpolation of Sebald's, whose purpose may be to signal a kinship with Virgil's boatsman; "He gave a start, then jumped over the shaft in order to be close to Amalia" is all Kafka writes of Sortini's leap.[28]

Elsewhere, Sebald accounts for desire by dismissing it as evidence of the characters' (above all the female characters') hetaeric origins: "It is well known," he insists, "that all the women characters in Kafka's novels remain tied to a stage of evolution that preceded the emergence of human life."[29] This recidivistic feature is manifest in their physical appearance. Thus Kafka's fictions are "permeated by the somberness of a world where the dark forces of matriarchal figures unsex their male partners."[30] To support this position, he declares that Frieda is an "etiolated creature who shuns the light"; Pepi, a character "who has risen from the chtonic [*sic*] depths of the Brückenhof"; Gardena, a woman "vegetating in her bed like a carnivorous plant."[31] A passage eventually removed from "Das unentdeckte Land" asserts that these "matriarchal figures . . . stand at the gates of Hell." Once again, Sebald bases his argument on *external,* rather than *primary,* sources—here, on a claim by Berthold von Regensburg (c. 1210–1272) that "Hell lies at the heart of earth's steamy swamps."[32]

For Sebald, the assistants, like Sortini, represent ambassadors of death. And so he emphasizes K.'s repulsion upon encountering Jeremias in a scene toward the end of the manuscript: "this flesh," thinks K. of his former aide: "which sometimes gave one the impression of not being properly alive."[33] The designation is a novel one in *The Castle;* up to this moment, Artur and Jeremias have actually been *too lively* for K.'s liking. But K. has an understandable reason for responding this way now—Jeremias has just stolen his fiancée.

Shortly after this encounter, K. arrives at a local inn for a hearing with a secretary of Klamm's. Distracted by a sudden sighting of Frieda, K. abandons his post by the door to try to regain her confidence—and nearly succeeds. After a long conversation during which K. calibrates every reply to win her back, the two stroll, arms entwined, up and down the hall of the inn. Frieda, leaning on K.'s shoulder, has just conceded that "your closeness is the only dream that I dream, none other," when Jeremias emerges from her room and breaks the spell. Sebald quotes the passage depicting his appearance (written in free indirect style from K.'s perspective) in full:

Standing there like that with his tousled hair, thin and seemingly rain-soaked beard, his eyes strenuously, pleadingly, reproachfully open, his dark cheeks reddish but as if consisting of extremely loose flesh, his bare legs trembling from the cold and the long fringes of his shawl trembling along with them, he was like a patient who had escaped from a hospital, so that one's only thought was how to get him back to bed.[34]

Sebald writes that Jeremias finds himself "in a state of decomposition"—an exaggerated claim he backs by asserting, in the next sentence, that Kafka himself refuses to distinguish between the living and the dead.

When Jeremias appears at the threshold of Frieda's room in the Herrenhof, he is indeed ill—literally, not symbolically ill, for the prosaic reason that he has stood out in the cold too long. Earlier, K. had dismissed the assistants and prevented them from reentering the heated schoolhouse. With a zeal that belies Sebald's characterization, Artur and Jeremias angle for K.'s attention in a manner that would seem to count for more than what the author dismisses as "sometimes importunate liveliness":[35]

Before long they appeared at the windows of the gymnasium, knocking on the panes and shouting, but their words were no longer audible. Yet they didn't stay there long either, in the deep snow they couldn't jump around as much as their restlessness demanded. So they rushed to the fence of the school garden, jumped up on the stone base, where, though only from afar, they could get a better view of the room, there they ran up and down, holding on to the fence, then halted, and stretched their clasped hands beseechingly toward K. They kept this up a long time, despite the futility of their efforts; it was as if they were blind, and they probably didn't even stop when K. lowered the curtains to get them out of his sight.[36]

Frieda and K. continue their discussion with the curtains closed, but when she peers out a few moments later the two assistants are still hanging from the fence in the school garden. They spring to life upon perceiving her glance: "Visibly tired though they were, summoning all their energy, they extended their arms beseechingly every now and then toward the schoolhouse. One of them, in order to avoid having to keep holding on, impaled the back of his coat to the fence."[37] It is difficult to reconcile such antics with Sebald's insistence that the assistants are "not . . . properly alive."

Jeremias and Artur are from the onset mischievous, keenly vital characters. Kafka's description places them in the very flush of youth: "two young men of medium height, both quite slender, in tight-fitting clothes, with very similar, dark-brown faces and strikingly black goatees." When K. encounters them for the first time, the assistants' animated effervescence compels him to think the two would make "good traveling companions [who] could cheer one up on his way to the inn."[38] They are a far cry from resident specters of that *undiscover'd country from whose bourn no traveller returns.*

Their first extended interview with K. confirms their presence in the novel as devilishly funny:

They saluted. Thinking of his time in the army, those happy days, he laughed. "Who are you?" he asked, glancing from one to the other. "Your assistants," they answered. "Those are the assistants," said the landlady softly in confirmation. "What?" asked K., "you are the old assistants whom I told to join me and am expecting?" They said yes. "It's a good thing," said K., after a little while, "it's a good thing you've come." "By the way," said K., after another little while, "you're very late, you've been most negligent!" "It was such a long way," said one of the assistants. "A long way," repeated K., "but when I met you, you were coming from the Castle." "Yes," they said, without further explanation. "Where did you put the instruments?" asked K. "We don't have any," they said. "The instruments I entrusted you with," said K. "We don't have any," they repeated. "Oh, you're a fine sort!" said K., "do you know anything about surveying?" "No," they said. "But if you are my old assistants, then you must know something about it," said K. They remained silent. "Well, come along then," said K., pushing them ahead into the inn.[39]

It is for scenes like this that Philip Roth lauded Kafka's facility as a "sit-down comic," envisioning in the same essay "the movie that could be made of *The Castle* with Groucho Marx as K. and Chico and Harpo as the two 'assistants.'"[40] The two serve as foils to K.'s overearnest severity. The above exchange effectively undermines our protagonist, who cannot help overestimating the extent of his own influence (not unlike his predecessor from *The Trial*). K.'s improvised playacting reveals his unreliability as a character, a factor I will discuss momentarily. Sebald's diagnosis, however, of Jeremias's illness—his claim that the latter's condition is that of a "corpse escaped from the grave"—sounds far more appropriate when applied to the narrators of his own novels.[41]

Sebald's response to his subject's "hovering trope" in this critical essay tells us worlds about the inner landscape he would ultimately re-create for *Vertigo, The Emigrants,* and other creative works. As we have already seen, Kafka's prose retains its resistance to penetration in part through an insistent conditionality; he is at home in the subjunctive, in journals as in letters, in philosophical meditations and in fictions. Critical readings such as Sebald's tend to disclose patterns of interpretation. Given the multiple paths that open before a sentence or phrase, an author is likely to select the one closest to him or herself—time after time after time. *The Castle* is without question a dark novel inhabited by unhappy characters, and it offers an array of suggestive gestures, symbols, and statements that can be readily identified with Sebald's death motif. By homing in on such passages while omitting the sentences shortly before or after that make their meaning more evasive, he projects his own vision onto the novel. It is a powerful, idiosyncratic vision, ostensibly trained at Kafka's text—the essay was written, after all, for refereed periodicals—but ultimately shooting past it.

The Castle dodges Sebald's incursions as effortlessly as it had earlier deflected the attempts of existentialists and even Kafka's closest friend "to wrest some positive meaning" from it.[42] The gravity Sebald attributes to this novel strikes me as incommensurate with its elastic narrative. Kafka's writing responds in like fashion to the excesses of affirmative *and* negative readings, pivoting consistently, as they do, on revisionary formulations like "No, it can't be done" (from "The Trees"), "Yet that isn't all true" (from "Excursion into the Mountains"), or the crucial "But since that is not so" (from "Up in the Gallery").[43] It is no coincidence that so much of Kafka's prose begins with *Als* or *Wenn*—"as" and "if" or "when."[44]

Sebald identifies closely with K's perspective, a viewpoint that is notoriously unreliable. Kafka's protagonist constantly challenges authorities to a game whose rules he cannot begin to comprehend. No wonder, then, that his exhaustion increases as he strives to override the intractable laws of an alien system. His conversation with Jeremias at the end of chapter 20, "Olga's Plans," leaves little doubt about this ignorance. In this scene, K. learns that the assistants have been assigned to him not by Klamm (as he had earlier believed) but by a substitute named Galater. Jeremias's explanation can be read as a gentle rebuttal to K. and perhaps, by extension, to those who side too readily with the supposed land surveyor. Informed that Artur has gone to the Castle to file a complaint, K. asks:

"What are you complaining about?" . . . "*We are complaining,*" said Jeremias, "*that you cannot take a joke.* Now then, what did we do? Joked a bit, laughed a bit, teased your fiancée a bit. And all this, by the way, in accordance with instructions. When Galater sent us to you . . . he said . . . 'You're being sent there as assistants of the surveyor.' We said: 'But we don't know anything about that kind of work.' At that he said: 'That isn't so important; if it becomes so necessary he will teach you. But it's important you should cheer him up a bit. From what I hear *he takes everything very seriously.* He has come to the village and right away thinks this is some great event, but in reality it's nothing at all.'" [My italics][45]

The professor in Sebald takes *everything* in Kafka's novel seriously too, drawing in these critical essays dramatic conclusions from a recalcitrant text. Strategic omission is of course a feature common to creative rewriting, a maneuver that creates myriad opportunities for self-fashioning. Sebald's rewriting of *The Castle* begins with his treatment of the two epigraphs that introduce "Das unentdeckte Land"—a Zürau aphorism by Kafka followed by a Yiddish proverb. The first reads: "Death is in front of us, rather as on the schoolroom wall there is a reproduction of Alexander's Battle" (*Der Tod ist vor uns, etwa wie im Schulzimmer an der Wand ein Bild der Alexanderschlacht*).[46] The second provides a kind of commentary to the first: "The feet carry, where the head should rest" (*Di fiss trogn, wu der kop sol run*). Together they insist that death, which lies before us at all times, is our rightful state. In this formulation, to stand upright—to live—is to defy the proper order of things. This is the fate of Sebald's K., who so ardently yearns for a respite. Though that respite is ever before him, it never arrives.

Yet Sebald leaves out the second half of the aphorism, effectively overturning its original import. Kafka's sentences announce a formidable task. In its entirety, the meditation reads: "Death is in front of us, rather as on the schoolroom wall there is a reproduction of Alexander's Battle. The thing is to darken, or even indeed to blot out, the picture in this one life of ours through our actions."[47] These lines underscore the individual's responsibility before the ineluctable. Death is always before us, yes, but this in turn requires us *to transform it through our actions.* Omitting the aphorism's second half performs the very interpretive turn Kafka cautions against: it fixes the picture, in darkness.

Arthur Lubow and James Wood were among the first to point out the relevance of Walter Benjamin's dictum in relation to Sebald's novels, namely that great writers either dissolve a prior genre or create a new one.[48] During the years of his essay's appearance (1972, then again in 1985), Sebald was chiefly regarded as a Germanist specialized in the field of Austrian literature. Nearly two decades later, the death motif expounded in "Das unentdeckte Land" has germinated fully; it holds together his first novel, *Schwindel. Gefühle* (*Vertigo*). Readers acquainted with Sebald's corpus will recognize the resonance of those twin epigraphs for his narrators, eternal wanderers all, haunted by the fear that they will be cheated of their deserved and final rest.

From Sebald's critical grappling with *The Castle,* a distinct narrative voice, persona, and storyteller emerges: the very narrator who debuted in 1990, seemingly from nowhere, with four variations on Kafka's Gracchus fragments. The final lines of "Das unentdeckte Land" thus forecast *Vertigo,* illuminating in the process the motives that drive his restless characters "Beyle," "Sebald," and naturally, "Dr. K.":

> The yearning for peace which in K.'s world only death itself can provide, and the fear of being unable to die (like the hero of Kafka's *Gracchus the Huntsman*), the fear of a perpetual habitation in the no-man's land between man and thing—that yearning, that fear must be reckoned the ultimate motive for K.'s journey to the village whose name we never learn.[49]

My analysis of Sebald's debut novel focuses precisely on his realization of these themes—the yearning for rest and the fear of eternal wandering on the wrong side of the Acheron—through the protean persona of his *Huntsman Gracchus.*

The Swindle of Fiction: Another Stendhal

Madame Gherardi continued: ". . . One is serious but one is not sad, and
there's a great difference."
—Stendhal, *Love*

K., writes Sebald in his essay on *The Castle,* is "merely a wanderer, a figure
who first appears with a 'minute rucksack' and a 'knotty stick.'"[50] This restless protagonist, incarnated as Gracchus at the essay's conclusion, wanders
through all the fiction Sebald would write over the next fifteen years. His
guise changes from book to book, even from chapter to chapter. In *The
Emigrants* he appears as the butterfly-chasing Nabokov, but also as the stories' four protagonists who are hounded, however indirectly, by the con-
vulsions of recent German history. In *The Rings of Saturn* the wanderer is
"W. G. Sebald" himself, sojourning through the Suffolk countryside and
making imaginary excursions into the lives of travelers as various as Joseph
Conrad and Chateaubriand. In *Austerlitz* Jacques' backpack triggers an
association in the narrator's mind (who himself treks from city to city) with
Ludwig Wittgenstein, yet another sufferer of transcendental homelessness
and object of identification. A photograph of an old rucksack—Austerlitz's? Wittgenstein's? the narrator's? Sebald's?—appears alongside this passage as if to unite all the figures in their migrations.[51]

By the time his review of Nicholas Shakespeare's Bruce Chatwin biography appeared in the November 2000 issue of *Literaturen,* Sebald had long
since discovered his form. His critical work, like his fiction, now seamlessly
incorporated photography, autobiographical reflection, travel writing, and
recurring motifs from his novels.[52] The photograph reproduced for Sebald's
review features a grinning Chatwin, walking stick in hand and backpack by
his side. Sebald admiringly depicts him in the review's opening paragraph
as a "tireless traveler" whose books, like Sebald's own, defy ready categori-
zation: "All that is obvious is that their structure and intentions place them
in no known genre."[53]

Stendhal is the subject of *Vertigo's* first chapter. For its duration, Sebald
fictionalizes him under his actual, rather than his pseudonymous, name,
Marie-Henri Beyle. Mark Anderson has advanced a useful hypothesis
regarding the author's choice of protagonist:

> If it is true, as Jorge Luis Borges suggested, that every author "creates"
> his or her own literary precursors, one can say that Sebald invented the

author . . . for his own purposes. A great European cosmopolitan who scattered English and Italian throughout his French; a writer who took a German pseudonym in order to escape the hated paternal name of Beyle; an "eternal traveler" hastening from one country to another all his life; and especially a melancholic who sought refuge in a form of writing halfway between autobiography and fiction—Stendhal was the writer who laid bare the vertiginous discrepancy between reality and representation that, 150 years later, would become Sebald's project in dealing with the legacy of Germany's Nazi past and his detested familial and provincial origins.[54]

In Sebald's vignette, Beyle is, like Gracchus, another "perennial traveler."[55] While writing his autobiography in Citavecchia between 1835 and 1836, Stendhal seems to have found himself in a no-man's-land of text and memory, "between man and thing," where the boundary between events experienced and imagined had become porous to the point of indistinguishability.[56]

Stendhal's *Life of Henry Brulard* (*Vie de Henry Brulard*) and *Love* (*De l'amour*), the literary works Sebald refers to explicitly in this chapter, resemble many of Chatwin's and all of Sebald's autobiographical writings insofar as they do not fit into generic conventions. Full of illustrations and diagrams, they revel in ludic identity games, teasing the reader with noms de plume that work to fracture the impression of an indivisible "I." Stendhal's deployment of multiple pseudonyms looks ahead to the semi-private play of modernists such as Kierkegaard and Fernando de Pessoa. What unifies these different autobiographical narratives is mainly their common sensibility and tone.[57]

The chapter's German title, "Beyle oder das merkwürdige Faktum der Liebe" ("Beyle, or the Remarkable Factum of Love"), recalls Sebald's catastrophic assessment in "The Undiscover'd Country," when he declared "the game of love" "not so much a bourgeois fantasy as a self-perpetuating natural historical disaster" (*ein sich selber perpetuierendes naturhistorisches Debakel*).[58] Its English rendering, "Beyle, or Love Is a Madness Most Discreet," derives, like the title of his early essay on the Kafka, from a celebrated passage in Shakespeare—in this case, the first scene of *Romeo and Juliet*: "Love is a smoke made with the fume of sighs, Being purg'd, a fire sparkling in lovers' eyes, Being vex'd, a sea nourish'd with loving tears. What is it else? a madness most discreet, a choking gall, and preserving sweet."[59]

Sebald links love to madness throughout the chapter, circulating allusions from diverse sources to reinforce his leading motif. In the appendix to *Love,* Stendhal's narrator observes the changes that overcome a young Bavarian falling in love. Stendhal invents a colorful figure to account for drastic transformations in the man's behavior. His trope of "crystallization" is inspired by the effect of salt prisms crystallizing, in a Salzburg mine, on a tree branch. (When the bough is removed, it resembles a wand decked in diamonds.) "What struck me was the undertone of madness which grew moment by moment in the officer;" writes Stendhal, "each moment he saw in this woman perfections more and more invisible to my eyes. Each moment what he said bore *less resemblance* to the woman he was beginning to love." The young soldier mistakes salt for precious stones, a twig for a treasure—conflations that indicate madness to an outside observer who, like the child of Andersen's fable, fails to apprehend the brilliant threads of the Emperor's dress.[60]

Stendhal concludes his anecdote by reproducing an exchange between the narrator and Madame Gherardi. The two debate a Milanese painter's infatuation with "the beautiful Marchesina Florenza." Relevant to Sebald's revision of these discussions is their difference of opinion on the topic of crystallization. If he is truly in love, are the emotional trials Oldofredi undergoes symptoms of sadness or signs of joy? Stendhal's Gherardi insists that even the momentary, delusional conviction that one is loved compels "moments of sublime happiness unlike anything else in this world." The narrator, in contrast, suspects that Oldofredi suffers terribly for all of his doubts. Unable to bridge their disagreement, the two lapse into uneasy silence.[61]

Stendhal illustrates both positions (madness most discreet, preserving sweet) in this scene convincingly, but refrains from overtly favoring either. The awkward stillness that opens up between his characters invites the reader's interpretation. And interpretation, so far as Bloom is concerned, "is implicitly hierarchical, and cannot proceed without a usurpation of authority."[62] Sebald confirms this view in *Vertigo*—in this scene, by relocating Stendhal's narrative to Lake Garda, location of the Hunter Gracchus's first appearance, for *Vertigo.*

"There is reason to suspect," he furthermore writes of Madame Gherardi,

that Beyle used her name as a cipher for various lovers . . . and that Mme Gherardi, whose life would easily furnish a whole novel . . . never really existed, despite all the documentary evidence, and was merely a phantom, albeit one to whom Beyle remained true for decades.[63]

His interpolation remakes the narrator of "The Salzburg Bough" into an autobiographical projection of its author. Sebald's narrator then confidently asserts that La Ghita (Gherardi's pseudonym in the story) is but a fictional cover for Métilde Dembrowski Viscontini, Beyle's great unrequited love. He also implies that the silence between her and Beyle has something to do with the latter's hopeless attraction, drawing attention to the suffering incurred as a result.

Sebald's Beyle is saturnine, ailing, inconsolable. His pursuit of love is the implied source of debilitations (e.g., unhappiness, syphilis) that dog him throughout the narrative. Absent from Sebald's vision is the cantankerous admirer of Benvenuto Cellini's "truthful" vitality, an author whose tremendous vigor touched every page of his writing.[64] Richard Howard's characterization of *The Charterhouse of Parma* as "a miracle of gusto, brio, élan, verve, panache" applies not only to *Brulard* but to the greater part of Stendhal's oeuvre.[65] Even the darkest moments of his memoirs are expressed with a kind of fundamental ebullience. Disillusions of love are addressed but not dismissed; "indeed," Stendhal writes, "for me love has always been the most important thing, or rather the only thing."[66] In *Vertigo*, catastrophe has annexed this central role. The Beyle of this novel comes closer to resembling Sebald's portrayal of K. in "The Undiscover'd Country" than the vigorous hero of *The Life of Henry Brulard*.

Sebald has him arrive in "a continuously elegiac frame of mind" at Desenzano on Lake Garda in September 1813.[67] A number of the thematic motifs immediately converge. The time of Beyle's arrival is clearly strategic (Stendhal does not appear to have traveled to Lake Garda that year), set precisely one century before Franz Kafka's arrival at Riva (September 1913) and two centuries before *Vertigo*'s apocalyptic conclusion (September 2013). Beyle and Madame Gherardi pass a number of evenings on the lake in search of refuge from the summer heat.

Their conversation borrows its subject and tenor from the "Salzburg Bough" episode of *Love*. Sebald now uses this setting to revise the ambiguity of Stendhal's conclusion. "Mme Gherardi maintained that love," he writes (these words never appear in Stendhal),

like most other blessings of civilization, was a chimera which we desire the more, the further we are removed from Nature . . . for love, she declared, is a passion that pays its debts in a coin of its own minting, and thus a purely notional transaction which one no more needs for one's fulfillment than one needs the instrument for trimming goose quills.[68]

In this rendition, Madame Gherardi no longer advocates her belief that love, despite the misery it may cause, inspires bursts of "sublime happiness unlike anything else in the world," moments that "are probably the best thing in life."[69] Her perspective is colder, less nuanced. A few days after this conversation, the two disembark for Riva, where the Huntsman Gracchus will make his ominous entrance.

Before discussing the repercussions of this episode, I think it important to consider some facts regarding Sebald's reception in relation to his development as a writer of fiction. In her review of *After Nature* (*Nach der Natur*) for the *New Republic*, Ruth Franklin noted an unforeseen "boon" for Sebald's English audience: the non-chronological publication of his books in translation exposed Anglophone readers to an experienced novelist at the height of his powers.[70] By the time his earlier, less finished work became available, readers had already been sensitized to characteristically Sebaldian themes and motifs. But to its original audience in 1988, *Nach der Natur* resembled nothing else in contemporary German letters—it seemed to spring from a void.[71]

Sebald enjoyed the advantage of having one of his most accomplished works, *The Emigrants,* appear as his debut abroad. Its enthusiastic reception in England and the United States led to a rapid succession of translations, which exposed readers in these countries to his modest corpus in a relatively short time. *The Emigrants* appeared three years after *Die Ausgewanderten,* in 1996. *The Rings of Saturn* (1998) was published more or less alongside *Die Ringe des Saturn* (1997), and then was followed by *Vertigo* (1999)—the slightly reworked translation of *Schwindel. Gefühle* (1990)— and the contemporaneous release of *Austerlitz* in both languages (2001).[72] The fourteen years spanning *Nach der Natur* and *Austerlitz* were reduced to five in English. As a result, it was much easier for admirers in the Anglo-American sphere to spot correspondences and interrelations between the works, to experience them as a series of what Goethe in his autobiography calls "fragments of a great confession."[73]

No other recent work of fiction has been better served by such coincidence than *Schwindel. Gefühle.* Sebald substantially improved the novel while translating it from the German with Michael Hulse nearly a decade after its initial publication. (Hulse alone is credited for the English version, but the effort was very much a collaborative one; in a communication from 2002, he informs me that Sebald declined his offer to be co-listed as translator.)[74] For all its creative license, "The Undiscover'd Country" still cites its sources, observing the protocol of a scholarly work. *Schwindel.Gefühle* showcases many of the same views, unbound by those earlier constraints.

Madame Gherardi and Beyle leave Desenzano for Riva, a journey whose route mimics the one Kafka will take in 1913. This alignment of coincidences is far from happenstance. Sebald systematically establishes associations between Stendhal, the characters featured in *Love*, Franz Kafka, and the hero of his Gracchus fragments. The alignments come in a variety of forms: they are geographical, situational, linguistic. Beyle and his companion set sail, for example, on a vessel that links them directly to the Hunter Gracchus and his ceaseless aquatic wandering:

> A few days after this conversation, Beyle and Mme Gherardi continued on their journey. . . . They first rode along the bank as far as Gargnano, halfway up the lake shore, and from there took a boat aboard which, as day broke, they entered the small port of Riva, where two boys were already sitting on the harbor wall playing dice. Beyle drew Mme Gherardi's attention to an old boat [*Kahn*], its mainmast fractured two-thirds of the way up, its buff-colored sails hanging in folds. It appeared to have made fast only a short time ago, and two men in dark silver-buttoned tunics were at that moment carrying a bier ashore on which, under a large, frayed, flower-patterned silk cloth, lay what was evidently a human form.[75]

The passage is an indirect adaptation, a rewriting and refiguring, of the opening to Kafka's fragment, in which Gracchus's vessel is not a *Kahn,* but a *Barke* like their own:

> Two boys were sitting on the harbor wall playing dice. On the steps of a monument a man was reading a newspaper, in the shadow of the sword-wielding hero. A girl was filling her tub at the fountain. A fruit-seller was lying beside his wares, looking out across the lake. Through the empty window and door openings of a tavern two men could be seen drinking their wine in the depths. Out in front the proprietor was sitting at a table dozing. A bark [*Barke*] glided silently into the little harbor, as if borne over the water. A man in a blue overall

climbed ashore and drew the ropes through the rings. Two other men, wearing dark coats with silver buttons, carried out past the boatman a bier draped with a great tasseled cloth of flower-patterned silk, beneath which there evidently lay a man.[76]

In Sebald's version, Beyle and Madame Gherardi witness (along with the reader) Gracchus's textual landing in *Vertigo*. Here and throughout the novel the lost huntsman performs the role of double as posited by Freud, namely, as an "uncanny herald of death."[77] The bier and its apparent corpse literalize Sebald's death motif. They also explain the defensive retreat of Beyle's companion: "The scene affected Mme Gherardi so adversely that she insisted on quitting Riva without delay."[78]

They travel through the mountains, then on to Innsbruck, where Madame Gherardi purchases "a broad-brimmed Tyrolean hat"—an allusion to Charon, according to Sebald's early essays.[79] Keeping to the formula, Beyle carries a telltale *Stock* (cane) nearly everywhere he goes.[80] Before the chapter ends, the genially optimistic Madame Gherardi of *Love* is redrawn once more as a wry and dolorous skeptic: "It seemed ultimately incomprehensible to him, when he wrote *De l'amour*, that whenever he tried to persuade Mme Gherardi to believe in love, she made him replies now of a melancholy sort, and now quite tart."[81]

The final paragraph underscores Beyle's physical torment between 1829 and 1842. Sebald catalogues syphilitic symptoms and the painful side effects of mercury treatment, suggesting that both are the inexorable consequences of his protagonist's pursuit of love. Stendhal, like Freud, entertained superstitions about the year of his death. Sebald reproduces one of his mathematical jottings to seal the thematic victory of Thanatos over Eros: "As had long been his habit, Beyle calculated, with growing frequency, the age to which he might expect to live in cryptographic forms which, in their scrawled, ominous abstraction, seem like harbingers of death."[82]

Beyle is released from his imprisonment this side of the "undiscover'd country" when he finally expires in the rue Danielle-Casanova, Paris. (The significance of this street name will become apparent within but a handful of pages.) But his spirit, which has masqueraded through the chapter in the persona of Sebald's Hunter Gracchus, cannot come to a full stop; it will continue its unhappy wanderings in another guise. The narrator of *The Life of Henry Brulard* offers a valuable insight into the nature of this metamorphosis, and seems to speak directly for Sebald, when he confesses: "I ruminate endlessly on what concerns me[;] by dint of looking at it from different *positions of soul* I finally find something new in it and cause it to *change its appearance.*"[83] "Beyle" is thus but a prelude to broodings and transformations to come.

Sebald's Italian Journey

I will be dead, not really dead, only dead in a certain way . . .
—Robert Walser, *Jakob von Gunten*

First Station: Vienna

Vienna may be to blame, though now you speak highly of it. . . . I couldn't imagine you so sad in Berlin, and I'm certain you weren't when you were there. Here, one could sometimes think, the gay ones become sad and the sad ones sadder still. . . . That one can well and truly suffer in Vienna was certainly proved by Grillparzer.
—Franz Kafka to Grete Bloch, February 14, 1914

In several writings from 1915 on, Kafka experimented with pronoun shifts that moved the first-person perspective into the third. From its first chapter to the second, *Vertigo* moves in the opposite direction, *toward* its ostensible author. "Beyle" is recounted by an all-knowing narrator, "All'estero" (and the later "Il Ritorno in Patria") by an *ich* who shares Sebald's name. Sebald assumes both positions in the novel, leaving it to the reader to deduce whether the "W. G. Sebald" of chapter 2 is also the shadowy chronicler of the book's opening chapter. All of these voices, *ich, Beyle,* and others to come, are mutually contained by Sebald's protean Gracchus figure.[84]

The section's opening is retrospective, and offers, in cursory form, an explanation for his initial departure: "In October 1980 I traveled from England," "All'estero" begins, "where I had then been living for nearly twenty-five years in a county which was almost always under grey skies, to Vienna, hoping that a change of place would help me get over a particularly difficult period in my life."[85] The desire to forget or even overcome personal difficulties by traveling is shared by many of the restless wanderers featured throughout Sebald's criticism and fiction—among them Beyle, hero of *Vertigo*'s previous section. But Vienna, a city better known for suicides and neuroses than for regenerative weather, exacerbates the narrator's gloominess. He paces its streets obsessively for ten days, mistaking local pedestrians for figures long deceased, incapable of all but the most essential communication: "The only creatures I talked to . . . were the jackdaws in the gardens by the city hall, and a white-headed blackbird that shared the jackdaws' interest in my grapes."[86]

"Jackdaw," as many now know, is *kavka* in Czech; Sebald thus identifies his eponymous protagonist with Franz Kafka from the start. But additional translations of the word reveal further levels of significance. Its Italian variant is *gracchio,* and all of the novel's principal characters are in some sense doubles or heirs of Kafka's huntsman. The German word for "jackdaw," *Dohle,* foreshadows the later appearance, or rather, disappearance of Herr Doll, a character who eventually acquires, in a hotel mix-up, the narrator's passport. It also resembles the word "dolor," an association Sebald encourages by reproducing a page from a nineteenth-century Italian-German phrasebook where *il dolóre* and its equivalent *der Schmerz* (pain, grief, sorrow) are neatly underlined.[87]

In Kafka's story, Gracchus's arrival is heralded by the appearance of a dove. "Yes," he admits to the mayor of Riva, "the doves fly on ahead of me."[88] In the Vienna of 1980, our narrator's colloquy with the jackdaws (*kavka / Dohle / gracchio*), which also occurs near a town hall, gives way to the appearance of an austere sea vessel: "Before I opened my eyes," he reports, "I could see myself descending the gangway of a large ferry."[89] Scenes like this evoke Sebald's vision of a Gracchus character who stands quite unambiguously for death. In "Love Is a Madness Most Discreet," a similar encounter hastens the departure of Beyle and his accomplice from Riva. The aquatic image has a comparable impact on "Sebald," who upon awakening determines to leave Vienna at once.

Before embarking for Italy, however, he visits the Austrian poet Ernst Herbeck in nearby Klosterneuburg. "Life in the family," writes Sebald of Herbeck, "and especially his father's incisive thinking, were corroding his nerves."[90] Sebald provides a summary description of Herbeck's breakdown and his subsequent wandering through the Vienna streets. The fact that his narrator was engaged in the same activity only a few pages earlier hints at his own identification with the poet—and by extension, with his madness.[91]

The letters and recollections of Reinbert Tabbert, a colleague of Sebald's from Manchester in the 1960s, attest to the latter's early preoccupation with literature and madness. In one passage, Tabbert discusses a conversation between the two on how to translate the opening of Saul Bellow's *Herzog*— "If I am out of my mind, it's all right with me"—into German.[92] Both had just attended a performance of Edward Albee's *Zoo Story.* Discussing the play over a drink, Sebald admits to having been tempted to succumb to madness. Tabbert quotes from a letter written at the time to his wife:

He sometimes feels close to the edge and would gladly give himself over were it not for three or four people, for whose sakes he resists. He feels himself breaking apart like Herzog and is filled with a maelstrom of pictures, ideas, and long-forgotten images and thoughts. In such a state he can write letters or talk as never before.[93]

A photograph of the young lecturer appears a few pages later. In it, we see Sebald playing billiards and wearing the red baseball cap "that he liked to wear in Didsbury after the example of J. D. Salinger's Holden Caulfield, yet another American anti-hero who is 'out of his mind.'"[94]

The trail of antecedents like Salinger, Bellow, and Albee disappeared in Sebald's later fiction. But his fascination with madness remained. In *Vertigo* it expresses itself urgently through the words of Casanova, the cosmopolitan antihero of eighteenth-century Europe. The lines apply directly to the unhappy lives of Sebald's broken protagonists:

Casanova considered the limits of human reason. He established that, while it might be rare for a man to be driven insane, little was required to tip the balance. All that was needed was a slight shift, and nothing would be as it formerly was. In these deliberations, Casanova likened a lucid mind to a glass, which does not break of its own accord. Yet how easily it is shattered.[95]

Sebald insists that the difference between the two states is negligible, even after the balance has been tipped. The so-called mad are so-called sane, the seemingly well-adjusted are wildly unstable. Sebald's readings of Herbeck's poems thus reveal them to be "expressions of an actually normal person."[96]

The narrator's account of his visit to Herbeck pays more than just a passing tribute to Robert Walser's life and work. It is, like much of Sebald's writing, an attempt at autobiography. Sebald would express this overtly in his later essay about Walser, where he reflects on how he

gradually learned to grasp how everything is connected beyond space and time. . . . Walser's strolls are connected with my excursions, birthdates, and death dates, happiness with unhappiness, natural history with the history of our industries, the history of homeland with that of exile. Walser has always accompanied me on all paths.[97]

Sebald identifies Walser (as he had earlier K. and the protagonist of Schubert's and Wilhelm Müller's *Winter Journey*) as another "unmistakable figure of the lonely wanderer." In *Wandering with Robert Walser*, Carl Seelig, Walser's friend (and ultimately the executor of his estate), recounts some twenty years of their extended jaunts and conversations.[98] His visits took place long after Walser had been institutionalized and ceased to write: "It is nonsense and crude," he is supposed to have told Seelig, "to expect me to be an author in the institute too."[99]

Sebald models the episodic structure of the Herbeck visit after Seelig's book. Both are composed like journal entries. They begin with a depiction of the poet's appearance. The narrator then recounts the content of their discussion while walking through the countryside. Herbeck and "Sebald" conclude their *Wanderung*, as Walser and Seelig so often do, over a drink in a rural tavern.

Though Kafka stands indisputably at the fore of Sebald's chosen antecedents, Robert Walser is never far behind, appearing regularly in his prose or interviews. These appearances are intensely personal. A later essay of Sebald's juxtaposes pictures of his grandfather with Seelig's of Walser, while a cropped photograph in "All'estero" shows a man's hand (ostensibly Herbeck's) holding a hat at his side—the text below assuring the reader that this mannerism is "just as my grandfather often used to do on summer walks."[100]

This manipulated photograph seems to portray neither Herbeck nor his grandfather, but Robert Walser. Eight years later, Sebald would offer an indirect explanation in "*Le promeneur solitaire: Zur Erinnerung an Robert Walser,*" his extended homage to the Swiss precursor. Seven snapshots marking various stations of Walser's life are accompanied by the following confession:

I feel closest to the pictures from Herisau which show Walser as a walker for the way that the poet, having long ago retired from his writing duties, stands there in the countryside; it brings to my mind spontaneously my grandfather Josef Egelhofer, with whom as a child I strolled, during those same years, for hours at a time through a region similar in many respects to the Appenzell. Every time I see these photographs . . . I think that I'm looking at my grandfather.[101]

Two sets of pictures bracket the prose. At the top of the page, a well-dressed gentleman and a child in lederhosen (presumably Egelhofer and Sebald) face the camera. Each brandishes a walking stick. Below we see two shots of Walser, taken during one of his ramblings. The one to the left bears a striking resemblance to the picture reproduced in *Vertigo*.

Sebald traced his sense of perpetual mourning to the loss of this same figure. "He dates his own fascination with the no longer living," wrote Arthur Lubow in a profile for the *New York Times*,

> to the death of his maternal grandfather. At the time Max was 12, and his gentle, soft-spoken grandfather had been his hiking companion and confidant. "My interest in the departed, which has been fairly constant, comes from that moment of losing someone you couldn't really afford to lose," he said. "I broke out in a skin disease right after his death, which lasted for years."[102]

Of the intersecting paths between Walser and his grandfather, Sebald wonders:

> What do such similarities, overlappings, and correspondences mean? Are they just the product of a memory's trick pictures, of self-deceptions or delusions, or are we dealing with the schema of an order, incomprehensible to us, programmed into the chaos of human relationships and extending likewise over the living and the dead?[103]

These questions correspond with an "astonishing coincidence" in *Wandering with Robert Walser:* Seelig and Walser sight Paul Klee's name in a mountain village shop window "less than a minute" after the former has asserted an affinity between the two. Sebald's *Vertigo* attempts to make sense of the "incomprehensible order" behind such unanticipated coincidences.[104]

Sebald draws ceaselessly on similar uncanny occurrences throughout "All'estero." Herbeck, like Kierkegaard and Beyle, employed a pseudonym for his poetic work. His self-selected name, Alexander, matches the Alexander of Kafka's aphorism as well as the painting by Albrecht Altdorfer that Sebald had so prominently featured at the conclusion of *After Nature*.[105] A passage from Franz Kafka's October 1913 letter to Felix Weltsch concisely expresses the organizing principle behind *Vertigo* and Sebald's other fictions, each of which is similarly fascinated by the workings of happenstance. In it, Kafka accounts for a tarot reading given to him during his stay at the Sanatorium Hoffmann: "To all appearances it would be folly to believe the cards literally. But there is a certain inherent rationale for using them or some other happenstance to introduce clarity into what is otherwise a confused and opaque realm."[106] Though he refuses to attribute objective truth to the reading, Kafka acknowledges the individual's need for clarity and order. It is precisely this desire that informs Sebald's methodical emphasis on "coincidence" and "uncanny repetition," both of which are to be found at what Tim Parks has called "the core of Sebald's vision."[107]

Robert Walser was, as Walter Benjamin astutely observed, "a favorite author of the implacable Franz Kafka."[108] Kafka's spectral presence hovers over the entire Klosterneuburg narrative, and not just because he is mentioned in Seelig's account.[109] The narrator and Herbeck start their walk after a short train ride to Altenberg, following a path to the Greifenstein fortress. Sebald's contrast between the elevated *Burg* and the village below is an explicit tribute to the lay of the land as depicted in Kafka's *The Castle.*

Only a few pages later, we encounter a series of events patterned identically after the one set into motion in Vienna by the narrator's exchange with *kavka*s near the city hall: a whiff of Gracchus, communicated by a watery vision, presages death. In this case, he is summoned by the narrator's recollection of a visit to his grandmother-in-law two years before in a Klosterneuberg nursing home. While looking out the window of her room on the fourth floor, he slips into a dreamlike state in which the treetops below become a "heaving sea."[110] This vision is immediately succeeded by a report of her demise. The narrator and Herbeck, "two strangers," conclude their outing in a dark inn modeled after those depicted in "The Undiscover'd Country," the *Winter Journey* of Schubert and Müller, and Adorno's *Minima Moralia.*[111]

Second Station: Venice

Herbeck returns to his pensioner's home, and the narrator reembarks for the world of the supposedly well. (Sebald refers to Herbeck's neighbors, that is, those inhabitants of the small town living *outside* of the institution, as *Insassen*—inmates.) Traveling southward, the narrator is haunted by thoughts of natural disasters that have struck the region in the past. Viewing the plains of Este from the train, he recalls Tiepolo's *Saint Tecla*

Liberating the City of Este from the Plague and is reminded that man, like art, is modeled "after nature"—that madness and disease are the enduring accomplices of human experience.

The change of setting in the novel brings about a shift in precursors. Franz Grillparzer and Giacomo Casanova adopt the Gracchus persona upon the narrator's arrival in Venice. During the second week of September 1913, Kafka acquired Heinrich Laube's *Franz Grillparzer's Life Story* in Vienna.[112] *Vertigo's* narrator purchases Grillparzer's *Diary of the Journey to Italy* in the same city and finds his own sadness reflected in the Austrian's sentences: "When I am traveling," writes the narrator, "I often feel as Grillparzer did on his journeys. Nothing pleases me, any more than it did him; the sights I find infinitely disappointing, one and all; and I sometimes think that I would have done far better to stay at home with my maps and timetables."[113]

Sebald channels Grillparzer (who was, like Kafka, a civil servant intimate with the law) to again demonstrate how easily catastrophes of the past, served by memory or the imagination, spill over into the present. In his journal, Grillparzer cannot pass the Doge's Palace and Bridge of Sighs without imagining condemned prisoners marching to their executions: "Among shadows only occasionally broken by streaks of light, the Bridge of Sighs, upon which criminals were once led to their deaths, hovered above me; a feverish shudder overtook me."[114] The stately tone, the unwanted confrontation with ancient ghosts, the convulsive tremor—all are pertinent for Sebald, who in this scene recasts Grillparzer's words to make the palace stand for the inscrutable laws of man, which prove to be no less incomprehensibly cruel than those of nature: "What is decided there, one thinks, must be mysterious and wise and merciless and hard."[115]

Josef K.'s education in *The Trial* consists in his gradual subjugation to an inscrutable law. He only acknowledges this after it is too late, a moment before his execution: "Logic is no doubt unshakable, but it can't withstand a person who wants to live. Where was the judge he had never seen? Where was the high court he'd never reached?"[116] Power invariably fills the gulf separating the law from its interpretation; it was with this in mind that Elias Canetti once deemed Kafka its greatest expert.[117]

One instance of this expertise appears in an unpublished fragment, "The Problem of Our Laws":

Our laws are not generally known; they are kept secret by the small group of nobles who rule us. We are convinced that these ancient laws are scrupulously administered; nevertheless it is an extremely painful thing to be ruled by laws that one does not know.[118]

Such is the crux of Josef K.'s dilemma in *The Trial*. The text's opening declaration is subjunctive, and there is no way to tell whether or not he has actually done something wrong. The ducal palace's authorities, like those of the court in *The Trial* or the administrators in *The Castle*, operate according to an "Invisible Principle": their law comes into view after a verdict has been reached. "The judgment isn't simply delivered at some point," as the chaplain from Kafka's *Trial* explains; "the proceedings gradually merge into the judgment."[119] By that novel's conclusion, Josef K.'s conscience has also started to assimilate the verdict of the court. He is a meeker, more compliant man than he had been on the morning of his arrest. In the final chapter, he comes to the aid of the hangmen assigned to carry out his execution—a sign of his increased identification with the sentence.

Having invoked this cluster of associations, Sebald shifts the narrator's focus from Franz Grillparzer to Giacomo Casanova, "one of the victims of Venetian justice" and another writer of significance in Kafka's reading history.[120] Kafka was familiar with his *Histoire de ma fuite des prisons de la République de Venise qu'on appelle les Plombs:* "Do you know Casanova's Escape from the Leads?" begins a letter to Milena Jesenská from 1920; "Yes, you know it."[121] In an article about these two writers, Michael Müller points to a line in the German translation of Casanova that reads like a prototype for *The Trial*'s opening sentence: "On the morning of July 25, 1755 I was awakened by the feared *Messer grande,* who burst into my room without warning and ordered me to rise, dress, hand over my papers at once, and—to follow him."[122] Müller's claim that Kafka must have read Casanova before starting *The Trial* during the summer of 1914 is buttressed by another piece of evidence, unmentioned in his article. Recounting a holiday spent in Riva with Kafka in 1909, Max Brod concedes his failure to convince his friend "to read more by Casanova than the account of his escape from the Leads."[123]

Casanova, like K., is thirty at the time of his arrest. The law apprehends Casanova on his name day; Josef K. on his birthday. Each is unexpectedly awakened in his bedroom. Most importantly for Sebald, both are left in the dark regarding what K. calls "the main question" in his repeated inquiries of Franz and Willem at the beginning of *The Trial*: "Who's accusing me? What authorities are in charge of the proceedings?"[124] "Casanova, like Josef K.," writes Müller, "never learns the real reason for his arrest, never sees one of his judges, never hears a verdict."[125] Once applied, the stain of guilt is irremovable, regardless of the defendant's prior conduct.

Sebald restates Casanova's own reflections on the law through direct translation and paraphrase. The passages he chooses reiterate motifs cited from Grillparzer and Kafka (e.g., "When the tribunal seized a criminal, it was already convinced of his guilt").[126] He revisits, too, the psychology of the accused that Kafka had exposited so trenchantly in *The Trial,* noting that even the indomitable Casanova's resolve weakens over time: "Soon he was prepared to forgive the injustice done to him, always providing some day he would be released."[127]

Casanova's story is a historical example of brute power masquerading as justice; Josef K.'s an existential one. The arrest of both characters raises questions regarding punishment and the law—hence Sebald's attentiveness to instances of *Verbrechen* (crime) in the chapter. Gracchus too is harshly sentenced for having taken a wrong turn. Imprisoned in purgatorial waters between life and death, he longs for the rest promised by the shores of an "undiscover'd country." The "terrible fate" Gracchus is condemned to endure originates in a principle beyond his comprehension. His response to the mayor's question in Kafka's story illustrates the inscrutable nature of his guilt:

"And you bear no blame for it?" [*Und Sie tragen gar keine Schuld daran?*] "None," said the hunter, "I was a hunter; am I to be blamed for that? I was assigned my place as a hunter in the Black Forest, where there were still wolves in those days; I used to lie in ambush, shoot, hit my mark, flay the skins from my victims: am I to be blamed for that? My labors were blessed. I was known as the great hunter of the Black Forest. Am I to be blamed for that?"[128]

The sin is original, but in a world from which God has absconded, its source must remain *unsichtbar*—invisible.

Years after this trip to Venice, the narrator discovers a surprising coincidence linking his own fate to those of Grillparzer and Casanova: the evening he had passed absorbed in Grillparzer's diary at a bar near the Doge's Palace (October 31, 1980) was the anniversary of Casanova's escape from the Leads (October 31, 1756). The next morning (November 1, 1980) he is visited by a *mémoire involontaire.* Lying in bed, he attentively heeds the stillness of Venetian daybreak: "The silence which hung over the city . . . that All Saint's morning seemed wholly unreal . . . while I lay submerged in the white air that drifted in at my half-open window."[129] This mist transports him back to his childhood: "The village of W., where I spent the first nine years of my life, I now remember, was always shrouded in the densest fog on All Saints' Day and on All Souls'."[130] Mayrbeck's *Seelenwecken* stand in as the Bavarian equivalent to Aunt Léonie's madeleines. (*Wecken,* the word for "rolls," also evokes the verb *wecken:* to wake, rouse, or call.) This unleashing of the past paralyzes the protagonist. After recalling the commemorative rolls and graveyard visits in his village, he is unable to move from his hotel room.[131]

He fantasizes crossing over to Venice's "island of the departed" and imagines "the hospital island of La Grazia with its circular panoptic building, from the windows of which thousands of madmen were waving, as though they were aboard a great ship sailing away."[132] Sebald's depiction of the narrator's state mimics his earlier portrayal of Castle villagers as living dead in "The Undiscover'd Country": "For, although I had closed the windows and the room was warm, my limbs were growing progressively colder and stiffer with my lack of movement, so that . . . I felt as if I had already been interred or laid out for burial."[133] Supine, aimlessly drifting over misty waters, "Sebald" assumes the mantle of the Gracchus persona.

Third Station: Verona

Two days later the narrator recovers, awakening from his state of immobility and departing directly for Verona, where he lodges at the Goldene Taube (Golden Dove). Here the soughing of the breeze through the branches of a cedar tree and the graceful flight of two Turkish doves provide momentary solace.

Before arriving at Dr. von Hartungen's sanitorium in Riva in September 1913, Franz Kafka traveled to Verona, where he visited the Church of Saint Anastasia. Sebald's narrator goes there as well, anxious to see Antonio Pisanello's fresco of Saint George and the Princess of Trebizond. Standing before it, he registers the terror evoked by the gaping lacunae to the left where Pisanello's painted monster had once stood. Gracchus's presence is teasingly suggested on the right wing, where "a ship with billowing sails" enters an inlet. Tellingly, Sebald attributes a sense of remoteness to the billowing sails while "the gallows with hanged man dangling from it . . . paradoxically impart something lifelike to the scene."[134]

The Huntsman, suggested by the still ship with extended sails and by these "lifelike" corpses, continues to stalk the narrator. After hours searching the city for a suitable place to eat, "Sebald" settles for the Pizzeria Verona. His increasing panic and sense of suffocation are exacerbated by the sight of a mural on one of the restaurant's walls: "As was commonly the case with such sea pieces, it showed a ship, on the crest of a turquoise wave crowned with snow-white foam, about to plunge into the yawning depths that gape beneath her bows."[135] Convinced that it is a sign of some impending catastrophe, he pushes aside his slice of pizza and grasps the edge of the table "as a seasick man might grip a sail's rail."[136] Everything he sees or hears seems to confirm him in his fears: his waiter's name is Carlo *Cadavero,* and the pizzeria's co-owner, we learn, is away hunting. A man of glass, teetering before an encroaching madness, the narrator hastily gathers his things, leaves ten thousand lire on the table, and takes flight, leaving Italy that very night.

Da Capo: Vienna–Venice–Verona

> Signs appear at all times, everything is filled with signs, but we notice them only when they are thrust upon us.
>
> —Franz Kafka to Felice Bauer, January 24/25, 1913

Sebald organizes "All'estero" around a seven-year cycle not unlike the one Kafka appears to have borrowed from Paul Zaunert's *Of Mermaids and Goblins and Other Spirits* while writing "The Hunter Gracchus." "One of the legends available to Kafka," reports Hartmut Binder, "tells of a hunter's posthumous fate. He hunts, 'driven by the wind until the end of the world, following his destined path. Every seven years he completes a rotation and reappears.'"[137] Seven years after abbreviating his journey to northern Italy, "Sebald" sets forth on a "journey from Vienna via Venice to Verona . . . to probe my somewhat imprecise recollections of those fraught and hazardous days and perhaps record some of them."[138] He returns to the continent, then, in an attempt to clarify his past—but also in search of material for his own writings. *Vertigo* is ostensibly the culmination of these efforts.

The narrator's arrival in 1987 marks another in the series of repetitions with a difference so essential to Sebald's approach. This becomes clear from the onset of the second journey, where the protagonist's stay in Vienna is omitted completely from the narrative; "Sebald" simply picks up the thread in Venice. The narrator's illness, less pronounced now than in 1980, has by no means been cured: the travelers in Venice's train station appear to him "as if they were preparing for the next stage of an arduous and never-ending journey."[139] Although he writes productively for half the morning, the sight of a rat diving into the water impels his premature departure from what he had earlier referred to as the "*città inquinata Venezia merda.*"[140]

Sebald deploys slight but significant variations of the Gracchus motif, reinforcing recurrent themes even as he revises them. "I am here," says the hunter Gracchus in Kafka's fragment, "more than that I do not know, more than that I cannot do. My boat has no rudder, it is driven by the wind that blows in the nethermost regions of death."[141] The narrator's impulsive decision to alter his itinerary by stopping in Padua to view Giotto's frescoes replicates the hunter's aimlessness. The barge from which the Venetian rat takes flight is also denoted by the same word in German as Gracchus's ship: "At one point a barge [*Kahn*] laden with heaps of rubbish came by. A large rat scuttled along its gunnel and, having reached the bow, plunged head-first into the water."[142]

The narrator's existence is very much, to use Kafka's expression, "directed toward literature."[143] His effort to make sense of his own past therefore entails a parallel study of literary antecedents. After viewing the Giotto frescos, "Sebald" leaves the Arena chapel for Padua's train station

> to take the very next train to Verona, where I hoped to learn something not only relating to my own abruptly broken-off stay in that city seven years before but also about the disconcerting afternoon, as he himself described it, that Dr. K. spent there in September 1913 on his way from Venice to Lake Garda.[144]

The afternoon he alludes to is September 20, 1913, the date of Kafka's visit to the Church of Saint Anastasia. Although Sebald has substituted Gracchus as a fictional hybrid for the Prague-born author (*gracchio* = *kavka*) since the beginning of the book, this is his first direct mention of Kafka.

Sebald collaborated extensively with Michael Hulse to render *Schwindel. Gefühle* into English almost a decade after its initial publication. While one of the aims of his revision was to make the work "easier to translate" (as editor Bill Swainson remarks in a letter to Hulse), Sebald took advantage of this opportunity to underscore certain themes and to diminish others.[145] The fictiveness of Franz Kafka falls into the former group; hence the "Dr. Kafka" of this scene of *Schwindel. Gefühle* is reborn as "Dr. K." in *Vertigo*—an amendment that also calls attention to the fictiveness of "W. G. Sebald."[146]

The narrator remains seated when the train arrives in Verona instead of disembarking as planned. He purchases a supplementary ticket to Desenzano, site of Kafka's brief layover en route to Riva during the afternoon of September 21, 1913. Kafka departed by steamer the same day, but not before writing a letter to Felice Bauer describing his disconsolate state. (He would not mail it to her until November.) The two had been engaged since early July, but Kafka's continued recalcitrance now threatened their wedding plans. By the time he departed for Vienna at the beginning of September, Felice had ceased to write. Kafka's letter from Desenzano expresses relief at his isolation: "The fact that no one knows where I am is my only happiness," he asserted:

If only I could prolong this forever! It would be far more just than death. I am empty and futile in every corner of my being, even in my unhappiness. Now for an island, with nobody on it, instead of the sanatorium. These complaints, however, do not relieve me; I remain entirely unmoved, am like a great stone at the very center of which there flickers a tiny soul.[147]

Sebald paraphrases parts of this letter, recounting a few basic facts about that afternoon in 1913. He virtuosically integrates Kafka's sentences into his own; they no longer jar and distract like his earlier transposition of the Gracchus story in "Beyle." The above letter is reported, not restated; Sebald places the locution in a long sentence that starts at the train station in Verona and ends with the first lines of Kafka's missive from Lake Garda's shore:

Strangely transfixed, I remained seated, and when the train had left Verona and the guard came down the corridor once more I asked him for a supplementary ticket to Desenzano, where I knew that on Sunday the 21st of September, 1913, Dr. K., filled with the singular happiness of knowing that no one suspected where he was at that moment, but otherwise profoundly disconsolate, had lain alone in the grass on the lakeside and gazed out at the waves in the reeds.[148]

Both of the narrators' Italian journeys are conducted under "profoundly desolate" conditions.[149] Although different fates have landed them in Desenzano, the paraphrase calls attention to the protagonist's identification with Dr. Kafka (and with the latter's unhappiness).

"Sebald" enters the train station of the small town, which he supposes had only recently been opened in 1913 when Kafka had arrived. Washing his hands in the lavatory, he gazes into the mirror and considers the likelihood that his precursor may have peered into the same glass seventy-four years before. A scrawl of graffiti beside the mirror, *Il cacciatore*—The Hunter—confirms their shared identity.[150] Beneath it, the narrator modernizes Dante's diction in the *Commedia* by adding "*nella selva nera*," a symbolic renewal that parallels his own revision of Kafka's *cacciatore*. Time itself seems momentarily abolished as they face one another in the narrator's fantasy; at this instant, Dr. Kafka and "Sebald," twin hunters, meet, having lost their way midlife in a dark wood.

Like Kafka, Sebald's narrator does not spend the night in town; he departs that afternoon for Riva by bus. Shortly after leaving the station, a youth "who bore the most uncanny resemblance imaginable to pictures of Franz Kafka as an adolescent schoolboy" boards the vehicle.[151] He is accompanied by a twin brother, a further extension of the ongoing double motif. Sebald's description of the twins' appearance seems to be based on the same photograph that he had written about in "Thanatos" and "The Undiscover'd Country": "The hairlines of both boys began well down their foreheads, they had the same dark eyes and thick brows, the same large and unequal ears, with the lobes growing into the skin of the neck."[152] This portrait can be found on page 32 of Klaus Wagenbach's *Pictures of a Life*. (Walter Benjamin, who rendered the same image in his essay on Kafka, also concluded with a remark about the author's ear.)

The narrator's initial bewilderment triggers a spell of dizziness (a *Schwindelgefühl*), reproducing the stunned response other fictive precursors have expressed upon recognizing their doubles. Freud insisted that this surprise informs the very phenomenon of the uncanny: "It is easy to see that . . . it is only this factor of involuntary repetition which surrounds with an uncanny atmosphere what would otherwise be innocent enough, and forces upon us the idea of something fateful and unescapable where otherwise we should have spoken of 'chance' only."[153] The narrator is overcome by a powerful nausea, which he attributes to motion sickness—an analogue for the seasickness Franz Kafka experienced while traveling from Desenzano to Riva.

Freud postulates that this reaction occurs in modern society because the double is no longer pertinent as a symbol for immortality (as it had once been for primitive man): "When this stage has been left behind the double takes on a different aspect. From having been an assurance of immortality, he becomes the ghastly harbinger of death."[154] This explains the uncanny reactions experienced by all of *Vertigo*'s protagonists whenever Gracchus surfaces: he is the living embodiment of Sebald's "death motif," a "ghastly harbinger of death."

This scene's "desperate comedy"—the twins' parents seem to take the narrator for an "English pederast traveling Italy for his so-called pleasure"— is generated by an incongruous gulf between the narrator's fascination with their resemblance to Kafka and the impression he makes on their parents, who know nothing about the Prague author and find the stranger's insistent demand for a photograph suspicious.[155] His futile attempt to explain his astonishment in Italian is as efficacious as Josef K.'s declaration to the prison chaplain in *The Trial*: "But I'm not guilty," says K. of the charge lodged against him. "It's a mistake. How can any person in general be guilty? We're all human after all, each and every one of us." "That's right," responds the chaplain, "but that's how guilty people always talk." The more ardently K. emphasizes his innocence, the less veracious he sounds—to the chaplain, even to himself.[156]

Sebald's humor in this scene recalls the opening section of "The Metamorphosis," when Gregor Samsa's explicit clarifications are relayed to the reader in plain German, but not to his auditors. For them, his voice does not clarify: it confounds. Similarly, the narrator's explanation, however sincere, cannot help but come across as "the most incomprehensible nonsense they had ever heard."[157] After his request for a photograph is rejected, "Sebald" returns to his seat pursued by the crude insinuations he has imagined on behalf of the parents and the sniggering of the boys, whose incessant giggling from behind the pages of a newspaper suggests an affinity with the assistants in *The Castle*. Ashamed, yet strangely consumed by an "impotent rage at the fact that I would now have no evidence whatsoever to document this most improbable coincidence," he disembarks early in Limone.[158]

No wonder the narrator regards himself "rather the worse for wear" when he finally approaches the desolate Hotel Sole.[159] Although it is only four in the afternoon, since daybreak he has written notes in Venice, visited the Arena chapel in Padua, boarded a train to Verona, traveled to Desenzano, and ridden the bus for three hours to the lakeside—all without having slept on the overnight train from Vienna. Exhausted but unable to rest, "Sebald" rents a boat after checking into a pension and stays on the water until nearly midnight. The tourists who fill the hotel upon his return resemble the villagers from "The Undiscover'd Country": "Unhappy they seemed, every one of them, condemned to haunt these streets night after night."[160]

August 2 proves to be calmer, and he works productively throughout the morning: "I sat at a table near the open terrace door, my papers and notes spread out around me, drawing connections between events that lay far apart but which seemed to me to be of the same order."[161] He tells Luciana, the proprietress, that he is assembling a book about "a series of unsolved murders [*Verbrechen*] and the reappearance of a person who had long been missing."[162] The word *Verbrechen* resonates in many directions, referring to the unexplained crimes already discussed in this chapter (others will follow before the novel ends) while evoking historical disasters, such as the Napoleonic Wars (encountered in "Beyle") and World War I. The second part of the narrator's reply—*das Wiederauftauchen einer seit langem verschollenen Person*—alludes to a search for self that necessarily encompasses the lives of important literary antecedents. The reader can now surmise that the notes "Sebald" arranges are the inchoate materials of *Vertigo,* that the "events that lay far apart" he endeavors to unite include the Lake Garda visits of Marie-Henri Beyle/Stendhal/Beyle in 1813, Franz Kafka/Dr. Kafka/Dr. K. in 1913, and Winfried Georg Maximilian Sebald/Max/W. G. Sebald in 1980 and 1987.

As the afternoon wanes, Luciana tends the bar below a large mirror while the narrator works at his notes (a pictorial quote of Édouard Manet's *Bar at the Folies-Bergère*). Her son Mauro arrives with the international newspapers, among which "Sebald" discovers an article announcing a piece of theater to be staged the following day in Bolzano. Its significance for the author is clear: the play's subject, Casanova's final years, is connected to the cluster of themes central to the narrator's work in progress. "Casanova, now old, lives in Bohemia," begins the section of the article marked off in the reproduction: "In 1798 he works alone as the librarian of the Castle Dux. He and a Mistress Sophie converse occasionally. Gradually, unintentionally, he seduces her. Just as she is about to fall into his arms, he suddenly dies."[163] "Sebald" keeps the clipping.

His intention to revisit Verona the next morning is thwarted, though now through no inclination of his own. Mauro has inadvertently handed the narrator's passport to a departing German—the aforementioned Herr Doll. "Sebald" will have to visit the consulate in Milan to acquire new papers. Luciana helps him obtain a document at the nearby police station, a provisional substitute for his "missing identity." Afterward, she drops him off at Limone's bus station, where he busies himself with notes until the bus arrives. His return to Desenzano is uneventful, but when he arrives in Milan two men try to strip him of his luggage as he looks up at an advertisement for Hertz rentals; with some effort, he manages to deflect them. The text captures his attention because it seems like a personal message. *LA PROSSIMA COINCIDENZA*—"The Next Connection"—is a phrase that refers at one level to the departure signboards of Milan's central train station. In the context of this novel, it evokes the constantly changing destinations of Sebald's perpetual traveler. It also points to coincidence, the phenomenon of accidental discovery that creates meaning from otherwise senselessly jumbled pieces of information. A new row of *coincidenze* unfolds when the narrator checks into the Hotel Boston. Its proprietor is named Orlando (Casanova determined the date of his escape from the Leads by consulting Ariosto's *Orlando Furioso*), and the hotel is located on the Via Lodovico (in Venice, "Sebald" takes a man on a bench for *Il re Lodovico,* Ludwig II, the mad king of Bavaria; the name is also shared by the Organizzazione Ludwig, a terrorist group of two members whose murders are surely among the *Verbrechen* the narrator has in mind for his work in progress).

At the consulate the next morning he inexplicably designates the parents of a friendly-looking troupe of entertainers "sleepwalkers."[164] The official who repatriates "Sebald" is dwarfish, like the sculpture Kafka had admired in Verona and like the pygmies we will read of in pages to come. The narrator's identification with Gracchus culminates in a moment when, having entered a cathedral in the Piazza della Scalla, he no longer knows "whether I was in the land of the living or already in another place."[165]

He finally arrives in Verona that evening, where he returns to the Golden Dove. The porter happens to resemble Ferdinand Bruckner (pen name: Theodor Tagger), founder of the Renaissance-Theater in Berlin and author of the late-1920s expressionist play *Die Verbrecher.*[166] The narrator chooses a pseudonym for himself, checking in under the name of Jakob Philipp Fallmerayer. (Fallmerayer was a well-traveled nineteenth-century historian whose lasting contribution was a study of the Trebizond empire; appropriate, since our narrator has just returned to Verona, site of Pisanello's *St. George and the Princess of Trebizond.*) As in 1980, he is reassured by his sighting of a dove. Comfortably nested "under the wing of a bird whose plumage I saw in the finest shades of brown and brick-red," he drifts out of consciousness and into a deep sleep.[167]

In the morning he visits the city library to examine a folio volume of local newspapers from 1913. He animates the advertisements, material artifacts of the past that were once the realia of Kafka's visit, into silent films in his imagination: "They were soundless and weightless, these images and words of times gone by, flaring up briefly and instantly going out, each of them its own empty enigma."[168] The mysteries contained in the pages of the old folios won't reveal their secret, but they do provide the narrator with new trails for unanswered tales. Characters like the missionary Giuseppe Ohrwalder, lost without a trace—*verschollen*—in Sudan, inspire "Sebald" in his ongoing search for "stories with neither beginnings nor end . . . which ought to be looked into more closely." The author hunts vestiges of the belle époque, remnants of a world inexorably altered by the outbreak of war one year later.[169]

In the journals from 1913, he detects a fiercely chauvinistic nationalism on the verge of exploding. He is particularly unsettled by the declaration of one journalist who, enthusing about the Arena's recent opening in Verona, declares that his own people are the true Titans of beauty, and the rest—pygmies. An atmosphere of just-barely contained violence pervades. Even Hans Castorp's isolated little Berghof community—another fictional world that turns on a seven-year cycle—could not evade the contagion rippling across the continent: "A rising temper. Acute irritability. A nameless rancor. A universal tendency to envenomed exchange of words, to outbursts of rage—yes, even to fisticuffs": these were the words Thomas Mann used in *The Magic Mountain* to describe the atmosphere at a Swiss sanatorium as war inched closer.[170] "Sebald" seems to have it in mind as he anxiously turns the pages of the old papers.[171] The narrator is rescued from his cataclysmic daydream by a reassuring glance at the librarian, whose quaint use of blotting sand refocuses him on his task.

Sebald's death motif nevertheless continues to resonate. One of the threads he considers pursuing is titled "*UCCISO SUL BANCO ANATOMICO*" ("Murder on the Anatomy Table"), an article whose "gruesome details" he associates with the postcard of a Genoese cemetery he finds lodged in one of the books.[172] He pockets the picture, examining it later with a magnifying glass. Its layout, "Sebald" tells us, looks strikingly familiar. He feels at home in the graveyard, a harbinger of Gracchus's return to the text. Both share a "yearning for peace which . . . only death itself can provide."[173]

After completing the day's *pensum*, "Sebald" heads to the Piazza Bra to meet an acquaintance named Salvatore Altamura. (The mayor of Riva in Kafka's Gracchus fragment is also called Salvatore.) Suddenly he finds himself in front of the Pizzeria Verona, the very location from whence he "had fled headlong that November evening seven years before."[174] The restaurant is now boarded up. When the narrator tries to recall its earlier appearance he realizes that his memory has been "strangely distorted."[175] The interference derives from Kafka's text, where "two other men, wearing dark coats with silver buttons, carried out past the boatman a bier draped with a great tasseled cloth of flower-patterned silk, beneath which there evidently lay a man."[176] These figures now reappear, in Verona, as "two men in black silver-buttoned tunics, who were carrying out from a rear courtyard a bier on which lay, under a floral-patterned drape, what was plainly the body of a human being."[177]

Lacking a camera, the narrator persuades a Bavarian tourist to photograph the closed pizzeria's shopfront, failing however to convince him to take a second snapshot of "the flock of pigeons that had just flown from the piazza into the Via Roma, and had settled on the balcony rail and the roof of the building."[178] The alighting doves prefigure Salvatore's entrance as they do the hunter's. In Kafka's fragment, a flock of doves announce Gracchus's arrival to the mayor, who then walks to a house by the quay to greet him.[179] Salvatore Altamura is the stationary figure in *Vertigo*, thoroughly absorbed by a book when "Sebald" arrives at their arranged meeting place on the piazza. A few minutes pass before Salvatore, deeply engrossed in a novel by Leonardo Sciascia, registers the narrator's arrival.

In Kafka's fragment, it is Gracchus who is slow to recognize Salvatore. The mayor introduces himself, and the hunter replies: "I knew that of course, Mr. Burgomaster, but for the first few moments I always find that I have forgotten everything, everything is in a whirl, and it is better for me to ask even if I do know the answers."[180] The narrator's synopsis of Sciascia's book, *1912+1*, reiterates motifs consonant with Sebald's own: the painter Giovanni Battista Tiepolo, the mystery of an unsolved crime, Venetian echoes of Casanova and Grillparzer, the law's "invisible principle," and finally, the ominous 13th year of the century, which Salvatore refers to as the last moment before the fall, a time when "everything was moving towards a certain point, at which something would have to happen, whatever the cost."[181]

The narrator has contacted Altamura in order to learn more about the trial of Wolfgang Abel and Marco Furlan, two young men captured while trying to set fire to a packed discotheque near Lake Garda in 1984. Both were charged with committing a series of grisly murders over the course of the past seven years, carried out in the name of a group called Organizzazione Ludwig. In January 1986 their sensational trial began. Abel and

Furlan were found guilty and sentenced to thirty years in prison. Midway through Altamura's summary, the author transfers the narrative reins—the first-person *ich*—from "Sebald" to Salvatore. Their conversation (or, as the reader experiences it, the old man's monologue) segues into a lament about the state of modern operagoing.

The change in subject is triggered by Salvatore's disdain for the teeming crowds of tourists come to Verona for the Arena's summer festival. The annual event was inaugurated by a performance of Giuseppe Verdi's *Aida* shortly before Kafka's 1913 stay in the city. Salvatore informs him that the costumes for 1987 performances are exact replicas of those worn the summer before the Great War began. *Aida's* 1871 premiere at the Royal Opera House in Cairo was delayed because the costumes were held up in Paris, a city under siege during the Franco-Prussian War. By the time *Aida* debuted on the eve of December 24, 1871, the Suez Canal, object of the "inexorable progress" it was intended to celebrate, had already opened.[182] With little transition and no explanation, Salvatore's narrative leaps forward one century into an apocalyptic depiction of the building's destruction by fire on October 28, 1971. In this passage an audience is engulfed in the flames, though no one was killed by the actual conflagration in Cairo. A disaster similar to the one depicted here was only narrowly averted when Abel and Furlan were apprehended while attempting to ignite a building filled with four hundred revelers in 1984. Sebald's inferno is an embellished conflation of the two.

His hellish vision concludes with the image of a lone figure descending through the smoke from the ceiling. Sebald interpolates a passage in Old Italian that announces the angel of death's descent. The passage is accompanied by a manipulated illustration of one of Giotto's frescoes in the Scrovegni chapel: it shows Leviathan devouring Jonah, but the image has been uprighted so that the prophet's legs, emerging from the jaws of the fish, point not to the sky but downward. Sebald's reversal is an oblique tribute to Paul Celan's inversion of Georg Büchner's *Lenz.* In the opening lines of that novella, Büchner's protagonist, strolling through the mountains one winter morning, regrets that "he could not walk on his head."[183] Celan overturns an already upended perspective: "He who goes on his head," he writes in his address, "ladies and gentlemen, he who goes on his head has the heavens as an abyss below him."[184]

The words that bring this scene to a close are lines recast from the final act of Verdi's opera. They provide a symbolic transition for the narrative's return to Klosterneuberg—site of the chapter's first station, and of Kafka's deathbed. Aida, having sneaked into the tomb where she and Rad-amès will perish, cries out at the angel of death's approach: "*Vedi? Di morte l'angelo radiante a noi s'appressa*" (You see? The angel of death, radiant, is approaching us).[185] The conversation deeply affects the narrator, and he remains seated in the piazza long after Altamura's departure. Words and images transport him back in time, first to 1913—he hears the sound of horse carriages—and then to a performance of *Aida* he had seen as a child in Augsburg. These thoughts follow him into a deep sleep from which, he notes in conclusion, "I did not awake till the morning after, in my room at the Golden Dove."[186]

In a brief postscript, we hear of Franz Werfel's visit to the dying Kafka during the spring of 1924, "bearing," as Sebald phrases it, "a bunch of roses and a copy of his newly published and universally acclaimed novel."[187] That Werfel actually shipped (not delivered) the bouquet of roses and an inscribed copy of *Verdi* hardly matters; Sebald is closing a circle in these final pages of "All'estero," doubling the point from whence his narrator had departed.[188] (He is also repeating with a difference the previous chapter's account of Beyle's suffering and demise.) A letter from Kafka to Brod indicates that Werfel embarked for Venice that very evening. On April 19 Kafka was moved to a private clinic in Kierling bei Klosterneuburg—the small town near Vienna that is the location of "Sebald's" encounter with Ernst Herbeck at the beginning of this section. Now, as it ends, he notes that the ex libris insignia inside of his copy of Werfel's *Verdi* depicts a giant pyramid—a monument of death that evokes yet again the two lovers in *Aida* and, more generally, the fate of being buried alive.[189]

Malcolm Pasley's 1965 article "Three Literary Enigmas in Kafka" pro-posed that Kafka saw Odradek, protagonist of "The Cares of a Family Man," as a cipher for his unfinished "Gracchus": "What they share in com-mon," Pasley observes, "is the remarkable quality that they, though never truly living, are incapable of dying."[190] The elusive Odradek appears most frequently in the vicinity of a staircase. When the frowning mayor asks Gracchus whether he has "no part in the other world," the latter responds: "I am forever . . . on the great stair that leads up to it. On that infinitely wide and spacious stair I clamber about, sometimes up, sometimes down, sometimes on the right, sometimes on the left, always in motion. The Hunter has been turned into a butterfly."[191]

The organizational principle behind Sebald's second novel can be found in these words of Gracchus. *The Emigrants* is another quartet of ostensibly disparate tales, threaded together by a narrator who flits in and out of each text: the Huntsman Gracchus-turned-butterfly here turns into the young butterfly catcher, Nabokov. Moments of transformation unite the four stories in both books, as do their common motifs. The third chapter of *Vertigo,* "Dr. K. Takes the Waters at Riva," assumes Gracchus's creator for its subject. By rendering an account of the historical Franz Kafka's death in the last pages of "All'estero," Sebald clears the path for an imaginative fusion of this literary father (Kafka) with his figurative sons (Gracchus, K., and finally, "Sebald"). The purpose of this metamorphosis is not to shed light on Kafka's 1913 trip to Riva—though the author cheerfully partakes, as we shall see, in specialized disputes about that journey—but to fix yet again, *by way of Dr. K.,* points of contrast that enable him to remake the master in his own image.

Almost Grounded in Fact

Menard (perhaps without wanting to) has enriched, by means of a new technique, the halting and rudimentary art of reading: this new technique is that of the deliberate anachronism and the erroneous attribution.

—Jorge Luis Borges, "Pierre Menard, Author of the *Quixote*"

Over the troublesome business of the quotations (Browne, Conrad, etc.) you must have cursed me more than once because of the "unreliable" way in which I deploy them. I often change them quite deliberately. . . . I therefore now changed your version, which goes back to the proper source, so that it follows more closely my own (partly fabricated) renditions of this passage. There is a great deal I simply made up.

—W. G. Sebald, letter to Michael Hulse, May 7, 1997

Less than two weeks before departing for Vienna in 1913, Franz Kafka confessed to Felice Bauer's father the grounds for his own unsuitability as a husband. He rested his justification on the following conclusion: "My whole being is directed toward literature . . . the moment I abandon it I cease to live. Everything I am, and am not, is a result of this."[192] Sebald's eponymous protagonist also resides in literature. His imagination capsizes reality, rematerializing long-dead authors and fictive characters (e.g., Dante or Theodor Tagger) as contemporaries. The narrator has internalized his reading history; memories of texts constantly shape his everyday perceptions. Hallucinations defy the order suggested by his meticulous anchoring of events to their historical dates, and the protagonist continuously senses the presence of the dead. Of all the characters to have ensconced themselves in the narrator's mind, none plays a role so pivotal or predominant as the subject of *Vertigo*'s third chapter, Franz Kafka.

Hartmut Binder has argued that Kafka's ownership of a study of supernatural creatures informs one of the chief motifs of the Gracchus fragment. Paul Zaunert's collection includes the tale of a game hunter whose unhappy lot is to wander the world eternally in seven-year cycles. Binder's exhaustive catalogue of sources is well known by most German-speaking scholars of Kafka. Sebald, for three decades a professor of German literature, credits Binder in his 1997 review of Zischler's book on Kafka and cinema as part of a group of critics "whose efforts have helped reconstruct a picture of the author and his time."[193] Binder published a lengthy monograph with historical photographs of Kafka's Riva before "The Undiscover'd Country" appeared in 1972. Further postulations by Binder (as well as those of other Kafka scholars) regarding the genesis of Gracchus find their way into Sebald's novel, among them the observation that Kafka's unfinished "In the Attic" was an early prototype of "The Hunter Gracchus." Kafka composed this brief sketch shortly before recording the first Gracchus fragment in a different octavo notebook. Its protagonist, the huntsman Hans Schlag, will appear as a character in "Il Ritorno in Patria," the final chapter of *Vertigo*.

In his initial readings of *The Castle*, Sebald portrayed K. as a sullen Hunter Gracchus figure, caught in a winter journey with a never-ending loop. The creative impulses that inspired those critical interpretations migrate here to a more hospitable generic climate, namely fiction. "Dr. K. Takes the Waters at Riva" and "Beyle, or Love Is a Madness Most Discreet" are ostensibly narrated by "Sebald," now in the third person. Although Sebald's working material for this chapter derives from Kafka's writing and life, Dr. K. is more a shadow figure of the narrator than a credible representation of a historical author. In "All'estero," the narrator follows Kafka's Italian journey in person, refracting his own vertiginous panic through a "Kafkan" lens. In "Dr. K.," the author pursues Kafka's *textual* trail and revises it through subtle variations that stress the death conceit exposited earlier in "The Undiscover'd Country."

Like the three other chapters of the novel, this one begins with a precise formulation of place and time: "On Saturday the 6th of September, 1913, Dr. K., the deputy secretary of the Prague Workers' Insurance Company, is on his way to Vienna to attend a congress on rescue services and hygiene."[194] Sebald unravels the certainty invoked by this pedantic specificity as his narrative proceeds—in this case immediately, with the sentence's very subject. Were "Franz Kafka" to appear instead of "Dr. K.," the passage would record a verifiable historical occasion. "Dr. K.," however, alludes directly to "K.," Kafka's protagonist in *The Castle*. Sebald's revision signals the fictionality of this chapter's hero and "Dr. K. Takes the Waters at Riva" as a whole.

Blending authentic data about Kafka's 1913 trip with inventions of his own, Sebald destabilizes the historical-biographical precedent and con- taminates it with his own projections.[195] In a 1997 letter to his translator, Sebald acknowledges his appropriation of Joseph Conrad's writing for *The Rings of Saturn,* conceding that "there is a great deal I simply made up." The same stands for his handling of Kafka's biography, in the critical stud- ies as in *Vertigo*. Though the self-contained fiction about Dr. K. is "almost entirely grounded in fact," Sebald alternates between recapitulating such facts directly from Kafka's writing and modifying them with his own sig- nificant deviations.[196] His revisions are usually modest enough to maintain a semblance of "the real" on the whole. Indeed, many reviewers appear not to have noticed the extent of Sebald's rewritings: Brigette Frase called the chapter a "vignette of Kafka in Italy";[197] "Dr. K. is Kafka," asserted Anthony Lane;[198] and W. S. Di Piero omitted this distinction entirely, referring to the protagonist as "Kafka" for the duration of his review.[199] Eventually, how- ever, the minor alterations contribute to an accumulative effect in which the fictional and historical characters become indistinguishable.

This technique is visible in the opening paragraph. Kafka indeed trav- eled to Vienna by train on September 6, 1913, as Sebald asserts, but Dr. K.'s "disquieted" response to a newspaper article on battlefield first aid and his conviction that a deserted station passed by the train is "ominous" are interpolations of the author. (These reactions reflect a sensibility congru- ous with the protagonists of the preceding two chapters.) Sebald's inven- tion is then countered by the next sentence, which reverts to Kafka's biog- raphy: "Dr. K. feels he has reached the end of the line and realizes that he should have begged the Director on his knees to let him stay in Prague."[200] This passage stems from a letter of Kafka's to Felice Bauer on September 9, 1913: "Instead of thanking my director for taking me along to Vienna, I wish I had begged him on my knees not to take me."[201] Sebald rephrases this excerpt in the third person and adds a wry afterthought—"But of course it is too late now"—that reclaims the tone, suffusing Dr. K.'s voice with the narrator's fatalism.[202]

In the previous chapter, "W. G. Sebald" purchased Franz Grillparzer's travel diaries in Vienna. Franz Kafka greedily read from Heinrich Laube's biography of Grillparzer while in the same city. And one week earlier he had counted the Austrian author alongside Dostoevsky, Kleist, and Flaubert among his "true blood relations."[203] Dr. K.'s dread while passing the deserted station can be explained by its location. Sebald places it in Heiligenstadt, a small town outside of Vienna where the young Grillparzer summered with his family. Grillparzer is a double of Dr. K.'s in the novel— they share, along with Werfel, the same first name. The latter's nausea can be attributed to his brief, uncanny recognition of Grillparzer's past, à la Freud's "The Uncanny." Stricken by incessant headaches and an insomnia that parallels the narrator's restless nights in "All'estero," Dr. K. checks in at the Hotel Matschakerhof. Upon noting that Grillparzer used to lunch there, Sebald literalizes, with license, a metaphor from a letter of Kafka's to Felice Bauer (composed on hotel letterhead): "I refuse invitations whenever possible," he had written of his social and literary engagements in the city, "but still meet a tremendous number of people and sit at meals like a ghost."[204] *Vertigo*'s author brings this "ghost at the table" to life, in the person of Grillparzer himself: "By his side, close enough to touch, as it were, sits Grillparzer, a man now so ancient that he has almost faded away. He indulges in all sorts of tomfoolery and on one occasion even lays a hand on Dr. K.'s knee." Dr. K.'s vision reenacts the narrator's in "All'estero," and draws freely from Kafka's experience.[205]

Sebald incorporates most of the moments in Kafka's texts that seem to reiterate the death motif as defined by "The Undiscover'd Country" and the first two chapters of *Vertigo*. The following excerpt derives from the same letter to Felice: "At night cold compresses around my head, but still toss about in vain, wishing I were lying several storeys down the ground."[206] Sebald transcribes it in the third person, welding this death wish to a diary entry of Kafka's (also eventually forwarded to Felice) that laments the impossibility of living independently with a woman outside of marriage. By fusing the two, Sebald again couples "the remarkable factum" of love with allusions to imprisonment, burial, and death.

Despite severe depression, Dr. K. (like "Sebald") continues to engage in worldly affairs. On the afternoon of September 7, 1913, he (like Kafka) accompanies Otto Pick to Ottakring to visit Albert Ehrenstein. Sebald's usurpation of meaning in Kafka's text is evident in this paragraph. The sudden aversion Dr. K. feels toward Pick and the remarkable locution used to express his disgust stem from a few lines by Kafka: "Antipathy toward P. On the whole a very decent man. Has always had an unpleasant little gap in his character, and out of this very gap—now that one is constantly on hand to see—he creeps out in his entirety."[207] Sebald transplants this observation into his book, adding a few alterations that modify the tone to fit his narrator's voice: "In the tram," he writes, "Dr. K. is suddenly convulsed by a violent aversion to Pick, because the latter has a small, unpleasant hole in his nature through which he sometimes creeps forth in his entirety, as Dr. K. now observes."[208] Sebald specifies the means of transportation, which breathes narrative life into Kafka's terse, declarative meditations. More significantly, he omits Kafka's apologetic reflection that Pick is actually a good man on the whole. Sebald's revisions disregard this essential reflex of Kafka's to acknowledge the inverse of every notion—to hold in suspension two ostensibly incommensurable positions. Sebald's portrayal of Kafka in *Vertigo* is purposely and methodically selective. His qualifying observations confirm that the thoughts about Pick recorded above belong not to Franz Kafka but to Dr. K. Phrases like "Dr. K. is suddenly convulsed by" and "as Dr. K. now observes" specify what Kafka leaves unsaid.

Dr. K. also expresses thoughts entirely fabricated by Sebald. The notion that Ehrenstein and Pick are twin brothers "as like as two eggs" appears nowhere in Kafka's writings. This is Sebald's latest variation of the double motif, a parallel of the giggling Kafka-like twins in the previous chapter.[209] Dr. K.'s astonishment at being the only one to smile for the gag photograph is also an interpolation: first, because Kafka looks directly at the camera and therefore cannot possibly see his companions' expressions, and second, because everyone in the picture but Ehrenstein does smile, only less broadly than Kafka. Though Kafka writes of accompanying them in a gondola nearby, the jarring insistence that "they might just as well have struck him dead with an oar" springs from Sebald—a line handpicked from the third canto of Dante's *Inferno* for its reference to the underworld (and because of the *Commedia*'s motific significance for *Schwindel. Gefühle* as a whole).[210]

The narrative recommences one week later. (Kafka wrote little during the week of the conference, no more than a short paragraph on September 8 and a handful of notes complaining of insomnia and relentless headaches.) Dr. K.'s train ride to Trieste recalls the narrator's voyage from Vienna to Venice in the previous chapter. Upon his arrival in Trieste, "Dr. K. is being driven to a harbor-front hotel,"

and sitting in the horse-drawn hackney cab, with the broad back of the coachman before him, he has a vision of himself as a most mysterious figure. It seems to him that people are stopping in the street, following him with their eyes, as if to say: there he is at last.[211]

Sebald endows Dr. K. with messianic qualities, a role stressed more overtly a few pages later. (In an analysis of *The Castle* published after "The Undiscover'd Country," he asserts that K. is "the unknown wanderer—his insignia the knapsack and the walking stick—traversing the country or sitting in wayside inns uttering truth upon truth." Sebald goes on to assert that an appearance such as K.'s announces the messiah's arrival in many Hasidic tales.)[212] As if to confirm that Dr. K. is not only a wanderer but a seer too, he transposes a visionary dream noted in Kafka's diary from June 25, 1914, shifting gently from first to third person and inflecting the tone to approximate the somberness of "W. G. Sebald." Sebald superimposes gravitas upon the childish wonder of Kafka's "'An angel, then!' I thought; 'it has been flying towards me all the day and in my disbelief I did not know it. Now it will speak to me.'"[213] "A veritable angel, thought Dr. K.," writes Sebald, "when he could breathe again, all day long it has flown towards me and I of little faith knew nothing of it. Now he will speak to me, he thought, and lowered his gaze."[214] (The descending angel in Sebald's revision also invokes the narrator's apocalyptic vision at the conclusion of "All'estero.")

Dr. K., like Franz Kafka, sets off for Venice the following morning, September 15, 1913. Both are aware of the literary precedents for this route by sea: Grillparzer, whose biography Kafka had procured the week before in Vienna, also traveled from Trieste to Venice by boat. The rough waters of the Adriatic make him seasick, as they had Grillparzer and the historical Franz Kafka. (The same happens to "W. G. Sebald" sixty-seven years later.) Kafka kept no diary during his stay there and posted few letters from the Hotel Sandwirth. On September 16 he notified Max Brod that he would tarry in the city longer than planned, but as Sebald (rightly) concedes, "how Dr. K. passed his few days in Venice in reality, we do not know."[215]

Though this admission of the author's calls attention to the text's artifice and opposes it to nothing less than "reality," Sebald refrains from recanting his authority in the matter. Reiner Stach's biography contests Ernst Pawel's assertion that Kafka "spent four utterly miserable days in Venice brooding over his fate."[216] Stach believes that Kafka's wish to emulate the Goethe of the *Italian Journey* by "throwing himself into" the city increases the likelihood of his having left the hotel room.[217] This may or may not have been true of Franz Kafka; Dr. K.'s saturninity, however, originates from the narrator's own Venetian paralysis in the previous chapter: "If, as he believed, it was impossible to be here at all, how much more was it impossible for him, on the brink of disintegration, to venture out beneath this watery sky under which the very stones dissolved."[218] Dr. K.'s immobility mimics the narrator's: "So Dr. K. remains in the hotel."

Sebald concludes his section on Venice with an excursion that deploys the first-person plural *wir*, semaphore of the scholar's authority. He concurs with Michael Müller that the Ducal Palace must have played a prominent role in Kafka's composition of *The Trial*.[219] Though this scene and the above are presented in the guise of fiction, they nevertheless propose a reading of Kafka's biography, disingenuously resisting the narrator's repeated insistence that nothing is known for certain. Sebald co-opts the novelist's license to address unresolved questions of Germanists.

The narrative skips to September 20, the day Kafka's trail picks up in Verona. Dr. K. visits the Church of Saint Anastasia, where he admires a marble sculpture of a dwarf and—unlike Kafka—caresses the locks of the figure's hair. Dr. K.'s bout of vertigo while standing at the threshold is also a fabrication of Sebald's:

> It might be shown, though, that when Dr. K. stood in the porch once again, on the threshold between the dark interior and the brightness outside, he felt for a moment as if the selfsame church were replicated before him, its entrance fitting directly with that of the church he had just left, a mirroring effect he was familiar with from his dreams, in which everything was forever splitting and multiplying, over and over, in the most terrifying manner.[220]

Kafka may have felt déjà vu upon entering the chapel, having viewed reproductions of its interior two years before at the Kaiserpanorama (Emperor's Panorama) in Friedland.[221] But Sebald's assertion is willfully misleading, since Dr. K.'s history necessarily invokes Kafka's.

Kafka fails to mention the *spettacol lirici all'Arena*, though the Veronese newspapers of 1913 do. The reader, familiar with the articles discussed in "All'estero," has been trained to view the following note (written by Kafka in Desenzano and later forwarded to Felice) from the narrator's perspective:

> Nothing happens to me to stir my inmost self. This applies even if I weep, as I did yesterday in a cinematographic theater in Verona. I am

capable of enjoying human relationships, but not experiencing them. This I can verify again and again: yesterday at a fiesta in Verona, before that with the honeymoon couples in Venice.[222]

Kafka thus functions as a new incarnation of the previous chapter's narrator. The Veronese festival recalls Salvatore's complaint in 1987—the festival was initiated on August 10, 1913, to celebrate the centenary of Verdi's birth—and the honeymooners recall the man from Erlangen (accompanied by his impatient bride) who had photographed the Pizzeria Verona. Sebald suggests that advertisements for *Aida* posted throughout the city lead Dr. K. to reflect on his need for human relationships.[223] He flees to the cinema, then, to escape the damning conviction that he is unable to partake in such basic sociability.

Sebald's *Vertigo* and "Kafka Goes to the Movies" insist that the work that moved Kafka to tears was Stellen Rye's *The Student of Prague*. The film features a young man named Balduin who seals a Faustian pact with Scapinelli, his diabolic doppelgänger. They face off when the latter follows him out of a mirror "and henceforth follows him as the ghostly shadow of his own restlessness."[224] Balduin shoots his double with a pistol and perishes from a wound that pierces his own heart. In his essay about Zischler's study, Sebald asserts that had Kafka seen the film, he would have recognized himself in the divided protagonist.

Sebald justifies this conjecture by invoking *Description of a Struggle*—the longer of two early fictions by Kafka that prominently feature a double. ("Unmasking of a Confidence Trickster" is the other.) The story relates a series of conversations between pairs of men whose speech is marked by verbal parrying that occasionally veers from playful to belligerent. Each figure's behavior toward his opposite vacillates between rivalry and a near-homoerotic intimacy. The fragment ends with a first-person narrator's admission, which Sebald quotes verbatim: "*Ich bin verlobt, ich gestehe es*" (Hulse and Sebald: "I am betrothed, I admit it"; Tania and James Stern: "I'm engaged, I confess it").[225] Upon hearing this, the interlocutor injures himself with a knife.

Sebald uses this quote to thread together the different themes and literary works featured in *Vertigo:* the double in Kafka's story reacts to learning that his other shall wed, implying that his engagement is (like Balduin's attempt to shoot his mirror image) a kind of suicide. This reading is Sebald's alone and can only elucidate Dr. K.'s motives—not Franz Kafka's. A quick comparison with the scene in *Description* confirms this difference, as Kafka's administrations of violence are comic and, like the beatings in *Don Quixote,* fail to arouse horror in the reader; Balduin's death in *The Student of Prague* was, for all of its melodramatics, intended as a terrifying twist.

Sebald adds messianic highlights to Kafka's brief stay in Desenzano, further evidence of his own interpretive predispositions. He reproduces a photograph twice: first in its entirety, then, on the following page, as a detail from the lower right-hand corner of the original. He has extracted the picture, which portrays a group of fifty or more citizens facing the camera, from Klaus Wagenbach's *Pictures of a Life.* Wagenbach's caption states that Kafka was scheduled to meet with citizens of Desenzano on the afternoon of the twentieth, thus implying that the photo was taken while Kafka neglected his appointment in favor of lying idly in the grass. Sebald works from this assertion, using Wagenbach's picture and caption for evidence: what Wagenbach insinuates Sebald affirms.[226] Of the town's residents, Sebald remarks that it is not known "how long the people of Desenzano continued their watch for the Deputy Secretary from Prague that afternoon."[227] Sebald ascribes the following remark to a disappointed resident of Desenzano: "that those in whom we invest our hopes only ever make their appearance when they are no longer needed"—a variation of Kafka's celebrated aphorism, "The Messiah will come only when he is no longer necessary, he will not come on the last day, but on the last day of all."[228]

Dr. K. travels by steamer to Riva, where he checks in at Dr. Hartungen's sanatorium to begin his cure. Sebald notes that Dr. K. continues to suffer implacable woe. The state of his unhappy engagement to Felice remains unresolved. An old general sits next to Dr. K. at the table. Though he was usually silent, one of his remarks sounds a familiar motif: "Tiny details imperceptible to us decide everything!"[229] The General, having cited an example from the Napoleonic Wars, goes on to assert that Stendhal knew this better than anyone else—including those in command above him. With this statement Sebald hitches yet another fiction to fact to bolster his effect of the real; the General's stress on contingency finds its parallel not in Kafka but in "Beyle," *Vertigo*'s first story.

Dr. K.'s other neighbor at the table is a teenage girl who apparently hails from Switzerland. The seasoned officer and young woman were actual guests at Dr. Hartungen's sanatorium. Scholars have identified the officer as General Ludwig von Koch; the latter, abbreviated "G. W." in Kafka's journal and believed at one time to be Gerti Wasner, remains unidentified.

Little is known about her relationship to Kafka, partly because they swore an oath of silence before her departure, partly since Kafka was by temperament exceptionally discreet. (Reiner Stach reminds us that even Max Brod knew next to nothing about his friend's second fiancée, Julie Wohryzek.)[230] The absence of sexual pressure in all likelihood encouraged their relationship's development. Kafka's few remarks on the subject appear to confirm this premise: "My evening intercourse with W. was carried on," he writes of their brief time together,

in a language of knocks whose meaning we never definitely agreed upon. I knocked on the ceiling of my room below hers, received her answer, leaned out of the window, greeted her, once let myself be blessed by her, once snatched at a ribbon she let down, sat on the windowsill for hours, heard every one of her steps above, mistakenly regarded every chance knock to be the sign of an understanding, heard her coughing, her singing before she fell asleep.[231]

A ceiling separates the two, but this division generates an otherwise impossible intimacy. A language of knocking, however misunderstood, effectively placates loneliness: what Kafka describes is still solitude, but solitude for two. Their relationship runs counter to the cheerless one-dimensional theory of love as madness sans balm, exposited by (*Sebald's*) Madame Gherardi. On the contrary: "The sweetness of sorrow and of love," Kafka noted a few weeks later in his journal, "to be smiled at by her in the boat. That was most beautiful of all."[232] Tellingly, Sebald refrains from including this passage.

This scene on Lake Garda recalls "Beyle," the novel's first chapter. Sebald furthermore identifies their restrained and virginal love as the pervading spirit of Robert Walser's corpus. Walser wrote a handful of vignettes on similar idyllic settings and even published a story called "From Stendhal" based on an episode from *Love*.[233] Sebald inserts a passage from Walser's "Kleist in Thun" verbatim here, depicting the lakeside scene "as if the entire location were an album and the mountains had been drawn on an empty page by some sensitive dilettante, as a remembrance for the lady to whom the album belongs."[234]

Sebald's manipulation of biographical data in the passage that follows preserves the austerity of tone. Reiner Stach has noted that Kafka identifies the moment of his enamorment with "the Swiss girl" quite precisely. In a long New Year's letter to Felice, Kafka confesses the affair, dating it ten days after Desenzano and ten before their departure. If true, the two must have met on or shortly before October 3, the day of General Koch's suicide.[235] By postponing Ludwig von Koch's death until *after* Wasner's departure, Sebald recasts whatever amelioration Kafka may have gained in her presence as a loss. Dr. K.'s mournful state continues unabated.

Dr. K. removes his hat at the funeral, another instance of Walserian counterpoint. Sebald's locution is nearly identical to the one he had already used to describe mannerisms shared by Walser and his narrator's grandfather—"On his head he wore a narrow-brimmed hat," he had written of Herbeck, "a kind of trilby, which he later took off when it grew too warm for him and carried beside him, just as my grandfather often used to do on summer walks."[236] In "*Le promeneur solitaire,*" Sebald would press the same point: "Grandfather and Walser resembled one another not only in appearance, but in their habits, the way each carried his hat by his side."[237] "The October sun shone so warm that day," he writes now of the funeral in Riva, "that Dr. K. was obliged to take off his hat and carry it in his hand."[238]

Koch's role in the novel is that of the aged bachelor; he is yet another "double" of Dr. K. and *Vertigo*'s narrator. His suicide echoes a September 2 letter to Felice in which Kafka declares that of Grillparzer, Dostoevsky, Kleist, and Flaubert—chosen relations, all—Kleist, "compelled by outer and inner necessity to shoot himself on the Wannsee, was the only one to find the right solution."[239] Koch's *felo-de-se* negates the consolations of G. W.'s presence. Kafka's conceit emerges from this darkness, along with a mysterious craft and its strange cargo. "Three whole years it takes," writes Sebald of the tale's gestation between September 1913 and January 1917, "until the vessel, as if it were being borne across the waters, gently drifts into the port of Riva."[240]

In *Vertigo,* Sebald accompanies his reference to Kafka's story pictorially with a reproduction of a ship, presumably Gracchus's. The image fills all but the eight lines of text on the page that center and frame it. Sebald now quotes the opening of Kafka's surviving fragment more extensively than he had in the previous two chapters, altering the details of the original at a couple of points (he sets the tale in the early morning, for instance, and furnishes Salvatore, mayor of Riva, with a walking stick). Dr. K.'s Gracchus reinforces the themes Sebald has enunciated throughout the novel. Though many of the words and biographical details originate from Kafka, the author has now annexed their significations, making them his own.

This Menardian rewriting of the precursor fulfills Sebald's reading of *The Castle* in "The Undiscover'd Country." Kafka's portrayal of the wandering hunter is sweetened by a gentle irony absent from *Vertigo*'s Gracchus. What the latter shares in common with the protagonist of *The Castle* is that both "take everything *too seriously.*"[241] Sebald claims that the question of guilt regarding the death ship's wrong turn remains "unresolved."[242] Kafka's Gracchus, on the other hand, offers a deadpan response to Salvatore's metaphysically charged question: "'But who, then, is to blame?' 'The boatsman,' said the hunter."[243]

Gracchus is no more dead than he is alive—this is a fact the hunter himself affirms in his lively exchange with the mayor (omitted by Sebald):

"Are you dead?" "Yes," said the hunter, "as you see. Many years ago, indeed it must be an uncommonly long time ago, I fell from a rock in the Black Forest—that is in Germany—when I was hunting a chamois. Since then I have been dead." "But you are alive too," said the burgomaster. "To some extent," said the hunter, "to some extent I am alive too."[244]

Gracchus lives, as Salvatore can see. In a certain sense—*gewissermaßen*—he cannot be dead, for having missed death amounts to nothing less than life itself. Sebald systematically neglects or obscures this suppleness of Kafka's text, even when he quotes from it directly.

His prose drifts through Kafka's Gracchus fragments. Author addresses reader, comments on the text, and, invariably, interprets it. He even uses this fictional setting to advance arguments begun in academic circles. His premise regarding Kafka's viewing of *The Student of Prague* is one example. Another is his challenge to Hartmut Binder's claim that "K.-H. Fingerhut's assumption that a hunter who plunges in pursuit of a chamois indicates the story's unrealism because this creature cannot be found in the Black Forest goes much too far."[245] Sebald's narrator insists that Kafka's placement of a chamois in the Black Forest remains "one of the strangest items of misinformation in all the tales that have ever been told."[246] The author, considering unresolved questions of guilt, enforces his own reading of the story in Dr. K.'s name. He interprets the Gracchus fragment psychologically with an eye to Dr. K./Kafka's biography, concluding that the incessant wandering of the hunter represents Dr. K.'s "penitence for a longing for love."[247]

The chapter ends on a curious note, a peculiar take on the terrors of desire and Kafka's compulsion to address them in writing. Sebald asserts that Dr. K. is haunted by a longing for love "where there is seemingly, and in the natural and lawful order of things, nothing to be enjoyed."[248] In the anecdote he quotes from (its source is a letter to Felice dated the night of February 23/24, 1913), Kafka follows a German Jewish bachelor down the streets of Prague. Sebald's reading of this episode turns on a word Kafka deploys to describe his pursuit: "Well, can you imagine, dearest, can you actually imagine (*tell me!*) what made me follow this man greedily [*lüstern*] along Zeltnergasse."[249] *Lüstern* can be rendered as "lewd" or "lecherous." For Sebald, this suffices to claim a parallel between the Hunter Gracchus's longing for love (*Sehnsucht nach Liebe*) and Dr. K.'s "illicit emotion"— "At this point Dr. K. surely came within an inch of admitting to a desire which we must assume remained unstilled," Sebald's narrator declares.[250] Kafka's anecdote contains incontestably homoerotic overtones, but they suffice to explain *Dr. K.'s* repressed homosexuality, nothing more. Neither Franz Kafka's biography nor the quotations summoned above bear out the narrator's insinuation.[251]

In the letter to Felice quoted above, Kafka observes that he can be "roused" (Stern and Duckworth's translation of *ergreifen*) "even when seemingly and legitimately there is nothing to enjoy."[252] This comment, however, has little to do with suppressed desire; Kafka is addressing his own remarks some lines earlier concerning a letter Felice had enclosed from her sister, Else Braun, in Budapest. Braun, he writes, possesses a surprisingly "candid disposition" that expresses itself "in a veritable flood, an inconceivable quantity of small, coherent, but above all monotonous detail." Perceiving pleasure in her enumeration of presents and customs charges, he shares an instance of his own making a great to-do about nothing.[253] Kafka ends his anecdote in a deprecating but affectionate tone, without any trace of a confession suppressed.

To seal his argument, Sebald calls up more excerpts from the Gracchus fragments for the chapter's last sentence. But Gracchus does not suffer from, as Sebald writes, "an illness that can only be cured in bed."[254] The sickness Kafka depicts refers to the very *thought* that the narrator might be helped, an action the text attributes to "Niemand" (No one): "The idea of wanting to help me is a sickness, and it has to be cured in bed."[255] Affirming this evidence of Dr. K.'s—and hence to a certain extent, Kafka's—repressed homosexuality is a blatant act of misreading, intended, presumably, to conjoin homosexuality and Judaism because of their social marginalization.

J. M. Coetzee observed a similar appropriative case while writing about *After Nature*. In the first of that poem's three sections, Sebald foists this desire upon the master of the Isenheim altar, Matthias Grünewald. According to the narrator, Grünewald's friendship with Mathis Nithart was ever "wavering between horror and loyalty."[256] Coetzee designates this assertion "highly contentious." Such speculation, he writes, indicates that Sebald's "aims . . . are not biographical or historical in any ordinary sense. Though the scholarship behind them is thorough . . . [it] takes second place to what he intuits about his subjects and perhaps projects upon them (this may give a clue as to how Sebald constructed characters in his later prose fictions)."[257] Sebald projects two such qualities in the final sentences of "Dr. K. Takes the Waters at Riva": latent homosexuality and fear of ceaseless wandering.

Doing so, he effectively transforms Gracchus into the narrator's alter ego, making him a composite of the many doubles already presented in the novel. Sebald experiments with the (textual) material at hand, here the elements of literature and personal history. But before he can reform them to shape his own fictional voice, he must consume and, in a certain sense, annihilate them. Freud accounts for this phenomenon in his essay on melancholy and mourning, a study that, alongside "The Uncanny," informs the symbolism Sebald applies in *Vertigo:*

> We have elsewhere shown that identification is a preliminary stage of object-choice, that it is the first way—and one that is expressed in an ambivalent fashion—in which the ego picks out an object. The ego wants to incorporate this object into itself, and, in accordance with the oral or cannibalistic phase of libidinal development in which it is, it wants to do so by devouring it.[258]

This particular response to aesthetic influence informs Sebald's development as a writer. His "is a style," Tim Parks has observed, "that recovers, devours, and displaces the past. . . . All these predecessors [e.g., Kafka, Stendhal, et al.] have been completely digested, destroyed, and remade."[259] It illuminates the idiosyncratic yet consistent deviations from Kafka's text in "The Undiscover'd Country" and other critical writings. Through Dr. K., Sebald blurs the distinction between Kafka and Kafka's characters radically. He then shapes his own fictional voice from what remains—a paradoxical tribute to the altered precursor, for this *Schwindel* ensures Kafka's continued circulation in the reading community. "It is a way," as Milan Kundera has written of Philip Roth's opportunistic use of the same author, "to preserve the past within the novel's horizons and not to abandon the characters of fiction to an empty void in which ancestral voices will no longer be audible."[260]

Gracchus in the Attic: The Homecoming of Dr. S.

> Leontes: The fixture of her eye has motion in't,
> As we are mocked with art.
> —Shakespeare, *The Winter's Tale*

> What am I doing here in this endless winter!
> —Franz Kafka, "A Country Doctor"

"Il Ritorno in Patria" features the same first-person singular narrator deployed in the earlier "All'estero." The return from abroad suggested here is misleading, since the narrator's *patria* is not the land he set off from in either 1980 or 1987—Suffolk County, England—but his uncanny *Heimat* (homeland), the Bavarian village of W. he had fled some thirty years before. In this chapter, Sebald's narrator undertakes an examination of his origins.

"Death," he had asserted in "The Undiscover'd Country," "has always been . . . the second home of mankind."[261] In this reading of *The Castle,* life is likened to a state of exile from his true *patria,* the grave. The narrator of "Il Ritorno" is related to the many other homeless characters in *Vertigo.* This chapter's title is doubly ironic, for its protagonist feels no less a foreigner in W., the village of his birth, than he does in the small English town where he has lived for the past three decades.[262] His sense of exile finds its most acute expression through the figure of Kafka's Hunter Gracchus.

The narrative picks up a little over a month after the second chapter's conclusion. It is November 1987, and "Sebald," having concluded his research in Verona, decides to visit W. before returning to England. He departs from the customs post in Oberjoch "carrying nothing but my small leather rucksack over my shoulder." Sebald had identified the backpack's symbolic import years earlier, in "The Undiscover'd Country." "K. is no land surveyor," he there writes of Kafka's protagonist: "He is merely a wanderer, a figure who first appears with a 'minute rucksack' and a 'knotty stick.'"[263] The trope of the alpine walker, invoked by Sebald in "All'estero" to recall Robert Walser via Ernst Herbeck (and, by way of Walser, the narrator's grandfather), is again yoked to a protean but all-encompassing persona: the Hunter Gracchus. After traversing a gorge whose surrounding spruces are seventy to eighty years old (that is, circa 1913), "Sebald" rests in the tiny chapel of Krummenbach:

Outside, snowflakes were drifting past the small window, and presently it seemed to me as if I were in a boat on a voyage, crossing vast waters. The moist smell of lime became sea air; I could feel the spray on my forehead and the boards swaying beneath my feet, and I imagined myself sailing in the ship out of the flooded mountains.[264]

The Alps thus mutate into the Acheron of the narrator's mind, waters he never quite manages to fully traverse. Traces of Charon the boatsman merge into his version of the Hunter Gracchus, eternal vagrant in a "no-man's land between man and thing."[265]

Winter is Sebald's seasonal analogue for this state of entrapment. Snowflakes strike the window of the Krummerbach chapel; the closer his narrator gets to the village, the more manifest the signs that winter has arrived. In "The Undiscover'd Country," Sebald had asserted a direct correspondence between this season (or its attributes) and death. The ground surrounding the Castle in Kafka's novel "is covered in frost and snow, a still-life, a *nature morte* which precludes any hope of regeneration; this is reinforced by Pepi's statement that winter is long in these parts."[266]

Sebald's W. appears modeled directly after the Castle village featured in that same essay. This becomes explicit when his protagonist pauses before its threshold: "I stood for a long time on the stone bridge a short distance before the first houses of W., listening to the steady murmur of the river and looking into the blackness which now enveloped everything." The passage recasts Kafka's opening to *The Castle*, which reads: "It was late evening when K. arrived. The village lay under deep snow. There was no sign of the Castle hill, fog and darkness surrounded it, not even the faintest gleam of light suggested the large Castle. K. stood a long time on the wooden bridge that leads from the main road to the village, gazing upward into the seeming emptiness."[267]

The most notable similarity between the two excerpts is the *Finsternis* of their atmosphere, though Sebald's subtle modulation of "*Nebel und Finsternis umgaben ihn*" (fog and darkness surrounded it [the Castle hill]) to "*die nun alles umgebende Finsternis*" (the blackness which now enveloped everything) registers a far more sinister view. Sebald conjures the Second World War with his insertion here of two photographs, one of a memorial erected for German soldiers killed in a local skirmish in April 1945 and the other of a detained gypsy woman, taken by his father during the "so-called Polish campaign." These reproductions imply that the darkness adheres no less to the landscape than to the memories it inspires, memories personal and collective. The narrator does not know what his father did while in the Wehrmacht—a mystery correspondingly ominous.[268] The symbolic darkness in Kafka's work bears no specific referent, certainly nothing as directly applicable as the above. Instead of corresponding to a particular object or event, it encourages and even invites the reader to submit his own.

"Sebald" recalls his enchantment as a young child by an amateur production of Friedrich Schiller's *The Robbers* staged outdoors in W. one February shortly after the war's end.[269] The snow-covered surroundings lead the author to refer to the play as a *Wintermärchen,* an intentional evocation of William Shakespeare's *A Winter's Tale* and Heinrich Heine's *Deutschland: Ein Wintermärchen.* Heine's highly ambivalent relation to his homeland places him alongside the other eternal wanderers who operate as doubles of "Sebald" in *Vertigo.* Heine's poem has special meaning for this last part of *Vertigo;* it too is a *ritorno in patria,* written in exile. The opening strophe could easily serve Sebald's "winter's tale" of 150 years later: "It was in November's dreary days:/The year grew heavy-hearted;/The wind stripped all the forest bare;/For Germany I departed."[270]

Elizabeth Stuart joins the constantly expanding crowd of Sebald's itinerant specters. Stuart, daughter of King James I (Scotland's James VI), became the titular queen of Bohemia six years after her marriage to Frederick V, elector of Palatine, in Heidelberg. A number of thematic threads link her back to the narrator and, by way of Gracchus, to Kafka, K., Heine, and the rest. "Sebald" recognizes her "without a shadow of a doubt" while traveling to London in early December.[271] Elizabeth acquired the sobriquet of "The Winter Queen" during her brief reign in Prague between 1619 and 1620. (Like many of the historical characters in this novel, she possessed more than one pseudonym.) The queen was an active patron of the arts, and her wedding to Frederick on Valentine's Day, 1613—a 13 hinged to the year is always a bad omen for Sebald—produced epithalamiums by John Donne and other distinguished poets of the court. Shakespeare's last play, *The Tempest* (alluded to a few times in this chapter), was performed before the couple in honor of their wedding. Frederick's defeat by the Catholic League at the Battle of the White Mountain one year after his crowning precipitated their exile. Elizabeth remained in the Netherlands for the next four decades, returning to England only shortly before her death.

The narrator's "Hoek van Holland" express stops in Heidelberg, where the young lady he identifies as the "Winter Queen" boards the train and takes an adjacent seat. She is thoroughly immersed in a work of Mila Štern's called *The Bohemian Sea,* a book that will eventually acquire a meaning for the narrator "of the greatest importance."[272] Shakespeare's *Winter's Tale* links this mysterious title to the verse recited by his fellow passenger. Shakespeare's geographical inversion of two settings explains Štern's title: Sicily is landlocked in the play, while Bohemia, land of Perdita's banishment, is an island.[273]

Sebald's Winter Queen gazes, from her window, at the same Rhine landscape of which Heine wrote so passionately in his introduction to the *Wintermärchen.* She utters a little verse to herself, the modification of a song that appears in *The Winter's Tale.* Her version illustrates Sebald's appropriative approach to preexisting texts. Shakespeare's troubadour is a comic rogue named Autolycus who pedals knickknacks for ladies to fools in the countryside; he enters the scene "singing, disguised with a false beard, and a pack slung open before him." Shakespeare's text follows:

Lawn as white as driven snow,
Cypress black as e'er was crow,
Gloves as sweet as damask roses,
Masks for faces and for noses:
Bugle bracelet, necklace amber,
Perfume for a lady's chamber:
Golden quoifs and stomachers
For my lads to give their dears:
Pins and poking-sticks of steel,
What maids lack from head to heel:
Come buy of me, come: come buy, come buy,
Buy lads, or else your lasses cry:
Come, buy![274]

Sebald transposes Autolycus's ebullient ditty into a minor key. The piece recited by the narrator's companion is practically a dirge:

Rasen weiß verweht von Schnee
Schleier schwärzer als die Kräh'
Handschuh weich wie Rosenblüten
Masken das Gesicht zu hüten.

[Grasses white as driven snow
Veils far blacker than a crow
Gloves as tender as the rose
Masks for faces no one knows][275]

Again we witness the creative process at work, as Sebald gives Shakespeare's figure for white linen in the first line a literal turn. The result: a landscape identical to that he had perceived in the *The Castle,* one wholly drained of the "brighter green of organic nature."[276]

This is a complete reversal of Autolycus's worldview, for when he makes his entrance a few pages earlier, Shakespeare's minstrel triumphantly asserts that "red blood reigns in the winter's pale."[277] The buried grass in *Vertigo,* then, is another reprise of Sebald's death motif. He *darkens* Shakespeare's black cypress by recasting the material as a veil (which connotes mourning) and by deepening its hue from *black as* a crow to *blacker than* a crow. Autolycus's gloves, once "sweet," are now "tender" and thereby vulnerable. Carnivalesque masks "for faces and for noses" now serve to protect (*hüten*) defenseless faces from exposure. He removes the remaining differences by simply omitting them.

The pattern of misreading here is consistent with the one already discussed in "The Undiscover'd Country." Of course, *The Castle* is not the only text of Kafka's that Sebald mines in this chapter. "A Country Doctor," the title work of Kafka's second collection of short prose pieces, also surfaces frequently in "Il Ritorno." Kafka wrote it alongside "Gracchus" during the winter of 1917.[278] The story begins as a country doctor receives an urgent call for care during a terrible snowstorm. His own horse has just perished from the cold, but he discovers two fresh steeds—and a crouching, blue-eyed servant—in the pig stall. Mounted on the powerful beasts, he is unable to aid his maid when the groom assaults her; the horses burst from the stall and arrive at their destination instantaneously. The doctor examines the bedridden boy, who appears at first glance to be well. A closer look, however, reveals a festering wound in his side. The family and other villagers strip the doctor and lay him next to the ailing child. He eventually rises, stumbles naked into the carriage, and tries to drive the coach homeward, but his horses now stagger like a pair of elderly men. The tale concludes as they are enveloped by the blinding snow.

Sebald transposes a number of details from this text into the final section of *Vertigo.* Rosina Zobel, landlady of the Engelwirt in "Il Ritorno," shares a name with the young maid from Kafka's fiction. (And significantly, with Sebald's actual mother, Rosa Genovefa Sebald, née Engelhofer.) In "A Country Doctor," Rosa, who is abandoned to the brutish desires of the stranger from the pigsty, shares much in common with the patient out in the countryside, another innocent child the doctor cannot save. Kafka emphasizes their kinship when the story's narrator is forced to concede that the boy is indeed seriously ill: "In his right side, near the hip, was an open wound as big as the palm of my hand. Rose-red [(r)osa], in many variations of shade, dark in the hollows, lighter at the edges, softly granulated, with irregular clots of blood, open as a surface mine to the daylight." The worms he sees writhing inside are also rosy. This floral trope culminates with the doctor's address to the boy: "Poor boy, you are past helping. I have discovered your great wound; this blossom will be your end."[279]

As a child, the narrator of Sebald's tale spends hours by the side of Rosina Zobel, a melancholy landlady who passes most days drinking in her parlor—waiting, it appears, to die. Like Rosa from "A Country Doctor," she is linked to a bedridden patient, in this case, her husband, who "lay in the room adjoining . . . and had a large wound in his hip which would not heal."[280] The injury stems from a burn he had acquired as a youth, having placed a lit cigar into his pocket to hide it from his father's sight. Decades later the wound inexplicably reopens, enlarging daily until it becomes apparent "that he might well . . . end up dying of gangrene."[281] Sebald never devoted a critical essay to this particular work of Kafka's. Previous chapters from *Vertigo,* however, suggest a fatalistic reading of life as an illness that can only be remedied by lying in bed—in other words, by dying. No wonder, then, the narrator recalls that for most of the day, Zobel "lay on the sofa," and that her husband "had now been bedridden for a number of years."[282] The wandering huntsman is the incarnation of these souls undone by the sickness unto death, one that, according to the narrator's earlier misquotation from Kafka's fragment, "can only be cured in bed."[283]

Other figures from "A Country Doctor" make an appearance in "Il Ritorno." Kafka's supernatural horses are evoked by the narrator's comments about the "somewhat crazed look" in the eyes of Karl Moor's steed during the outdoor finale of *The Robbers.* This same expression is shared by the chargers in a picture, viewed by "Sebald" as a child, depicting the Battle of Lechfeld. They then resurface more benignly in the upper right-hand corner of Pisanello's *The Virgin and Child with Saint George and Saint Anthony Abbot,* the painting Sebald visits in the basement of the National Gallery after his departure from W.[284]

"Il Ritorno" features two country doctors, Dr. Rambousek and Dr. Piazolo. Sebald's characterization of the pair is informed by historical and biographical publications about Kafka's favorite uncle, Siegfried Löwy, who practiced medicine in the small Moravian town of Triesch. Dr. Rambousek hails from Moravia and may share the same ethnicity with Löwy; Sebald, who never shied from physiognomic readings in his scholarly writings, here describes Rambousek's countenance as "melancholy and foreign features, perhaps best described as Levantine."[285] Löwy's temperament better matches the liveliness of Dr. Piazolo, W.'s local doctor who, though nearly seventy, can be heard at all hours buzzing up and down the mountain roads on his motorbike. In 1907 Siegfried Löwy was one of only a few thousand residents in the Austrian monarchy licensed to own a motorcycle. Wagenbach's *Pictures of a Life* features a gag photograph of Uncle Siegfried on his bike, pushed along by four smiling girls (among them, Franz's youngest sister Ottla). Sebald owned a copy.[286]

Dr. Piazolo possesses another "double or shadow" in *Vertigo,* the parish priest Father Wurmser. Though aging in years, Piazolo and Wurmser travel by motorcycle. Both carry their instruments in "an old rucksack."[287] On one occasion the two packs are inadvertently confused. As a result, Dr. Piazolo appears at the bedside of an ill patient with the instruments of sacrament, while Father Wurmser finds the doctor's tools to give last rites. Kafka's country doctor laments the conflation of tasks suggested by this anecdote. The villagers have lost "their ancient beliefs," he complains: "The parson sits at home and unravels his vestments, one after the other; but the doctor is supposed to be omnipotent with his merciful surgeon's hand."[288] This loss of faith in religion itself is finally echoed by Father Wurmser's name, which recalls the rosy *Würmer* of the young boy's wound.

Kafka's doctor is no better equipped to heal it than the priest. After being stripped of his clothes by "village elders" as well as the boy's family, he flees the house: "Naked," he concludes, "exposed to the frost of this most unhappy of ages, with an earthly vehicle, unearthly horses, old man that I am, I wander astray."[289] The wanderers of *Vertigo* are similarly driven into the hostile elements. Sebald uses Kafka's Gracchus to embody their condition. Eric L. Santner has noted that the importance of this particular character for Sebald lies in the huntsman's evocation of "the uncanny animation we associate with the realm between real and symbolic deaths," a state that Walter Benjamin had once referred to as "petrified unrest."[290] "The Hunter Gracchus" was preceded, in Kafka's imagination, by a character trapped in a similar dilemma—Hans Schlag, the protagonist of a sketch posthumously titled "In the Attic."

Kafka composed it in December 1916, approximately a month before drafting the first version of his Gracchus story into a separate octavo notebook.[291] The fragment tells of a lawyer's son who one day finds a stranger seated on a chest in the attic of his house. The man extends a hand to the boy, who, startled, retreats until curiosity draws him close once more. In a gesture that mirrors the visitor's, he reaches out to touch the man and discovers that he is coated entirely in dust. A brief exchange ensues: "'I'm Hans,' he said, 'the advocate's son. And who are you?' 'I see,' the stranger said, 'I am a Hans too, my name's Hans Schlag, I'm a huntsman from Baden and come from Kossgarten on the Neckar. Old stories.'" Upon recording this mysterious echo of names, Kafka's handwriting abruptly breaks off.[292]

Sebald resurrects this unfinished character and resettles him in W. during the years of his narrator's childhood. Once a week, young "Sebald" accompanies his grandfather to visit Mathild Ambrose at the Alpenrose. He occupies himself with a large atlas while the adults chat or play cards. When the weather is pleasant, he carries it outside and reads in the garden. In winter, he settles down with the book on the top landing of the staircase, stationed beneath an oleograph entitled *Im Ardennerwald*.[293] "The secret contained in the word 'Ardennerwald,'" Sebald writes,

was deepened by the fact that Mathild had expressly forbidden me to open any of the doors on the top floor. Above all, I was not to climb up into the attic, which, as Mathild had given me to understand in her peculiarly persuasive manner, was the dwelling of someone she referred to as the grey *chasseur*, about whom she would not tell me any more.[294]

Kafka's fragment begins "The children had a secret."[295] In *Vertigo,* the secret is withheld by an adult. The latter one, however, possesses a menacing, historical dimension; the silence in the attic, Sebald writes, harbors a noiseless process of disintegration.[296] His choice of diction links this material decomposition to the Holocaust; *Auflösung* can denote "liquidation." It also restates an issue familiar to Sebald's readers: namely, the German public's willful suppression of recent traumas, such as the Final Solution and the destruction of Hamburg and Dresden through aerial warfare. Hence the narrator's remark: "And yet that silence was not to be trusted."[297]

In a 1998 interview, Sebald admitted to being "very taken with the business of ashes and dust," above all because of the substance's material location on the "borderline between being and nothingness."[298] The color grey befits this indefinite state. Now, in the final chapter of *Vertigo,* Sebald's protagonist returns to the staircase to meet the "grey *chasseur,*" ghost of the Alpenrose attic. Accompanied by Mathild's nephew Lukas, Sebald's narrator enters the room and begins to wade through what Kafka had called the "rubbish accumulated during a whole century."[299]

Eventually, the narrator becomes aware of an apparition, "which now could be seen more clearly, now more faintly behind the blade of light that slanted through the attic window."[300] It is a soldier's uniform, mounted onto a tailor's dummy. Like Hans in Kafka's story, the narrator reaches forward and touches the figure. To his horror, the object crumbles into dust. He learns that the uniform once belonged to a Tyrolean ancestor of the Ambrose family who had led an attack against the French at the beginning of the previous century. The alpine soldier was a scout—a *Jäger*—who journeyed southward through the Austrian Alps by way of the Brenner Pass and Lake Garda.[301] He fell in combat that June at the Battle of Merango. (Beyle traverses this same landscape in Sebald's first chapter, and returns years later to revisit the battle site.)

The narrator notes his surprise upon finally confronting the *chasseur* in the attic, conceding that his childhood fantasies had not so much envisioned a victim of history as they had conjured

a tall stranger with a high round cap of astrakhan fur set low on his forehead, dressed in a brown greatcoat fastened with broad straps reminiscent of a horse's harness. Lying in his lap he had a short curved saber with a sheath that gleamed faintly. His feet were encased in spurred jackboots. One foot was on an overturned wine bottle, the other he rested up-angled on the floor, the heel and spur rammed into the wood. Time and again I dreamed, and occasionally I still do, that this stranger reaches out his hand to me and I, in the teeth of my fear, venture ever closer to him, so close that, at last, I can touch him. And every time, I then see before me the fingers of my right hand, dusty and even blackened from that one touch, like the token of some great woe that nothing in the world will ever put right.[302]

Sebald has lifted this passage directly from "In the Attic," expanding its sentences while infusing a lugubrious world-weariness into the tone consonant with the voice of his own narrator (as in the last sentence). Compare Kafka's original:

A big round cap made of Crimean lambskin was pulled far down on his head. He had a thick mustache, which stood out stiffly. He was wearing a loose brown cloak held together by a tremendous system of straps, reminiscent of a horse's harness. On the lap there lay a short scimitar in a dimly shining sheath. His feet were shod in spurred high boots, one foot was placed on a wine bottle, which had rolled over, the other, on the floor, was slightly tilted, heel and spur rammed into the wood. "Go away!" Hans screamed, as the man stretched out his hand slowly to take hold of him.[303]

The narrator's discovery of the uniform triggers a memory of Hans Schlag, the huntsman "of whom it was said that he hailed from other parts, from Koßgarten on the Neckar in fact, and that he managed extensive hunting grounds in the Black Forest for several years."[304] Sebald thus explains the hunter's arrival in W. while playfully accounting for the character's migration from Kafka's "In the Attic" to "The Hunter Gracchus." (Kafka's Hans Schlag stems from Koßgarten; his Gracchus from the Black Forest.)

This figure's appearance in *Vertigo* always indicates a return of the repressed, a character's confrontation with death. The two episodes Sebald recounts concerning Schlag reinforce this pattern. In the first, the young narrator discovers the huntsman in coitus with Romana, a young woman employed in the Engelwirt taproom. Sebald's depiction of their sex serves as yet another reprise of the death motif: Romana's eyes, he declares, resemble Rombousek's after the doctor's suicide. The next morning, the hunter is found dead at the bottom of a ravine on the Tyrolean side of the border, having fallen from an icy footbridge. It may have been an accident, although the decision to venture such a risky crossing in the midst of winter—not to mention his having gone so far off course in familiar territory—suggests otherwise.

That afternoon, the young narrator encounters the corpse on his way home from school. Schlag's appearance on the sled initiates the fourth and final reprise of the opening scene from Kafka's "Hunter Gracchus," in which "two other men, wearing dark coats with silver buttons, carried out past the boatman a bier draped with a great tasseled cloth of flower-patterned silk, beneath which there evidently lay a man": "I had heard the jingling of a horse's harness for some time before," Sebald writes; "out of the grey air and the gently swirling snow, a woodcutters' sledge drawn by the heavy bay belonging to the proprietor of the sawmill appeared, bearing upon it what was plainly the body of a man under a wine-colored horse blanket."[305]

A comment of Sebald's from "The Undiscover'd Country" helps illuminate this scene. Likening the assistant Jeremias to a corpse escaped from his grave, Sebald had insisted that "apparently dead or apparently living remains a sophistic question, since life and death in this novel are not separated from one another but rather, one is an allegory of the other and vice versa."[306] This statement seems to clarify the young narrator's belief that, were it not for the glazed stillness of the corpse's frozen face, one could believe "Schlag had simply fallen asleep."[307]

An autopsy uncovers a sailing ship tattooed onto Schlag's arm—final confirmation that this figure is yet another incarnation of Kafka's hunter. Gracchus "dies" after plunging into a ravine in pursuit of a chamois. This fall is repeated in various guises throughout "Il Ritorno." Lena Ambrose escapes W. by emigrating to California, but perishes with her husband when their Oldsmobile drives off a cliff. A picture young "Sebald" sees at the Alpenrose depicts a pair of lovers about to jump from a precipice. The mural artist Hengge dies while painting a woodcutter on a sledge, "hurtling down into the valley below."[308] In most of the examples Sebald cites, love is the elusive object signified by the chamois. He conjoins it with the death motif throughout *Vertigo*—whether through the entombment of ill-fated lovers (as in *Romeo and Juliet* or *Aida*) or by way of the pleasure principle's capitulation to the death drive (as in all of the book's suicides).

Sebald's revision of the Gracchus myth points to a worldview more explicit and more funereal than the one expressed by Kafka's fictions. As a work of analysis, "The Undiscover'd Country" counters the reductive optimism of Max Brod's affirmative interpretations with reductive pessimism. Harold Bloom has written eloquently about Kafka's evasive prose, which ebbs from the negative nearly as often as it flows toward it:

> How admirable Gracchus is, even when compared to the Homeric heroes! They know, or think they know, that to be alive, however miserable, is preferable to being the foremost among the dead. But Gracchus wishes only to be himself, happy to be a hunter when alive, joyful to be a corpse when dead . . . So long as everything happens in good order, Gracchus is more than content. The guilt must be the boatman's, and may not exceed mere incompetence.[309]

In *Vertigo,* guilt is existential and deadly; it always exceeds incompetence. Christian eschatology underpins Sebald's themes of apocalypse and salvation. This is especially true of his early considerations of *The Castle,* which are marked by insistent movement away from the object of study. Driven by a deeply personal vision, these studies frequently seem hampered by scholarly protocol (footnotes, for example). Nevertheless, it was here that Sebald developed the themes and motifs that would come to dominate his creative writing.

Gracchus's condition has literary resonances too; his state of petrified unrest evokes the way a work of art remains vital years after its author's death. Kafka's ambivalence toward this kind of afterlife was expressed in "The Cares of a Family Man": "He does no harm to anyone that one can see," he wrote of Odradek, a personified stand-in for his unfinished Gracchus project; "but the idea that he is likely to survive me I find almost painful."[310] Although Sebald identifies his protagonist with both Odradek and Gracchus, he uses these personae to express something other than the uneasiness of being outlived by one's progeny—his concern is rather "the fear of being unable to die."[311]

Instead of dying, Odradek shares the fate of all literary works that survive the test of time: he becomes something new through the eyes of others. As a crossed-out passage from Kafka's first draft of "Gracchus" has it: "On that infinitely wide and spacious stair I clamber about, sometimes up, sometimes down, sometimes on the right, sometimes on the left, always in motion. The Hunter has been turned into a butterfly."[312] These lines well depict Sebald's predatory approach to his own literary fathers, hunted down and transformed through his own prose. As the narrator's train to East Anglia pulls out of Liverpool Station, "Sebald" catches sight of the embutterflied hunter: "And I could hardly believe my eyes, as the train was waiting at a signal, to see a yellow brimstone butterfly flitting about from one purple flower to the other, first at the top, then at the bottom, now at the left, constantly moving."[313]

Though Sebald has referred to allusions like this as "tributes," I hope to have demonstrated the destructive, and not merely regenerative, features of such transformations—how such identifications willfully remake the father in the image of the son. Harold Bloom insists that this process is an inevitable one for "strong voices." Sebald's example, like that of pre-Zuckerman Roth, appears to confirm it.

4. J. M. Coetzee: *Elizabeth Costello*

In December 1983, Christopher Lehmann-Haupt's review of J. M. Coetzee's third novel appeared in the *New York Times*. After praising *Life & Times of Michael K* for its "elemental" universalism and gripping prose, Lehmann-Haupt deems the book inferior to its predecessor, *Waiting for the Barbarians*. *Michael K*'s impact, he maintains, is vitiated to no small degree by the author's devotional attentiveness to a literary antecedent:

> There is, to begin with, the novel's heavy debt to Franz Kafka—not only the references to "K" and even once to a telephone call placed to "the Castle," but also the insistent comparisons of Michael K to various insects, and his gradual mastery of the role of hunger artist. These are doubtless meant to be tributes to a master as much as borrowings from him, but they are overdone and call an unnecessary amount of atten-tion to themselves.[1]

Though it is true that Coetzee alludes to Kafka often in the novel, his ref-erences are less obtrusive than Lehmann-Haupt suggests—David Attwell characterizes them aptly in his full-length study, calling them "nods" to the Prague master.[2] They are not nearly so insistently incorporated into the work as in, say, W. G. Sebald's *Vertigo*. Nor do they attempt, like Philip Roth's "Looking at Kafka," to domesticate Kafka's life and fiction by rei-magining both in absurdly incongruent contexts. Coetzee's nods are open ciphers, ever subordinate to the novel's intrinsic concerns.

Despite this oversight, Lehmann-Haupt is right to highlight Coetzee's debts and tributes to this prominent literary father. Thematic or stylistic resemblances to Samuel Beckett, Daniel Defoe, and Fyodor Dostoevsky have flitted in and out of Coetzee's prose over the years, but Franz Kafka's influence has been by far the most consistently salient of the group. Coetzee's fictional debut, *Dusklands* (1974), contains several allusions to Kafka.[3] *Waiting for the Barbarians* (1980) pronounces them more distinctly through its allegorical structure and nameless characters, both of which hark back to "In the Penal Colony."[4] So does *Life & Times of Michael K,* which draws, in addition to the fictions mentioned above, from *The Trial,* "The Burrow," and "A Report to an Academy." Although Coetzee launches *Foe* (1986) from Defoe's *Robinson Crusoe,* the novel utilizes parable in a manner patterned after the gatekeeper legend in *The Trial.*[5] Kafka's Red Peter is the central figure of a lecture Coetzee presented at Bennington College in 1996 titled "What Is Realism?" (eventually revised for adoption in *Elizabeth Costello*). *Disgrace* (1999) features a character whose intransigence often mirrors Josef K.'s.[6] *The Lives of Animals* (1999), another Costello "lesson," makes extensive use of "Report to an Academy." Kafka's fictions pepper the landscape of *Elizabeth Costello*'s (2003) climactic chapter, "At the Gate," whose concentration on poetic belatedness I shall discuss in greater detail at the conclusion of this chapter.

Coetzee also published articles on Kafka: "Time, Tense, and Aspect in Kafka's 'The Burrow'" appeared first in *Modern Language Notes* (1981), then alongside an extended interview with David Attwell about the essay (and, more broadly, Kafka's impact on his writing) in *Doubling the Point* (1992). Coetzee's 1998 review of Mark Harman's rendering of *The Castle,* "Kafka: Translators on Trial," was reprinted as "Translating Kafka" for the collection *Stranger Shores: Literary Essays, 1986–1999* (2001).

Like the other two authors considered in this study, Coetzee has approached Kafka professorially. Among the three, his academic writings exhibit the greatest integrity. He is intimate, as was W. G. Sebald, with different German editions of the Kafkan corpus and the scholarship it has generated on the Continent. (Numerous indispensable studies, like Klaus Wagenbach's biography of Kafka's early years, remain unavailable in English.) He has written authoritatively on other key figures to emerge from the Austro-Hungarian Empire's dissolution, and demonstrated an intimate familiarity with authors scarcely read today outside of central Europe, many of whom had a detectable effect on Kafka's prose.[7]

Although Philip Roth taught Kafka in his classes at the University of Pennsylvania and studied him carefully for many years, "I Always Wanted You to Admire My Fasting; or, Looking at Kafka" never aspires to academic standards, not even in its essayistic opening section. It was published in Ted Solotaroff's *American Review* (whose cover advertises it as "a biographical story") alongside fictions by Harold Brodkey and Malcolm Lowry, and targeted a readership whose literary interests favored contemporary Anglophone writing.

Sebald's studies, on the other hand, were presented at conferences, appeared in specialized journals, and eventually filled out two volumes on Austrian literature published by the German equivalent of a university press. They were addressed mainly to a community of scholars. Barring a few exceptions, creative manipulations akin to those discussed in my analysis of "The Undiscover'd Country" mar his critical work.[8] Most of the essays in *Describing Misfortune* (*Beschreibung des Unglücks*) and *Uncanny Homeland* (*Unheimliche Heimat*) fall short of the scrupulous standards exemplified by Coetzee. They are too fictive to convince as research, and too fettered by convention to successfully execute the sort of autobiographical exegesis pursued in later volumes (*Lodgings in a Country House*, *Campo Santo*).

Roth's and Sebald's earliest writings on Kafka incline toward self-reflection. Like all projections, they inevitably distort. Harold Bloom claims this process is essential to the poet's development when he avers that the "strong imagination comes to its painful birth through savagery and misrepresentation."[9] Yet in reading Coetzee we are reminded that the Oedipal pattern is a model, not a template. Although literary history offers plenty of instances confirming the Bloomian archetype, other patterns of absorption coexist beside them. Goethe's precedent may have indeed impeded Kafka's writing at times, but he was affected profoundly by other writers (e.g., Flaubert, Kleist, Dostoevsky, and Cervantes) whose imprint was never accompanied by a patricidal resistance.

Coetzee's fiction and scholarly essays demonstrate another type of literary influence. He thematizes the ambivalence an author feels about writing in the shadows of one's precursors (in, say, "At the Gate"), yet avoids savage misrepresentation. In *Foe* and *The Master of Petersburg* (1994), two novels which share canonical texts as their points of departure (*Robinson Crusoe* and *The Demons*), Coetzee draws from the life histories of their authors with something like circumspection. This is not to claim that either book shies from invention or misrepresentation; merely that

Coetzee does not overtly seek to overthrow his models. We detect in his revisions a reserve conspicuously absent from *Vertigo* and "Looking at Kafka."

In the first section I shall provide an overview of Coetzee's essay on "The Burrow" (making recourse, when useful, to the Attwell interview in *Doubling the Point*) and discuss the qualities of Kafka's work that compel the author. I then shift my attention to *Elizabeth Costello*, where some of these techniques are illustrated. I conclude by discussing Coetzee's representation of belatedness (poetic and otherwise) in the novel, and why Kafka's fictions are invariably embedded at the heart of it.

Writing in the Tracks: On "Time, Tense, and Aspect in Kafka's 'The Burrow'"

David Attwell commences his introduction to *Doubling the Point: Essays and Interviews* (1992) by recalling an article published nearly two decades earlier in the *New York Times Book Review*. In it, John Leonard laments a then-recent analysis of Samuel Beckett's *Lessness* based on a computer-generated mapping of the text's repetitions. The article was by J. M. Coetzee, then a young professor at the University of Cape Town.[10]

Given the plaintiveness of Leonard's critique, few of those who read it could have guessed that Coetzee's seemingly cold analysis of Beckett was born of exultation. In conversation with Attwell, Coetzee declares that "Beckett's prose, up to and including *The Unnamable,* has given me a sensuous delight that hasn't dimmed over the years. The critical work I did on Beckett originated in that sensuous response, and was a grasping after ways in which to talk about it: to talk about delight."[11]

The experience Coetzee describes here is sensual, not technical, and evinces a heuristic project much closer to literature than Leonard could have imagined. "Most writers," Coetzee continues,

absorb influence through their skin. With me there has also been a more conscious process of absorption. Or shall I say, my linguistic training enabled me to see the effects I was undergoing with a degree of consciousness. The essays I wrote on Beckett's style aren't only academic exercises, in the colloquial sense of that word. They are also attempts to get closer to a secret, a secret of Beckett's that I wanted to make my own. And discard, eventually, as it is with influences.[12]

Stylistics offered him intimacy with the language of a significant precursor without requiring him to take a stance. Coetzee tunnels toward the source of his delight in order to learn from it. Although he approaches Beckett's "secret," his method circumvents its heart, thereby preserving its inviolability. (Incidentally, "assimilate" strikes me as a more pertinent descriptor for this process than "discard"; Beckett's imprint remains as a dim yet visible palimpsest in Coetzee's later, terse prose.)

Coetzee, like many of his colleagues in literary studies during the 1970s, acquired a thorough command of seminal structuralist and post-structuralist thought, as will be evident in the summary below. A reverence for literature, however, has always set him apart from his contemporaries. This holds true for the writings on Beckett, and is especially pronounced in his interview with Attwell on Kafka. "You ask about the impact of Kafka on my own fiction," Coetzee answers a query about *Life & Times of Michael K:* "I acknowledge it, and acknowledge it with what I hope is a proper humility. As a writer I am not worthy to loose the latchet of Kafka's shoe."[13] It is hard to imagine Philip Roth confessing a like inadequacy, and one searches in vain throughout Harold Bloom for an account of a strong writer conceding his inferiority. (Sebald's case is a strange one, for although he spoke self-effacingly about his own writing in relation to anteriority, his "tributes" distort the texts of forebears more than do any others considered in this study.)

The study of linguistic stylistics featured in his early scholarship on Beckett is prominent in "Time, Tense, and Aspect in Kafka's 'The Burrow.'" Coetzee again refuses to violate the subject: his surgical analysis of the story's verb tenses and mode of narration enables him to examine Kafka's prose closely without having to account for its meaning.[14] (The only positions he assumes in the article are aimed toward critical, not literary, models—namely those of Dorrit Cohn and Heinrich Henel.) He follows Kafka into "The Burrow's" verbal labyrinth in order to learn from it, to witness at close range the mechanics behind, or rather beneath, its unsettling effect: "What engaged me then and engages me still in Kafka," Coetzee tells Attwell, "is an intensity, a pressure of writing that . . . pushes at the limits of language and specifically of German."[15] In "Time, Tense," Coetzee focuses on *how* Kafka's language creates this "pressure of writing" and, in doing so, hints at methods his later novels would assume to establish their own concentrated intensity.

The recapitulation below reveals an instance of influence manifested as restraint—a distinct counterexample to Philip Roth's "Looking at Kafka" and W. G. Sebald's "The Undiscover'd Country." The aim here is not to evaluate Coetzee's Guillaumean analysis, which would hardly be relevant to my arguments about literary paternity. Instead, I reproduce the stances taken in "Time, Tense," inserting remarks from Coetzee's conversation with David Attwell or his essay about "Translating Kafka" when relevant. My primary consideration is to demonstrate the author's critical engagement with a work of Kafka's and his attendant "refusal to succumb completely to the interpretive drive."[16] Many of the qualities he exhibits in "Time, Tense" resurface, in fictional form, in *Elizabeth Costello*.

After a brief introduction, Coetzee outlines the scope of his essay: "I am concerned," he writes, "to explore the relations between the verb-system of German (which, in the features I shall be commenting on, is very close to the verb-system in English), the narrative (and narratorial) structure of 'The Burrow,' and the conception of time we can postulate Kafka held in 1923."[17] He divides his paper into four parts: the first illustrates how the "temporal order" of the story is "riddled with difficulties"; the second critiques prior attempts by two scholars (Cohn and Henel) to surmount them; the third proposes Gustave Guillaume's distinction between tense and aspect as a way of resolving the confusion; and the fourth concludes that "The Burrow" exemplifies "a radical treatment . . . of narrative time" in which "the ever-lasting present is nothing but the moment of narration itself."[18]

Kafka's story appears, at first glance, to be set in the immediate present. The narrator has completed the construction of his burrow and, his opening sentence affirms, finds it good: "I have completed the construction of my burrow and it seems to be successful."[19] Like so many beginnings by Kafka, this seemingly assertive declaration harbors a qualifier that will ultimately undermine the certainty of its claim. Here it is the third-person indicative *er scheint* (it seems), which fixes (or seems to fix) the narrative present "a moment after the completion of the burrow but not so long after it that final judgment on its success can be given."[20]

For six paragraphs this retrospective first-person narration remains stable. The manner of speech, a concatenation of antithetical musings, is consistent with Kafka's late style.[21] The creature describes his burrow's entrance, a decoy nearby, different stratagems of fortification. We are acclimated to his extreme vulnerability, which is also the story's true subject: "And it is not only by external enemies that I am threatened," the narrator relates. "There are also enemies inside the earth."[22]

At the heart of his underground structure lies the *Burgplatz* (Castle Keep), the space for provisions that is the burrow's most capacious chamber. The creature describes his nervous vacillations regarding their storage: Is it safe to accumulate them in a single location? Or should he disperse them throughout the burrow instead? If so, where and in what manner? Kafka portrays this dilemma in an iterative, recurrent present. I quote here from the selection reproduced by Coetzee: "It sometimes seems risky to make the Castle Keep the basis of defense," Kafka's narrator begins.

> Therefore I mark off every third room . . . as a reserve storeroom . . . or I ignore certain passageways altogether . . . or I choose quite at random a very few rooms . . . Each of these new plans involves of course heavy work . . . True, I can do [it] at my leisure . . . But it is not so pleasant when, as sometimes happens, you suddenly fancy, starting up from your sleep, that the present distribution of your stores is completely and totally wrong . . . and must be set right at once, no matter how tired or sleepy you may be; then I rush, then I fly, then I have no time for calculation; and although I was about to execute a perfectly new, perfectly exact plan, I now seize whatever my teeth hit upon and drag or carry it away, sighing, groaning, stumbling . . . Until little by little full wakefulness sobers me, and I can . . . return to my resting place . . . Then again there are times when the storing of all my food in one place seems the best of all . . . and so . . . I begin once more to haul all my stores back . . . to the Castle Keep. For some time afterwards I find a certain comfort in having all the passages and rooms free . . . Then I usually enjoy periods of particular tranquillity . . . until at last I can no longer restrain myself [*bis ich es nicht mehr ertrage*] and one night [*eines Nachts*] rush into the Castle Keep, mightily fling myself upon my stores, and glut myself.[23]

The *now* of this utterance is synchronous with the perpetual crisis it delineates. "Episodes of panic," Coetzee continues, "are part of the life of the creature, they have occurred in the past, they are expected to recur." But the impulsive quality of these episodes disrupts our sense of a habitual present. In the passage above, Kafka's narrator recounts four discrete actions:

1. He distributes rations into different chambers of the burrow.
2. Struck by sudden anxiety, he rearranges them.

3. He returns everything to the Castle Keep.
4. After a period of tranquillity, he abruptly gluts himself on the goods.

Because the experience conveyed by iterative speech is cyclical, these motions generalize how the creature has acted in the past and forecast how he will behave in the future. The problem lies in the sudden change of mind that impels each redistribution, since "the act of prediction conflicts with the notion of the impulsive."[24]

Coetzee offers two explanations for this contradiction. The first points to the limitations of the language(s) applied: "German, like English," he writes, "lacks a specific morphological form to signify iterative action." If not preceded by a signaling modifier or modal construction (e.g., "sometimes," or "used to"), verbs are generally read as non-iterative. Habitual time in both languages depends upon a "continual pressure of emphasis"— an emphasis whose unintermittent semaphoring would invariably result in stylistic awkwardness. To circumvent such "clumsiness," Kafka writes in an unmarked, non-iterative time marked by irruptions like the one above which "*dramatize a typical event* from the iterative cycle." Coetzee calls this a "rhetorical" explanation, then promptly dismisses it.[25]

Instead, he proposes that "the conception of time that reigns in 'The Burrow' is truly aberrant, that it can be domesticated only with a degree of rhetorical violence amounting to traduction, and that it is better understood as the reflection of a time-sense that does not draw the line between iterative and noniterative senses of the verb, or does not draw the line in the usual place." For evidence, Coetzee highlights two episodes from Kafka's text. In the first, the creature voices his anxiety about a labyrinth that lies directly beneath the main entrance. Having built it long before, he worries whether it can effectively obstruct an attack from outside. The moment of utterance in this passage is the same, Coetzee argues, as the *now* of the story's opening sentence: it is set in "a present time after the completion of the burrow, a point from which the creature looks back to a cycle of habitual past behavior and forward to a future in which the burrow will probably not be rebuilt."[26]

When the creature lifts the mossy trapdoor, exits his burrow, and dashes away from the telltale spot, the time of narration seems to change from that at the tale's start to the moment of this excursion. Coetzee quotes the next few pages at length, emphasizing the turbulent time sequence and providing the German original in brackets when the Muirs' version fails to adequately represent Kafka's ambiguous tense.[27] This inadequacy is in many respects no fault of theirs, since "there are unavoidable moments when they have to choose between progressive and nonprogressive English forms (*die ich hier beobachte* becomes 'which I am looking at here' rather than 'which I look at here') and between perfect and preterite (*bin fortge-laufen* becomes 'fled' rather than 'have fled'). There is no way, in fact," he continues,

> of translating the passage without committing oneself from moment to moment to an interpretation of its time structure, in particular of the situation in time of the moment at which the narrator speaks: are the events beheld from the perspective of the *now* of the first sentence of the story . . . a so-called historical present . . . or has the moment of nar-ration shifted decisively, for the time being, to a time out in the fresh air where the burrowing creature waits indecisively, unable to venture the descent back into the earth?[28]

The resistance to exegesis in Kafka's texts already discussed repeats itself, here at the level of time and tense.

The wavering narration persists as long as the creature hesitates out-side of his burrow. A paralysis of indecision precedes his reentry, which he accomplishes only after fatigue overcomes his anxiety that an enemy will witness it and thus discover his secret opening. The moment this happens, "'now' entrance is achieved."[29] In the pages that follow, the creature hauls his hunted game through the labyrinth into the Castle Keep, where he finally allows himself to rest.

He is awakened by a faint, steady whistling noise whose identification becomes the object of his worried musings for the remainder of the story. Although the protagonist's speech is mainly "cotemporal with the *now* of the action," it continues to lapse into an iterative tense, causing further consternation to the reader.[30] If the episode recited is cyclical, then the nar-rator ought to be able to learn from his experience. He should not be so prone to hoping that an idea which has already failed may in fact provide a solution. Yet the creature is, Coetzee remarks, "in some sense condemned to these iterations,"

> and that part of being condemned (as the example of Sisyphus might teach) is that the torments of hope are part of the sentence. What should interest us particularly in an investigation of tense and time, however, is

that the inability to learn from past failure is a reflection of the fact that iterations are not ordered: none of them being earlier in time than any other, no iteration encompasses a memory of an earlier one.[31]

Kafka's time of narration remains unstable until the tale breaks off, its hero having convinced himself that the noise originates from an enemy tunneling toward his burrow. Coetzee concludes this first part of his analysis by again stressing the prose's iterative connotations: "Perhaps it is possible that the beast has never heard him," he writes, "in which case there is hope. '*But all remains unchanged*'" (my italics).[32]

After demonstrating the challenges posed by Kafka's representation of temporal order in the story, Coetzee considers the efforts of two contemporary scholars to make sense of it. The first is Dorrit Cohn, whose 1968 article "Kafka's Eternal Present: Narrative Tense in 'Ein Landarzt' and Other First-Person Stories" and *Transparent Minds* (1978) reach a conclusion Coetzee concedes is similar to his own, namely that "a constantly repeated present" prevails in "The Burrow."[33] His disagreement stems from *how* she arrives at it. Cohn claims that the text fissures when the creature first hears (or articulates hearing) the hissing noise. "Up to this point the animal has described his habitual subterranean existence in durative-iterative present tense," Cohn writes. After this point "the static time of the first part of the story . . . becomes an evolving time, its durative tense a punctual tense."[34] She then marshals an aphorism of Kafka's in support of her postulation: "The decisive moment of human development is everlasting."[35]

Coetzee criticizes both approaches. He contends that Cohn's division of the text into two parts—one in which time is static and another in which it evolves—is too simplistic a generalization. Kafka's fiction, he writes, defies such a neat mapping of tenses; Coetzee has already provided sufficient examples drawn from "The Burrow" to prove this the case. Later in the essay, he takes issue with Cohn's haphazard appropriation of the 1917 aphorism, noting that Kafka had composed it in a context different from the one implied. Cohn's annexation of the passage (not dissimilar, in fact, from Sebald's method of "proving" arguments in critical essays) "misses the point," he maintains, and disregards the strategy's more radical implications.[36]

Heinrich Henel's article "The End of Kafka's 'The Burrow'" posits the endless temporality of Kafka's tale. He too separates the story into two sections (in Henel they are joined by a transitional passage), and asserts that the present tense in "The Burrow" fills "no less than five distinct functions."[37] Coetzee parries by insisting that Henel's division, like Cohn's, takes the text's radical aberrance too lightly—that it tries to "smooth out" difficulties instead of accounting for them. These "five functions" demur from probing deeper into the problems of time and tense provoked by "The Burrow." Henel's classificatory system raises the question to which Coetzee will devote the remainder of his essay: "Is there a temporal coherence to the story, or does the mind behind the story shift from one temporal subsystem to another?"[38]

Coetzee begins by "refining" the notion of tense in his essay's third section, making a distinction between "*two* elements of verb inflection," time and aspect. He follows here the work of the Canadian linguist Gustave Guillaume, whose *Time and Verb* (*Temps et verbe,* 1929) and 1948–49 lectures maintain that time and aspect *cannot be reconciled* "in the familiar unidirectional arrow of infinite time of Newtonian physics. The verb system," Coetzee continues,

> instead rests upon two simultaneous and complementary ways of conceiving time: as universe time, a limitless linear time along whose axis any event can be situated; and as event time, the span of time that an event takes to achieve itself. . . . Verbal aspect is a system of representing event time. Once this mental representation has been achieved, . . . the system of tense serves to combine the representations of event time and universe time.[39]

Having established these basic features, Coetzee highlights a few corollaries before embarking on an examination of how Guillaumean tense and aspect help resolve some of the formal challenges presented by Kafka's narrative. I encapsulate them below in chronological sequence.

- Event time occurs in two phases: "a *coming-to-be* phase extending over successive instants," then "a *result* phase during which no further development . . . can take place."[40]
- The point where a verb intercepts event time on the temporal continuum determines aspect.
- Although an iterative verb form "may be thought of as shorthand for a succession of single events each with a beginning and an end, . . . it does not intercept the result phase of any of these single events, and at most may or may not intercept only the result phase of their totality."[41]

- The "morphological means of time specification" in an iterated event are "impoverished . . . because what is under normal circumstances a tense marker with a secondary aspectual function . . . is now charged primarily with marking iterative aspect." "Time relations" in such cases, the author concludes, "have to be specified by syntactic means." Coetzee quotes passages from the story that demonstrate Kafka's use of syntax "to involve the reader in the narrative as an event, and to challenge conventional notions of time."[42]

Concentrating on the section of "The Burrow" set above the labyrinth in the open air, Coetzee shows Kafka's narration alternating between two competing experiences of time. The first represents the protagonist's cyclical experience of (1) exiting the burrow, (2) undergoing terrestrial life's exhilaration and terror, (3) hesitating before his return underground, and (4) finally accomplishing reentry and descent. The author indicates iterativity by combining present-tense verbs with adverbials like "sometimes" and "usually." This temporality is punctured repeatedly by another whose "time of . . . iteration [is] experienced from the inside, with a past and an unknown future of its own . . . as though the iterative nature became invisible or were erased from knowledge."[43]

"The movement of these pages," Coetzee observes of 176–85 of "The Burrow" (pages 476–84 in *The Collected Stories*),

is . . . a continual slide from an outside view of the cycle safety-danger-safety to an inside view in which the danger is experienced from the inside and from which it seems impossible to reattain safety, followed by an abrupt and temporary return to the safer outside view. This back-and-forth occurs not only at the level of the narrator's experience; it is also explicitly thematized in the passage as a "problem."[44]

Only when the creature is too exhausted to think can he surmount his inertia and return to the burrow:

As long as consciousness has been in control, the creature has been unable to achieve this transition from above to below and has remained stuck in a condition that is not only unendurable but logically impossible: the iterative forms have already promised that ascent and descent form a cycle; therefore, the creature cannot remain stuck halfway. Exhaustion and incapacity for thought are the sole means that overcome the arguments (or rationalizations) of the conscious mind that keep him from his burrow; they also constitute the "absurd device" that solves the problem of getting stuck during the cycle.[45]

The creature's mental fatigue implies that consciousness itself generates *both* his intricate fortifications *and* the impasse that deters him from returning underground.

Coetzee proposes that these intermittent ruptures of temporality emerge from the narrator's ongoing struggle for self-preservation. He likens them to the paradoxical notion of time evinced by Kafka in prior fictions ("The Great Wall of China," "The Next Village," "Advocates"), one whose laws conform not to Newtonian linearity but to Zeno's paradox. The subjects who inhabit this temporality are constantly exposed to sudden transformation: "no amount of watchfulness will reveal how one moment becomes another; all we know is that the next moment happens."[46] "Kafka's concern," Coetzee explains to David Attwell, "is with the experience of a breakdown . . . of the time-sense: one moment does not flow into the next—on the contrary, each moment has the threat or promise of being (not becoming) a timeless forever, unconnected to, ungenerated by, the past."[47] For this story's burrowing narrator, existence requires perpetual guardedness against such transitionless change.

To counter its threat, Kafka's creature attempts to contain linear time—and the oblivion it implies—in an *iterative pseudo-present.* In Guillaumean terminology, this entails moving from universe time toward event time, "away from linear past-present-future tense organization toward a cyclic aspectual organization of time."[48] This move is enabled by "peculiarities" of the German language (shared by English); with no morphological form to indicate iteration, the author can move easily from tense to aspect and—as we so often witness in "The Burrow"—back again. The temporal breakdowns, the ruptures of time that foil a flawless configuration or distinct sequence of events confirm the inevitable failure of this enterprise.

Coetzee briefly notes the visceral effect of the narrator's "ruse" on the reader. The uneasy oscillation between incommensurable temporalities appears to amplify the prose's intensity.[49] So do the syntactic maneuvers required to signal iteration. *Narrative* time feeds on *narrated* time until "the adventures of the creature seeking a way into his burrow become identical with the adventures of the signifying subject seeking to find a way to keep the narrative moving."[50]

"Time, Tense" concludes with Coetzee's return to Dorrit Cohn's postulation that "Kafka's paradoxical conception of human time . . . is based on the denial of the distinction between repetitious and singular events."[51] Cohn claims that if this distinction no longer exists, then the hissing noise first mentioned halfway through the manuscript must therefore be present in the silence preceding its mention (or notice). She finds this premise affirmed by an earlier aphorism of Kafka's: "The decisive moment of human development is everlasting." Coetzee has already contested her assertion that Kafka "effaces" the difference between these two modes of temporality. He does, however, agree with her general conclusion, which he now refines by looking more closely at the aphorism invoked.[52]

His first step illustrates the perils of interpretation, a temptation that Coetzee for the most part resists in this essay. The apothegm Cohn alludes to is number 6 of the 109 Kafka gathered in one of his octavo notebooks ("G"). Together, they constitute a series known in English by the misleading title Max Brod selected for a volume of posthumous writings: "Reflections on Sin, Suffering, Hope, and the True Way."[53] Marshaling the support of aphorisms that precede and succeed the one chosen by Cohn, Coetzee asserts that "the passage as a whole . . . contrasts two kinds of awareness of time," one historical (i.e., linear, continuous with present), the other eschatological (nonlinear, discontinuous).

But his contextualization poses new difficulties. Coetzee's encapsulation of the fifth aphorism on pages 230–31 of "Time, Tense, and Aspect"—"We die at every moment, but blindly do not recognize our death and are spat back into life"—reveals, however subtly, a distinct poetic license over the original which reads:

> Many shades of the departed are occupied solely in licking the waves of the river of death because it comes from our direction and still has the salty taste of our seas. Then the river rears up in disgust, flows the opposite way, and washes the dead back to life. They however are happy, sing songs of thanksgiving, and stroke the indignant theme.[54]

Coetzee substitutes a literal meaning for Kafka's open and ambiguous parable. It is unclear precisely where the alleged *recognition* in this passage occurs. And even if the "shades of the departed" are indeed souls that die at every moment, Coetzee's elision of the opening qualifier (*Viele,* that is, "many") significantly alters the image of shades shuttling back and forth between the living and the dead.

Having noted the aphorism antecedent to the one quoted by Cohn,[55]

Coetzee cites this successor: "Human history is the second between two steps of a traveler."[56] Coetzee infers that, considered together, the four assert "the paradox that history is over in 'a second,' while the present moment is 'everlasting.'" He implies that their proximity supports this view.[57] Yet a quick glance at the critical edition reveals how different versions of Kafka's unpublished manuscripts further compound the texts' built-in resistance to generalized theorization.

In *Wedding Preparations in the Country,* the volume of prose arranged by Brod and published in 1953, the first three aphorisms appear side by side. No space in the text divides them; they seem to be one and the same entry. Kafka's maxim about human history being an instant between two steps follows it. One searches in vain, though, for this latter entry in the relevant copy of *Posthumous Writings and Fragments.* Why? *Because Kafka had crossed the passage out.*

Brod inserted it in his reproduction of the octavo notebooks—an understandable though problematic admission. Had it not appeared in this edition, it would have remained out of sight for decades longer. (As scholars and enthusiasts already know, Kafka's cross-outs—many of which exceed a paragraph in length—reveal how methodically he worked to evade interpretation. Many are equivalent in literary value to lines that he allowed to stand.) Conforming to the editorial policy of S. Fischer's critical edition, Jost Schillemeit consigns this passage to a companion volume of textual variants, accounts of composition, and additional notes and observations.[58]

This revelation does not annul Coetzee's claim that "The Burrow" advances a "radical treatment" of narrative time in which "the everlasting present is nothing but the moment of narration itself."[59] Though his familiarity with the biographical, historical, and material circumstances surrounding "The Burrow's" composition is evident, Coetzee secures the validity of his argument in the close textual analysis that precedes these closing remarks. Moreover, the aphorisms summoned *did* appear next to one another in Kafka's octavo notebook; the contemporary reader, however, will recognize that the final one's inclusion (which no longer appears in standard editions of his work) was purely arbitrary, that is, subject to Max Brod's selective restitution of crossed-out passages.

Coetzee foresaw such risks, even at the time of this paper's composition. Earlier in the essay, he concedes it "foolhardy to dismiss out of hand the possibility that 'The Burrow' is incomplete."[60] Now, in a footnote conjoined to his account of Kafka's aphorism, he issues a caveat against the very sort of selective appropriation he has just engaged in. It offers a most cogent demonstration of the caution inherent in Coetzee's approach:

Quite aside from the literary-biographical problem of relating a journal entry to a story written some six years later, we should be wary of erecting large interpretive edifices upon journal entries that may be no more than fleeting, partial insights developed in greater precision by the fiction. Cohn perhaps places too much reliance on this particular entry in her reading of "The Burrow."[61]

This advice becomes even more significant when we consider the regularity with which commentators have attempted to treat the aphorisms as a skeleton key to Kafka's entire corpus.[62] Only three years after the first publication of *The Great Wall of China: Unpublished Stories and Prose from the Posthumous Papers,* Walter Benjamin disclaimed the tendency of critics to overestimate the authority emanated by these particular writings: "Hardly had this volume appeared," he remarked, "when the reflections served as the basis for a Kafka criticism which concentrated on an interpretation of these reflections to the neglect of his real works."[63] The aphorisms obstinately deflect all attempts at systemization. They constitute no theory of time, historical or otherwise; at best, they *register* (like many of Kafka's other fictions, i.e., his "real work") aporias that occur when a linear, unidirectional model is presumed. Coetzee's footnoted admission again exhibits the critical reserve so carefully sustained throughout the paper.

Reading Coetzee's essay on "The Burrow," we witness an earnest disciple schooling himself on the writings of a selected mentor. Critical essays by Sebald and Roth exhibit Kafka's influence through their exaggeration of certain qualities (saturninity in Sebald's case, physical desire in Roth's). Coetzee's affinities, at least with this author, can be measured in units of likeness. By "writing in the tracks" of Kafka's burrowing narrator, Coetzee absorbs numerous lessons and strategies that his novels would later reflect, exhibiting all the while an interpretative restraint that defies the Oedipal scheme laid out by Bloom.

Going Over: "Realism" and the Task of Embodiment

It is safe to surmise that many of the spectators in the Stockholm audience attending J. M. Coetzee's Nobel lecture in November 2003 expected to hear the new laureate deliver a fiction in place of the customary lecture.

Coetzee's address confounded, however, those anticipating Elizabeth Costello's report to the academy; "He and His Man" did not spotlight the protagonist Coetzee had featured in public talks over the previous seven years, but a host of figures and conceits drawn from Daniel Defoe's *The Life and Strange Adventures of Robinson Crusoe* (1719), *Journal of the Plague Year* (1722), and *Tour Through the Whole Island of Great Britain* (1724–26).

Before beginning the address proper, Coetzee related an anecdote about his first encounter with *Robinson Crusoe*. I reproduce here his introduction, transcribed from an archived webcast:

Before I begin to read to you the lecture proper, the piece called "He and His Man" or "His Man and He" (I cannot remember which comes first, he or his man), I want to say a word about certain events that must have taken place in 1948 or 1949 when I, that is to say, the one I call I, not the one I call he, was a boy of eight or nine, reading for the first time the book called *Robinson Crusoe*, more accurately, the *Strange and Surprising Adventures of Robinson Crusoe,* to distinguish it from the book called *The Further Adventures of Robinson Crusoe,* about whose existence I knew nothing at the time. *Robinson Crusoe,* the story first of Robinson Crusoe shipwrecked alone on a desert island and later of Robinson Crusoe and his man Friday after Friday had made his appearance. I read with the fullest attention this story, the story of the desert island that is turned into an island kingdom. Robinson Crusoe became a figure in my imagination. So I was puzzled when some months later I came across a statement in the children's encyclopedia to the effect that someone else besides Robinson Crusoe and Friday was part of the island story, a man with a wig named Daniel Defoe. What was not clear from the children's encyclopedia was exactly how this man fitted into the story. The encyclopedia referred to the man as the author of *Robinson Crusoe* but this made no sense, since it said on the very first page of *Robinson Crusoe* that Robinson Crusoe told the story himself. Who was Daniel Defoe? What had he done to get into the children's encyclopedia along with Robinson Crusoe? Was Daniel Defoe perhaps another name for Robinson Crusoe, an alias that he used when he returned to England from his island and put on a wig?[64]

Given Crusoe's adamant insistence that his story is true, who then is "Defoe"? The riddle unsettles Coetzee long after he consults an encyclopedia. Crusoe, a fictive author, has taken up residence in his imagination.

And there he continues to exist, alongside Coetzee's knowledge that Daniel Defoe (1660–1731), née Foe, son of a Cornhill Ward chandler, intentionally promoted this deception.

A late work of Kafka's best known by its posthumously appended title, "On Parables," offers an apposite commentary. I quote it in full:

Many complain that the words of the wise are always merely parables and of no use in daily life, which is the only life we have. When the sage says: "Go over" [*Gehe hinüber*], he does not mean that we should cross to some actual place, which we could do anyhow if the labor were worth it; he means some fabulous yonder, something unknown to us, something he cannot designate more precisely either, and therefore cannot help us in the very least. All these parables set out to say merely that the incomprehensible is incomprehensible, and we know that already. But the cares we have to struggle with every day: that is a different matter.

Concerning this a man once said: Why such reluctance? If you only followed the parables you yourselves would become parables and with that rid of all your daily cares.[65]

Another said: I bet that is also a parable.

The first said: You have won.

The second said: But unfortunately only in parable.

The first said: No, in reality: in parable you have lost.[66]

"On Parables" pivots on the ambiguity of an expression, *gehe hinüber*. The mystic traversal Kafka invokes in his parable draws first from this imperative's literal meaning: without an "actual place to cross," no "fabulous yonder" can exist. *Elizabeth Costello*'s leading sentence also proposes a "going over": "There is first of all the problem of the opening," Coetzee writes, "namely, how to get us from where we are, which is, as yet, nowhere, to the far bank." Though the problem of crossing here seems to address the discrete tasks faced by a writer at the beginning of a new work—finding the right materials (words) for "knocking together a bridge"—the "far bank" will acquire, by *Costello*'s end, symbolic resonance.[67]

Coetzee frequently uses Kafkan models to reinforce this novel's main concerns. For the greater part of this section, I handle the topics individually. They include: the stakes of literary realism at the beginning of the twenty-first century; the phenomenon of divine inspiration (also referred to as "embodiment"); and the conflicted view of origins—in life as in art—that *Elizabeth Costello* expresses. After exploring these themes, I will focus exclusively on the first chapter of Coetzee's novel, which shares its title, "What Is Realism?" with a talk given by the author at Bennington College in November 1996.[68]

Coetzee's omniscient narrator in *Elizabeth Costello* begins by divulging a convention of fiction-making, namely, that an opening must transport its reader from his world of daily cares ("*das womit wir uns . . . jeden Tag abmühn,*" in Kafka's parable) to an imaginary realm created by the author. Abruptly, his speaker then preempts that process by announcing that he will skip it: "Let us assume that," Coetzee writes, "however it may have been done, it is done. . . . We have left behind the territory in which we were. We are in the far territory, where we want to be."[69] This announcement draws in the reader as effectively as the traditional approach he so openly rejects. Throughout "What Is Realism?" Coetzee repeatedly confirms what postmodern fictions of the past three and a half decades have proven: "that the realistic illusion can survive the author's showing of his or her hand."[70]

The chapter proceeds, a present-tense account of events punctuated by the narrator's occasional interpolations. During these interruptions he comments on the principal story, which centers on the brief stay of Australian novelist Elizabeth Costello and her son John in a small American town, where Elizabeth has arrived to claim an important prize. One such disruption occurs shortly after they check in at their hotel. The long flight has sapped Costello of her strength. Mother and son adjourn to their rooms to recuperate before convening for dinner with the panel that has conferred the award. When John stops by her room that evening to collect her, she exits in her "lady novelist's uniform": a "blue costume and silk jacket" worn in tandem with a white pair of shoes. Coetzee glosses over her appearance, noting that her washed-back hair looks "greasy, but honourably greasy, like a navvy's or a mechanic's," and that her countenance has assumed a passive expression evocative—to her son, at least—of Keats's "blank receptiveness."[71]

The narrator calls attention to these specific details and how they conspire to establish an effect of the real upon the reader. "Supply the particulars," maintains Coetzee's somewhat pedantic speaker: "allow the significations to emerge themselves." He then credits Daniel Defoe with developing this technique:

Robinson Crusoe, cast up on the beach, looks around for his shipmates. But there are none. "I never saw them afterwards, or any sign of them," says he, "except three of their hats, one cap, and two shoes that were not fellows." Two shoes, not fellows: by not being fellows, the shoes have ceased to be footwear and become proofs of deaths, torn by the foaming seas off the feet of drowning men and tossed ashore. No large words, no despair, just hats and caps and shoes.[72]

It behooves us to note that Coetzee cited the same passage in his foreword to the Oxford World Classics edition of *Robinson Crusoe* (1999) a few years after the Bennington lecture appeared in print. "In representing the distress of the castaway," he had written of Defoe's realism,

the method of bald empirical description works wonderfully. . . . For page after page—for the first time in the history of fiction—we see a minute, ordered description of how things are done. It is a matter of purely writerly attentiveness, pure submission to the exigencies of a world which, through being submitted to in a state so close to spiritual absorption, becomes transfigured, real.[73]

In highlighting the items belonging to Crusoe's drowned companions, Coetzee points to two aspects of realism that inform his own project in *Elizabeth Costello:* first, how gaps and absences effectively shape the parameters of a fictional world, and second, verisimilitude's debt to mundane details.

Elizabeth Costello's speculations on embodiment echo this premise. So does Defoe's evocation of Crusoe's dead comrades neither with the aid of "large words" nor "despair," but with "hats and caps and shoes." The opposition in this sentence stresses the importance of seemingly superfluous objects, bits of empirical data used by the author to construct a plausible scene.[74] Modernist novels would eventually develop Defoe's emphasis on minor but significant details. In *The Voyage Out* (1915), for example, Virginia Woolf, Costello's literary forebear, included a scene in which a character pares his toenails—a moment Coetzee alludes to in a later scene.[75]

Authors can also convey *thoughts* to make their characters seem credible. As John accompanies Susan Moebius to her room after their conversation in the hotel bar, it strikes him as strange that the building has a thirteenth floor: "He is surprised . . . He thought that floors went twelve-fourteen, that that was the rule in the hotel world."[76] When he sees an overweight woman stuffing herself with popcorn at the airport he thinks: "Without ceasing to chew, the fat woman removes her eyes from them. He thinks of the cud of mashed corn and saliva in her mouth and shudders. Where does it all end?"[77] Both moments contribute to Coetzee's portrayal of John as a highly attentive, somewhat unlikeable individual. Like the author's description of Costello's outfit, passages such as these labor to produce an aura of verity around the character.

In a different interpolation, Coetzee's speaker declares that "realism has never been comfortable with ideas."

> It could not be otherwise: realism is premised on the idea that ideas have no autonomous existence, can exist only in things. So when it needs to debate ideas, as here, realism is driven to invent situations . . . in which characters give voice to contending ideas and thereby in a certain sense embody them. The notion of *embodying* turns out to be pivotal.[78]

Although the subject of this passage—the embodiment of ideas *an sich* in a prose narrative—lies one degree apart from the mere depiction of a figure's characteristic thoughts, we observe Coetzee here pointing the way to an even more modern variety of realism. Earlier, in his essay on *Robinson Crusoe* for the Oxford World Classics edition, Coetzee had claimed that Defoe's novel "look[s] forward to a later realism" that "reveal[s] inner life in unconscious gesture, or in moments of speech or action whose meaning is unguessed-at by its subject."[79] The author's task is to find the gesture or action that can give life to an idea.

Of course, this second, nonempirical approach to realism allows for greater ambiguity. It is easier to discern the significance of a shoe found near a shipwreck than to pin down the meaning of an "unconscious gesture." Uncertainty plays a far greater role in Coetzee's fiction than it does for either Roth or Sebald. Consequently, his take on generational strife contains greater nuance than, say, either "Looking at Kafka" (i.e., early, combative Roth) or *Vertigo*. Like these works, "Realism" thematizes the ambivalence that arises between parents and children. And as in *The Ghost Writer*, tropes of genealogy intermingle freely. What emerges from the struggle here, however, varies considerably from the aggressive path-clearing emphasized by Harold Bloom.

Consider, for example, what Coetzee tells us of James Joyce's influence on Costello's writing. We quickly learn that her reputation as an author was secured by her fourth book, *The House on Eccles Street*, a novel "whose main character is Marion Bloom, wife of Leopold Bloom, principal character of another novel, *Ulysses*."[80] At the time of events narrated, her son John teaches physics and astronomy at a New England college. We learn that he had deliberately avoided reading her work until his thirty-third year— "This was his reply . . . his revenge on her for locking him out [emotionally, devoted to her vocation]." When he finally discovers her writing, it delivers the proverbial blow to the head that Kafka once demanded of all serious fiction.[81]

As his mother fends off crassly reductive questions about *Eccles Street* in an interview conducted the morning of their arrival in Williamstown, John reflects on the work that has "made her name." His thoughts progress fluidly from the book's debt to progenitor Joyce to the enigma of his own descent: "*Eccles Street* is a great novel," he muses, "it will live, perhaps, as long as *Ulysses;* it will certainly be around long after its maker is in the grave. He was only a small child when she wrote it. It unsettles him to think that the same being that engendered this book engendered him."[82] John's concern closely resembles that of the narrator in Kafka's "Cares of a Family Man," particularly in his uneasiness confronting the likelihood that his mother's handiwork—an inanimate object—will ultimately outlast him. (Not coincidentally, Kafka saw Odradek, his odd-looking, thread-trailing, star-shaped, spool-like creation as a cipher for some of his own unfinished writings.)[83]

That same morning Susan Moebius moderates a discussion with the author for a radio program called *Writers at Work*. After posing a few formulaic questions about Costello's most recent novel, Moebius shifts the discussion to *The House on Eccles Street*. "Critics have concentrated," she begins, "on the way you have claimed or reclaimed Molly from Joyce, made her your own. I wonder whether you would comment on your intentions in this book, particularly in challenging Joyce, one of the father-figures of modern literature, on his own territory."[84] Similar to Coetzee, Costello nurtures a more nuanced position toward the nature of literary influence. She perceives *Eccles Street* as corollary to *Ulysses,* rather than as an attempt to usurp it. "I don't see myself challenging Joyce" she says; "certain books are so prodigally inventive that there is plenty of material left over at the end, material that almost invites you to take it over and use it to build something of your own."[85] Therewith she is, as her son elsewhere attests, "measuring herself against the illustrious dead" and "paying tribute to the powers that animate her."[86]

And yet she acknowledges, in nearly the same breath as above, the need to create something new—to beget characters or worlds independent of previous examples. "Seriously," she tells Moebius, "we can't go on parasitizing the classics for ever. I am not excluding myself from the charge. We've got to start doing some inventing of our own."[87] *The House on Eccles Street* thus both refutes and confirms Ecclesiastes' pronouncement that nothing is new under the sun. Costello launched her novel from *Ulysses,* just as Joyce had launched his from Homer's *Odyssey.* In this fashion, the nothing-new renews itself, from one generation to the next. Still, her ambivalence toward Joyce is in distinct contrast to the more aggressive "challenges" mounted in early Roth or Sebald. There, the actual biography of the forebear in question is parasitized as well, aggressively redrawn to propagate the successor's vision.

Similar, however, to these other sons of Kafka is Coetzee's decision to allow literary tropes of kinship to emerge alongside their literal prototypes. Costello's remarks about Joyce parallel John's conflicted feelings as the "flesh of her flesh" and "blood of her blood." The temperamental affinities shared by both Costellos—each is skeptical, ironic, and unrelentingly earnest—are as plain to the novel's other characters as they are to Coetzee's reader. ("You really are her son, aren't you," Susan tells John the next morning at breakfast: "Do you write too?")[88]

Despite this, the filial bond remains unfathomable to John. Their differences seem absolute: "What is the truth of his mother? He does not know, and at the deepest level does not want to know."[89] The aversion expressed by this line culminates in a gesture of recoil at chapter's end, as he watches Elizabeth slumber during their return flight to Australia:

> He can see up her nostrils, into her mouth, down the back of her throat. And what he cannot see he can imagine: the gullet, pink and ugly, contracting as it swallows, like a python, drawing things down to the pear-shaped belly-sac. He draws away, tightens his own belt, sits up, facing forward. No, he tells himself, that is not where I come from, that is not it.[90]

Her body, organic and profane, repulses him. It is incommensurate with the greatness that emanates from her work.

Indeed, when asked whether he writes, John distinguishes his literary aptitude from his mother's by declaring hers trans-mundane: she is "touched with the god," a "mouthpiece for the divine."[91] He formulates this conceit in another conversation with Moebius, who, like the committee that has awarded Costello the prize, cannot fathom *Eccles Street* as the product of a perennial conversation with one's chosen masters. They can only seem to appreciate it for political—or worse, essentialist—reasons. John attempts to explain the irrelevance of gender (at an evaluative level, at least) for someone endowed with the transfiguring gift.

"My mother has been a man," he persists. "She has also been a dog. She can think her way into other people, into other existences. I have read her; I know. It is within her powers. Isn't that what is most important about fiction: that it takes us out of ourselves, into other lives?"

"Perhaps. But your mother remains a woman all the same. Whatever she does, she does as a woman. She inhabits her characters as a woman does, not a man."[92]

There is, John acknowledges, some truth to this response, but he is unwilling to cede an impersonal, trans-historical quality to Costello's inhabitations.

Later that night he awakes in Moebius's bed, gripped by a powerful sadness. He has a vision of his mother alone, and is overcome by the desire to return to his own room in the hotel. Yet he is averse to being by himself at this moment, and besides, "he wants to sleep." The word "sleep"—Coetzee uses free indirect speech to chronicle his thoughts—summons a passage from *Macbeth* to the surface of his consciousness:

Sleep, he thinks, *that knits up the ravelled sleeve of care.* What an extraordinary way of putting it! Not all the monkeys in the world picking away at typewriters all their lives would come up with those words in that arrangement. Out of the dark emerging, out of nowhere: first not there, then there, like a newborn child, heart working, brain working, all the processes of that intricate electrochemical labyrinth working. A miracle.[93]

John's meditation marvels before what the philosopher Lev Shestov once referred to as "creation out of the void."[94] Neither reading history nor literary descent suffice to account for Shakespeare's powerful metaphor. Poetic insight of this magnitude finally defies rational explanation. John is convinced that this phenomenon lies behind Moebius's attraction to his mother's work: "I think you are baffled, even if you won't admit it, by the mystery of the divine in the human," he tells her the following morning. "You know there is something special about my mother—that is what draws you to her—yet when you meet her she turns out to be just an ordinary old woman. You can't square the two. You want an explanation. You want a clue, a sign, if not from her then from me."[95] But no degree of intimacy, whether immediate or secondhand, can unlock her secret: "Costello is . . . touched with a godly or ungodly power," as Judith Schulevitz observes, despite being "off-puttingly fallible" in person.[96]

To a certain extent these considerations of John's do little more than restate what Kafka's narrator says "On Parables": "[merely] that the incomprehensible is incomprehensible, and we know that already." But we, the readers of *Elizabeth Costello,* are still too close to the near bank to draw conclusions; the "far territory, where we want to be," lies at the other end of the novel.[97] Every time Coetzee returns to this paradox of divine embodiment—and he does so in every one of the book's eight lessons—it acquires a new, compounded effect.

Before looking closely at Costello's use of "Report to an Academy" in her Stowe Award lecture and its relevance to the topic of realism, I would like to mention a couple of other traces left by Kafka's fiction in this chapter. As in Coetzee's earlier critical essay on "The Burrow," they demonstrate a thoughtful, non-Oedipal instance of literary influence.

In *J. M. Coetzee and the Ethics of Reading,* Derek Attridge points out discrepancies in *Elizabeth Costello* that seem to have arisen from Coetzee's revision of prior lectures. Many of them pivot on Costello's son. When Coetzee delivered "What Is Realism?" at Bennington College in November 1996, John taught in "the department of astronomy at the Australian National University." By the time of the Tanner Lectures at Princeton University one year later, he has become an "assistant professor of physics and astronomy" at Appleton College in Massachusetts.[98] John keeps this position in the United States for *Elizabeth Costello,* though "for reasons of his own [he] is on leave for the year." He can thus accompany his mother to Pennsylvania and back for the award ceremony.

"Coetzee appears to have overlooked a couple more places where adjustments needed to be made," writes Attridge.

> He has John, who lives permanently in the U.S.A., still referring to North America as a "foreign continent" (23) and an "unexplored continent" (27). There is also the puzzle of John's marriage: what does he mean when he tells the woman he has slept with in Pennsylvania that he has, or is, "Married and unmarried," when in "Lives of Animals" and "As a Woman [Grows Older]" . . . he lives with his wife and children?[99]

Some of these shifts are indeed "slightly awkward," as Attridge attests. But this reason alone is not sufficient for presuming the textual incongruities to be accidental. On the contrary, Coetzee's obscure representation of John's marital status appears deliberate, especially when we observe how these inconsistencies parallel particular episodes from Kafka's *The Castle*.

The passage Attridge refers to does not appear in the Bennington lecture. Coetzee either omitted it at the time (1996) or composed it while adapting "Realism" for the novel. The dialogue added—spoken by Susan Moebius and John the morning after they sleep together—is preceded by the following exchange (identical in both versions): "You really are her son, aren't you," Moebius remarks; "Do you write too?" "You mean, am I touched by the god?" he answers; "No. But yes, I am her son. Not a foundling, not an adoptee. Out of her very body I came, caterwauling."[100] "Realism" appends to these lines the following:

> "And you have a sister."
> "A half-sister, from the same place. The real thing, both of us. Flesh of her flesh, blood of her blood."
> "And you have never married."
> "Wrong. Married and unmarried. What about you?"
> "I have a husband. A husband, a child, a happy marriage."
> "That's good then."
> There is nothing more to be said.[101]

John's response is open-ended. He never claims to be a single man, as Moebius assumes: only that he has married *and* unmarried. This is certainly not a sign of authorial carelessness. Costello's son is under no obligation to speak with greater specificity.[102]

If we take Coetzee at his later word—that is, that he is married with children—then John misleads Moebius with his ambiguous reply.[103] His equivocal claim bears direct resemblance to the land surveyor K.'s in *The Castle*. Shortly after arriving in the snow-covered village, Kafka's protagonist tells the innkeeper that he has traveled far from wife and child.[104] But only a few chapters later he proposes to Frieda, the barmaid at a nearby establishment patronized by Castle employees.

John's insistence that America, his host country, remains both foreign and strange resembles K.'s persisting sense of his own difference in the Castle village. It also recalls his feeling of having drifted irreparably far from home. Kafka uses free indirect speech to ascribe these thoughts to his protagonist in the scene that depicts K.'s congress with Frieda on the floor of the Gentleman's Inn:

> Hours passed there, hours breathing together with a single heartbeat, hours in which K. constantly felt he was lost or had wandered farther into foreign lands than any human being before him, so foreign that even the air hadn't a single component of the air in his homeland and where one would inevitably suffocate from the foreignness but where the meaningless enticements were such that one had no alternative but to go on and get even more lost.[105]

In his *New York Review of Books* essay about Kafka, Coetzee scrutinized Mark Harman's translation of this very passage. Although his purpose was to subject the latest English version to "microscopic attention" (following Milan Kundera, who critiqued French renderings of the same scene in *Testaments Betrayed*), Coetzee asserts that this moment is paradigmatic of Kafka's "groping to record moments of transcendental insight"—an instance where the author "visibly reaches the limits of expression."[106]

Elsewhere, he has credited assaults on linguistic thresholds like this for having inspired his admiration: "What engaged me then and engages me still in Kafka is an intensity, a pressure of writing that . . . pushes at the limits of language," he says in one of his interviews with David Attwell:

> Kafka . . . hints that it is possible, for snatches, however brief, to think outside one's language, perhaps to report back on what it is like to think outside language itself. . . . I work on a writer like Kafka because he opens for me, or opens to me, moments of analytic intensity. And such moments are, in their lesser way, also matters of grace, inspiration.[107]

Rightly, Jennifer Szalai has observed that the "ineffability that lies beyond language" is a theme Coetzee "has pursued in all his novels." His character Elizabeth Costello discusses it explicitly in the part of her award talk that addresses realism and embodiment. "What Is Realism?" initiates an interrogation (which Coetzee then sustains for the duration of the novel) of whether reality can be adequately represented with a material as flawed as language.

Costello's vehicle for worrying this question is Kafka's "A Report to an Academy." The first words of her address allude lightly to his story: "Ladies and gentlemen" updates Red Peter's greeting to an exclusively male establishment, "*Hohe Herren von der Akademie!*" (Esteemed Gentlemen of the Academy!)[108] Her real engagement with Kafka's text occurs during the lecture's second half. For now she begins by relating a story about the anxiety she had experienced four decades before, when her first novel was published. Costello reports that while she had been pleased to hold a copy in her hands, the feeling of general uneasiness did not subside until she received confirmation that deposit copies had been dispatched to leading British libraries.

Costello now submits that fear to scrutiny, admitting that her "great ambition" at the time had been "to have my place on the shelves of the British Museum, rubbing shoulders with the other Cs, the great ones: Carlyle and Chaucer and Coleridge and Conrad," company that reminds us of her filial identification with the classics.[109] She then cites a second reason for this allegiance—namely, to preserve her name after death through literary progeny: "What lay behind my concern about deposit copies was the wish that, even if I myself should be knocked over by a bus the next day, this first-born of mine would have a home . . . if I, this mortal shell, am going to die," goes the consideration in sum, "let me at least live on through my creations."[110] Costello's hope for her issue discloses an unusual modesty. Her wish is not that the book be read, but that it simply continue to *be*—a vessel abandoned and obscure, a hidden Golem, safe from oblivion and yet secure enough from meddlers who might "come poking with a stick to see if it was still alive."

The narrator intercedes to inform us that he will skip Costello's further reflections "on the transience of fame." He resumes at the point in her speech where she admits to the folly of such aspirations. Her desire for a protective obscurity is no less defensive than her desire for celebrity; both are ineffective against the perennial wheeling of years. Costello declares that the buildings housing a culture's tomes will eventually "crumble and decay." The works kept in their collections are destined to "turn to powder." She concludes this portion of her talk by reminding her audience of the vanity of institutions and awards. "We can rely on the British Library or the Library of Congress," she declares, "no more than on reputation itself to save us from oblivion."[111]

Having thus admonished her listeners, Costello turns to the topic of her lecture, realism. She invokes Kafka's "Report to an Academy" and subjects his story to a literalist rigor that would seem to exclude symbolic interpretation. She also attempts to outmaneuver her audience, preemptively ruling out an allegorical reading of her own performance: "Why am I reminding you of Kafka's story? Am I going to pretend I am the ape, torn away from my natural surroundings, forced to perform in front of a gathering of critical strangers? I hope not. I am one of you, I am not of a different species."[112]

Kafka's story invites various readings. His text consists solely of a protagonist's monologue, that is, the transcript of Red Peter's speech to an assembly of experts. "Within this form," Costello asserts, "there is no means for either speaker or audience to be inspected with an outsider's eye." Although we presume we are reading a lecture penned by an ape who has mastered the skills necessary for rational discourse, the tale's speaker and audience are in fact unclear. Might "Red Peter" not be a human being "deluded" into believing himself an ape? Or someone who assumes this position intentionally, "with heavy irony, for rhetorical purposes"? Or is he an intelligent ape after all, but speaking to an audience composed not of scientists but of other trained apes, or untrained apes, or perhaps even parrots? "We don't know," concludes Costello. "We don't know and will never know, with certainty, what is really going on in this story."[113]

Costello's observation about the open-endedness of Red Peter's monologue is well-made, but we, Coetzee's readers, can already perceive the instability of her argument. Her subject is supposed to be realism—in particular, how conceptions of a unified "reality" were forever disrupted by the onset of modernity.[114] In a free re-creation of the crisis described by the Austrian writer Hugo von Hofmannsthal, she asserts that

there used to be a time when we knew. We used to believe that when the text said, "On the table stood a glass of water," there was indeed a table, and a glass of water, and we had only to look into the word-mirror of the text to see them. But all that has ended. The word-mirror is broken, irreparably, it seems. . . . The words will no longer stand up and be counted, each proclaiming "I mean what I mean!" . . . There used to be a time, we believe, when we could say who we were. Now we are just performers speaking our parts. The bottom has dropped out. We could think of this as a tragic turn of events, were it not that it is hard to have respect for whatever was the bottom that dropped out—it looks to us like an illusion now, one of those illusions sustained only by the concentrated gaze of everyone in the room. Remove your gaze for but an instant, and the mirror falls to the floor and shatters.[115]

Representative truth, then, turns out to have been a collective delusion. What had sustained it up to the twentieth century was mere magical thinking. Her consideration of Kafka and literary realism fail to develop a particular position. The examples she raises emphasize, more than anything else, the limits of human knowledge—especially her own. Costello winds up her talk by affirming once more that time will vanquish her work and her person, an indirect rebuff of the committee that has selected her for recognition. In claiming that "there must be some limit to the burden of remembering that we impose on our children and grandchildren," she calls this transience just.[116] Her award lecture ends awkwardly on this self-abnegating note.

"A Report to an Academy" may well have given Coetzee the idea to make his heroine's lecture the centerpiece of this lesson. But he diverges from Kafka by preceding and succeeding her monologue with dialogue. Other characters grapple, in conversation, with Costello's contradictory and at times parabolic references to his work. Susan Moebius, for example, finds fault in Costello's illustrative reliance on Kafka. She detects too much protective "armour" in the open form of a story like "Report," and an excessive tendency toward "heavy historical self-ironization." Such discourse strikes her as overly defensive; it has had its day, she thinks, and is no longer relevant: "This is America, the 1990s. People don't want to hear the Kafka thing yet again."[117]

Moebius's assessment does not suit John, who remains deeply puzzled by his mother's choice of subject. Awaiting their flight to Los Angeles, he asks her directly: "Why literary history?"

> "And why such a grim chapter in literary history? Realism . . . no one in this place wanted to hear about realism. . . . When I think of realism," he goes on, "I think of peasants frozen in blocks of ice. I think of Norwegians in smelly underwear. What is your interest in it? And where does Kafka fit in? What has Kafka to do with it all?"
>
> "With what? With smelly underwear?"
>
> "Yes. With smelly underwear. With people picking their noses. You don't write about that kind of thing. Kafka didn't write about it."[118]

Costello evades his question as she answers it, declining to provide an explanation that will neatly account for the relation between time, fame, and death (probed in the first part of her lecture), Kafka's ape, and a literary method "pioneered by Daniel Defoe":[119]

"No, Kafka didn't write about people picking their noses. But Kafka had time to wonder where and how his poor educated ape was going to find a mate. And what it was going to be like when he was left in the dark with the bewildered, half-tamed female that his keepers eventually produced for his use. Kafka's ape is embedded in life. It is the embeddedness that is important, not the life itself. His ape is embedded as we are embedded, you in me, I in you. That ape is followed through to the end, to the bitter, unsayable end, whether or not there are traces left on the page. Kafka stays awake during the gaps when we are sleeping. That is where Kafka fits in."[120]

Kafka's skill at portraying psychological thought-processes is so great that even implausible situations in his fiction (e.g., an ape learns how to speak, a man wakes transformed into a monstrous vermin) produce illusions as compelling as Defoe's. Red Peter *lives* in Costello's imagination.

Costello uses two sentences from the penultimate paragraph of "Report" to underline this vitality. Having recited the history of his fantastic education, Red Peter describes his daily life: his reception of visitors, interactions with an impresario, attendance of formal gatherings, and so on. "When I come home late at night," Kafka writes,

from banquets, from scientific receptions, from social gatherings, there sits waiting for me a half-trained little chimpanzee and I take comfort from her as apes do. By day I cannot bear to see her; for she has the insane look of the bewildered half-broken animal in her eye; no one else sees it, but I do, and I cannot bear it.[121]

Kafka renders the sadness and depth of Red Peter's isolation indirectly. Like the hats, caps, and shoes of *Robinson Crusoe,* the above details conjure a life while inviting readers like Costello to fill in what has been left unsaid.

It is a tribute to Coetzee's accomplishment that "What Is Realism?" moves along briskly, despite frequent interruptions by the narrator. His characters share Red Peter's embeddedness in our "daily cares." We can also recognize how this chapter acknowledges, by its very execution, a method of formal ambiguity mastered by Kafka. Viewed alongside some of the other examples considered in this study, Coetzee's borrowings are altogether reticent. They express an anxiety of influence, of course—Costello insists that contemporary writers have "got to start doing some inventing of our own." But Coetzee's own stance is much less combative. In "At the

Gate," the novel's final lesson, Coetzee confronts the problem of originality head-on. To illustrate the burden of belatedness, he again uses Kafka as a model.

Poetic Belatedness in "At the Gate"

For the first six "lessons" of *Elizabeth Costello,* Coetzee uses a monologue form styled after Red Peter's report to mediate his protagonist's thoughts and provisional beliefs on a variety of topics pertinent to her work (the future of the novel, the writer's relationship to evil in the world). In some cases ("The Philosophers and the Animals," "The Problem of Evil"), we are led to presume that the narrator has reproduced her lecture in the text at length, if not in full; in others ("What Is Realism?" "The Poets and the Animals"), Coetzee signals his omissions up front;[122] and on one occasion ("The Humanities in Africa"), Costello sits among the auditors while her sister Blanche (Sister Bridget) delivers a commencement address to the graduates of a Johannesburg university.

Not until the seventh chapter do we encounter a narrative set in private rather than on a public stage. "Eros" registers Costello's musings on desire, embodiment, and—most importantly—divine possession. It is a brief chapter, but efficiently gathers the disparate themes of prior sections into the final lesson, "At the Gate." In its pages Costello muses on the dilemma of belatedness as it is formulated by Friedrich Hölderlin. His conceit that God has abandoned modern man recurs in several poetic works (*Hyperion,* "The Titans," et al.). Costello, who regards the Romantic poet with fondness, settles on one line in particular: "We come too late."[123]

Its provenance lies in the seventh stanza of his elegy "Bread and Wine," which begins:

> But, my friend, we have come too late. Though the gods are living,
> Over our heads they live, up in a different world.
> Endlessly they act and, such is their kind wish to spare us,
> Little they seem to care whether we live or do not.
> For not always a frail, a delicate vessel can hold them,
> Only at times can our kind bear the full impact of gods.[124]

The concern of having been born too late is of direct pertinence to Costello's claim to artistic originality. As we have already seen in "Realism," she wavers between believing that great literature invites renewal (as Joyce had renewed *The Odyssey* by writing *Ulysses,* or Costello *Ulysses* through *The House on Eccles Street*) and believing that it has to be unfettered by the past.[125]

"At the Gate" deposits its reader at the far bank of the allegorical crossing mentioned in the novel's opening paragraph.[126] It is narrated in an omniscient third-person voice that slides in and out of free indirect speech. Now Costello travels alone. No major foil accompanies her. And her appeals are no longer directed at professional academies or general audiences, but toward what appears to be a higher authority. Here Costello faces a panel of judges in a court of undisclosed nature—undisclosed, that is, beyond its uncanny evocation of scenes from classic modern literature, above all in the fiction of Kafka. In the pages below, I will parse Coetzee's representation of literary belatedness as well as the ambivalence engendered by the notion of "coming too late." Both are thrust into relief by the story's conspicuous references to Kafka.

"At the Gate" is an extraordinary tribute to the generative yet constraining nature of literary influence. By placing his protagonist in an environment that so closely resembles Kafka's imaginary world—and then granting her a critical awareness of that resemblance—Coetzee openly acknowledges his own indebtedness to a precursor whose writings have touched his fiction since the late 1960s. It seems clear that had Kafka never been born, "At the Gate" and the rest of this novel could hardly exist. Again, as in his earlier novels (*Waiting for the Barbarians, Life & Times of Michael K*) and critical essays ("Time, Tense, and Aspect in Kafka's 'The Burrow'"), Coetzee refrains from violating the integrity of his antecedent.[127]

Tokens of Kafka's influence appear in two manifestations, one formal, the other thematic. In what follows I consider structural features of "At the Gate" which mimic, with only the slightest of swervings, those present in *The Trial* and the celebrated fable at the heart of that novel, "Before the Law." These formal likenesses very much account for parallel developments of plot, their appeal to and evasion of interpretation, and tonal and rhythmic affinities. I then comb the story to highlight Coetzee's restaging of scenes borrowed from Kafka (and other literary precursors).

When the priest in *The Trial* relates the parable, Josef K. makes vigorous attempts to decipher it. He is eager to grasp its relevance for his own proceedings. Kafka omitted this framing device entirely for his publication of "Before the Law," which commences with the man from the country's arrival. The man is refused permission to enter by a custodian of the Law, who then warns him against trying to penetrate the thresh-

old by force. Convinced, the man accepts a stool provided by the doorkeeper to wait for his admission. "Days and years" go by. His appeals
are refused, his bribes taken but to little avail.[128] Shortly before dying,
he finally asks the doorkeeper why no one else has ever come, seeking ingress to the law. "No one else could ever be admitted here," the
guard replies, "since this gate was made only for you. I am now going
to shut it."[129]

"At the Gate" opens with Elizabeth Costello's arrival in a small, vaguely
Austro-Hungarian town. Like the man from the country in "Before the
Law," she heads to the portal, where she is denied entry by a reticent
guard. For the time being, that is: "First," she is told, "you must make a
statement"—a pronouncement of her beliefs.[130] Whether she will then be
allowed to pass, he cannot say. "It [entry] is possible," the doorkeeper in
Kafka's tale remarks of this indefiniteness, "but not at the moment."[131]

She drafts a declaration asserting that her vocation, that of the writer,
forbids her the strict maintenance of any single belief. The guard, however, waves off her plea for an exemption. Her explanation will not suffice: "We all believe," he tells her. "We are not cattle. For each of us there is
something we believe. Write it down, what you believe. Put it in the statement."[132] And hence the deferrals begin. She moves into a dormitory "for
long-term petitioners," unpacks her bag, and ensconces herself in the town.
Like Kafka's man from the country or Moses on Mount Moriah, Costello
finds herself held up just short of her destination.

Time passes—though not, as in Kafka's legend, an entire lifetime.
Coetzee's protagonist ventures several attempts to gain passage beyond the
gate, but they falter. The chapter ends with the guard's impatient reply to a
query of Costello's. He "has evidently had enough of questions," which is a
virtual echo of "Before the Law," whose guardian is also irked by a suppli-
cant's insistent beckoning: "What do you want to know now? . . . You are
insatiable."[133] By refusing to resolve the period of waiting for his petitioner,
Coetzee swerves away from Kafka. "Before the Law" concludes with the
doorkeeper shutting the portal as the man from the country dies; in "At the
Gate," Costello's case stays unclosed.

Kafka's legend is riddled with lacunae that invite but never satisfy interpretation. Has the doorkeeper fulfilled his duty or exceeded it? Is he superior or of subordinate rank to the man from the country? "Who is freer,"
Frederick Karl has asked, "the man from the country or the doorkeeper?"[134]
The legend will not tell: it stands as written, inscrutable. Even Josef K.
realizes that his assessment of the Law—*Lies are made into a universal*

system—requires qualification: "K. said that with finality, but it was not his final judgment."[135]

Coetzee retains this ambiguity in "At the Gate." He never defines what lies beyond the barrier. It could be the afterlife, but the text contains no definitive indication that its heroine has died. Perhaps the Gate is a metaphor meant to stand for a broader conceit, like the Law in "Before the Law." And yet the author has chosen not to elaborate. For all we know, this entire lesson—and even the letter from Lady Chandos that serves as the novel's postscript—might well be a fiction Costello herself has composed. Which goes to reinforce the central point of her lecture on realism, namely that the damage inflicted upon the tacit, premodern understanding between author and reader—the breaking of the "word-mirror"—is irreparable.[136] The protagonist in "At the Gate" puzzles her way through a world of uncertainty, trying to make sense of the signs before her. But her extensive training as a reader grants her few advantages.

Coetzee's formal debt to Kafka also extends to the quality of his prose, namely, to his sentences' transparency and precision, their cadences and poise. At a talk given at the University of California at Berkeley in 1991 devoted to "some of the writers without whom I would not be the person I am," Coetzee places "the elements of rhythm and syntax" at the fore of his discussion, "the rhythm and syntax not only of words but . . . of thought too. This is proper," he affirms, since "the deepest lessons one learns from other writers are, I suspect, matters of rhythm, broadly conceived."[137] The essays in stylistics Coetzee wrote on Beckett and Kafka between the late 1960s and the early 1980s concentrate precisely on this aspect of their work.

It is evident that a related feature of their writing appealed to him, namely their purity of tone. Reviewing the latest translation of Kafka's *The Castle* in 1998, Coetzee accurately describes the author's German as "generally clear, specific, and neutral," distinctive for its exceptional "spareness and apparent matter-of-factness."[138] He elucidates his appreciation in the Berkeley address when he locates the "peculiar strength" of another pivotal forebear, the Polish poet Zbigniew Herbert, in his "dryness to the point of desiccation," a "removed, cerebral stance expressed in ironies that mask the most intense ethical and indeed lyrical passion":

> What one learns from Herbert is not a body of ideas but a certain style, hard, durable: a style that is also an approach to the world and to experience . . . . Ideas are certainly important—who would deny that?—

but the fact is, the ideas that operate in novels and poems, once they are unpicked from their context and laid out on the laboratory table, usually turn out to be uncomplicated, even banal. Whereas a style, an attitude to the world, as it soaks in, becomes part of the personality, part of the self, ultimately indistinguishable from the self. [139]

In Kafka as in Coetzee, the filtering of absurd or even horrific events through a "desiccated" prose devoid of ornament is enhanced by the author's sensitivity to cadence and his discriminating application of punctuation. Consider, for example, how this concatenation of declarative statements at the beginning of "Before the Law" works to establish a tone "clear, specific, and neutral" within a few sentences:

Before the law stands a doorkeeper. To this doorkeeper there comes a man from the country and prays for admittance to the Law. But the doorkeeper says that he cannot grant admittance at the moment. The man thinks it over and then asks if he will be allowed in later. "It is possible," says the doorkeeper, "but not at the moment." [140]

The start of "At the Gate" is similarly brisk and declarative: "It is a hot afternoon. The square is packed with visitors. Few spare a glance for the white-haired woman who, suitcase in hand, descends from the bus. She wears a cotton frock; her neck, in the sun, is burned red and beaded with sweat." [141] As each tale advances toward its narrative climax, the third-person present speaker maintains this distanced, objective tone. [142] The friction generated by this contrast produces an intensity that drives the prose relentlessly forward. It is no coincidence, then, that Coetzee, responding to a question of David Attwell's in *Doubling the Point*, acknowledges that "what engaged me then [i.e., 1981, when he published his stylistic analysis of "The Burrow"] and engages me still in Kafka is an intensity, a pressure of writing that, as I have said, pushes at the limits of language." Nor is James Wood's observation that "Costello at one point commends Kafka for taking things 'to the end, to the bitter, unsayable end whether or not there are traces left on the page.' Coetzee," he resumes, "is constantly pushing here against the unsayable, and we can only faintly feel his traces on the page. But they are certainly there." [143] Coetzee writes "at the limits of language" in a style whose contours have been molded by his extensive readings of—and critical excursions writing *after*—Kafka.

One factor that distinguishes Elizabeth Costello from Kafka's man from the country is the fact that Costello has already read "Before the Law." She is well aware that her scenario is a flagging imitation of the original. It only takes one brief exchange with the guard for her to know that she has been deposited in someone else's story:

> There is no more doubt in her mind about where she is, who she is. She is a petitioner before the gate. The journey that brought her here, to this country, to this town, that seemed to reach its end when the bus halted and its door opened on to the crowded square, was not the end of it at all. Now commences a trial of a different kind. Some act is required of her, some prescribed yet undefined affirmation, before she will be found good and can pass through. But is this the one who will judge her, this ruddy, heavy-set man on whose rather sketchy uniform (military? civil guard?) she can detect no mark of rank but on whom the fan, swinging neither left nor right, pours a coolness that she wishes were being poured on her?[144]

We witness in this passage what Andrew Riemer has designated the "scholar's temperament" of Elizabeth Costello: "analytical, often detached, sometimes legislative."[145] Costello is an experienced close reader, and she promptly recognizes the resemblance between her situation and that of the man from the country in "Before the Law."

Although Kafka is unnamed, his language touches this and other aspects of the diction cited above. Coetzee refers to Costello as a "petitioner" in a newly commenced "trial." She will be "judged." Given their context, the words cannot help evoking "The Judgment," "In the Penal Colony," and *The Trial.* They also gesture toward a notion of "the Kafkaesque," one that increasingly overshadows Costello as this fiction proceeds.[146]

Like the K.s of *The Trial* and *The Castle,* Costello calibrates her questions to elicit information and exert influence. In the passage below (which occurs before she asks her guard whether an "imitation of belief" will suffice), Costello attempts to unknot the tangle of preexisting stories that confront her here, before the gate: "She pauses, then brings out the next sentence, the sentence that will determine whether this is her judge, the right one to judge her, or, on the contrary, merely the first in a long line leading to who knows what featureless functionary in what chancellery in what castle."[147] Into which fiction has she fallen? Will this doorkeeper forever prevent her trespass, like the one from Kafka's parable? Is his line of communication to his superiors modeled after the endlessly receding path from emperor to subject in "The Great Wall of China" and "An Imperial Message"? Are these "castle functionaries" obstreperous and elusive, as in *The Castle*? All the above fictions converge in this scene.

Coetzee utilizes literary devices discussed in the novel's first chapter to animate this otherwise allegorical—"unreal"—town. Many of his details are attentive observations that rank alongside Defoe's "two shoes that were not fellows" for their power of embodiment.[148] Some he bases on the physical appearance of her surroundings, others on processes of her thought. Both bestow verisimilitude to an otherwise fantastic setting. Upon learning that her guard never goes "off duty," for instance, she reflects that "this town where she finds herself, where the guardian of the gate never sleeps and the people in the cafés seem to have nowhere to go, no obligation other than to fill the air with their chatter, is no more real than she: no more but perhaps no less."[149] Her sober assessment of this "unrealistic" situation lends veracity to her as a character.

As do many of the ruminating questions she poses to herself:

> Am I going to become an institution, she wonders: the old woman who says she is a writer exempt from the law? The woman who, with her black suitcase always beside her (containing what?—she can no longer remember), writes pleas, one after the other, that she puts before the man in the guardhouse and the man in the guardhouse pushes aside as not good enough, not what is required before one can pass?

Costello wants to evade the man from the country's end. She therefore tries to use her knowledge of Kafka's legend to gain leverage. By asking the guard for permission to "glance through" the doors to see whether "it is worth all this trouble," she alters the earlier story and thus—at least conceivably—its ending.

Coetzee also incorporates numerous concrete details, all of which distinguish Costello's experience from the hero's in Kafka's legend, that make it more "realistic." She describes the guard's uniform and deduces, not without mordant wit, how uncomfortable it must be to wear in summer ("how hot he must be!") and winter ("how cold!"). The guard leads her to "the gate itself, massive enough to hold back an army": "From a pouch at his belt he takes a key nearly as long as his forearm. Will this be the point where he tells her the gate is meant for her and her alone, and moreover that she is destined never to pass through? Should she remind him, let him know she knows the score?"[150]

Costello refers directly to the last lines of "Before the Law," but her familiarity with that tale does not, in fact, ensure that she "knows the score." Her brief vision of the territory on the other side baffles: what she sees—a light "not more brilliant than, say, a magnesium flash sustained endlessly"—is mundane, a letdown from what she "despite her unbelief" had hoped to encounter. It is remarkably "imaginable" compared to her anticipation of "a light so blinding that earthly senses would be stunned by it."

This scene recalls the moment in Kafka shortly before the petitioner's death. After years of waiting for permission to enter, the man from the country perceives—rather, *thinks* he perceives—a light emitting behind the gate: "At length his eyesight begins to fail, and he does not know whether the world is really darker or whether his eyes are only deceiving him. Yet in the darkness he is now aware of a radiance that streams indistinguishably from the gateway of the Law."[151] Kafka does not disclose whether the radiance exists beyond the man's perception—whether, for example, the doorkeeper can see it as well.

Coetzee's heroine is disappointed by this preview, but it nevertheless convinces her that she should revise her statement of belief. She takes residence in a dormitory built "for long-term petitioners," and it is here, among the two-tiered bunks and mattresses of straw that resemble so distinctly the prisoners' barracks of concentration camps and gulags, that she first elucidates what disturbs her about the uncanny familiarity of her surroundings: "The whole thing [is] put together from clichés, with not a speck of originality."[152] She is reading her environment like a book and finding it poor, an unsatisfactory blending of historical and literary narratives.

A gap intercedes, and Coetzee recommences with her first hearing. He has supplied her courtroom with images borrowed from Kafka. Excepting some chairs and a high bench upon which nine microphones have been neatly aligned, the chamber is unfurnished, its shabby makeshift appearance evoking the room in *The Trial* where Josef K.'s initial inquiry takes place. Her judges file in, garbed in black. Like Josef K. during his initial inquiry, Costello recognizes that a "performance will be required of her." In "Realism," her son John compares her lecture delivery to the act of "a seal, an old, tired circus seal."[153] If she seems sharper in this chapter and more keenly responsive to her interrogation, this is because she finds herself not in another lecture hall but in unfamiliar territory. She must learn new cues, master a different game. The stakes of her performance have definitely risen.

Josef K. presumes a false command of both. During his hearing, he justifies his reckless conduct (e.g., insulting the chief magistrate, mocking the court's authority) on the mistaken assumption that his auditors are "people . . . easily won over."[154] A study in contrast, Costello conducts herself prudently. She takes the proceedings seriously. Her aim is not exculpation, but merely "to pass the gate. To pass through. To get on with what comes next."[155]

She recites her statement of belief, which pivots on the argument that her vocation necessarily precludes the assumption of fixed positions. Its dominant figure is that of the amanuensis:

> "I am a writer, and what I write is what I hear. I am a secretary of the invisible, one of many secretaries over the ages. That is my calling: dictation secretary. It is not for me to interrogate, to judge what is given me. I merely write down the words and then test them, test their soundness, to make sure I have heard right.
>
> "Secretary of the invisible: not my own phrase, I hasten to say. I borrow it from a secretary of a higher order, Czesław Miłosz, a poet, perhaps known to you, to whom it was dictated years ago."[156]

The poem she alludes to is titled "Secretaries," and was published in Miłosz's 1981 collection *Hymn of the Pearl*. I reproduce it here in a translation by the author and Robert Haas:

> I am no more than a secretary of the invisible thing
> That is dictated to me and a few others.
> Secretaries, mutually unknown, we walk the earth
> Without much comprehension. Beginning a phrase in the middle
> Or ending it with a comma. And how it all looks when completed
> Is not up to us to inquire, we won't read it anyway.[157]

A brief look at this and one other document by Miłosz about the poet's calling helps to clarify her position. The weakness at the heart of Costello's statement, as one of her judges quickly detects, is that the self-abnegation requisite for relaying messages from invisible *"powers beyond us"* by nature forfeits the conduit's ethical agency.

To some extent, this lack may reveal itself through the artist's relation to her contemporaries and family. Coetzee unveils Costello's parental shortcomings in an earlier chapter, when John recalls her (with little if any attending bitterness or resentment) as a wildly unstable woman who *"stormed around the house in Melbourne, hair flying in all directions, screaming at her children, 'You are killing me! You are tearing the flesh from my body!'"*[158]

Succumbing to the muse, the author is obligated to transmit what she hears truthfully, repugnant or obscene as it may be. Hence the urgency bristling from these lines of Miłosz's 1968 tour de force rejoinder to Horace, *"Ars Poetica?"* (I begin my citation with the second strophe):

In the very essence of poetry there is something indecent:
a thing is brought forth which we didn't know we had in us,
so we blink our eyes, as if a tiger had sprung out
and stood in the light, lashing his tail.

That's why poetry is rightly said to be dictated by a daimonion,
though it's an exaggeration to maintain that he must be an angel. . . .

What reasonable man would like to be a city of demons,
who behave as if they were at home, speak in many tongues,
and who, not satisfied with stealing lips, or hand,
work at changing his destiny for their convenience? . . .

The purpose of poetry is to remind us
how difficult it is to remain just one person,
for our house is open, there are no keys in the doors,
and invisible guests come in and out at will.

What I'm saying here is not, I agree, poetry,
as poems should be written rarely and reluctantly,
under unbearable duress and only with the hope
that good spirits, not evil ones, choose us for their instrument.[159]

This is, in effect, Costello's point in "The Problem of Evil" when she argues that Paul West's imagined account of the slow, gruesome execution of the Stauffenberg plotters transgresses the victims' privacy. "I believe," she asserts at a conference in Amsterdam, "that bars should be erected over

the cellar mouth, with a bronze memorial plaque saying *Here died . . .* followed by a list of the dead and their dates, and that should be that."[160] By
chronicling the suffering of his subjects to their bitter end, West contami-
nates both himself and those readers who follow him into the Berlin bun-
ker with pure, unadulterated evil.[161]

The key word here is "follow," a term Coetzee has often used to illustrate
the activity of writing and, to a lesser extent, of deeply sympathetic reading. In the interview with David Attwell that precedes his essay on Kafka's
"The Burrow," he speaks of "the kind of writing-in-the-tracks one does in
criticism" and his methodical approach of taking up the pen and, "step by
step, writ[ing] my way after him [i.e., Kafka]."[162] The same goes for non-
literary topics. In "Apartheid Thinking," his analysis of select texts written
by Geoffrey Cronjé, an Afrikaner theorist of apartheid, Coetzee affirms
that "a reading position is not a position at all: it is only what I can call a
following."[163]

Costello's celebrated novel *The House on Eccles Street* is one instance
of such following. So is the way she processes reality, filtered as it is by
years of reading. The judges thus remind her of grotesque creatures from
J. J. Grandville; her panel is *"excessively literary,"* *"a characterist's idea of
a bench of judges."* Their buffoonish appearance seems to complicate the
boundary, as Coetzee once wrote of the assistants in Kafka's *The Castle,*
"between the clownish and the evil."[164]

Her elaboration of the secretarial imperative follows another precedent
adopted from a literary precursor. "Of course, gentlemen," Costello tells
the panel, "I do not claim to be bereft of all belief":

> "I have what I think of as opinions and prejudices, no different in kind
> from what are commonly called beliefs. When I claim to be a secretary
> clean of belief I refer to my ideal self, a self capable of holding opinions
> and prejudices at bay while the word which it is her function to conduct
> passes through her."[165]

Costello's depiction of her "ideal self" is, as one of her judges correctly
notes, based on the notion of "Negative Capability" exposited by John
Keats in a December 1817 letter to his brothers George and Thomas:

> that is when man is capable of being in uncertainties, Mysteries,
> doubts, without any irritable reaching after fact & reason—Coleridge
> for instance, would let go by a fine isolated verisimilitude caught from

the Penetralium of mystery, from being incapable of remaining content with half knowledge. This pursued through Volumes would take us no further than this, that with a great poet the sense of Beauty overcomes every other consideration, or rather obliterates every other consideration.[166]

And this is not the last of the literary allusions mentioned by the panel, all of whom appear as shrewd as she—they are certainly well-briefed!—in their dialectic exchanges. The same judge, a "wizened little fellow" she silently thinks of as Grimalkin, counters with a suggestion drawn from Kafka's "An Imperial Message": "And what if the invisible does not regard you as its secretary?" he asks. "What if your appointment was long ago discontinued, and the letter did not reach you?"[167]

"An Imperial Message" was originally part of a longer, unfinished prose narrative titled "The Great Wall of China." Kafka extracted it for publication in his 1917 collection *A Country Doctor: Little Stories,* where it appeared alongside "Before the Law," another illustrious fable from an incomplete manuscript. A quick summary: the emperor has addressed a message to you from his deathbed. Although he has assigned its delivery to the most able of couriers, an infinite continuum of obstacles prevents the messenger from ever arriving at your doorstep. "Nobody could fight his way through here," the narrator concludes, "even with a message from a dead man. But you sit at your window when evening falls and dream it to yourself."[168]

The work exemplifies a principle of infinite regress. This messenger's non-arrival produces the "physical aporia" that Walter Benjamin found so characteristic of Kafka's fiction.[169] Grimalkin cites this parable in order to suggest that the defendant's anticipation may be deluded. But Coetzee's protagonist is well acquainted with such doubts: they are corollary to her profession. What torments her most about the judge's parody of Kafka is the *obviousness* of its referentiality: "She cannot stand the literariness of it all. Have they not the wit to come up with something new?"[170]

Either "they" haven't, or Costello cannot help but interpret her surroundings in literary terms. Some time after her first hearing adjourns, she sees a brass band in uniform playing marches and waltzes in the town square. They too are unoriginal; she recognizes them, presumably, from a prior reading of Joseph Roth's novel about the Austrian Empire's decline, *The Radetzky March.* "Is it all being mounted for her sake," she thinks, "because she is a writer? Is it someone's idea of what hell will be like for a writer, or at least purgatory: a purgatory of clichés?"[171]

Costello tests this hypothesis by considering the prominence of Kafka's tread. "The wall," she reflects,

the gate, the sentry, are straight out of Kafka. So is the demand for a confession, so is the courtroom with the dozing bailiff and the panel of old men in their crows' robes pretending to pay attention while she thrashes around in the toils of her own words. Kafka, but only the superfices of Kafka; Kafka reduced and flattened to a parody.[172]

Dislocation is what makes her experience superficial: the work has been removed from its original context and placed in an unfamiliar setting. But of all writers, why Kafka? Why should elements of *his* fictional imagination permeate her surroundings so completely?

She is no devotee of Kafka. Most of the time she cannot read him without impatience. As he veers between helplessness and lust, between rage and obsequiousness, she too often finds him, or at least his K selves, simply childish. So why is the *mise en scène* into which she has been hurled so— she dislikes the word but there is no other—so Kafkaesque?[173]

She entertains the possibility that her disinclination might be the reason for this arrangement—"*You do not like the Kafkaesque, so let us rub your nose in it*"—but the reader who comes to this chapter by way of the previous seven lessons already knows that she is more devoted to Kafka than she cares to admit.[174] As Janet Maslin makes clear, Costello's relation to the "Kafkaesque" is in fact an *affinity*.[175] It is Kafka, not Woolf or Joyce, whom she appropriates in lectures that probe her beliefs about the feasibility of realism in the twentieth century and about animal suffering. She cannot divest herself of his influence, cannot let go of his creations.

Nor can she dismiss the burden of belatedness so lightly, since it causes her to react adversely to the derivative environment. It is not within her powers to simply "hand back her ticket" like Ivan Karamazov. Even her figures of speech, as this last statement shows, originate elsewhere.[176] Writing about belatedness in Gnosticism, Harold Bloom envisions this fear as the "nightmare sense of coming *after the event,* of trying to occupy ground where others have stood more significantly. To have come too late *into* the story," he continues, "is necessarily to fear that one is too late in the story."[177] Such an awareness haunts Costello throughout "At the Gate."

Days pass while she revises her statement ("we call them confessions here," a fellow roomer tells her), trying to infuse it with a passion that will impel "the effect of belief" among her judges. She notes that her appetite has waned since her arrival, but this observation triggers yet another allusion to Kafka:

> Is a new career beginning to beckon: as one of the thin folk, the compulsive fasters, the hunger artists? Will her judges take pity if they see her waste away? She sees herself, a sticklike figure on a public bench in a patch of sunlight scribbling away at her task, a task never to be completed. *God save me!* she whispers to herself. *Too literary, too literary! I must get out of here before I die!*[178]

Because Coetzee records his protagonist's thoughts as they move through her mind, the reader can witness not only her involuntary invocation of "A Hunger Artist" but the nausea this recognition induces, which the author conveys through her italicized whisperings.[179]

Costello's second hearing is unsuccessful, despite her impassioned appeal. She recites a "lamentably literary" allegory (disguised as autobiographical recollection), depicting to her panel the magical awakening of thousands of hibernating frogs in her native Australia after a flood. She believes in *them,* she says, because of their very indifference to *her* belief. This absence of reciprocity is central to her confession.[180]

As before, she fares poorly in cross-examination. When asked by her judges whether she, "this person before our eyes, this person petitioning for passage, this person here and nowhere else," speaks for herself, Costello responds: "Yes. No, emphatically no. Yes and no. Both."[181] Her admission (consistent with the thesis proposed by Miłosz in "Secretaries" and "*Ars Poetica*")[182] makes her instability transparent to the judges. When she denies being "confused," the panel of judges howls in laughter—not unlike Red Peter's apes before the acrobats—confirming therewith her initial suspicion that this is neither "a court of law" nor a "court of logic," but "a court out of Kafka or *Alice in Wonderland,* a court of paradox."[183]

This final "lesson" of the novel finishes with Costello's imagining the other side of the gate, where she conjures a haggard, drowsing dog "blocking the way" on the far side. Literary associations, constructs, and precedents once again color her vision. Her reaction to this contamination is predictably visceral: "It is her first vision in a long while, and she does not trust it, does not trust in particular the anagram GOD-DOG. *Too literary,* she thinks again. A curse on literature!" Costello's imprecation, thought but not spoken, constitutes her last words in the story.[184]

———

There is a moment after her second hearing when, ruminating on the properties of belief, a vision comes to Costello of "a girl crossing a stream." Her thoughts add to it a line from a poem, *"Keeping steady her laden head across a brook."*[185] This merging of image and word inspires a metaphoric understanding of belief that culminates in an epiphany: "Her mind, when she is truly herself, appears to pass from one belief to the next, pausing, balancing, then moving on." At no other point in the novel does Coetzee's protagonist come closer to achieving a level of self-understanding that so evenly accommodates the different stations of belief through which she moves.[186]

John Keats's "Autumn" provides the linguistic precedent for this insight. In Keats's poem, however, the subject (as Costello recalls it) is the season personified:

Who hath not seen thee oft amid thy store?
　　Sometimes whoever seeks abroad may find
Thee sitting careless on a granary floor,
　　Thy hair soft-lifted by the winnowing wind;
Or on a half-reap'd furrow sound asleep,
　　Drows'd with the fume of poppies, while thy hook
　　Spares the next swath and all its twined flowers:
And sometimes like a gleaner thou dost keep
　　Steady thy laden head across a brook;
　　Or by a cyder-press, with patient look,
Thou watchest the last oozings hours by hours.[187]

Her recollection of this text transforms Keats's representation of the season's fragile pause before the onset of winter to a projection of herself, precariously balancing the beliefs of others. This movement away from the original is an exemplary model of Harold Bloom's *clinamen:* it implies her own corrective rearrangement of an anterior text. Costello responds to Keats in a manner whose pattern echoes precisely those of her Kafkan misreadings heretofore. She may harbor ambivalence toward her literary forebears, but her revisions of them eschew the reconstructive violence perpetrated in the writings of, say, W. G. Sebald or in early Philip Roth.

Coetzee thus stages belatedness as burden and boon alike. (Had Costello never engaged with Keats, her arrival at this particular view of belief would necessarily have taken a different route.) But he refrains from demonstrating one effect at the expense of the other. The image in this scene comes to her like those that have preceded it in the novel. Although altered, it preserves the spirit of its origin, acting, for as long as a reader contemplates this work, like the fragile vessel that ferries Keats and her other masters over the extinguishing rapids of time.

Notes

Introduction

1. W. H. Auden, "The Wandering Jew," in *The Complete Works of W. H. Auden: Prose, 1939–1948*, ed. Edward Mendelson (Princeton, N.J.: Princeton University Press, 2002), 110.

2. London: *The Castle*, 1930; *The Trial*, 1935/1937; *America*, 1938. New York: *The Castle*, 1930; *The Trial*, 1937. Norfolk, Conn.: *Amerika*, 1946. Paris: *Le Procès*, 1933; *Le Château* 1938; *L'Amérique*, 1946.

3. London: *The Great Wall of China and Other Pieces*, 1933; *In the Penal Settlement: Tales and Short Prose Works*, 1949. New York: *The Great Wall of China: Stories and Reflections*, 1946; *The Penal Colony: Stories and Short Pieces*, 1948. Paris: *La Métamorphose* [and other stories], 1938; *La Colonie Pénitentiare* [and other stories] 1945/1948; *La Muraille de Chine* [with other posthumously published stories], 1950.

4. Edmund Wilson, "A Dissenting Opinion on Kafka," in *Kafka: A Collection of Critical Essays*, ed. Ronald D. Gray (Englewood Cliffs, N.J.: Prentice-Hall, 1962), 97.

5. Ibid. Wilson's complaint was echoed with greater vigor by a German-speaking contemporary, Günther Anders, who went so far as to assert that the "self-doubting" political impotence of Kafka and his enthusiasts unwittingly facilitated the rise of fascism. See Günther Anders, *Kafka—Pro und Contra: Die Prozeßunterlagen* (Munich: Verlag Beck, 1951).

6. J. M. Coetzee, "What Is a Classic?" in *Stranger Shores: Literary Essays, 1986–1999* (New York: Viking, 2001), 16.

7. A position shared by Marxist critics as well, the most famous expression of which remains Georg Lukács' "Franz Kafka or Thomas Mann?" in *The Meaning of Contemporary Realism* (London: Merlin, 1962), 47–92.

8. Philip Roth, "The Story Behind *The Plot Against America*," *New York Times*, September 19, 2004.

9. For a thorough overview of Kafka's reception in Germany, England, France, and the United States—as well as elsewhere around the globe—see "Die Aufnahme in den einzelnen Ländern" in Hartmut Binder's *Kafka-Handbuch, Band 2: Das Werk und seine Werkung* (Stuttgart: Alfred Kröner, 1979), 624–786. Jürgen Born's *Franz Kafka: Kritik und Rezeption* (Frankfurt am Main: S. Fischer, 1983) handily reproduces the most important German-language reviews from 1912 through 1938. The most extensive bibliographical reference work to date is the three-volume *Franz Kafka: Internationale Bibliographie der Primär- und*

Sekundärliteratur (Munich: K. G. Saur, 2000), edited by Maria Luise Caputo-Mayr and Julius Michael Herz.

10. Gary Adelman, "Beckett's Readers: A Commentary and Symposium," *Michigan Quarterly Review* 43, no. 1 (Winter 2004): 55.

11. Harold Bloom, *The Western Canon: The Books and School of the Ages* (New York: Riverhead Books, 1994), 428.

12. This remains true today. The latest generation of Anglophone stars (Jonathan Safran Foer, Zadie Smith) has published tributes to the Prague author in recent years, and the international success of Hakiro Murakami's *Kafka on the Shore* (2002) and Orhan Pamuk's *Snow* (2002) attest to the ongoing power of Kafka's writings in translation.

13. Hans-Ulrich Treichel, Ilse Aichinger, and Imre Kertész, "Kafka und seine Kinder," *Literaturen*, January/February 2003, 35–36, 41–43, 41.

14. Jonathan Lethem, "The Figure in the Castle," *New York Times Book Review*, May 1, 2005, 16. Lethem must be mistaken, since every edition of *The Castle* to appear before 1998 printed Brod's editorial intervention (he completed Kafka's final sentence). Not until Mark Harman's translation appeared in 1999 did an English-language version reproduce the unfinished ending "in full."

15. Thomas Bernhard, *Auslöschung: Ein Zerfall* (Berlin: Verlag Volk und Welt Berlin, 1989), 113.

16. Harold Bloom, *A Map of Misreading*, 2nd ed. (New York: Oxford University Press, 2003), xiii.

17. James Wood, *The Broken Estate: Essays on Literature and Belief* (New York: Modern Library, 2000), 18.

18. Harold Bloom, *Poetry and Repression: Revisionism from Blake to Stevens* (New Haven, Conn.: Yale University Press, 1976), 21.

19. Harold Bloom, *The Breaking of the Vessels* (The Wellek Library Lectures at the University of California, Irvine) (Chicago: University of Chicago Press, 1982), 44.

20. Harold Bloom, *Agon: Towards a Theory of Revisionism* (Oxford: Oxford University Press, 1982), 273.

21. Bloom, *Poetry and Repression,* 25.

22. Harold Bloom, *The Anxiety of Influence: A Theory of Poetry,* 2nd ed. (New York: Oxford University Press, 1997), xxiii.

23. Ibid., 6.

24. Ibid., 8.

25. Ibid., 11.

26. Bloom, *Poetry and Repression,* 7.

27. Bloom, *Breaking of the Vessels,* 66.

28. Harold Bloom, *Ruin the Sacred Truths: Poetry and Belief from the Bible to the Present* (Cambridge, Mass.: Harvard University Press, 1989), 125.

29. Bloom, *Agon,* viii.

30. Bloom, *Anxiety of Influence*, 140–41.

31. Bloom, *Agon*, 241.

32. Volumes of essays such as *Lodgings in a Country House* (2000) and *Campo Santo* (2005) differ from previous collections in so far as Sebald here incorporates techniques perfected in his prose fiction: reproductions accompany the narrative, allusions to the author's personal history occur with greater frequency, and annotations have been dropped.

33. William J. Dodd, *Kafka and Dostoyevsky: The Shaping of Influence* (London: Macmillan, 1992), 2.

34. Bloom, *Anxiety of Influence*, 14.

35. Franz Kafka, *Briefe 1913–1914*, ed. Hans-Gerd Koch (Frankfurt am Main: S. Fischer, 2001), 275.

36. Johann Wolfgang von Goethe, vol. 2 of *Gedichte in zeitlicher Folge: Eine Lebensgeschichte Goethes in seinen Gedichten*, 2 vols. (Frankfurt am Main: Insel, 1978), 2:238.

37. Johann Wolfgang von Goethe et al., *West-Östlicher Divan*, ed. Karl Richter et al., Munich edition, vol. 11.1.2 of *Sämtliche Werke nach Epochen Seines Schaffens*, 20 vols. (Munich: Carl Hanser Verlag, 1998), 744. The quotation marks cite an excerpt from Norbert Altenhofer's "Poesie als Auslegung" in *Für Rudolf Hirsch: Zum Siebzigsten Geburtstag* (Frankfurt am Main: S. Fischer, 1975), 110.

Chapter I

1. For a biographical account of this strategy (which dates from the spring of 1915), see the first chapter of Reiner Stach, *Kafka: Die Jahre der Entscheidungen* (Frankfurt am Main: S. Fischer, 2002), 17–41.

2. Hartmut Binder, *Kafka-Kommentar zu den Romanen, Rezensionen, Aphorismen und zum Brief an den Vater* (Munich: Winkler, 1976), 14.

3. Ross Posnock, *Philip Roth's Rude Truth: The Art of Immaturity* (Princeton, N.J.: Princeton University Press, 2006), 336.

4. Klaus Wagenbach, *Franz Kafka mit Selbstzeugnissen und Bilddokumenten* (Reinbek bei Hamburg: Rowohlt, 1998), 121.

5. Franz Kafka, *Tagebücher, Band 1: 1909–1912*, ed. Hans-Gerd Koch, vol. 9 of *Gesammelte Werke in zwölf Bänden*, 12 vols. (Frankfurt am Main: Fischer Taschenbuch Verlag, 1994), 231.

6. Mark Anderson, ed., *Reading Kafka: Prague, Politics, and the Fin de Siècle* (New York: Schocken, 1989), 17.

7. Johann Wolfgang von Goethe, *Dichtung und Wahrheit*, ed. Klaus-Detlef Müller, vol. 5 of *Werke*, 6 vols., Jubilee ed. (Frankfurt am Main.: Insel, 1998), 256; Robert Walser, *Für die Katz*, ed. Jochen Greven, vol. 20 of *Sämtliche Werke in*

Einzelausgaben, 20 vols. (Frankfurt am Main: Suhrkamp, 1985), 322. The Walser quotation is taken from "Eine Art Erzählung" ("A Kind of Story"), translation by J. M. Coetzee.

8. Franz Kafka, *Tagebücher, Band 3: 1914–1923,* ed. Hans-Gerd Koch, vol. 11 of *Gesammelte Werke in zwölf Bänden,* 12 vols. (Frankfurt am Main: Fischer Taschenbuch Verlag, 1994), 179–80.

9. Ibid., 180.

10. Ibid., 177.

11. Franz Kafka, *Briefe 1902–1924,* ed. Max Brod, vol. 8 of *Gesammelte Werke,* 8 vols. (Frankfurt am Main: Fischer Taschenbuch Verlag, 1998), 269–71.

12. Karl Erich Grözinger, Stéphane Mosès, and Hans Dieter Zimmermann, eds., *Kafka und das Judentum* (Frankfurt am Main: Jüdischer Verlag bei Athenäum, 1987), 8.

13. Ritchie Robertson, *Kafka: Judaism, Politics, and Literature* (Oxford: Clarendon, 1985), 2.

14. Mark Twain, *The Complete Essays of Mark Twain,* ed. Charles Neider (Garden City, N.J.: Doubleday, 1963), 235.

15. Mark Twain, *Mark Twain's Letters,* ed. Albert Bigelow Paine (New York: AMS, 1975), 2:647.

16. Quoted in Klaus Wagenbach, *Franz Kafka: Eine Biographie seiner Jugend, 1883–1912* (Bern: Francke, 1958), 75.

17. Peter Gay, *Freud: A Life for Our Time* (New York: Norton, 1988), 139.

18. Robert Musil, *Der Mann ohne Eigenschaften, Erstes und zweites Buch,* ed. Adolf Frisé, 2 vols. (Reinbek bei Hamburg: Rowohlt Taschenbuch Verlag, 1999), 1:203.

19. Kafka, *Briefe 1902–1924,* 336.

20. Sander L. Gilman, *Jewish Self-Hatred: Anti-Semitism and the Hidden Language of the Jews* (Baltimore: Johns Hopkins University Press, 1986), 139.

21. Ernst Pawel, *The Nightmare of Reason: A Life of Franz Kafka* (New York: Farrar, Straus and Giroux, 1984), 227.

22. Mark Anderson, *Kafka's Clothes: Ornament and Aestheticism in the Hapsburg Fin de Siècle* (Oxford: Clarendon, 1992), 227.

23. Kafka, *Briefe 1902–1924,* 336.

24. Ibid., 337–38. For an insightful consideration of the linguistic and historical-cultural parameters of this conflict, see chapter 3 of Scott Spector, *Prague Territories: National Conflict and Cultural Innovation in Franz Kafka's Fin de Siècle* (Berkeley: University of California Press, 2000), 68–92.

25. Franz Kafka, *Briefe an Ottla und die Familie,* ed. Hartmut Binder and Klaus Wagenbach (Frankfurt am Main: Fischer Taschenbuch Verlag, 1981), 82. Kafka's "The Trees," offers an interesting counterpoint (and another instance of his hovering trope at work): "For we are like tree trunks in the snow. In appearance they lie sleekly and a little push should be enough to set them rolling. No, it can't be done,

for they are firmly wedded to the ground. But see, even that is only appearance." Franz Kafka, *Ein Landarzt und andere Drucke zu Lebzeiten,* ed. Hans-Gerd Koch, vol. 1 of *Gesammelte Werke in zwölf Bänden,* 12 vols. (Frankfurt am Main: Fischer Taschenbuch Verlag, 1994), 30.

26. Kafka, *Briefe 1902–1924,* 403–4.

27. Link to video interview at http://www.sueddeutsche.de/kultur/artikel/369/183795/ (accessed September 9, 2008).

28. Franz Kafka, *Briefe an Milena, Erweiterte und neu geordnete Ausgabe,* ed. Jürgen Born and Michael Müller (Frankfurt am Main: Fischer Taschenbuch Verlag, 1986), 26.

29. Franz Kafka, *Beim Bau der chinesischen Mauer und andere Schriften aus dem Nachlaß,* ed. Hans-Gerd Koch, vol. 6 of *Gesammelte Werke in zwölf Bänden,* 12 vols. (Frankfurt am Main: Fischer Taschenbuch Verlag, 1994), 215.

30. Christoph Stölzl, *Kafkas böses Böhmen: Zur Sozialgeschichte eines Prager Juden* (Munich: Edition Text + Kritik, 1975), 22.

31. Pawel, *Nightmare of Reason,* 41.

32. Sander L. Gilman, *Franz Kafka, the Jewish Patient* (New York: Routledge, 1995), 121–24; Franz Kafka, *Briefe an Felice und andere Korrespondenz aus der Verlobungszeit,* ed. Erich Heller and Jürgen Born (Frankfurt am Main: Fischer Taschenbuch Verlag, 1976), 735–36.

33. Stölzl, *Kafkas böses Böhmen,* 67.

34. For more about the future president's complex relationships with Czech assimilationists and Zionists, see Hillel Kieval's "Masaryk and Czech Jewry: The Ambiguities of Friendship" in *Languages of Community: The Jewish Experience in the Czech Lands* (Berkeley: University of California Press, 2000), 198–216.

35. Peter Demetz, *Prague in Black and Gold: The History of a City* (London: Penguin, 1997), 337.

36. In a 1920 letter to Milena Jesenská, Kafka wrote feverishly about the affair, imagining himself in relation to Hilsner: "I don't understand how whole nations of people could ever have thought of ritual murder before these recent events (at most they may have felt general fear and jealousy, but here there is no question, we see 'Hilsner' committing the crime step by step; what difference does it make that the virgin embraces him at the same time?). But on the other hand, I also don't understand how nations could believe that the Jew might murder without stabbing himself in the process, for that is what he does—but of course the nations don't need to worry about that." See Kafka, *Briefe an Milena,* 68.

37. Hillel Kieval, *The Making of Czech Jewry: National Conflict and Jewish Society in Bohemia, 1870–1918* (New York: Oxford University Press, 1988), 73.

38. Several extraordinary portraits of Jesenská have come to light during the past few decades, most notably in Margarete Buber-Neumann, *Milena: Kafkas Freundin: Ein Lebensbild* (Frankfurt am Main: Ullstein, 1996); Reiner Stach, *Kafka: Die Jahre der Erkenntnis* (Frankfurt am Main: S. Fischer, 2008); and Alena

Wagnerová, *Milena Jesenská* (Frankfurt am Main: Fischer Taschenbuch Verlag, 1997). For a self-portrait of sorts, see Milena Jesenská, ed., *"Ich hätte zu antworten tage- und nächtelang": Die Briefe von Milena* (Frankfurt am Main: Fischer Taschenbuch Verlag, 1999).

39. Kafka, *Briefe an Milena*, 26; Franz Kafka, *Zur Frage der Gesetze und andere Schriften aus dem Nachlaß*, ed. Hans-Gerd Koch, vol. 7 of *Gesammelte Werke in zwölf Bänden*, 12 vols. (Frankfurt am Main: Fischer Taschenbuch Verlag, 1994), 36.

40. Hans-Gerd Koch, *"Als Kafka mir Entgegenkam": Erinnerungen an Franz Kafka* (Frankfurt am Main: Fischer Taschenbuch Verlag, 2000).

41. Kafka's performance in this sphere has been closely documented. See, for example, Franz Kafka, *Franz Kafka: The Office Writings*, ed. Stanley Corngold, Jack Greenberg, and Benno Wagner (Princeton, NJ.: Princeton University Press, 2008); and Hans-Gerd Koch and Klaus Wagenbach, "Kafkas Fabriken," *Marbacher Magazin*, no. 100 (2002).

42. Pawel, *Nightmare of Reason*, 175.

43. Kafka, *Tagebücher 3*, 98.

44. Ibid., 179–80.

45. Kafka, *Tagebücher 1*, 14–15.

46. Franz Kafka, *Tagebücher, Band 2: 1912–1914*, ed. Hans-Gerd Koch, vol. 10 of *Gesammelte Werke in zwölf Bänden*, 12 vols. (Frankfurt am Main: Fischer Taschenbuch Verlag, 1994), 15.

47. He mentions one after the other in a 1912 letter to Felice Bauer. See Franz Kafka, *Briefe 1900–1912*, ed. Hans-Gerd Koch (Frankfurt am Main: S. Fischer, 1999), 271.

48. Max Brod, *Über Franz Kafka: Franz Kafka, Eine Biographie; Franz Kafkas Glauben und Lehre; Verzweiflung und Erlösung im Werk Franz Kafkas* (Frankfurt am Main: Fischer Bücherei, 1974), 53. Brod's attribution is confirmed in the Critical Edition's last volume of posthumous papers. Here Kafka pluralizes the obstacle (*Hindernis→Hindernisse*): "On the handle of Balzac's walking stick: I crush all obstacles, on mine: all obstacles crush me. In common is the 'all.'" Franz Kafka, *Das Ehepaar*, ed. Hans-Gerd Koch, vol. 8 of *Gesammelte Werke in zwölf Bänden*, 12 vols. (Frankfurt am Main: Fischer Taschenbuch Verlag, 1994), 132.

49. Kafka, *Tagebücher 1*, 42.

50. "In Hebrew my name is Anschel, like my mother's maternal grandfather," the passage begins, "whom my mother, who was six years old when he died, can remember as a very pious and learned man with a long, white beard." See ibid., 247.

51. Kafka, *Briefe an Milena*, 201. "There's no more intimate relationship," Italo Svevo asserted in a letter to his wife, "than the one between a sufferer and the inflictor of suffering." Livia Veneziano Svevo, *Memoir of Italo Svevo*, trans. Isabel Quigly (Marlboro, Vt.: Marlboro, 2001), 27.

52. Kafka, *Briefe 1913–1914*, 152. Elsewhere, Kafka imagines the first moment of a suicide: "To awaken on a cold autumn morning full of yellowish light. To force your way through the half-shut window and while still in front of the panes, before you fall, to hover [*schweben*], arms extended, belly arched, legs curved backwards, like the figures on the bows of ships in old times." Kafka, *Tagebücher 1*, 193.

53. Kafka, *Tagebücher 2*, 177.

54. Gilman, *Jewish Patient*, 88.

55. Kafka, *Briefe an Milena*, 79.

56. Georg Christoph Lichtenberg, *Sudelbücher*, ed. Franz H. Mautner (Frankfurt am Main: Insel, 1984), 170.

57. Clayton Koelb, *Kafka's Rhetoric: The Passion of Reading* (Ithaca, N.Y.: Cornell University Press, 1989), 143.

58. Kafka, *Briefe 1902–1924*, 192.

59. Kafka, *Tagebücher 2*, 193.

60. Kafka, *Zur Frage*, 47.

61. Kafka, *Ein Landarzt*, 52.

62. Kafka, *Zur Frage*, 47.

63. Ibid., 38–39. Reiner Stach writes insightfully about this aspect of the Kafka family romance—particularly, of Kafka's relation to his sister Ottla—in *Die Jahre der Erkenntnis*. For an in-depth analysis, see Hartmut Binder, "Kafka und seine Schwester Ottla," *Jahrbuch der deutschen Schillergesellschaft* 12 (1968): 403–56.

64. Kafka, *Zur Frage*, 41.

65. Kafka, *Ein Landarzt*, 50.

66. Kafka, *Zur Frage*, 64.

67. Kafka, *Ein Landarzt*, 51.

68. Kafka, *Briefe an Milena*, 75.

69. Kafka, *Tagebücher 2*, 15.

70. Kafka, *Ein Landarzt*, 85.

71. Hans Dieter Zimmermann, *Kafka für Fortgeschrittene* (Munich: C. H. Beck, 2004), 69. Zimmermann and Alena Wagenrová have sought to redress vilifications of Hermann Kafka in the critical literature by taking the reports of other contemporaries into account. See Alena Wagnerová, "Nachwort," in *Franz Kafka: Brief an den Vater*, ed. Hans-Gerd Koch (Berlin: Wagenbach, 2004); Zimmermann, *Kafka für Fortgeschrittene*, 17–22.

72. Kafka, *Zur Frage*, 42.

73. Kafka, *Briefe 1902–1924*, 337.

74. Kafka, *Das Ehepaar*, 66.

75. In "Up in the Gallery," this state is structurally and grammatically represented as well—the story's two sentences balance opposed visions of her performance.

76. Kafka, *Tagebücher 1*, 93.

77. "So you think the man wasn't deceived?" Josef K. asks the prison chaplain in their discussion of "Before the Law." "Don't misunderstand me," the priest responds, "I'm just pointing out the various opinions that exist on the matter. You musn't pay too much attention to opinions. *The text is immutable,* and the opinions are often an expression of despair over it" (my italics). Franz Kafka, *Der Proceß,* ed. Hans-Gerd Koch, vol. 3 of *Gesammelte Werke in zwölf Bänden,* 12 vols. (Frankfurt am Main: Fischer Taschenbuch Verlag, 1994), 230.

78. Kafka, *Briefe an Felice,* 719–20.

Chapter 2

1. "I think of you," says Zuckerman to Lonoff at the beginning of *Zuckerman Bound,* "as the Jew who got away." Martin Green addresses this phenomenon in his comparison of Roth to Saul Bellow: "One crucial likeness is between their senses of themselves as overprivileged, burdened with others' love or envy, too lucky by half." Philip Roth, *The Ghost Writer* (New York: Vintage, 1995), 50; Philip Roth, *A Philip Roth Reader,* ed. Philip Roth (New York: Farrar, Straus and Giroux, 1980), xxi–xxii.

2. Sigmund Freud, *Der Humor,* ed. Anna Freud, Edward Bilbring, and Ernst Kris, vol. 14 of *Gesammelte Werke,* 18 vols. (Frankfurt am Main: Fischer Taschenbuch Verlag, 1999), 386.

3. Philip Roth, "The Breast," in *A Philip Roth Reader,* ed. Philip Roth (New York: Farrar, Straus and Giroux, 1980), 480.

4. Kafka, *Briefe 1902–1924,* 337.

5. Philip Roth, *The Anatomy Lesson* (New York: Vintage, 1996), 40.

6. Hermione Lee, *Philip Roth* (London: Methuen, 1982), 34.

7. Epigraph taken from Philip Roth, *Shop Talk: A Writer and His Colleagues and Their Work* (Boston: Houghton Mifflin, 2001), 80.

8. I have decided not to devote equal attention to his "epilogue," *The Prague Orgy,* which differs significantly in content and scope from the preceding three novels. Roth uses this coda of sorts to introduce thematic concerns that move his protagonist beyond the generational conflict that is the subject of this study.

9. J. M. Coetzee, *Stranger Shores: Literary Essays, 1986–1999* (New York: Viking, 2001), 16.

10. Kafka, *Tagebücher 1,* 247.

11. Jonathan Safran Foer, "Jeffrey Eugenides Interviewed by Jonathan Safran Foer," *BOMB Magazine,* Fall 2002, http://www.bombsite.com/issues/81/articles/2519 (accessed September 9, 2008).

12. Martin Green, "Introduction," in *A Philip Roth Reader,* ed. Philip Roth (New York: Farrar, Straus and Giroux, 1980), ix.

13. Philip Roth, "In Search of Kafka and Other Answers," *New York Times Book Review*, February 15, 1976, 6.

14. Philip Roth, *Reading Myself and Others*, rev. ed. (New York: Penguin, 1985), 303.

15. Ibid., 303–4.

16. Philip Roth, *Conversations with Philip Roth*, ed. George J. Searles (Jackson: University Press of Mississippi, 1992), 233; Roth, *Reading Myself*, 304.

17. Roth, *Reading Myself*, 303–5.

18. Roth, *Conversations*, 243.

19. Roth, "In Search of Kafka and Other Answers," 6–7.

20. Roth, *Reading Myself*, 308.

21. Ibid., 311.

22. Malcolm Pasley, "Kafka and the Theme of 'Berufung,'" *Oxford German Studies*, no. 9 (1978).

23. Joachim Unseld, *Franz Kafka: Ein Schriftstellerleben* (Frankfurt am Main: Fischer Taschenbuch Verlag, 1984), 220. "His friend's continuing urgent need" refers to the cost of Kafka's hospitalization and treatment.

24. Kafka, *Tagebücher 2*, 252.

25. Roth, *Conversations*, 243. "Dostoevsky and Parricide" is a prominent example, though outrageous "misreadings"—especially of Shakespeare—persist throughout Freud's body of work. See "Freud: A Shakespearean Reading" in Bloom, *Western Canon*.

26. Roth, *Reading Myself*, 313.

27. "Roth's view of Kafka," writes Morton P. Levitt of the above passage, "shares some of the familiar clichés: he fails as would-be husband with Felice, as lover with Milena, is "chaste" with Dora Diamant. . . . Written by some psychoanalytical critic . . . [these] words would seem portentous and foolish. Coming from Roth, who also means them seriously, they retain a certain comic potential." See Morton P. Levitt, "Roth and Kafka: Two Jews," in *Critical Essays on Philip Roth*, ed. Sanford Pinsker (Boston: Hall, 1982), 249. I agree with the above implication that this potential is never fully realized.

28. Lee, *Philip Roth*, 67.

29. Roth, *Reading Myself*, 314.

30. Ibid., 315.

31. Ibid., 317.

32. Ibid., 318.

33. Ibid., 320.

34. Although Kafka mentions Chekhov favorably in one of his letters to Milena, the ardent enthusiasm belongs to Roth; Chekhov's example is overtly featured as a foil to Kafka's in his novel of a few years later, *The Professor of Desire*.

35. Roth, *Reading Myself*, 323.

36. Ibid., 324.

37. Ibid., 325.

38. See "On *Portnoy's Complaint*" (*New York Times Book Review,* 1969); *The Breast* (1972); "On *The Breast*" (*New York Review of Books,* 1972); "Looking at Kafka" (*American Review,* 1973); "Our Castle" (*Village Voice,* 1974); "In Search of Kafka and Other Answers" (*New York Times,* 1976); and *The Professor of Desire* (1977). A new maturity and change in approach become increasingly apparent beginning with the *New York Times* article of 1976.

39. Roth, *Reading Myself,* 325.

40. Ibid., 326.

41. Sanford Pinsker, *The Comedy That "Hoits": An Essay on the Fiction of Philip Roth* (Columbia: University of Missouri Press, 1975), 20, 123; Harold Bloom, ed., *Philip Roth (Bloom's Modern Critical Views),* (New York: Chelsea House, 1986), 1; Bernard F. Rodgers, *Philip Roth* (Boston: Twayne, 1978), 18, 123. In a March 2004 conversation, Bloom expressed reservations about the story.

42. Peter Demetz, "Mit Franz Kafka in den Straßen von Newark," *Frankfurter Allgemeine Zeitung,* March 23, 2002; Lee, *Philip Roth,* 18, 82.

43. Roth, *Conversations,* 175.

44. Ibid., 181.

45. Ross Posnock assigns *The Counterlife* (1986) a pivotal position in Roth's corpus: "The rigor of the novel," he argues, "is its fidelity to the making of counterlife, to enacting bruising antagonisms out of which emerge revisions and redirection inside and beyond the book." See Posnock, *Philip Roth's Rude Truth,* 137. Signs that Roth's combative agonism was moving inward were already apparent halfway through the first Zuckerman trilogy. In "Looking at Kafka," this aggression is still targeted outward.

46. Roth, *Reading Myself,* 22. Alan Cooper identifies Kafka's "comic self-deflation" as the "saving grace" that proved so attractive to Roth. See *Philip Roth and the Jews* (Albany: SUNY Press, 1996), 18–19.

47. Roth, *Conversations,* 98.

48. Ibid., 242.

49. Bloom, *Philip Roth,* 1.

50. Roth, *Ghost Writer,* 79.

51. Ibid., 82. Sidney is resurrected in *The Plot Against America* as Alvin, the disgruntled cousin who boards with the Roth family.

52. Among them, Saul Bellow, Bernard Malamud, and Isaac Bashevis Singer. Leslie Fiedler noted that Bellow's *Seize the Day,* published in 1956, "emerges at the moment when the Jews for the first time move into the center of American culture," a time when the Jew has become a fashionable "image for what the American longs to be or fears he is being forced to become." Leslie A. Fiedler, *A New Fiedler Reader* (Amherst, N.Y.: Prometheus Books, 1999), 109–10. *The Ghost Writer* takes place on the evening of December 10, 1956.

53. Roth, *Ghost Writer,* 83.

54. Ibid., 80.

55. Ibid., 81.

56. Ibid., 103.

57. Ibid., 88.

58. Ibid., 92.

59. Ibid., 94.

60. Debra B. Shostak, *Philip Roth: Countertexts, Counterlives* (Columbia: University of South Carolina Press, 2004), 126.

61. Roth, *Shop Talk*, 23–24.

62. Roth, *Ghost Writer*, 111.

63. Ibid., 95–96.

64. Ibid., 106. Five years earlier, Roth published "Imagining Jews" in the *New York Review of Books*. His essay reveals that Judge Wapter's "question" almost certainly derived from a real one posed by the "well known American Zionist leader" Marie Syrkin in *Commentary* one year before. There, Syrkin had argued that Roth's depiction of oral intercourse between Portnoy and "a rich and pretty Wasp girl" comes "straight out of the Goebbels-Streicher script"—"the anti-semitic indictment straight through Hitler is that the Jew is the defiler and destroyer of the Gentile world. . . . Hitler, Goebbels, Streicher," Roth concludes: "Had she not been constrained by limitations of space, Syrkin might eventually have had me in the dock with the entire roster of Nurenberg defendants." See Roth, *Reading Myself*, 300.

65. Roth, *Ghost Writer*, 106.

66. This passage is comparable in tone and combativeness to *Portnoy's Complaint*'s notorious: "Weep for your own pathetic selves, why don't you, sucking and sucking on that sour grape of a religion! Jew! Jew! Jew! Jew! Jew! Jew! It is coming out my ears already, the saga of the suffering Jews! Do me a favor, my people, and stick your suffering heritage up your suffering ass—*I happen also to be a human being!*" It is lines like these that so offended Gershom Scholem, the eminent scholar of Jewish mysticism (and insightful reader of Kafka) who remained convinced until the end of his life that Roth's novel would eventually be co-opted by enemies of the Jews: "This is the book for which all anti-Semites have been praying," Scholem wrote in an article for the Israeli daily *Ha'aretz*. "I daresay that with the next turn of history, not long to be delayed, this book will make all of us defendants at court. We will pay the price, not the author . . . I wonder what price *k'lal yisrael* [the world Jewish community]—and there is such an entity in the eyes of the Gentiles—is going to pay for this book. Woe to us on that day of reckoning." Philip Roth, *Portnoy's Complaint* (London: Cape, 1969), 76. See also David Remnick, "Into the Clear: Philip Roth," in *Reporting: Writings from the New Yorker* (New York: Knopf, 2006), 101–24.

67. Roth, *Ghost Writer*, 95.

68. Ibid., 102.

69. Ibid., 108–9.

70. Ibid., 10. "In order to be a writer," observes Hermione Lee of families in Roth and Joyce, "one must cease to be a son." Lee, *Philip Roth,* 34.

71. Hence the resonance of these lines by Kafka about the Castle's administrators: "Nowhere else had K. ever seen one's official position and one's life so intertwined as they were here, so intertwined that it sometimes seemed as though office and life had switched places." Later in that novel, a secretary named Bürgel adds, "We don't acknowledge any distinction between ordinary time and work time." Franz Kafka, *Das Schloß,* ed. Hans-Gerd Koch, vol. 4 of *Gesammelte Werke in zwölf Bänden,* 12 vols. (Frankfurt am Main: Fischer Taschenbuch Verlag, 1994), 94, 411.

72. Roth, *Ghost Writer,* 13.

73. The likenesses between Lonoff's compositional method and Babel's merit notice. Roth may have known Konstantin Paustovsky's *Years of Hope,* in which the following is attributed to Babel: "I go over each sentence, time and again." Compare this to Lonoff's "I turn sentences around. That's my life. I write a sentence and then I turn it around." Roth, *Ghost Writer,* 17–18. Lonoff's isolated routine resembles Flaubert's, as well as those of Roth's close friend, the painter Philip Guston. For more on the latter, see Musa Mayer, *Night Studio: A Memoir of Philip Guston* (New York: Da Capo, 1997), 176–77.

74. Kafka, *Briefe 1902–1924,* 337.

75. Kafka, *Briefe 1913–1914,* 275.

76. Roth, *Ghost Writer,* 47.

77. Isaac Babel, *The Collected Stories of Isaac Babel,* ed. Nathalie Babel and Peter Constantine, trans. Peter Constantine (New York: W. W. Norton, 2002), 108; Roth, *Ghost Writer,* 47–48. Zuckerman's reading of Lonoff's "dreaming," "reporting," and "writing" explains the transition from Kafka to Babel in their conversation, and perhaps also Roth's inclusion of Bruno Schulz and Isaac Bashevis Singer in the web of "blood relations" he has spun for himself over the past four decades.

78. Babel, *Collected Stories,* 48. Peter Constantine's translation of the above reads: "How late I learned the essential things in life! In my childhood, nailed to the Gemara, I led the life of a sage, and it was only later, when I was older, that I began to climb trees." Babel, *Collected Stories,* 630–31.

79. A variation of Kafka's "What have I in common with Jews? I have hardly anything in common with myself." Kafka, *Tagebücher 2,* 252.

80. Roth, *Ghost Writer,* 49.

81. Ibid., 50. "I understood the celebrated phenomenon for the first time," the narrator later notes: "a man, his destiny, and his work—all one. What a terrible triumph!" Roth, *Ghost Writer,* 73.

82. Roth, *Ghost Writer,* 51.

83. Ibid., 29, 72.

84. Ibid., 56–57.

85. Ibid., 78.

86. Henry James, *Complete Stories, 1892–1898* (New York: Library of America, 1996), 354; Roth, *Ghost Writer*, 76. Roth's novel pays tribute to James's "Master and acolyte" tales from the mid-1880s through the turn of the century. Twenty-three years after *The Ghost Writer*'s publication, Roth cited this passage upon winning the American Academy's Gold Medal in Fiction: "This is a great honor and an enormous pleasure . . . I'd like to quote a few lines from the work of one of our most distinguished members, and then to hurry back to my chair to look at my medal. The lines are from Henry James. They are spoken by Dencombe, an aging novelist, in the James story 'The Middle Years.' They furnish the most telling description of the literary vocation that I know of. Dencombe says, 'We work in the dark—we do what we can—we give what we have. Our doubt is our passion, and our passion is our task. The rest is the madness of art.' Thank you." Philip Roth, "An Acceptance," *Paris Review*, no. 167 (Fall 2003).

87. Roth, *Ghost Writer*, 79.

88. Roth, *Reading Myself*, 269.

89. Roth, *Ghost Writer*, 23.

90. Ibid., 28.

91. Ibid., 112.

92. *The Ghost Writer* and *The Prague Orgy* were the last of Roth's fictions to insistently demonstrate the author's engagement—till then persistent—with James's work.

93. Roth, *Ghost Writer*, 121; Roth, *Reading Myself*. "Writing American Fiction" was first published in *Commentary* in 1961.

94. Roth, *Ghost Writer*, 121.

95. Sigmund Freud, *Der Dichter und das Phantasieren*, ed. Anna Freud, Edward Bilbring, and Ernst Kris, vol. 7 of *Gesammelte Werke*, 18 vols. (Frankfurt am Main: Fischer Taschenbuch Verlag, 1999), 218.

96. Roth, *Ghost Writer*, 102, 107.

97. One wonders how the author who here asserts that "any projection of Anne Frank as a contemporary figure is an unholy speculation: it tampers with history, with reality, with deadly truth" responded initially to the "Femme Fatale" chapter of *The Ghost Writer*. Roth's Frank projections do not end with this novella, but with the final installment of *Zuckerman Bound*. See Cynthia Ozick, *Quarrel and Quandary* (New York: Knopf, 2000), 75, 77, 80.

98. Zuckerman imagines that the person who identified her corpse has either "confused her with her older sister" or "figured that she was dead after seeing her so long in a coma." Roth, *Ghost Writer*, 125, 28.

99. Quoted in Ozick, *Quarrel*, 74; Roth, *Ghost Writer*, 132.

100. James, *Complete Stories, 1892–1898*, 354.

101. Roth, *Ghost Writer*, 135. The Catholic orphanage near Roth's childhood home in Newark remains an enduring symbol in his imagination. See, for example, the juvenile stories "Orphans" and "The Fence." It reappears in *Zuckerman*

Unbound and plays a pivotal role in the childhood of *The Plot Against America*'s protagonist, "Philip Roth."

102. Roth, *Ghost Writer,* 147. Zuckerman's invention is a wish-fulfillment in which the two wed, thus reconciling him with his father while proving his goodwill to the Jewish community: "Heedless of Jewish feeling? Indifferent to Jewish survival? Brutish about their well-being? Who dares to accuse of such unthinking crimes the husband of Anne Frank!" Roth, *Ghost Writer,* 171.

103. Gilman, *Jewish Self-Hatred,* 380; Shostak, *Philip Roth: Countertexts, Counterlives,* 126.

104. Roth, *Ghost Writer,* 152.

105. Ibid., 70.

106. Martin Buber, *Briefwechsel aus sieben Jahrzehnten,* ed. Grete Schaeder, 3 vols. (Heidelberg: L. Schneider, 1972), 1:491–92.

107. See the famous octavo notebook entry from February 25, 1918, where Kafka declares: "I have vigorously absorbed the negative element of the age in which I live, an age that is, of course, very close to me, which I have no right ever to fight against, but as it were a right to represent." Kafka, *Beim Bau,* 215. Roth's *The Prague Orgy,* epilogue to *Zuckerman Bound,* and *The Counterlife,* its successor, echo this pattern by turning Zuckerman's inward dilemmas outward. "In this nation of narrators [Czechoslovakia]," Zuckerman writes, "I'd only just begun hearing all their stories; I'd only just begun to sense myself shedding *my* story, as wordlessly as possible snaking away from the narrative encasing me." Philip Roth, *The Prague Orgy* (New York: Vintage, 1996), 83–84.

108. Kafka, *Ein Landarzt,* 52.

109. Some contemporaries noted this reflexivity upon the work's appearance in 1981. "Roth's previous four books," wrote George Stade in the *New York Times,* "were also rites of appeasement, gestures of self-exculpation, explanation, and excuse. . . . Some critics had charged [them] with both narcissism and self-hatred, with beastliness to women and, above all, with anti-Semitism. To these charges Roth's recent books had answered Not Guilty or Guilty with Cause. His new book accepts the indictment and sentences his younger self to death." Stade's exaggeration (no one besides Zuckerman's father dies in Roth's novel) points to the novel's kinship with "The Judgment." George Stade, "Roth's Complaint," *New York Times,* May 24, 1981.

110. Kafka, *Ein Landarzt,* 168.

111. Roth, *Ghost Writer,* 107.

112. Ibid., 73. The writing continues to perplex the elder Zuckerman: "*Mixed Emotions* had been the title of his second book. It had confused his father no less than *Higher Education,* his first. Why should emotions be mixed? They weren't when he was a boy." Philip Roth, *Zuckerman Unbound* (New York: Vintage, 1995), 185.

113. *Carnovsky* is narrated, like Roth's *Portnoy's Complaint,* by a Newarker whose

obsession with sex is accompanied by equally intense pangs of guilt. Gilbert Carnovsky's name derives from Israel Joshua Singer's 1943 novel *Di mishpokhe Karnovski* (*The Carnovsky Family*).

114. "As anyone over forty knows," Roth wrote in an essay marking the twenty-fifth anniversary of *Portnoy's Complaint's* publication, "the Law of 26 postulates, with illuminating if chilling accuracy, that the minimum number of repercussions, not only of every last thing one does or says, but of everything one fails to do or say, is 26; that these 26 repercussions occur *in addition to* whatever repercussions one is ever feebly able to foresee; and that these repercussions are *by necessity* opposed diametrically to the repercussions one had hoped to effectuate." Philip Roth, "Juice or Gravy? How I Met My Fate in a Cafeteria," *New York Times,* September 18, 1994.

115. Roth, *Reading Myself,* 162.

116. I count one. Zuckerman quotes a celebrated line from Kafka's 1904 letter to Oskar Pollak: "I believe we should read only those books that bite and sting us. If a book we are reading does not rouse us with a blow to the head, why read it?" Roth omits its most memorable simile, that of a book being an axe for the frozen sea inside us. In full the passage reads: "I think we ought to read only the kind of books that wound and stab us. If the book we're reading doesn't wake us up with a blow on the head, what are we reading it for? So that it will make us happy, as you write? Good Lord, we could be happy precisely if we had no books, and the kind of books that make us happy are the kind we could write ourselves if we had to. But we need the books that affect us like a disaster, that grieve us deeply, like the death of someone we loved more than ourselves, like being banished into forests far from everyone, like a suicide. A book must be the axe for the frozen sea inside us. That is my belief." Kafka, *Briefe 1900–1912,* 36; Roth, *Zuckerman Unbound,* 200.

117. Hana Wirth-Nesher, "From Newark to Prague: Roth's Place in the American-Jewish Literary Tradition," in *Reading Philip Roth,* ed. Asher Z. Milbauer and Donald G. Watson (London: Macmillan, 1994), 24–25. Writing about "Looking at Kafka," Wirth-Nesher continues: "But the real Kafka is an overwhelming father-figure both in terms of the drama of his own life and the place he now occupies in the post-Holocaust view of that life and art. So Roth can claim him as a literary father and then minimize that threat by making Kafka an unpublished author, a pathetic elderly man with comic elements, the subject of mockery by his Hebrew school pupils. This leaves room for Roth's life and art, while also diminishing it." Martin Green similarly notes that until the late 1970s, Roth "appropriates his literary and ideological heroes by domesticating them, K. becomes his Hebrew teacher, his Aunt Rhoda becomes a Chekhov actress, Anne Frank becomes his girlfriend and wife." Martin Green, "Half a Lemon, Half an Egg," in *Reading Philip Roth,* ed. Asher Z. Milbauer and Donald G. Watson (New York: St. Martin's, 1988), 76.

118. Kafka, *Ein Landarzt,* 235.

119. Ibid., 238. The Muirs translate *Kistenwand* as "locker." Joachim Neugro-schel's version is clearer; Red Peter's description of his cage in the latter reads: "The cage did not have four sides; it consisted of only three sides and was attached to a crate [*Kiste*], which formed the fourth wall [*Wand*]." Franz Kafka, *The Meta-morphosis and Other Stories*, trans. Joachim Neugroschel (New York: Simon and Schuster, 1993), 284.

120. Roth, *Ghost Writer*, 33. To this extent he resembles the hero (also a devel-oping writer) of Saul Bellow's *The Adventures of Augie March*. Augie too seems pli-ant on the surface, and is taken aback when his crippled boss—no distinguished writer like Lonoff, though equally memorable—reveals otherwise: "'But wait. All of a sudden I catch on to something about you. You've got *opposition* in you. You don't slide through everything. You just make it look so.' This was the first time anyone had told me anything like the truth about myself. I felt it powerfully. That, as he said, I did have opposition in me, and great desire to offer resistance and to say '*No!*' which was as clear as could be, as definite a feeling as a pang of hunger. The discoverer of this, who had taken pains to think of me—to *think* of me—I was full of love of him for it. But I was also wearing the discovered attribute, my opposition. I was clothed in it. So I couldn't make any sign of argument or indi-cate how I felt." Saul Bellow, *The Adventures of Augie March* (New York: Penguin, 1999), 126.

121. Edward Rothstein, "The Revenge of the Vrai," *New York Review of Books* 28, no. 11 (1981): 21.

122. Roth, *Zuckerman Unbound*, 120.

123. Roth, *Ghost Writer*, 49.

124. Roth, *Zuckerman Unbound*, 120, 25.

125. Ibid., 182. Kafka's story pivots, of course, on Herr Bendemann's query: "'Am I well covered up now?' asked his father, as if he couldn't see whether his feet were properly tucked in or not. 'So you like it in bed, don't you?' said Georg, and tucked the blanket more closely around him. 'Am I well covered up?' the father asked once more, seeming to be particularly intent on the answer. 'Don't worry, you're well covered up.'" Kafka, *Ein Landarzt*, 48.

126. Roth, *Zuckerman Unbound*, 181–83.

127. Ibid., 186–88.

128. Ibid., 192–93.

129. "The hallowing of Pain/Like hallowing of Heaven,/Obtains at a corpo-real cost—/The Summit is not given/to Him who strives severe/At middle of the Hill—/But He who has achieved the Top—/All—is the price of All— ." Emily Dickinson, *The Complete Poems of Emily Dickinson*, ed. Thomas H. Johnson (Bos-ton: Little, Brown, 1960), 377.

130. Roth, *Zuckerman Unbound*, 199–200.

131. J. M. Coetzee, *Elizabeth Costello* (New York: Viking, 2003), 215.

132. Kafka, *Ein Landarzt,* 238; Roth, *Zuckerman Unbound,* 197.

133. Roth, *Zuckerman Unbound,* 198. Compare the final sentence in Roth's 1991 account of his father's death: "You must not forget anything." Philip Roth, *Patrimony: A True Story* (New York: Vintage, 1996), 238.

134. No surprise then, that Henry becomes Nathan's double in *The Counterlife,* the first novel published by Roth after *Zuckerman Bound.*

135. Roth, *Zuckerman Unbound,* 212–13, 15.

136. Ibid., 217.

137. Ibid., 218.

138. Quoted in Wood, *Broken Estate,* 123.

139. In 1969 Arnold H. Lubasch spoke with Roth's former classmates for a *New York Times* article titled "Philip Roth Shakes Weequahic High": "Dr. Martin Weich," Lubasch writes, "a Manhattan psychiatrist who has maintained his friendship with Mr. Roth since high school, suggested that the author possessed a gift for taking fragments of several people and fashioning them into a single fictional character that conveyed truth." Arnold H. Lubasch, "Philip Roth Shakes Weequahic High," *New York Times,* February 28, 1969. See also Christopher Goffard, "Philip Roth Unbound," *St. Petersburg Times,* July 4, 2004.

140. Wood, *Broken Estate,* 123. In *Confessions of Felix Krull, Confidence Man,* Mann explicitly links his artistic protagonist with Hermes. Roth may have had Krull in mind when he named one of Zuckerman's literary fathers Felix Abravenel.

141. Philip Guston, "Faith, Hope and Impossibility," in *Philip Guston Retrospective,* ed. Michael Auping (New York: Thames and Hudson, 2003).

142. Kafka, *Briefe 1913–1914,* 322.

143. Roth, *Zuckerman Unbound,* 223.

144. Ibid., 219–20.

145. Ibid., 221, 24.

146. Kafka, *Ein Landarzt,* 238–39.

147. Lee, *Philip Roth,* 33–34.

148. Roth, *Anatomy Lesson,* 5.

149. George Herbert, *Complete English Works,* ed. Ann Pasternak Slater (London: Everyman, 1995), 149–50.

150. Roth, *Anatomy Lesson,* 10.

151. Red Peter forsakes his cage on the Hagenbeck steamship by learning to speak. In joining the human community, he commits himself to the new restraint of reason and speech. Zuckerman, on the other hand, "had shaken free at an early age from the sentimental claims of a conventional, protective, worshipful family, he had surmounted a great university's beguiling purity, he had torn loose from the puzzle of passionless marriages to three exemplary women and from the moral propriety of his own early books; he had worked hard for his place as a

writer—eager for recognition in his striving twenties, desperate for his serenity in his celebrated thirties—only at forty to be vanquished by a causeless, nameless, untreatable phantom disease." Ibid., 28.

152. Saul Bellow, *It All Adds Up: From the Dim Past to the Uncertain Future* (New York: Penguin, 1995), 11.

153. Roth, *Anatomy Lesson*, 5–6.

154. Roth, *Patrimony*, 237.

155. Roth, *Roth Reader*, 270, 79.

156. "The body contains the life story just as much as the brain," asserted the Irish writer Edna O'Brien to Roth in a 1984 conversation published in the *New York Times Book Review*. Roth, *Shop Talk*, 105. Seventeen years later, Roth used O'Brien's assertion as the epigraph to his novel *The Dying Animal*.

157. Kafka, *Ein Landarzt*, 161; Roth, *Roth Reader*, 272.

158. "It consists, as you see, of three parts. . . . The lower one is called the 'Bed,' the upper one the 'Designer,' and this one here in the middle . . . is called the 'Harrow.' . . . As soon as the man is strapped down, the Bed is set in motion. It quivers in minute, very rapid vibrations, both from side to side and up and down. You will have seen similar apparatus in hospitals." Kafka, *Ein Landarzt*, 163–65.

159. Roth, *Anatomy Lesson*, 24.

160. See especially the fourth case history in Freud's *Studien* ("Fräulein Elisabeth v. R . . ."), his breakthrough examination of a "pain" of "undetermined nature." Roth's ending for *The Anatomy Lesson*—Zuckerman, who cannot stop ranting, breaks his jaw, which must then be sewn shut—seems to lampoon the therapeutic development championed in this section, namely, that "the only way to get rid of [her] pain was to talk it away." Sigmund Freud, *Studien über Hysterie*, ed. Anna Freud, Edward Bilbring, and Ernst Kris, vol. 1 of *Gesammelte Werke*, 18 vols. (Frankfurt am Main: Fischer Taschenbuch Verlag, 1999), 196–251; Gay, *A Life for Our Time*, 71–72.

161. "I was teaching a lot of Kafka in a course I gave once a week at the University of Pennsylvania," Roth tells George Plimpton of the period of *Portnoy's Complaint*'s gestation during the mid- to late 1960s. "When I look back now on the reading I assigned that year, I realize that the course might have been called 'Studies in Guilt and Persecution'—'The Metamorphosis,' *The Castle*, 'In the Penal Colony,' *Crime and Punishment*, 'Notes from Underground,' *Death in Venice, Anna Karenina*." Roth, *Reading Myself*, 21.

162. Compare the conclusion of James's "The Middle Years," quoted by Roth in *The Ghost Writer*. Doctor Hugh tries to convince the dying Dencombe of his work's value: "'If you've doubted, if you've despaired, you've always 'done' it,' his visitor subtly argued. 'We've done something or other,' Dencombe conceded. 'Something or other is everything. It's the feasible. It's *you*!' 'Comforter!' poor Dencombe ironically sighed." James, *Complete Stories, 1892–1898*, 116.

163. Roth, *Anatomy Lesson*, 34.

164. Kafka, *Ein Landarzt*, 166.

165. See Kafka's letters to Verlag Kurt Wolff from October 15, 1915 and July 28, August 14, and August 19, 1916 (*Briefe 1914–1917*, 142–43, 191, 201, 207–8).

166. The same can also be said for *The Counterlife*, which was published two years after *The Prague Orgy*. In a 1987 letter to Mary McCarthy, Roth accounts for Zuckerman's confrontations with English anti-Semitism thus: "I wanted him astonished, caught off-balance, *educated.*" Roth, *Shop Talk*, 116–17.

167. Kafka, *Der Proceß*, 223–24.

168. Frieda, the barkeep in Kafka's *The Castle*, exerts a similar appeal for K. when he learns that she is the lover of a prominent Castle official.

169. Kafka, *Der Proceß*, 261.

170. Samuel Beckett, *Three Novels: Molloy, Malone Dies, The Unnamable* (New York: Grove, 1995). This is yet another variation of the "Dedalian formula" young Zuckerman aspires to in *The Ghost Writer*. For the relevant passage in Beckett, see *Malone Dies* in Beckett, *Three Novels*, 238–46.

171. Roth, *Anatomy Lesson*, 11–12. Compare the advocate Huld on the correspondence between guilt and attraction—"defendants are indeed often attractive," and so on—in "Block, the Merchant/Dismissal of the Lawyer." Kafka, *Der Proceß*, 194.

172. Roth, *Anatomy Lesson*, 14.

173. Ibid., 155.

174. Kafka, *Der Proceß*, 113.

175. Precisely the opposite of the elaborate advice Huld provides: "Just don't attract attention! Keep calm, no matter how much it seems counter to good sense. Try to realize that this vast judicial organism remains, so to speak, in a state of eternal equilibrium, and that if you change something on your own where you are, you can cut the ground out from under your feet and fall, while the vast organism easily compensates for the minor disturbance at some other spot . . . and remains unchanged, if not, which is likely, even more resolute, more vigilant, more severe, more malicious." Ibid., 126.

176. Roth, *Anatomy Lesson*, 6.

177. Ibid., 24, 35.

178. Roth, *Reading Myself*, 132.

179. Shostak, *Philip Roth: Countertexts, Counterlives*, 167; Roth, *Reading Myself*, 108.

180. Kafka, *Der Proceß*, 224–25. I revert here to the Willa and Edwin Muir translation which Roth quotes in the interview.

181. Guston, "Faith, Hope and Impossibility," 93. Of "The Stoker"—one of his three "sons"—he writes in his diary on May 24, 1913: "This evening I read it to my parents, there is no better critic than I when I read to my father, who listens with the most extreme reluctance." Kafka, *Tagebücher 2*, 178.

182. Robert Kiely, "Roth's Writer and His Stumbling Block," *New York*

Times, October 30, 1983; Sanford Pinsker, *Critical Essays on Philip Roth* (Boston: G. K. Hall, 1982). For a concise recapitulation of this debate, see Mark Shechner's "Only a *Weltanschauung:* Howe's Lost Young Intellectual" in *Up Society's Ass, Copper: Rereading Philip Roth* (Madison: University of Wisconsin Press, 2003), 44–50.

183. Roth, *Anatomy Lesson,* 70.

184. Ibid., 71.

185. Ibid., 72.

186. Shechner, *Up Society's Ass, Copper,* 86.

187. Roth, *Anatomy Lesson,* 74–75.

188. Ibid., 69.

189. Ibid., 71–72.

190. Ibid., 73.

191. Kafka, *Briefe 1902–1924,* 337.

192. "What else have you underlined?" Zuckerman asks Caesara O'Shea about her copy of Kierkegaard in *Zuckerman Unbound.* "What everybody underlines," she responds. "Everything that says 'me.'" Roth, *Zuckerman Unbound,* 92.

193. Roth, *Anatomy Lesson,* 104–5.

194. Roth, *Reading Myself,* 5. Roth launches Zuckerman's story from the same presumption: "I'd slammed a lot of doors and declared a few wars, but still loved them like their child. And whether or not I wholly knew just how extensive the addiction, I was much in need of their love for me, of which I assumed there was an inexhaustible supply." Roth, *Ghost Writer,* 81.

195. Roth, *Reading Myself,* 325.

196. Kafka, *Zur Frage,* 49. "No new Newark was going to spring up again for Zuckerman," Roth asserts, "not like the first one: no fathers like those pioneering Jewish fathers bursting with taboos, no sons like their sons boiling with temptations, no loyalties, no ambitions, no rebellions, no capitulations, no clashes quite so convulsive again. Never again to feel such tender emotion and such a desire to escape. Without a father and mother and a homeland, he was no longer a novelist. No longer a son, no longer a writer. Everything that galvanized him had been extinguished, leaving nothing unmistakably his and nobody else's to claim, exploit, enlarge, and reconstruct." Roth, *Anatomy Lesson,* 39–40.

197. Kafka, *Zur Frage,* 48.

198. Milbauer and Watson, *Reading Philip Roth* (1988), 8.

199. Green, "Introduction," in *A Philip Roth Reader,* xiv.

200. "The last of the old-fashioned fathers," the novel concludes. "And we, thought Zuckerman, the last of the old-fashioned sons. Who that follows after us will understand how midway through the twentieth century, in this huge, lax, disjointed democracy, a father—and not even a father of learning or eminence or demonstrable power—could still assume the stature of a father in a Kafka story? No, the good old days are just about over, when half the time, without even know-

ing it, a father could sentence a son to punishment for his crimes, and the love and hatred of authority could be such a painful, tangled mess." Roth, *Anatomy Lesson*, 280.

201. Ibid., 74.

202. Maksim Gorky, *Literary Portraits*, trans. Ivy Litvinov (Moscow: Foreign Languages Publishing House, n.d.), 13.

203. Roth, *Patrimony*, 238.

Chapter 3

1. Sven Meyer, "Das Fähnlein auf der Brücke," *Akzente: Zeitschrift für Literatur* 50.1, special issue, "W. G. Sebald zum Gedächtnis" (2003): 51. A reference to Gottfried Keller's story "The Banner of the Upright Seven."

2. Bloom, *Anxiety of Influence*, 5.

3. The poet is furthermore incapable of recognizing his distortions. Bloom notes that "to be turned the right way in regard to the precursor"—that is, to read him accurately—"means not to swerve at all, so any bias or inclination perforce must be perverse *in relation to the precursor* . . . Yet the strong poet's imagination *cannot see itself as perverse;* its own inclination must be health, the true priority." Ibid., 85–86.

4. *Literatur und Kritik* published a German version of "The Undiscover'd Country" that same year. See W. G. Sebald, "Thanatos—Zur Motivstruktur in Kafkas *Schloß*," *Literatur und Kritik*, no. 66/67 (1972).

5. Andreas Isenschmid, "Melancolia: W. G. Sebalds *Schwindel.Gefühle*," in *W. G. Sebald*, Porträt 7, ed. Franz Loquai, (Eggingen, Ger.: Isele, 1997), 73.

6. Marcel Atze, "Koinzidenz und Intertextualität: Der Einsatz von Prätexten in W. G. Sebalds Erzählung 'All'estero,'" in *W. G. Sebald*, Porträt 7, ed. Franz Loquai, (Eggingen, Ger.: Isele, 1997), 151.

7. A reproduction of this photograph appears in Klaus Wagenbach, *Franz Kafka*, Bilder aus seinem Leben, 3rd ed. (Berlin: Wagenbach, 2008), 32.

8. W. G. Sebald, "The Undiscover'd Country—The Death Motif in Kafka's 'Castle,'" *Journal of European Studies*, no. 2 (1972): 22.

9. At least such readings had begun to ebb by the time "The Undiscover'd Country" was published. Until the mid-1960s Brod's influence (which emphasized the redemptive aspect of Kafka's fiction) remained authoritatively pervasive.

10. Bloom, *Anxiety of Influence*, 42.

11. Sebald, "Undiscover'd Country," 22. Virgil's *Aeneid* suggests a possible explanation for Sebald's emphasis on the years 1813, 1913, 2013 in his first novel: "That ferryman is Charon," Sybil tells Aeneas in the underworld. "And the waves will only carry souls that have a tomb. Before his bones have found their rest, no one may cross the horrid shores and the hoarse waters. *They wander for*

a hundred years and hover about these banks until they gain their entry, to visit once again the pools they long for" (my italics). Virgil, *The Aeneid of Virgil: A Verse Translation,* trans. Allen Mandelbaum (Berkeley: University of California Press, 1982), 143.

12. These boundaries are equally conflated in Sebald's own fiction and nonfiction, where it is no less difficult to distinguish between W. G. Sebald and "W. G. Sebald" than it is to do so here between Franz Kafka and K.

13. W. G. Sebald, "Das unentdeckte Land: Zur Motivstruktur in Kafkas *Schloß,*" in *Die Beschreibung des Unglücks* (Frankfurt am Main: Fischer Taschenbuch Verlag, 2003), 78.

14. Sebald's reading of Freud clearly inspired his title for the first German version of this essay, "Thanatos." His emendation, extracted from Hamlet's "To be or not to be" soliloquy, probably derived from the same studies; "Das Abreisen bedeutet im Traum Sterben," writes Freud in the tenth chapter of the *Introductory Lectures on Psycho-Analysis:* "Der Dichter bedient sich derselben Symbolbeziehung, wenn er vom Jenseits als vom unentdeckten Land spricht, von dessen Bezirk kein Reisender (*no traveller*) wiederkehrt." The translation Sebald uses at the conclusion of this essay reads: "Das unentdeckte Land, von des Bezirk kein Wandrer wiederkehrt." Sigmund Freud, *Vorlesungen zur Einführung in der Psychoanalyse,* ed. Anna Freud, Edward Bilbring, and Ernst Kris, vol. 11 of *Gesammelte Werke,* 18 vols. (Frankfurt am Main: Fischer Taschenbuch Verlag, 1999), 163; W. G. Sebald, *Die Beschreibung des Unglücks: Zur Österreichischen Literatur von Stifter bis Handke* (Frankfurt am Main: Fischer Taschenbuch Verlag, 1994), 92.

15. Sebald, "Das unentdeckte Land," 79; Wood, *Broken Estate,* 254.

16. Sebald, "Das unentdeckte Land," 79. Sebald expurgated this passage from the English version.

17. Kafka, *Der Proceß,* 233.

18. Søren Kierkegaard, *Fear and Trembling/Repetition,* trans. and ed. Edna H. Hong and Edward V. Hong, vol. 6 of *Kierkegaard's Writings* (Princeton, N.J.: Princeton University Press, 1983), 163. Since my primary concern is to demonstrate Sebald's appropriation of this passage, I reproduce here a translation by Kierkegaard scholars Howard and Edna Hong instead of the author's—which is itself a poeticized version of Adorno's German in "Zweimal Chaplin," in *Ohne Leitbild: Parva aesthetica* (Frankfurt am Main: Suhrkamp, 1967).

19. Sebald, "Das unentdeckte Land," 80.

20. Kierkegaard, *Repetition,* 163.

21. Beckett's project was highly relevant for Sebald. "The Undiscover'd Country" is preceded, in fact, by an epigraph from *Molloy:* "And in the end, or almost, to be abroad alone, by unknown ways, in the gathering of the night, with a stick. It was a stout stick, he used it to thrust himself onward, or as a defence, when the time came, against dogs and marauders. Yes, night was gathering, but the man was innocent, greatly innocent, he had nothing to fear, though he went in fear, he had

nothing to fear, there was nothing they could do to him, or very little." Sebald, "Undiscover'd Country," 22.

22. Ibid., 23; Sebald, "Das unentdeckte Land," 79, 81.

23. Sigmund Freud, *Jenseits des Lustprinzips,* ed. Anna Freud, Edward Bilbring, and Ernst Kris, vol. 13 of *Gesammelte Werke,* 18 vols. (Frankfurt am Main: Fischer Taschenbuch Verlag, 1999), 40.

24. Gay, *A Life for Our Time,* 401.

25. Sebald, "Undiscover'd Country," 25–26.

26. Sebald, "Das unentdeckte Land," 83 (my translation). In both versions of the essay, Sebald insists that Kafka was influenced by Murnau's *Nosferatu. Vertigo* makes a similar claim about a different product of German expressionism, namely the film *The Student of Prague.* (See page 181.)

27. Sebald, "Undiscover'd Country," 26.

28. Kafka, *Das Schloß,* 233.

29. Sebald, "Undiscover'd Country," 28. Sebald expands on this evolutionary theory in his "Tiere, Menschen, Maschinen—Zu Kafkas Evolutionsgeschichte," *Literatur und Kritik* 66/67 (1972): 399–411.

30. Sebald, "Das unentdeckte Land," 88.

31. Sebald, "Undiscover'd Country," 28.

32. Ibid., 29. Quoted from Hanns Bächtold-Stäubli, ed., *Handwörterbuch des deutschen Aberglaubens,* 10 vols. (Berlin: Walter de Gruyter, 1938–41), 4:196.

33. Kafka, *Das Schloß,* 286; Sebald, "Das unentdeckte Land," 81.

34. Kafka, *Das Schloß,* 306; Sebald, "Das unentdeckte Land," 81. Compare his translation of the same passage: "As he stood there, his hair rumpled, his thin beard lank as if dripping with wet, his eyes painfully beseeching and wide with reproach, his sallow cheeks flushed, but yet flaccid, his naked legs trembling so violently with cold that the long fringes of the wrap quivered as well, he was like a patient who had escaped from hospital, and whose appearance could only suggest one thought, that of getting him back in bed again." Sebald, "Undiscover'd Country," 25.

35. Sebald, "Undiscover'd Country," 24. In German: "Die Gehilfen selber, Inkarnationen antiker larvae, erwecken, *trotz ihrer bisweilen aufdringlichen Leb-endigkeit,* den Eindruck, als seien sie nicht recht am Leben" (my italics). Sebald, "Das unentdeckte Land," 81.

36. Kafka, *Das Schloß,* 166–67.

37. Ibid., 169–70.

38. Ibid., 23.

39. Ibid., 27.

40. Roth, *Reading Myself,* 21–22. Evelyn Torton Beck has drawn informative parallels between the comic improvisations between K., Jeremias, and Artur and the Yiddish theater as Kafka experienced it in Prague. "The assistants," she writes, "described as dark-skinned young men, seem duplicates of Tsingitang, the wild, dark, youth who serves the hero of *Shulamit.* Like the assistants, Tsingting's

intelligence appears limited (attributable to his being a 'native'), but like them, he is good-natured, childlike, and always ready to serve his master. Tsingting and the assistants weep easily, dance, jump about, gesticulate with exaggeration, and laugh at their master's lovemaking, which they openly envy." Evelyn Torton Beck, *Kafka and the Yiddish Theater: Its Impact on His Work* (Madison: University of Wisconsin Press, 1971), 198.

41. Sebald, "Das unentdeckte Land," 81.

42. Sebald, "Undiscover'd Country," 22.

43. Kafka, *Ein Landarzt*, 30, 21, 207.

44. A selection culled from works published during Kafka's lifetime: "*Wenn* man sich am Abend entgültig entschlossen zu haben scheint, zu Hause zu bleiben" ("The Sudden Walk"); "*Wenn* man in der Nacht durch eine Gasse spazieren geht" ("Passers-by"); "Oft *wenn* ich Kleider mit vielfachen Falten, Rüschen und Behängen sehe" ("Clothes"); "*Wenn* ich einem schönen Mädchen begegne und sie bitte" ("Rejection"); "*Wenn* man doch ein Indianer wäre" ("The Wish to Be a Red Indian"); "*Als* es schon unerträglich war" ("Unhappiness"); "*Als* der sechzenjährige Karl Roßmann" ("The Stoker"); "*Als* Gregor Samsa eines Morgens aus unruhigen Träumen erwachte" ("The Metamorphosis").

45. Kafka, *Das Schloß*, 283.

46. Taken from the aphorism numbered eighty-eight in the sequence; see Kafka, *Beim Bau*. A copy of the famous first-century mosaic depicting Alexander in the Battle of Issus hung in Kafka's gymnasium; see Klaus Wagenbach, *Franz Kafka, Bilder aus seinem Leben,* 3rd ed. (Berlin: Wagenbach, 2008), 43. In *After Nature,* the long poem published only three years after *Describing Unhappiness,* Sebald fixes his eye on an *Alexanderschlacht* of his own, namely, the painting by Albrecht Altdorfer (c. 1480–1538) that now hangs in the Alte Pinakotek, Munich. He mentions, in the work's final pages, an oleograph of the picture he viewed as a child: "Since then I have read in another teacher's writings that we have death in front of us rather like a picture of Alexander's battle on the classroom wall." Kafka is clearly the unnamed *Lehrer,* or teacher, credited above. W. G. Sebald, *Nach der Natur: Ein Elementargedicht* (Nördlingen, Ger.: Greno, 1988), 98.

47. Kafka, *Beim Bau,* 243.

48. Geoff Dyer et al., "A Symposium on W. G. Sebald," *Threepenny Review,* Spring 2002; Wood, *Broken Estate,* 248.

49. Sebald, "Das unentdeckte Land," 92.

50. Ibid., 78.

51. Wittgenstein's eyes appear in a reproduction early on in the book. W. G. Sebald, *Austerlitz* (Frankfurt am Main: Fischer Taschenbuch Verlag, 2003), 11, 63.

52. See, for example, *Lodgings in a Country House,* the collection of critical essays closer in form to his "prose fictions" of the 1990s than either of his previous volumes on Austrian literature.

53. W. G. Sebald, *Campo Santo*, ed. Sven Meyer (Munich: Hanser, 2003), 215; W. G. Sebald, "Das Geheimnis des Rotbraunen Fells: Annäherung an Bruce Chatwins aus Anlass von Nicolas Shakespeares Biographie," *Literaturen*, November 2000, 72. Sebald borrows Adorno's figure of a streaking meteor—used to depict Chaplin in the essay discussed above—to conjure Chatwin's constant movement across the globe.

54. Mark Anderson, "The Edge of Darkness," *October* 106 (2003): 117–18.

55. W. G. Sebald, *Schwindel.Gefühle.* (Frankfurt am Main: Fischer Taschenbuch Verlag, 1994), 17.

56. "In dem Niemandsland zwischen Mensch und Ding": Sebald, "Das unentdeckte Land," 92.

57. The same holds for Walter Benjamin's *One-Way Street* (1928), which probably exerted an influence on Sebald's own approach to writing personal history. Reinbert Tabbert, a former colleague of Sebald's at the University of Manchester, notes the following: "In connection with Sebald's way of seeing and representing the world, Sigrid Löffler makes mention only of Walter Benjamin, though rightly so, for Sebald had appreciated him quite early on." Reinbert Tabbert, "Max in Manchester," *Akzente: Zeitschrift für Literatur* 50.1, special issue, "W. G. Sebald zum Gedächtnis" (2003): 22.

58. Sebald, "Das unentdeckte Land," 87.

59. William Shakespeare, *The Tragedy of Romeo and Juliet*, ed. G. Blackmore Evans, in *The Riverside Shakespeare* (Boston: Houghton Mifflin, 1974), 1061. Hulse's translations for this title in initial drafts—jettisoned later for the Shakespearean equation—included "the notable fact of love" and "that curious thing known as love."

60. Stendhal, *Love*, trans. Gilbert Sale and Suzanne Sale (New York: Penguin, 1975), 285. Contrary to the impression given by Sebald's narrator, the "Salzburg Bough" section is the only section of Stendhal's book in which Mme Gherardi appears.

61. Ibid., 291–92.

62. Bloom, *Agon*, 43.

63. Sebald, *Schwindel.Gefühle*, 27.

64. Stendhal, *The Life of Henry Brulard*, trans. John Sturrock (New York: Penguin, 1995), 8.

65. Richard Howard, "Translator's Afterword," in Stendhal, *The Charterhouse of Parma* (New York: Modern Library, 1999), 503.

66. Stendhal, *Brulard*, 256. "His notion was that *passion*," Henry James keenly observed, "the power to surrender one's self sincerely and consistently to the feeling of the hour, was the finest thing in the world." Henry James, *Literary Criticism, Volume 2: European Writers and Prefaces to the New York Edition*, ed. Leon Edel, 2 vols. (New York: Library of America, 1984), 817.

67. Sebald, *Schwindel.Gefühle*, 28.

68. Ibid., 29–30.

69. Stendhal, *Love*, 292.

70. Ruth Franklin, "Rings of Smoke," *New Republic* (2002): 32.

71. This can be confirmed by contemporary reviews of *Nach der Natur* and *Schwindel.Gefühle,* several of which are reprinted in Loquai, *W. G. Sebald,* Porträt 7 (Eggingen: Isele, 1997).

72. For an overview of the publicizing role of "Holocaust literature" and the success of *The Emigrants,* see Peter C. Pfeiffer, "Korrespondenz und Wahlver-wandtschaft: W. G. Sebalds *Die Ringe des Saturn,*" in *Gegenwartsliteratur: Ein germanistisches Jahrbuch* 2, ed. Paul Michael Lützeler and Stephan K. Schindler (Tübingen: Stauffenburg, 2003), 226–44.

73. Goethe, *Dichtung und Wahrheit,* 306. I have yet to read a negative high-profile review of his major fictions at the time of their first appearance. Sebald's supporters included many of the Anglophone world's most celebrated novelists, poets, and critics, for example, Paul Auster, Michiko Kukatani, Anthony Lane, Cynthia Ozick, Tim Parks, Charles Simic, Susan Sontag, and James Wood. Their admiration quickly established his renown outside of Germany.

74. Sebald's books were taken up by his readers in English as literary works in that same language. When the *Guardian* undertook to determine the greatest novel published in the Commonwealth between 1980 and 2005, Robert McCrum reported that "an anguished minority argued for the inclusion of the German writer W.G. Sebald, whose translations of his own work (*The Emigrants, Vertigo, Rings of Saturn, Austerlitz*) render a prose so classical as to be quasi-native." Robert McCrum, "What's the Best Novel in the Past 25 Years?" *Guardian* (1996), http://www.guardian.co.uk/books/2006/oct/08/fiction.features1 (accessed September 9, 2008).

75. Sebald, *Schwindel.Gefühle,* 29–31.

76. Kafka, *Beim Bau,* 40. All translations from "The Hunter Gracchus" by Malcolm Pasley. See Franz Kafka, *The Great Wall of China and Other Short Works,* ed. and trans. Malcolm Pasley (London: Penguin, 1991).

77. Sigmund Freud, *Das Unheimliche,* ed. Anna Freud, Edward Bilbring, and Ernst Kris, vol. 12 of *Gesammelte Werke,* 18 vols. (Frankfurt am Main: Fischer Taschenbuch Verlag, 1999), 247.

78. Sebald, *Schwindel.Gefühle,* 31.

79. Ibid.; Sebald, "Undiscover'd Country," 22; Sebald, "Thanatos—Zur Motivstruktur in Kafkas *Schloß,*" 399.

80. Sebald, *Schwindel.Gefühle,* 33.

81. Ibid., 33–34.

82. Ibid., 36.

83. Stendhal, *Brulard,* 314.

84. Sebald set a precedent for deferring the entrance of a first-person narrator in *After Nature.* The triptych's first part, ". . . As the Snow on the Alps,"

recounts the life and work of the German painter Matthias Grünewald. "And if I Remained by the Outermost Sea" relates the history of Georg Wilhelm Stiller, an eighteenth-century botanist (and namesake of the author, Winfried Georg Sebald). Only in "Dark Night Sallies Forth," the poem's final section, does the autobiographical "I" finally emerge as the central narrative perspective.

85. Sebald, *Schwindel. Gefühle*, 41.

86. Ibid., 44–45.

87. Ibid., 125.

88. Kafka, *Beim Bau*, 42.

89. Ibid., 46.

90. Sebald, *Schwindel. Gefühle*, 47. These lines about Herbeck echo Stendhal's sentiments in *The Life of Henry Brulard*.

91. Marcel Atze has noted correspondences between "All'estero" and Wilhelm Waiblinger's *Friedrich Hölderlin's Life, Poetry, and Madness* near the time of *Schwindel's* publication. Though his analysis makes a strong case for Hölderlin's relevance to this section, Atze underestimates Walser's importance when he claims that "the intertextual relationships" pertaining to Carl Seelig's memoir of Robert Walser are thinner and less significant. It is nevertheless to Atze's credit to have observed this connection among many others in his 1997 article. (Sebald's lengthy autobiographical essay on Walser in *Lodgings in a Country House* did not appear until 1998.) See Atze, "Koinzidenz und Intertextualität," 151–75; Wilhelm Waiblinger, *Friedrich Hölderlins Leben, Dichtung und Wahnsinn,* http://www.guenther-emig.de/waiblinger/hoelderlin.html (accessed September 9, 2008); Carl Seelig, *Wanderungen mit Robert Walser,* ed. Elio Fröhlich (Frankfurt am Main: Suhrkamp, 1996).

92. Saul Bellow, *Herzog* (London: Penguin, 2001), 1.

93. Tabbert, "Max in Manchester," 25.

94. Ibid., 27–28.

95. Sebald, *Schwindel. Gefühle*, 68.

96. W. G. Sebald, "Eine kleine Traverse: Das poetische Werk Ernst Herbecks," in *Die Beschreibung des Unglücks* (1994), 132. Compare Cervantes's "Glass Graduate," who, "were it not for the cries of anguish he uttered when anyone touched or approached him, or his manner of dress, the frugality of his diet, the way he drank, his unwillingness to sleep anywhere but out of doors in summer and in hay-lofts in winter, as was stated earlier, no one would have thought he was anything but one of the sanest men on earth." Miguel Saavedra de Cervantes, *Exemplary Stories,* trans. Lesley Lipson (Oxford: Oxford University Press, 1998), 128.

97. W. G. Sebald, "*Le promeneur solitaire: Zur Erinnerung an Robert Walser,*" in *Logis in einem Landhaus* (Frankfurt am Main: Fischer Taschenbuch Verlag, 2000), 163.

98. Sebald correctly notes that without Seelig—who was in this respect to Walser as Max Brod was to Kafka—"Walser's rehabilitation would have never succeeded, and the memory of him would have probably passed." W. G. Sebald, *Logis*

in einem Landhaus: Über Gottfrid Keller, Johann Peter Hebel, Robert Walser und andere (Frankfurt am Main: Fischer Taschenbuch Verlag, 2000), 130–31.

99. Robert Mächler, *Das Leben Robert Walsers: Eine dokumentarische Biographie* (Frankfurt am Main: Suhrkamp, 1978), 188.

100. Sebald, *Schwindel. Gefühle,* 48.

101. Sebald, *"Le promeneur solitaire,"* 135–36.

102. Arthur Lubow, "Preoccupied with Death, but Still Funny," *New York Times,* December 11, 2001. This assessment is confirmed in Sebald's essay on Walser. See Sebald, *"Le promeneur solitaire,"* 137.

103. Sebald, *"Le promeneur solitaire,"* 137–38.

104. Seelig, *Wanderungen mit Robert Walser,* 53.

105. Sebald, *Nach der Natur.* For more on the role of the pseudonym, see "Eine kleine Traverse: Das poetische Werk Ernst Herbecks." The essay also includes a discussion of bricolage highly relevant to the author's own method of composition. Sebald expresses his personal enthusiasm for Herbeck's work in "Des Häschens Kind, der kleine Has: Über das Totemtier des Lyrikers Ernst Herbecks." See Sebald, *Campo Santo,* 171–78.

106. Kafka, *Briefe 1913–1914,* 288.

107. Tim Parks, "The Hunter," *New York Review of Books* 47, no. 10 (June 15, 2000): 53.

108. Walter Benjamin, *II: Aufsätze, Essays, Vorträge,* ed. Rolf Tiedemann and Hermann Schweppenhäuser, vol. 2 of *Gesammelte Schriften,* 3 vols. (Frankfurt am Main: Suhrkamp, 1991), 351.

109. Carl Seelig mentions Kafka on two occasions in *Wandering with Robert Walser.*

110. Sebald, *Schwindel. Gefühle,* 55.

111. *"Landesfremden gleich"* connotes foreignness in a way that "stranger" does not. The German makes it clear that both men are aliens. Ibid., 56.

112. Kafka, *Briefe 1913–1914,* 245; Franz Kafka, *Reisetagebücher,* ed. Hans-Gerd Koch, vol. 12 of *Gesammelte Werke in zwölf Bänden,* 12 vols. (Frankfurt am Main: Fischer Taschenbuch Verlag, 1994), 112.

113. Sebald, *Schwindel. Gefühle,* 65. "One has so often described the first view of Venice as wonderful, I have scarcely found it so," writes Grillparzer. "The first impression Venice made on me was alienating, cramped, unpleasant." Franz Grillparzer, "Tagebücher" in *Ausgewählte Briefe, Gespräche, Berichte,* ed. Peter Frank and Karl Pörnbacher, vol. 4 of *Sämtliche Werke,* 4 vols. (Munich; Carl Hanser, 1965), 283.

114. Grillparzer, "Tagebücher," 284.

115. Ibid.

116. Kafka, *Der Proceß,* 241.

117. Elias Canetti, *Der andere Prozeß: Kafkas Briefe an Felice* (Munich: Carl

Hanser, 1984), 76. Roberto Calasso contributes admirably to this discussion in the chapter of his monograph titled "Powers." See Roberto Calasso, *K.*, trans. Geoffrey Brock (New York: Vintage International, 2005), 109–27.

118. Kafka, *Zur Frage*, 166.

119. Kafka, *Der Proceß*, 223.

120. Sebald, *Schwindel.Gefühle*, 66.

121. Kafka, *Briefe an Milena*, 151.

122. Quoted in Michael Müller, "Kafka und Casanova," *Freibeuter*, no. 16 (1983): 68.

123. Brod, *Über Franz Kafka*, 92.

124. Kafka, *Der Proceß*, 20.

125. Müller, "Kafka und Casanova," 71.

126. Sebald, *Schwindel.Gefühle*, 68.

127. Ibid., 69.

128. Kafka, *Beim Bau*, 43.

129. Sebald, *Schwindel.Gefühle*, 76.

130. W. G. Sebald, *Vertigo*, trans. Michael Hulse (New York: New Directions, 2000), 64.

131. Pico Iyer refers to this phenomenon as "À la fuite du temps perdu." Paralysis recurs in much of Sebald's work; the opening to *The Rings of Saturn* (1955) relates a similar but more drastic attack that leaves the narrator hospitalized in a state of near immobility. At the Norwich hospital, his inability to penetrate the grey haze beyond his window reminds him of Gregor Samsa's encroaching blindness in "The Metamorphosis." Pico Iyer, "Dead Man Writing: The Strange, Haunted World of W. G. Sebald," *Harper's Magazine*, October 2000, 86; W. G. Sebald, *Die Ringe des Saturn: Eine englische Wallfahrt* (Frankfurt am Main: Fischer Taschenbuch Verlag, 1997), 11–12; Kafka, *Ein Landarzt*, 123–24.

132. Sebald, *Schwindel.Gefühle*, 79.

133. Ibid., 78.

134. Ibid., 90. Kafka noted this paradoxical fusion of liveliness and stillness in the lantern slides of Verona he viewed at the Kaiserpanorama (Emperor's Panorama) in Friedland. A journal entry from 1911 prefigures Sebald's remarks concerning Pisanello's "lifelike" fresco: "The pictures more alive than in the cinema because they offer the eye all the repose of reality." Kafka, *Reisetagebücher*, 16. Sebald read Kafka's travel diaries with fondness, and knew them well. See "Via Schweiz ins Bordell: Zu den Reisetagebüchern Kafkas" in Sebald, *Campo Santo*, 179–83.

135. Sebald, *Schwindel.Gefühle*, 92.

136. Ibid., 93.

137. The book was listed in Klaus Wagenbach's 1958 register of Kafka's library. Wagenbach, *Eine Biographie seiner Jugend*, 262. See also Jürgen Born, *Kafkas Bibliothek: Ein beschreibendes Verzeichnis mit einem Index aller in Kafkas Schriften*

erwähnten Bücher, Zeitschriften und Zeitschriftenbeiträge (Frankfurt am Main: S. Fischer, 1990), 170; Hartmut Binder, "'Der Jäger Gracchus': Zu Kafkas Schaffensweise und poetischer Topographie," *Jahrbuch der deutschen Schillergesellschaft,* no. 15 (1971): 422; Hartmut Binder, *Kafka-Kommentar zu sämtlichen Erzählungen* (Munich: Winkler, 1975), 194–95.

138. Sebald, *Schwindel.Gefühle,* 97.

139. Ibid., 99.

140. Ibid., 64.

141. Kafka, *Beim Bau,* 44.

142. Sebald, *Schwindel.Gefühle,* 99.

143. Kafka, *Briefe 1913–1914,* 271.

144. Sebald, *Schwindel.Gefühle,* 101.

145. Sebald–Hulse Translation Manuscripts (Letters and Drafts), *2003 M-20, Houghton Library, Harvard University, Cambridge, Mass. By permission of the Houghton Library, Harvard University. At the time of publication, this collection was unprocessed. Box locations may change.

146. Compare this to Sebald's "The Undiscover'd Country," where the historical Franz Kafka is frequently conflated with K., protagonist of *The Castle*—and less explicitly, with the author himself. Shortly after securing his reputation as a novelist, Sebald dropped the footnotes from his literary essays and began to speak openly of his identification with literary precursors. See, for example, his 1995 article "To the Brothel by Way of Switzerland: On Kafka's Travel Diaries," where he confesses that events described in Kafka's journals are "as real to me as if I myself had been there, and not just because 'Max' is so frequently mentioned." Sebald, *Campo Santo,* 179–80.

147. Kafka, *Briefe 1913–1914,* 295.

148. Sebald, *Schwindel.Gefühle,* 101–2.

149. Sebald, *Vertigo,* 85. Italy was attractive to Kafka, and is mentioned often with longing in his diaries and letters. See, for example, this letter to Max Brod from April 1921, where he states that given three wishes he would choose "approximate recovery," "a foreign land in the south," and "a modest handicraft." Kafka, *Briefe 1902–1924,* 315. There is also a wonderful comic fragment in the octavo notebooks about a man who one day returns from work and finds a large egg in his room. A stork-like bird hatches; the narrator consents to raise it in return for a later trip to the "southern countries" on its back. Kafka, *Beim Bau,* 85–87. Kafka's travels, like Sebald's, were occasionally shaped by literary precedents. A 1913 postcard to Ottla describes following the footsteps of Goethe with his copy of *The Italian Journey* in Malcesine. Kafka, *Briefe, 1913–1914,* 287. See also Hanns Zischler, "Kafkas Sätze (14): 'Im Süden Ist, Glaube Ich, Alles Möglich,'" *Frankfurter Allgemeine Zeitung,* July 18, 2008.

150. Sebald, *Schwindel.Gefühle,* 103.

151. Ibid., 105.

152. Ibid., 106.

153. Freud, *Unheimliche*, 250.

154. Ibid., 247.

155. Wood, *Broken Estate*, 252; Sebald, *Schwindel.Gefühle*, 107.

156. Kafka, *Der Proceß*, 223.

157. Sebald, *Vertigo*, 90–91.

158. Sebald, *Schwindel.Gefühle*, 108.

159. Sebald, *Vertigo*, 91.

160. Sebald, *Schwindel.Gefühle*, 111.

161. Ibid., 112.

162. Ibid., 113.

163. Sebald, *Schwindel.Gefühle*, 115.

164. Ibid., 133.

165. Ibid., 136.

166. Ibid., 137. Hartmut Binder and Joachim Unseld have both noted that Kafka sent two short manuscripts to Tagger, then editor of the journal *Marsyas*, during the spring of 1917. "The Hunter Gracchus" fragments were written in two spurts, the first in January and the second in April.

167. Sebald, *Schwindel.Gefühle*, 138.

168. Ibid., 142.

169. Ibid.

170. Thomas Mann, *Der Zauberberg*, ed. Peter de Mendelssohn, Frankfurt edition (Frankfurt am Main: S. Fischer, 1981), 958.

171. Mann also depicted this tension in the opening sentence of *Death in Venice*. The bellowing chant of *"Pig-me-i, Pig-me-i, Pig-me-i"* Sebald's narrator hears in his daydream distinctly echoes the nightmare of Gustav von Aschenbach toward the end of Mann's novella. For more on Sebald's use of Mann in *Vertigo*, see Atze, "Koinzidenz und Intertextualität," 158–62.

172. Sebald, *Schwindel.Gefühle*, 123.

173. Sebald, "Das unentdeckte Land," 92.

174. Sebald, *Schwindel.Gefühle*, 146.

175. Sebald, *Vertigo*, 125. This is not unlike Beyle's recollection of Ivrea, which has been distorted by his memory of an engraved portrait of the town. Sebald, *Schwindel.Gefühle*, 12; Stendhal, *Brulard*, 453.

176. Kafka, *Beim Bau*, 40.

177. Sebald, *Schwindel.Gefühle*, 147.

178. Ibid., 149.

179. Kafka, *Beim Bau*, 40–42.

180. Ibid., 42.

181. Ibid., 152.

182. Ibid., 156.

183. Georg Büchner, *Dichtungen*, ed. Henri Poschmann and Rosemarie

Poschmann, Bibliothek Deutscher Klassiker edition, vol. 1 of *Georg Büchner: Sämtliche Werke, Briefe und Dokumente in zwei Bänden,* 2 vols. (Frankfurt am Main: Deutscher Klassiker Verlag, 1992), 225.

184. Paul Celan, *Gedichte, Prosa, Reden,* ed. Beda Allemann and Stefan Reichert, vol. 3 of *Gesammelte Werke,* 3 vols. (Frankfurt am Main: Suhrkamp, 2001), 195.

185. Translation by William Weaver. This is an echo of the Veronese lovers in *Romeo and Juliet,* who are likewise entombed as the consequence of a "madness so discreet."

186. Sebald, *Schwindel.Gefühle,* 158.

187. Sebald, *Vertigo,* 136; Stach, *Kafka: Die Jahre der Erkenntnis,* 601.

188. Brod reports that Werfel tried to use his fame to improve the quality of Kafka's medical care. See Brod, *Über Franz Kafka,* 178.

189. Compare Sebald's 1983 essay on Elias Canetti, where he links Hitler's enthusiasm for these "stony extensions of death's irreversibility and reign" with the Castle authorities in Kafka's novel. Sebald, *Beschreibung,* 95.

190. Malcolm Pasley, "Drei literarische Mystifikationen Kafkas," in *Kafka-Symposion,* ed. Jürgen Born et al. (1990), 22.

191. Ibid., 23–24. I have extracted this quotation from Brod's version of the story, which fuses the four fragments together. The critical edition omits this line about metamorphosis, since Kafka crossed it out in the original manuscript; Brod's, however, was the only one available to Sebald at the time of *Schwindel. Gefühle*'s composition. See Franz Kafka, *Nachgelassene Schriften und Fragmente I: Apparatband,* ed. Hans-Gerd Koch, vol. 10 of *Kritische Ausgabe in 15 Bänden,* 15 vols. (Frankfurt am Main: Fischer Taschenbuch Verlag, 2002), 272.

192. Kafka, *Briefe 1913–1914,* 271. The note was enclosed in a letter to Felice, though—like the later *Brief an den Vater*—it probably never made it into the hands of its addressee.

193. First published in shortened form for the January 18 issue of the *Frankfurter Rundschau,* Sebald's essay was reprinted in full six years later. See "Kafka im Kino" in Sebald, *Campo Santo,* 193–209.

194. Sebald, *Schwindel.Gefühle,* 163.

195. Sebald admits as much in a 1997 review of Zischler's book on Kafka and cinema: "To me at least," he there writes, *"—and I cannot claim to be entirely innocent of the fatal inclination to speculate about meanings*—it seems increasingly that Malcolm Pasley, Klaus Wagenbach, Hartmut Binder, Walter Müller Seidel, Christoph Stölzl, Anthony Northey, and Ritchie Robertson, all of whom have concentrated mainly on reconstructing a portrait of the author in his own time, have made a greater contribution to elucidating the texts than those exegetes who dig around in them unscrupulously and often shamelessly" (my italics). Sebald, *Campo Santo,* 196.

196. Sebald and Hulse, letters dated May 7, 1997 and June 19, 1995, Sebald-Hulse Translation Manuscripts (Letters and Drafts), *2003 M-20, Houghton Library,

Harvard University, Cambridge, Mass. By permission of the Houghton Library, Harvard University.

197. Brigette Frase, "*Vertigo* by W. G. Sebald," *Salon,* June 26, 2000, http://archive.salon.com/books/review/2000/06/26/sebald/ (accessed September 9, 2008).

198. Anthony Lane, *Nobody's Perfect* (New York: Vintage, 2000), 495.

199. W. S. Di Piero, "Another Country," *New York Times,* June 11, 2000, http://www.nytimes.com/books/00/06/11/reviews/000611.11dipiert.html (accessed September 9, 2008).

200. Sebald, *Schwindel.Gefühle,* 163.

201. Kafka, *Briefe 1913–1914,* 278.

202. Sebald, *Schwindel.Gefühle,* 163.

203. Kafka, *Briefe 1913–1914,* 275. Kafka was deeply affected by anecdotes about Grillparzer's failed engagement to Katharina Fröhlich. Max Brod later reported that Kafka was familiar with Grillparzer's autobiographical writings. Moreover, he owned a volume devoted exclusively to the poet's relationship with Fröhlich. See footnote 437 in Wagenbach, *Eine Biographie seiner Jugend,* 217.

204. Kafka, *Briefe 1913–1914,* 278.

205. Sebald, *Schwindel.Gefühle,* 164. It also showcases the author's knowledge of Kafka's life and work. The gesture Sebald attributes to Grillparzer has three sources: Kafka's own "Hunter Gracchus," a 1914 letter to Bauer's friend Grete Bloch, and Laube's biography, from which Kafka extracted the following anecdote: "The engagement had been broken off ages ago . . . One evening G. goes to see the sisters, as he does most evenings; K. is particularly nice to him, partly out of pity he makes her sit on his lap . . . whereupon he discovers, and later writes it down, that he feels utterly indifferent to K., that at the time he had to force himself, that he would have been glad to have experienced the slightest emotion, but that he had no alternative but to keep her on his lap and then after a while to extricate himself again." Franz Kafka, *Briefe 1914–1917,* ed. Hans-Gerd Koch (Frankfurt am Main: S. Fischer, 2005), 57.

206. Kafka, *Briefe 1913–1914,* 278.

207. Ibid., 280.

208. Sebald, *Schwindel.Gefühle,* 165.

209. To reinforce this point, Sebald reproduces the gag photograph taken of Kafka, Ehrenstein, Pick, and Lise Kanzelson at the Prater and centers them in an ovular frame. See Sebald, *Schwindel.Gefühle,* 165; Wagenbach, *Franz Kafka, Bilder aus seinem Leben,* 198.

210. Sebald, *Schwindel.Gefühle,* 165. For more about Dante's role in the novel, see R. J. A. Kilbourn, "Kafka, Nabokov . . . Sebald: Intertextuality and Narratives of Redemption in *Vertigo* and *The Emigrants,*" in *W. G. Sebald: History, Memory, Trauma,* ed. Scott Denham and Mark McCulloh (Berlin: De Gruyter, 2006).

211. Sebald, *Schwindel.Gefühle,* 167.

212. W. G. Sebald, "Das Gesetz der Schande—Macht, Messianismus und Exil in Kafkas *Schloß*," in *Unheimliche Heimat* (Frankfurt am Main: Fischer Taschenbuch Verlag, 1995), 92.

213. Kafka, *Tagebücher 2*, 163.

214. Sebald, *Schwindel. Gefühle*, 168.

215. Ibid., 170.

216. Pawel, *Nightmare of Reason*, 301.

217. Kafka, *Briefe, 1913–1914*, 281; Stach, *Kafka: Die Jahre der Entscheidungen*, 418–19.

218. Sebald, *Schwindel. Gefühle*, 169.

219. Müller, "Kafka und Casanova." Sebald stands by this assertion despite conceding that "there is not even a reference to the Doge's Palace." Sebald, *Schwindel. Gefühle*, 170.

220. Sebald, *Schwindel. Gefühle*, 171.

221. See Hanns Zischler, *Kafka geht ins Kino* (Reinbek bei Hamburg: Rowohlt, 1996), 39–46, 129–34.

222. Kafka, *Briefe 1913–1914*, 295.

223. Sebald, *Schwindel. Gefühle*, 172.

224. Ibid., 174. For more on the historical connotations of representation in the film, see Stefan Andriopoulos, "The Terror of Reproduction: Early Cinema's Ghostly Doubles and the Right to One's Own Image," *New German Critique* 33, no. 3 (2006).

225. Franz Kafka, *Beschreibung eines Kampfes und andere Schriften aus dem Nachlaß*, ed. Hans-Gerd Koch, vol. 5 of *Gesammelte Werke in zwölf Bänden*, 12 vols. (Frankfurt am Main: Fischer Taschenbuch Verlag, 1994), 95; Sebald, *Schwindel. Gefühle*, 174.

226. Klaus Wagenbach, *Franz Kafka, Bilder aus seinem Leben*, 2nd ed. (Berlin: Wagenbach, 1994), 186. Wittingly or unwittingly, Sebald seems to have fallen for a prank of the editor's. No citation follows this caption. Wagenbach removed this picture for his third (and presumably final) expanded edition of the picture book, remarking in small print at the end that "the frequently posed question concerning the Desenzano reception is no longer answerable: the inhabitants have in the meantime dispersed." Wagenbach, *Franz Kafka, Bilder aus seinem Leben*, 253.

227. Sebald, *Schwindel. Gefühle*, 176.

228. Kafka, *Beim Bau*, 182; Sebald, *Schwindel. Gefühle*, 177. The subject of messianism in Kafka had long been a preoccupation of Sebald's critical writings. Some of his arguments were toned down in revision; an earlier English version of an essay on *The Castle* asserts that "the aspirations and weaknesses" of messianism "form a central issue of the Castle novel." Revised in German fifteen years later, this passage reads more modestly: "Das vielleicht komplexeste Beispiel . . . bietet der Messianismus, von dessen Aspirationen und Schwächen Kafka im *Schloß*-Roman zwar

nicht ausdrücklich, aber nichtdestoweniger ausführlich handelt." Sebald, "Gesetz der Schande," 91; W. G. Sebald, "The Law of Ignominy—Authority, Messianism, and Exile in Kafka's *Castle*," in *On Kafka—Semi-Centenary Prespectives*, ed. Franz Kuna (London, 1976), 46.

229. Sebald, *Schwindel. Gefühle*, 178–79.

230. Stach, *Kafka: Die Jahre der Erkenntnis*, 297.

231. Kafka, *Tagebücher 2*, 198.

232. Ibid., 199.

233. "Der Nachen" ("The Dinghy"), for example, was published in 1914 and opens with an admission of this very nature: "I believe I've already described this scenario, but I want to write it one more time." Walser's "Aus Stendhal" ("From Stendhal") appeared a year earlier in *Essays*, a volume that Kafka owned and, according to Max Brod, recited from with gusto. Brod, *Über Franz Kafka*, 294; Robert Walser, *Aufsätze*, ed. Jochen Greven, vol. 3 of *Sämtliche Werke in Einzelausgaben*, 20 vols. (Frankfurt am Main: Suhrkamp, 1985), 102–4; Robert Walser, *Kleine Dichtungen*, ed. Jochen Greven, vol. 4 of *Sämtliche Werke in Einzelausgaben*, 20 vols. (Frankfurt am Main: Suhrkamp, 1985), 12.

234. Sebald, *Schwindel. Gefühle*, 180; Robert Walser, *Geschichten*, ed. Jochen Greven, vol. 2 of *Sämtliche Werke in Einzelausgaben*, 20 vols. (Frankfurt am Main: Suhrkamp, 1985), 71.

235. Stach, *Kafka: Die Jahre der Entscheidungen*, 425.

236. Sebald, *Schwindel. Gefühle*, 48.

237. Sebald, *"Le promeneur solitaire,"* 136–37.

238. Sebald, *Schwindel. Gefühle*, 185.

239. Kafka, *Briefe 1913–1914*, 275.

240. Sebald, *Schwindel. Gefühle*, 186.

241. Kafka, *Das Schloß*, 283.

242. Sebald, *Schwindel. Gefühle*, 188.

243. Kafka, *Beim Bau*, 43. This is a reply that reminds me of the legendary exchange reported by Max Brod: "He: 'We are nihilistic thoughts that came into God's head.' I quoted in support the doctrine of the Gnostics concerning the Demiurge, the evil creator of the world, the doctrine of the world as a sin of God's. 'No,' said Kafka, 'I believe we are not such a radical relapse of God's, only one of his bad moods. He had a bad day.' 'So there would be hope outside our world?' He smiled: 'Plenty of hope—for God—no end of hope—only not for us.'" Brushing aside Brod's Gnostic comparison, Kafka makes a mysterious deity instantly accessible, *allzumenschlich:* God was simply having a bad day. Brod, *Über Franz Kafka*, 71.

244. Kafka, *Beim Bau*, 42–43.

245. Binder, "Zu Kafkas Schaffensweise," 422.

246. Sebald, *Schwindel. Gefühle*, 188.

247. Ibid.

248. Ibid., 189.

249. Kafka, *Briefe 1913–1914*, 108. For a short biography of this man, see Hartmut Binder, *Kafkas Welt: Eine Lebenschronik in Bildern* (Reinbek bei Hamburg: Rowohlt, 2008), 138.

250. Sebald, *Schwindel.Gefühle*, 190.

251. I disagree with Anthony Heilbut, whose *Thomas Mann: Eros and Literature* proposes that Kafka, like Mann, coded homosexual desire in his writings. There is a huge disparity between the number of Mann's allusions to "inversion" and the handful of homoerotic passages in Kafka's journals and letters. For a finer analysis of their significance, see Mark Anderson, "Kafka, Homosexuality and the Aesthetics of 'Male Culture,'" in *Gender and Politics in Austrian Fiction*, ed. Ritchie Robertson and Edward Timms (Edinburgh: Edinburgh University Press, 1996).

252. Franz Kafka, *Letters to Felice*, ed. Jürgen Born and Erich Heller, trans. James Stern and Elisabeth Duckworth (New York: Schocken Books, 1973), 203.

253. Kafka, *Briefe 1913–1914*, 107.

254. This is a literal translation of "Krankheit, die nur im Bett geheilt werden kann." Sebald, *Schwindel.Gefühle*, 190. In an early draft, Michael Hulse rendered this passage as "sickness that can only be cured if we are confined to our bed." Sebald ultimately recast it as "confined to a bed in our sickness." Sebald-Hulse Translation Manuscripts (Letters and Drafts), *2003 M-20, Houghton Library, Harvard University, Cambridge, Mass.; Sebald, *Vertigo*, 167.

255. Kafka, *Beim Bau*, 44. The passage very closely resembles Kafka's earlier short prose work, "Excursion into the Mountains," published in 1912 in *Meditation*. In a different sketch from the same octavo notebook, Kafka again plays with the personification of a word, here, the feminine noun *Ohnmacht;* "Yesterday I was visited by a swoon. She lives in the house next door; I have quite often seen her disappearing through the low gateway, bent down, in the evenings." Kafka, *Beim Bau*, 57.

256. Sebald, *Nach der Natur*, 18.

257. J. M. Coetzee, "Heir of a Dark History," *New York Review of Books* 49, no. 16 (October 24, 2002): 26.

258. Sigmund Freud, *Trauer und Melancholie*, ed. Anna Freud, Edward Bilbring, and Ernst Kris, vol. 10 of *Gesammelte Werke*, 18 vols. (Frankfurt am Main: Fischer Taschenbuch Verlag, 1999), 436.

259. Parks, "The Hunter," 56.

260. Milan Kundera, "Some Notes on Roth's *My Life as a Man* and *The Professor of Desire*," in Milbauer and Watson, *Reading Philip Roth* (1988), 166.

261. Sebald, "Undiscover'd Country," 27.

262. "A good thirty years had gone by since I had last been in W. In the course of that time," remarks the narrator upon his arrival, "many of the localities I associated with it. . . had continually returned in my dreams and daydreams and had become more real to me than they had been then, yet the village itself, I reflected, as I arrived

at that late hour, was more remote from me [*weiter für mich in der Fremde*] than any other place I could conceive of." Sebald, *Schwindel. Gefühle*, 211.

263. Sebald, "Das unentdeckte Land," 78; Sebald, *Schwindel. Gefühle*, 202.

264. Sebald, *Schwindel. Gefühle*, 203–4.

265. Sebald, "Das unentdeckte Land," 92.

266. Ibid., 78–79.

267. Kafka, *Das Schloß*, 9; Sebald, *Schwindel. Gefühle*, 209.

268. Sebald's allusions to the Second World War are accompanied by a quieter one to its predecessor: the narrator recalls a sign on the forester's villa with the inscription "1913." Sebald, *Schwindel. Gefühle*, 210–11.

269. The cast of Schiller's play teems with allusions to other writers and texts important to Sebald's novel, e.g., Maximilian (Winfried Georg Maximilian Sebald), Franz (Kafka, Grillparzer, Werfel), Karl (Robert Walser's *The Robber,* Kafka's *The Man Who Disappeared*), and Amalia (*The Castle*).

270. Heinrich Heine, *Gedichte,* ed. Hans Mayer, vol. 1, *Werke* (Frankfurt am Main.: Insel, 1968), 424.

271. Sebald, *Schwindel. Gefühle*, 289.

272. Ibid., 286–87, 91.

273. Galater's reproach, *He takes everything very seriously,* can here be applied to Shakespeare's contemporary Ben Jonson, who was reportedly unsettled by his rival's freewheeling approach to geography: "Shakespeare," he is said to have told William Drummond, "wanted art," but mistakenly "brought in a number of men saying they had suffered shipwreck in Bohemia, where th[e]r[e] is no sea by some 100 miles." William Shakespeare, *The Winter's Tale: Texts and Contexts,* ed. Stephen Orgel (Oxford: Oxford University Press, 1998), 38.

274. William Shakespeare, *The Winter's Tale,* ed. G. Blackmore Evans, in *The Riverside Shakespeare,* 1590–91.

275. Sebald, *Schwindel. Gefühle*, 291; Sebald, *Vertigo,* 256. Sebald's English translation maintains this distortion, despite the slight change of meaning in the last line.

276. "Kafka deliberately avoided introducing the brighter green of organic nature into his landscape as a source of comfort." Sebald, "Undiscover'd Country," 78.

277. Shakespeare, *Winter's Tale,* 1586.

278. Kafka composed the first of the Gracchus fragments in January 1917; "A Country Doctor" was completed between December and January. See Malcolm Pasley and Klaus Wagenbach, "Datierung Sämtlicher Texte Franz Kafkas," in *Kafka-Symposion* (Munich: Deutscher Taschenbuch Verlag, 1969), 63–65; Stach, *Kafka: Die Jahre der Erkenntnis,* 171.

279. I have amended the Muir translation slightly to conform with verb tenses in the original. Kafka, *Ein Landarzt,* 204.

280. Sebald, *Schwindel. Gefühle*, 224.

281. This is a fitting metaphor for the sudden return of repressed childhood memories experienced by so many of Sebald's protagonists (e.g., Dr. Henry Selwyn and Paul Bereyter in *The Emigrants,* or Jacques Austerlitz in *Austerlitz*). In each case, a long-forgotten trauma, or "wound," unexpectedly comes to light.

282. Sebald, *Schwindel.Gefühle,* 222, 24. "Sleep is the brother of death and is assiduously cultivated by the inhabitants of the Castle," writes Sebald of the bedbound functionaries in Kafka's novel; see Sebald, "Das unentdeckte Land," 82.

283. Sebald, *Schwindel.Gefühle,* 190–91. Sebald revised Hulse's initial rendering of this line, "confined to a bed in our sickness." Sebald-Hulse Translation Manuscripts (Letters and Drafts), *2003 M-20, Houghton Library, Harvard University, Cambridge, Mass.

284. Sebald, *Schwindel.Gefühle,* 216, 36, 93.

285. Ibid., 260.

286. Wagenbach, *Franz Kafka, Bilder aus seinem Leben,* 3rd ed., 54. On page 47 of the 1st edition of *Pictures* owned by Sebald (one of the 1,255 volumes from Sebald's library acquired by the German Literary Archives in Marbach), Wagenbach ventures that Löwy's model might have been called the *Odradek.* He amended this claim for a later edition.

287. Sebald, *Schwindel.Gefühle,* 261, 62.

288. Kafka, *Ein Landarzt,* 205. Sebald refers to this passage in his 1985 "To the Edge of Nature: Essay on Stifter": "And if Stifter was really a priest who once again celebrated the liturgy of an absolute order, he secretly remained quite occupied, like the poor clergyman from Kafka's *Country Doctor,* with the unraveling of his vestments." Sebald, *Beschreibung,* 18.

289. Kafka, *Ein Landarzt,* 206.

290. Excerpted from "W. G. Sebald and the Politics of Exposure," Santner's keynote address for "Approaching W. G. Sebald," a graduate symposium sponsored by the German Department at Yale University, March 26–27, 2004. See also Eric L. Santner, *On Creaturely Life: Rilke, Benjamin, Sebald* (Chicago: University of Chicago Press, 2006), xx, 81.

291. Binder, *Kafka-Kommentar zu sämtlichen Erzählungen,* 194.

292. Kafka, *Beim Bau,* 14.

293. The Arden Forest was the birthplace of Mary Arden, Shakespeare's mother. The playwright set his *As You Like It* there. And the scene portrayed in the Alpenrose oleograph—a wild boar frightens a group of hunters—evokes *Venus and Adonis,* another history of "madness most discreet."

294. Sebald, *Schwindel.Gefühle,* 252–53.

295. Kafka, *Beim Bau,* 13.

296. Sebald, *Schwindel.Gefühle,* 254.

297. Ibid.

298. Quoted in Santner, *On Creaturely Life,* 102.

299. Kafka, *Beim Bau*, 13. The author notes that the hundred or so books they find belonging to Mathild's library would later come into his possession. His remark concerning their great importance can be connected to Sebald's own work: the "accounts of expeditions to the polar regions" alludes to Georg Wilhelm Steller, subject of the second poem in *After Nature*. The narrator is also astonished to find a copy of Lily Braun's *Memoires of a Socialist* in the collection; Kafka gifted this book to Felice Bauer and enthused about it to both family and friends. See Kafka, *Briefe 1914–1917*, 134, 98; and Kafka, *Briefe 1902–1924*, 282.

300. Sebald, *Schwindel. Gefühle*, 257.

301. Michael Hulse translates it as *chasseur*, an appropriate choice given Sebald's application of related words in different languages throughout the work (e.g., hunter/*Jäger*/*chasseur*/*cacciatore*; jackdaw/*kavka*/*gracchio*/*Dohle*).

302. Sebald, *Schwindel. Gefühle*, 259–60.

303. Kafka, *Beim Bau*, 13.

304. Sebald, *Schwindel. Gefühle*, 269.

305. Kafka, *Beim Bau*, 40; Sebald, *Schwindel. Gefühle*, 280.

306. Sebald, "Das unentdeckte Land," 81. Sebald omitted this passage from his English version.

307. Sebald, *Schwindel. Gefühle*, 281.

308. Ibid., 240, 48, 36.

309. Bloom, *Ruin the Sacred Truths*, 173.

310. The figure of literary paternity is also at work in the title, a literal translation of which would be "The Cares of a Housefather." Kafka, *Ein Landarzt*, 223.

311. Similar to Odradek, the younger "Sebald" of "Il Ritorno" "lurks by turns in the garret, the stairway, the lobbies, the entry hall." See Kafka, *Ein Landarzt*, 223; Sebald, "Das unentdeckte Land," 92.

312. Quoted in Kafka, *Nachgelassene Schriften und Fragmente I: Apparatband*, 272.

313. Sebald, *Schwindel. Gefühle*, 296.

Chapter 4

1. Christopher Lehmann-Haupt, review of *Life & Times of Michael K*, by J. M. Coetzee, *New York Times*, December 6, 1983, C22.

2. David Attwell, *J. M. Coetzee: South Africa and the Politics of Writing* (Berkeley and Los Angeles: University of California Press, 1993), 101.

3. *Dusklands* consists of two novellas. Eugene Dawn, narrator of "The Vietnam Project," paraphrases Kafka's remark that books should strike the frozen sea inside their readers like an axe. "The Narrative of Jacobus Coetzee" alludes delicately to *The Castle*. J. M. Coetzee, *Dusklands* (New York: Penguin Books, 1985), 14, 110–11.

4. Shades of "The Great Wall of China" and "An Imperial Message" are detectable in Coetzee's characterization of communication between the Empire's isolated outposts and its distant center.

5. See especially Foe's parable of the chaplain and condemned thief. His recounting of this tale to Susan Barton and their subsequent interpretative sparring mimics the encounter between the prison chaplain and Josef K.—another condemned prisoner—in the cathedral chapter of *The Trial*. J. M. Coetzee, *Foe* (New York: Penguin Books, 1987), 123–24, 226–33.

6. The novel also quotes directly from Kafka's *The Trial*, ending (for example) with the same phrase. "Yes . . . it is humiliating," remarks David Lurie. "Perhaps that is what I must learn to accept. To start at ground level. With nothing. . . . No cards, no weapons, no property, no rights, no dignity. . . . Yes, like a dog." "Like a dog!" utters the dying Josef K.; "it seemed as though the shame was to outlive him." J. M. Coetzee, *Disgrace* (New York: Viking, 1999), 205; Kafka, *Der Proceß*, 241.

7. Coetzee's essays on Robert Musil, Joseph Roth, Sándor Márai, Rainer Maria Rilke, and Italo Svevo have all appeared in the *New York Review of Books* over the past decade. Kafka was familiar with works by Hugo von Hofmannsthal ("Letter to Lord Chandos," "Conversation About Poetry") and Robert Walser (*Jakob von Gunten, Essays*), authors who have enjoyed rather limited success in English.

8. "Wo die Dunkelheit den Strick zuzieht," Sebald's essay on Thomas Bernhard is a deeply perceptive analysis of that author and his early fictions. See *Die Beschreibung des Unglücks*, 103–14.

9. Bloom, *Anxiety of Influence*, 86.

10. J. M. Coetzee and David Attwell, *Doubling the Point: Essays and Interviews* (Cambridge, Mass.: Harvard University Press, 1992), 1, 20. Coetzee had taught at the State University of New York in Buffalo for three years (1968–71), but returned to South Africa after his visa was not renewed. See J. M. Coetzee, "Samuel Beckett's *Lessness:* An Exercise in Decomposition," *Computers and the Humanities* 7, no. 4 (1973); John Leonard, "Beckett Safe from Computers," *New York Times Book Review,* August 19, 1973.

11. Coetzee and Attwell, *Doubling the Point,* 20.

12. Ibid., 25.

13. Ibid., 199.

14. "I am intensely uncomfortable with questions," Coetzee remarks in the interview, "that call upon me to *answer for* (in two senses) my novels, and my responses are often taken as evasive. To defend against that judgment I suppose I should, as a preliminary step, explain my difficulties, explain myself, spell out my position with regard to *answering for.* But my difficulty is precisely with the project of stating positions, taking positions." I believe this extraordinary statement highly pertinent to all of Coetzee's writing, creative and otherwise. For more on the subject, see his discussion of Erasmus in *Giving Offense.* J. M. Coetzee, *Giv-*

ing *Offense: Essays on Censorship* (Chicago: University of Chicago Press, 1996), ix, 83–103; Coetzee and Attwell, *Doubling the Point*, 205.

15. Coetzee and Attwell, *Doubling the Point*, 198. A crisis Coetzee re-creates through his protagonists'—e.g., Magda (*In the Heart of the Country*), Elizabeth Cullen (*Age of Iron*), David Lurie (*Disgrace*), and most recently, C (*Diary of a Bad Year*)—exasperation before the limits of English.

16. Derek Attridge, *J. M. Coetzee and the Ethics of Reading: Literature in the Event* (Chicago: University of Chicago Press, 2004), 47. Derek Attridge employs this phrase in a different but analogous context, namely to describe the Magistrate's dreams in *Waiting for the Barbarians*.

17. J. M. Coetzee, "Time, Tense, and Aspect in Kafka's 'The Burrow,'" in Coetzee and Attwell, *Doubling the Point*, 211.

18. Ibid., 231.

19. Kafka, *Das Ehepaar*, 165.

20. Coetzee, "Time, Tense, and Aspect," 210.

21. Compare "A Little Woman," "Investigations of a Dog," and "Josephine the Singer, or the Mouse Folk"—other works of Kafka composed between 1923 and early 1924 that share the same density of narrative reflectiveness.

22. I have slighted amended the Muirs' translation; "in the bowels of the earth" dodges Kafka's literal juxtaposition of dangers faced from without (*äußern*) and from within (*im Innern*). Kafka, *Das Ehepaar*, 167.

23. Quoted in Coetzee, "Time, Tense, and Aspect"; 212, Kafka, *Das Ehepaar*, 471–73.

24. In another instance of a concerted effort not to abuse the text, Coetzee acknowledges that he has grounded his argument mainly on "connotations": "Kafka does not unequivocally provoke this contradiction in the passages I have quoted," he writes. "Nevertheless . . . the verbs carry connotations of the impulsive, the uncontrollable, the unpredictable, and therefore sit uneasily in a narratorial framework of iterated time." Coetzee, "Time, Tense, and Aspect," 213.

25. Ibid.

26. Ibid., 214.

27. Ibid., 215; Franz Kafka, *Collected Stories*, trans. Edward Muir and Willa Muir (New York: Everyman's Library, 1993), 476–80; Kafka, *Das Ehepaar*, 176–81.

28. Coetzee, "Time, Tense, and Aspect," 216.

29. Ibid.

30. Ibid., 217.

31. Ibid., 218.

32. Ibid.; the original ends mid-sentence: "Aber alles blieb unverändert, das"; see Kafka, *Das Ehepaar*, 208.

33. *Ein Landarzt* is "A Country Doctor." Coetzee, "Time, Tense, and Aspect," 220; Dorrit Cohn, "Kafka's Eternal Present: Narrative Tense in 'Ein Landarzt' and

Other First-Person Stories," *PMLA: Publications of the Modern Language Association of America* 83, no. 1 (1968).

34. Quoted in Coetzee, "Time, Tense, and Aspect," 219.

35. Kafka, *Beim Bau*, 229.

36. Ibid., 231.

37. Quoted in Coetzee, "Time, Tense, and Aspect," 221; Heinrich Henel, "Das Ende von Kafkas 'Der Bau,'" *Germanisch-Romanische Monatsschrift*, no. 22 (1972).

38. Coetzee, "Time, Tense, and Aspect," 221. In fairness to Henel, "Das Ende von Kafkas 'Der Bau'" (literally, "The End of Kafka's 'The Burrow'") concerns itself not with Kafka's manipulation of tense—the focus of Cohn's analysis—but with the story's ending.

39. Coetzee, "Time, Tense, and Aspect," 221–22.

40. Ibid., 222.

41. Ibid., 223.

42. Attridge, *Ethics of Reading*, 40; Coetzee, "Time, Tense, and Aspect," 224.

43. Coetzee, "Time, Tense, and Aspect," 224.

44. Ibid., 225.

45. Ibid.

46. Ibid., 227.

47. Coetzee later accedes to Attwell's suggestion that this "horror of chronicity" may have evolved as a response to the stagnancy of South African history during their lifetimes, when laws were passed to prevent so-called normal development in order to freeze time in the colonial, apartheid past. He adds, however, that this horror "is also a horror of death . . . It is not just time as history that threatens to engulf one: it is time itself, time as death." This second reply seems more relevant to a reading of "The Burrow"—a story that the terminally ill Kafka composed during the terrible winter of 1923–24 in Berlin. J. M. Coetzee, "Interview with David Attwell (Kafka)," in Coetzee and Attwell, *Doubling the Point*, 203, 209.

48. Coetzee, "Time, Tense, and Aspect," 229.

49. The relevance of intensity to his own later narratives is direct. "I work on a writer like Kafka," Coetzee tells Attwell in the interview that precedes the essay's republication in *Doubling the Point*, "because he opens for me, or opens me to, moments of analytic intensity" (199). Analogous moments of piercing analysis aided by syntactic strategies and calculations of verb-tense resound in his fiction, from the early *In the Heart of the Country* (1977) through more recent publications, *Disgrace* (1999), *Youth: Scenes from a Provincial Life II* (2002), and *Elizabeth Costello* (2003).

50. Coetzee, "Time, Tense, and Aspect," 226.

51. Quoted ibid., 219, 30.

52. "The most we can say," Coetzee corrects, "is that at certain points in the text where we would expect the one form we encounter the other, and vice versa. If the

distinction were indeed effaced, if the durative and singular forms were used inter-changeably, the result would very probably be nonsense." Ibid., 220.

53. Kafka composed them between October 1917 and February 1918, while con-valescing from the hemorrhage that announced his tuberculosis. "Late in 1920," writes Malcolm Pasley, "Kafka copied out these aphorisms on separate num-bered sheets; he then made a further fair copy, in typescript, on which this text is based. It seems likely that he considered publication." Malcolm Pasley, *Great Wall of China*, xvi.

54. Kafka, *Beim Bau*, 228, 163. Translated by Ernst Kaiser and Eithne Wilkins.

55. "From a certain point on, there is no more turning back. This is the point to be reached." Translated by Malcolm Pasley (Kafka, *Beim Bau*, 229, 164; quoted in Coetzee, "Time, Tense, and Aspect," 231).

56. Quoted in Coetzee, "Time, Tense, and Aspect," 231; Franz Kafka, *Hochzeits-vorbereitungen auf dem Lande*, ed. Max Brod, vol. 6 of *Gesammelte Werke*, 8 vols. (Frankfurt am Main: Fischer Taschenbuch Verlag, 1998), 54.

57. Coetzee, "Time, Tense, and Aspect," 231.

58. For the excerpt in question, see the reference to page 34, lines 10–12, in Franz Kafka, *Nachgelassene Schriften und Fragmente II: Apparatband*, ed. Hans-Gerd Koch, vol. 12 of *Kritische Ausgabe in 15 Bänden*, 15 vols. (Frankfurt am Main: Fischer Taschenbuch Verlag, 2002), 201.

59. Coetzee, "Time, Tense, and Aspect," 231.

60. Ibid., 226.

61. Ibid., 417.

62. The most compelling attempt I know is Ritchie Robertson's analysis of "the indestructible" in "Reflections from a Damaged Life: The Zürau Aphorisms, 1917–1918." See Robertson, *Kafka: Judaism, Politics, and Literature*, 185–217. Har-old Bloom expands on Robertson's idea in the chapter entitled "Kafka: Canonical Patience and 'Indestructibility'" in Bloom, *Western Canon*, 416–30.

63. Benjamin, *Aufsätze, Essays, Vorträge*, 425.

64. J. M. Coetzee, "He and His Man" (2003). See, for example, Defoe's pref-ace to volume 3, *Serious Reflections During the Life and Surprising Adventures of Robinson Crusoe: With His Vision of the Angelic World* (1720), where the book's hero asserts that he and he alone is author of the novel: "I, Robinson Crusoe . . . do affirm that the story, though allegorical, is historical . . . Farther, that there is a man alive, and well known too, the actions of whose life are the just subject of these volumes, and to whom all or most part of the story most directly alludes; this may be depended upon for truth, and to this I set my name." In his essay on Defoe, Coetzee rates this "bravado worthy of Cervantes"—an apt comparison, since "Crusoe" alludes twice to this precursor in his preface. Coetzee, *Stranger Shores*, 18; Daniel Defoe, *Serious Reflections During the Life and Surprising Adven-tures of Robinson Crusoe: With His Vision of the Angelic World*, ed. G. H. Maynadier, vol. 3 of *The Works of Daniel Defoe*, 16 vols. (Boston: D. Nickerson, 1903), ix–x.

65. Elizabeth Costello responds to this proposition circuitously in the separately published lesson, "As a Woman Grows Older." When son John urges her to stay with his family in the United States "in the spirit of paradox" if for no other reason, Costello declines: "As for paradox, the first lesson of paradox, in my experience, is not to rely on paradox. If you rely on paradox, paradox will let you down." J. M. Coetzee, "As a Woman Grows Older," *New York Review of Books* 51, no. 1 (January 15, 2004).

66. Kafka, *Das Ehepaar*, 131–32.

67. Coetzee, *Elizabeth Costello*, 1. For an acute analysis of the relation between the figurative and the literal in this parable, see Michael Wood, "Kafka's China and the Parable of Parables," *Philosophy and Literature* 20, no. 2 (October 1996): 334.

68. J. M. Coetzee, "What Is Realism?" *Salmagundi*, no. 114–15 (1997): 60-81.

69. Coetzee, *Elizabeth Costello*, 1.

70. Attridge, *Ethics of Reading*, 201. "Asked if he regarded himself as a 'metaphysical novelist' who also gives the reader 'all the enjoyment of reading a novel,' [Coetzee] replied . . . 'All attempts to eradicate storytelling from the novel are doomed . . . and here I think particularly of the Nouveau Roman . . . I would regard these as philosophical experiments, immensely important for philosophical experiment with the nature of fiction, but experiments from which we finally have to retreat . . . if we are ever going to go back to the novel, go back to storytelling." Dick Penner, *Countries of the Mind: The Fiction of J. M. Coetzee* (New York: Greenwood, 1989), 130.

71. Coetzee, *Elizabeth Costello*, 3–4.

72. Ibid., 4; Virginia Woolf, "Robinson Crusoe," in *The Common Reader, Second Series* (London: Hogarth, 1965), 57–58.

73. Coetzee, *Stranger Shores*, 20.

74. "Defoe is a realist," Coetzee states early in his essay on *Robinson Crusoe*, "in that he is an empiricist, and empiricism is one of the tenets of the realist novel." Ibid., 19.

75. Namely, when he silently acknowledges that the woman with whom he has just spent the night values him chiefly for his relation to his mother, whose fiction she admires. He therefore likens himself to "[a] toenail clipping, that one steals and wraps in a tissue and takes away, for one's own purposes." Coetzee, *Elizabeth Costello*, 30; Virginia Woolf, *The Voyage Out* (San Diego, Calif.: Harcourt Brace, 1948), 107.

76. Coetzee, *Elizabeth Costello*, 24.

77. Ibid., 33.

78. Ibid., 9.

79. Coetzee, *Stranger Shores*, 20.

80. Coetzee, *Elizabeth Costello*, 1. Critics have observed parallels between Costello's novel, which reimagines Joyce, and Coetzee's own *Foe*, which incorporates and corrects elements from Defoe's *Robinson Crusoe, Roxana*, and "A True Revela-

tion of the Apparition of One Mrs Veal." For a postcolonial analysis of this intertextuality, see "The Maze of Doubting" in Dominic Head, *J. M. Coetzee* (Cambridge, Eng.: Cambridge University Press, 1997), 112–28.

81. Coetzee, *Elizabeth Costello*, 5.

82. Ibid., 11.

83. "Can he possibly die?" Kafka's paterfamilias asks: "Am I to suppose, then, that he will always be rolling down the stairs, with ends of thread trailing after him, right before the feet of my children, and my children's children? He does no harm to anyone that one can see; but the idea that he is likely to survive me I find almost painful." Kafka, *Ein Landarzt*, 223. See "Die Sorge des Hausvaters" in Pasley, "Drei literarische Mystifikationen Kafkas," 21–24.

84. Coetzee, *Elizabeth Costello*, 12.

85. Ibid., 13.

86. Ibid., 26.

87. Ibid., 15.

88. Ibid., 28.

89. Ibid., 30.

90. Ibid., 34.

91. Ibid., 28, 31.

92. Ibid., 22–23. Costello wants to be evaluated vis-à-vis her masters (Woolf, Joyce) and therefore has little taste for dubious accolades such as *best Australian novelist* or *leading woman writer*. The exchange I quote is of course pertinent to contemporary discourse on Coetzee as a white African author, and runs parallel to the frustrations of Jewish (Roth, Bellow, Malamud) and African-American (Ellison, Baldwin, Morrison) artists in the United States whose work is frequently pigeonholed into ethnic sub-categorizations.

93. Ibid., 27. The words are Macbeth's, spoken in act 2, scene 2: "Methought I heard a voice cry, 'Sleep no more!/Macbeth does murther sleep'—the innocent sleep,/Sleep that knits up the ravell'd sleave of care,/The death of each day's life, sore labor's bath,/Balm of hurt minds, great nature's second course,/Chief nourisher in life's feast." William Shakespeare, *The Tragedy of Macbeth*, ed. G. Blackmore Evans, in *The Riverside Shakespeare*, 1320.

94. Lev Shestov, *Chekhov, and Other Essays*, ed. Sidney Monas (Ann Arbor: University of Michigan Press, 1966), 36.

95. Ibid., 28.

96. Judith Schulevitz, "Author Tour," *New York Times*, October 26, 2003.

97. Coetzee, *Elizabeth Costello*, 1.

98. Ibid., 2; J. M. Coetzee, *The Lives of Animals* (London: Profile Books, 2001), 11; Coetzee, "What Is Realism?" 60.

99. Attridge, *Ethics of Reading*, 194.

100. Coetzee, *Elizabeth Costello*, 28; Coetzee, "What Is Realism?" 77.

101. Coetzee, "What Is Realism?" 77.

102. Nor is Coetzee. There was much ado concerning the uncertainty of his middle name—it had appeared in print as Marie, Maxwell, and Michael—after he was awarded the Nobel. ("Maxwell" appears in the official announcement.)

103. See Coetzee, *Lives of Animals*, 60–61.

104. Kafka, *Das Schloß*, 14.

105. Ibid., 55.

106. J. M. Coetzee, "Translating Kafka," in *Stranger Shores*, 82–83. As already stated in my second chapter, Kafka changed *The Castle* from a first-person to a third-person narrative (*I* to *K.*) during the writing of this scene. Interestingly enough, Coetzee's revision of "What Is Realism?" enacts a distancing pronominal shift as well. In "Realism," he switches the first-person singular to the first-person plural (*I* to *we*): "There is a scene in the restaurant, mainly dialogue, which I will skip" (64), hence becomes "There is a scene in the restaurant, mainly dialogue, which we will skip." See Coetzee, *Elizabeth Costello*, 7; Coetzee, "What Is Realism?" 64.

107. Coetzee, "Interview with David Attwell (Kafka)," 198–99. Both Derek Attridge and Andrew Mars-Jones have addressed the significance of grace in Coetzee's work. See "Age of Bronze, State of Grace" in Attridge, *Ethics of Reading*, 162–91; and Andrew Mars-Jones, "It's Very Novel, but Is It Actually a Novel?" *The Observer*, September 14, 2003.

108. Coetzee, *Elizabeth Costello*, 16; Kafka, *Ein Landarzt*, 234.

109. Coetzee, *Elizabeth Costello*, 16.

110. Ibid., 17.

111. Ibid., 17–18. This passage does not appear in Coetzee's first version of "Realism." Throughout the novel, Costello constantly reiterates her own—and a more general, collective—need for salvation. It is fitting that the last words of *Elizabeth Costello*'s are "Save us."

112. Ibid., 18.

113. Ibid., 19.

114. For more on the relation between the two, see "Realism, Modernism, and the Aesthetics of Interruption"—a topic highly relevant to strategies deployed by Coetzee in this chapter—in Astradur Eysteinsson's *The Concept of Modernism* (179–241).

115. Coetzee, *Elizabeth Costello*, 19–20. See Hugo von Hofmannsthal, *The Lord Chandos Letter*, trans. Joel Rotenberg (New York: New York Review Books, 2005).

116. Coetzee, *Elizabeth Costello*, 20.

117. Ibid., 25.

118. Ibid., 31–32.

119. Ibid., 4.

120. Ibid., 32.

121. Kafka, *Ein Landarzt*, 245.

122. As when he interrupts Costello's first lecture, "What Is Realism?" with

these words: "Elizabeth Costello proceeds to reflect on the transience of fame. We skip ahead." Coetzee, *Elizabeth Costello*, 17. In the second part of "The Lives of Animals," her son John, the chapter's principal consciousness, misses her talk and arrives in mid-discussion.

123. Ibid., 188.

124. Friedrich Hölderlin, *Selected Poems and Fragments*, ed. Jeremy Adler, trans. Michael Hamburger (London: Penguin, 1998), 156.

125. Coetzee, *Elizabeth Costello*, 14.

126. "There is first of all the problem of the opening," writes Coetzee: "namely, how to get us from where we are, which is, as yet, nowhere, to the far bank" (ibid., 1).

127. According to the notion of violation as established by Samuel Beckett in his searing critique of Eduard Mörike's treatment of Mozart "as a compound of Horace Skimpole and Wagner in half-hose." See "Schwabenstreich: Mozart on the Way to Prague" in Beckett, *Disjecta: Miscellaneous Writings and a Dramatic Fragment*, ed. Ruby Cohn (New York: Grove, 1984), 62.

128. Kafka, *Ein Landarzt*, 211.

129. Ibid., 212.

130. Coetzee, *Elizabeth Costello*, 193.

131. Elizabeth Costello receives a reply equally ambiguous in her final confrontation with the guard. To her query of whether she stands a chance of being "deemed good enough to pass," the man shrugs and then replies: "We all stand a chance." Ibid., 224; Kafka, *Ein Landarzt*, 211.

132. Coetzee, *Elizabeth Costello*, 194.

133. Ibid., 225; Kafka, *Ein Landarzt*, 212.

134. Frederick Robert Karl, *Franz Kafka, Representative Man* (New York: Ticknor and Fields, 1991), 272.

135. Kafka, *Der Proceß*, 233.

136. Coetzee, *Elizabeth Costello*, 19.

137. J. M. Coetzee, "Homage," *Threepenny Review*, Spring 1993, 6–7.

138. Coetzee, "Translating Kafka," 81.

139. Coetzee, "Homage," 7. Dryness has always been well-suited to Coetzee's subject (and perhaps, his temperament). Little surprise, then, that the Polish poet turns up in *Youth* and as the subject of an essay in *Giving Offense*.

140. Kafka, *Ein Landarzt*, 211.

141. Coetzee, *Elizabeth Costello*, 193.

142. This is a strategy that Kafka emulated during his lifelong "apprenticeship" to Flaubert. Compare, for example, the opening of the Gracchus fragment with *Sentimental Education, Bouvard and Pécuchet*, or any one of the *Three Stories*.

143. Coetzee, "Interview with David Attwell (Kafka)," 198; James Wood, "A Frog's Life," *London Review of Books* 25, no. 20 (2003).

144. Coetzee, *Elizabeth Costello*, 194.

145. Andrew Riemer, "A Marriage of One," *Sydney Morning Herald,* September 13–14, 2003, 14.

146. Shimon Sandbank neatly summarizes this appellation as an indicator for "the thematics of alienation and anxiety, the décor of labyrinthine corridors and offices, the prophecies of totalitarianism." See Sandbank, *After Kafka: The Influence of Kafka's Fiction* (Athens: University of Georgia Press), 11.

147. Coetzee, *Elizabeth Costello,* 194.

148. Daniel Defoe, *Robinson Crusoe,* ed. John Richetti (New York: Penguin, 2003), 39. Costello's fondness for this line seems to have been inspired by a reading of Virginia Woolf's essay on *Robinson Crusoe,* which singles out this passage (and the kind of realism it represents) for praise.

149. Coetzee, *Elizabeth Costello,* 195. Compare Coetzee's formulation in this response to a question of David Attwell's about Kafka's impact on *Life & Times of Michael K:* "There is no monopoly on the letter K; or to put it another way, it is as much possible to center the universe on the town of Prince Albert in the Cape Province as on Prague. *Equally*—and the moment in history has perhaps come at which this must be said—it is as much possible to center the universe on Prague as on Prince Albert. Being an out-of-work gardener in Africa in the late twentieth century is no *less,* but also no *more,* central a fate than being a clerk in Hapsburg Central Europe." Coetzee, "Interview with David Attwell (Kafka)," 199.

150. Coetzee, *Elizabeth Costello,* 196.

151. Kafka, *Ein Landarzt,* 212.

152. Coetzee, *Elizabeth Costello,* 197–98.

153. Ibid., 3.

154. Kafka, *Der Proceß,* 49.

155. Coetzee, *Elizabeth Costello,* 199.

156. Ibid.

157. Czesław Miłosz, *New and Collected Poems, 1931–2001* (New York: Ecco, 2003), 343.

158. Coetzee, *Elizabeth Costello,* 30.

159. Miłosz, *New and Collected Poems,* 240–41.

160. Coetzee, *Elizabeth Costello,* 173.

161. Costello's "thesis"—"that writing itself, as a form of moral adventurousness, has the potential to be dangerous" (162)—reiterates the comments of Miłosz recorded in an interview with Aleksander Fiut: "I just think that various demons or beings inhabit me; they take me over, and I regret it afterward" (*Conversations with Czesław Miłosz,* 322).

162. Coetzee, "Interview with David Attwell (Kafka)," 199.

163. Coetzee, *Giving Offense,* 184.

164. Coetzee, *Elizabeth Costello,* 200; Coetzee, "Translating Kafka," 80.

165. Coetzee, *Elizabeth Costello,* 200.

166. John Keats, *The Letters of John Keats, Volume 1: 1814–1818,* ed. Hyder

Edward Rollins, vol. 1 of *The Letters of John Keats, 1814–1821,* 2 vols. (Cambridge, Eng.: Cambridge University Press, 1958). Costello has earlier referred to Keats as "the great advocate of blank receptiveness." In *Youth,* Coetzee describes the effect of Ezra Pound and T. S. Eliot on his prior tastes: "How he could once have been so infatuated with Keats as to write Keatsian sonnets he cannot comprehend. Keats is like watermelon, soft and sweet and crimson, whereas poetry should be hard and clear like a flame. Reading half a dozen pages of Keats is like yielding to seduction." Coetzee, *Elizabeth Costello,* 4; J. M. Coetzee, *Youth* (London: Secker and Warburg, 2002), 21.

167. Coetzee, *Elizabeth Costello,* 201.

168. Kafka, *Ein Landarzt,* 222.

169. Walter Benjamin, *Benjamin über Kafka: Texte, Briefzeugnisse, Aufzeichnungen,* ed. Hermann Schweppenhäuser, (Frankfurt am Main: Suhrkamp, 1981), 86.

170. Coetzee, *Elizabeth Costello,* 204.

171. Ibid., 206. Coetzee wrote about Joseph Roth for the *New York Review of Books,* well before *Elizabeth Costello*'s publication. A version of "The Emperor of Nostalgia" appears in J. M. Coetzee, *Inner Workings: Essays 2000–2005* (London: Harvill Secker, 2007), 79–93.

172. Coetzee, *Elizabeth Costello,* 209.

173. Ibid.

174. A phenomenon duly noted by several critics. See John Banville, "Being and Nothingness," *The Nation,* November 3, 2003; John Bayley, "Dispensing with Realism, We Can See Reality," *Los Angeles Times Book Review,* November 22, 2003; Anita Brookner, "A Brave Stance to Take," *The Spectator,* September 13, 2003; and Siddhartha Deb, "Mind into Matter," *Boston Globe,* October 26, 2003.

175. Janet Maslin, "The Mockery Can Still Sting with a Target in the Mirror," *New York Times,* October 21, 2003.

176. Coetzee, *Elizabeth Costello,* 214. Dostoevsky's grappling with the suffering of children was alluded to earlier in the chapter (202, 204). Costello is quoting from *The Brothers Karamazov* here, but Coetzee has other texts in mind as well ("The Dream of a Ridiculous Man," *The Insulted and the Injured, The Idiot,* and *The Demons*), all of which contain variations on the same issue. Coetzee has devoted many pages to Dostoevsky: two essays (one in *Doubling the Point,* the other in *Stranger Shores*), a biographical novel (*The Master of Petersburg*), and *Diary of a Bad Year* (2007), a section of which, "On Dostoevsky," contains this extravagant praise: "*Slava, Fyodor Michailovich! May your name resound forever in the halls of fame!*" J. M. Coetzee, *Diary of a Bad Year* (London: Harvill Secker, 2007), 226.

177. Bloom, *Agon,* 81.

178. Coetzee, *Elizabeth Costello,* 214–15.

179. Costello probably has this story in mind when she argues, in "Realism," that animals like Red Peter do not possess a right to privacy: "Not if they are in a

zoo, . . . not if they are on show. Once you are on show, you have no private life." Ibid., 33.

180. Coetzee implies that this episode is fictional when one of the judges remarks that "it says nothing here, in your docket, about a childhood on the Dulgannon. . . . Is childhood on the Dulgannon," he continues, "another of your stories, Mrs Costello? Along with the frogs and the rain from heaven?" Ibid., 217–18.

181. Ibid., 221.

182. "The purpose of poetry is to remind us/how difficult it is to remain just one person,/for our house is open, there are no keys in the doors,/and invisible guests come in and out at will."

183. Coetzee, *Elizabeth Costello*, 223. Compare this scene from "Report to an Academy": "I have often watched, before my turn came on, a couple of acrobats performing on trapezes high in the roof. They swung themselves, they rocked to and fro, they sprang into the air, they floated into each other's arms, one hung by the hair from the teeth of the other. 'And that too is human freedom,' I thought, 'self-controlled movement.' What a mockery of holy Mother Nature! Were the apes to see such a spectacle, no theater walls could stand the shock of their laughter." Kafka, *Ein Landarzt*, 239.

184. Coetzee, *Elizabeth Costello*, 225.

185. Ibid., 222.

186. Coetzee complicates this scene of revelation with a shadowy conditional: "when she is truly herself." In doing so, he evades easy apotheosis through qualification—a device frequently employed by Kafka.

187. John Keats, *Poetical Works of John Keats,* ed. H. W. Garrod (Oxford: Clarendon, 1958), 273.

Bibliography

Translations of Kafka

Translations of Kafka originate from the editions listed below unless otherwise noted. I have used Malcolm Pasley's versions of "The Hunter Gracchus" and "Eleven Sons."

Kafka, Franz. *The Blue Octavo Notebooks.* Translated by Ernst Kaiser and Eithne Wilkins. Edited by Max Brod. Cambridge, Mass.: Exact Change, 1991.

————. *The Castle.* Translated by Mark Harman. New York: Schocken, 1998.

————. *Collected Stories.* Translated by Edward Muir and Willa Muir. New York: Everyman's Library, 1993.

————. *The Diaries, 1910–1923.* Translated by Joseph Kresh. Edited by Max Brod. New York: Schocken, 1976.

————. *Franz Kafka: The Office Writings.* Edited by Stanley Corngold, Jack Greenberg, and Benno Wagner. Princeton, N.J.: Princeton University Press, 2008.

————. *The Great Wall of China and Other Short Works.* Translated and edited by Malcolm Pasley. London: Penguin, 1991.

————. *Letters to Felice.* Translated by James Stern and Elisabeth Duckworth. Edited by Jürgen Born and Erich Heller. New York: Schocken, 1973.

————. *Letters to Friends, Family, and Editors.* Translated by Richard Winston and Clara Winston. Edited by Max Brod, Beverly Colman, Nahum N. Glatzer, Christopher J. Kuppig, and Wolfgang Sauerlander. New York: Schocken, 1987.

————. *Letters to Milena.* Translated by Philip Boehm. New York: Schocken, 1990.

————. *Letters to Ottla and the Family.* Edited by Nahum N. Glatzer. New York: Schocken, 1982.

————. *The Sons: "The Judgment," "The Stoker," "The Metamorphosis," and "Letter to His Father."* Translated by Edward Muir, Willa Muir, Ernst Kaiser, Eithne Wilkins, and Arthur S. Wensinger. New York: Schocken, 1989.

————. *The Trial.* Translated by Breon Mitchell. New York: Schocken, 1999.

General Bibliography

Adelman, Gary. "Beckett's Readers: A Commentary and Symposium." *Michigan Quarterly Review* 43, no. 1 (Winter 2004): 54–70.

Adorno, Theodor W. *Minima Moralia: Reflexionen aus dem beschädigten Leben.* Frankfurt am Main: Suhrkamp, 2001.

——. *Ohne Leitbild. Parva aesthetica.* Frankfurt am Main: Suhrkamp, 1967.

Alighieri, Dante. *The Divine Comedy 1: Inferno.* Translated by John D. Sinclair. Oxford: Oxford University Press, 1961.

——. *The Divine Comedy 2: Purgatorio.* Translated by John D. Sinclair. Oxford: Oxford University Press, 1961.

——. *The Divine Comedy 3: Paradiso.* Translated by John D. Sinclair. Oxford: Oxford University Press, 1961.

Anders, Günther. *Kafka: Pro und Contra: Die Prozeß-Unterlagen.* Munich: Beck, 1951.

Anderson, Mark. "The Edge of Darkness." *October* 106 (2003): 102–21.

——. *Kafka's Clothes: Ornament and Aestheticism in the Hapsburg Fin de Siècle.* Oxford: Clarendon, 1992.

——. "Kafka, Homosexuality and the Aesthetics of 'Male Culture.'" In *Gender and Politics in Austrian Fiction,* edited by Ritchie Robertson and Edward Timms, 79–99. Edinburgh: Edinburgh University Press, 1996.

——, ed. *Reading Kafka: Prague, Politics, and the Fin de Siècle.* New York: Schocken, 1989.

——. "Wo die Schrecken der Kindheit verborgen sind: W. G. Sebalds Dilemma der zwei Väter." *Literaturen* (July/August 2006): 32-39.

Andriopoulos, Stefan. "The Terror of Reproduction: Early Cinema's Ghostly Doubles and the Right to One's Own Image." *New German Critique* 33, no. 3 (2006): 151–70.

Arnold, Heinz Ludwig, ed. *Text + Kritik* 158, special issue, "W. G. Sebald." Munich: Edition Text + Kritik, 2003.

Attridge, Derek. *J. M. Coetzee and the Ethics of Reading: Literature in the Event.* Chicago: University of Chicago Press, 2004.

Attwell, David. *J. M. Coetzee: South Africa and the Politics of Writing.* Berkeley and Los Angeles: University of California Press, 1993.

Atze, Marcel. "Koinzidenz und Intertextualität. Der Einsatz von Prätexten in W.G. Sebalds Erzählung 'All'estero.'" In *W. G. Sebald,* Porträt 7, edited by Franz Loquai, 151–75. Eggingen, Ger.: Isele, 1997.

Auden, W. H. "The Wandering Jew." In *The Complete Works of W. H. Auden: Prose, 1939–1948,* edited by Edward Mendelson, 110–13. Princeton, N.J.: Princeton University Press, 2002.

Babel, Isaac. *The Collected Stories of Isaac Babel.* Translated by Peter Constantine. Edited by Nathalie Babel and Peter Constantine. New York: W. W. Norton, 2002.

Bächtold-Stäubli, Hanns, ed. *Handwörterbuch des deutschen Aberglaubens.* 10 vols. Vol. 4. Berlin: Walter de Gruyter, 1938–41.

Baioni, Giuliano. *Kafka—Literatur und Judentum.* Translated by Gertrud Billen and Josef Billen. Stuttgart: J. B. Metzler, 1994.

Banville, John. "Being and Nothingness." *The Nation,* November 3, 2003.

Bayley, John. "Dispensing with Realism, We Can See Reality." *Los Angeles Times Book Review*, November 22, 2003, R16.

Beck, Evelyn Torton. *Kafka and the Yiddish Theater: Its Impact on His Work*. Madison: University of Wisconsin Press, 1971.

Beckett, Samuel. *Disjecta: Miscellaneous Writings and a Dramatic Fragment*. Edited by Ruby Cohn. New York: Grove, 1984.

———. *The Complete Short Prose, 1929-1989*, edited by S. E. Gontarski. New York: Grove, 1997.

———. *Three Novels: Molloy, Malone Dies, The Unnamable*. New York: Grove, 1995.

Bellow, Saul. *The Adventures of Augie March*. New York: Penguin, 1999.

———. *Herzog*. London: Penguin, 2001.

———. *It All Adds Up: From the Dim Past to the Uncertain Future*. New York: Penguin, 1995.

Benjamin, Walter. *Benjamin über Kafka: Texte, Briefzeugnisse, Aufzeichnungen*. Edited by Hermann Schweppenhäuser. Frankfurt am Main: Suhrkamp, 1981.

———. *II: Aufsätze, Essays, Vorträge*. Edited by Rolf Tiedemann and Hermann Schweppenhäuser. Vol. 2 of *Gesammelte Schriften*, 3 vols. Frankfurt am Main: Suhrkamp, 1991.

Bernhard, Thomas. *Auslöschung: Ein Zerfall*. Berlin: Verlag Volk und Welt, 1989.

Binder, Hartmut. "'Der Jäger Gracchus': Zu Kafkas Schaffensweise und poetischer Topographie." *Jahrbuch der deutschen Schillergesellschaft*, no. 15 (1971).

———, ed. *Kafka-Handbuch, Band 2: Die Werk und seine Wirkung*. Stuttgart: Alfred Kröner, 1979.

———. *Kafka-Kommentar zu den Romanen, Rezensionen, Aphorismen und zum Brief an den Vater*. Munich: Winkler, 1976.

———. *Kafka-Kommentar zu sämtlichen Erzählungen*. Munich: Winkler, 1975.

———. *Kafkas Welt: Eine Lebenschronik in Bildern*. Reinbek bei Hamburg: Rowohlt, 2008.

Bleikasten, André. *Philip Roth: Les Ruses de la fiction*. Paris: Berlin, 2001.

Bloom, Harold. *Agon: Towards a Theory of Revisionism*. Oxford: Oxford University Press, 1982.

———. *The Anxiety of Influence: A Theory of Poetry*. 2nd ed. New York: Oxford University Press, 1997.

———. *The Breaking of the Vessels (The Wellek Library Lectures at the University of California, Irvine)*. Chicago: University of Chicago Press, 1982.

———, ed. *Franz Kafka (Bloom's Modern Critical Views)*. New York: Chelsea House, 1986.

———, ed. *Franz Kafka's The Castle (Bloom's Modern Critical Interpretations)*. New York: Chelsea House, 1988.

———, ed. *Franz Kafka's "The Metamorphosis" (Bloom's Modern Critical Interpretations)*. New York: Chelsea House, 1988.

————, ed. *Franz Kafka's The Trial (Bloom's Modern Critical Interpretations)*. New York: Chelsea House, 1987.

————. *Kabbalah and Criticism*. New York: Continuum, 1983.

————. *A Map of Misreading*. 2nd ed. New York: Oxford University Press, 2003.

————, ed. *Philip Roth (Bloom's Modern Critical Views)*. New York: Chelsea House, 1986.

————, ed. *Philip Roth (Bloom's Modern Critical Views)*. New York: Chelsea House, 2003.

————, ed. *Philip Roth's* Portnoy's Complaint *(Bloom's Modern Critical Interpretations)*. New York: Chelsea House, 2004.

————. *Poetry and Repression: Revisionism from Blake to Stevens*. New Haven, Conn.: Yale University Press, 1976.

————. *Ruin the Sacred Truths: Poetry and Belief from the Bible to the Present*. Cambridge, Mass.: Harvard University Press, 1989.

————. *Shakespeare: The Invention of the Human*. New York: Riverhead Books, 1998.

————, ed. *Stendhal (Bloom's Modern Critical Views)*. New York: Chelsea House, 1989.

————. *The Strong Light of the Canonical: Kafka, Freud, and Scholem as Revisionists of Jewish Culture and Thought*. New York: The City College Papers, 1987.

————. *The Western Canon: The Books and School of the Ages*. New York: Riverhead Books, 1994.

Borges, Jorge Luis. *Labyrinths: Selected Stories and Other Writings*. Edited by James E. Irby and Donald A. Yates. Translated by Anthony Kerrigan. New York: New Directions, 1964.

Born, Jürgen. *Franz Kafka: Kritik und Rezeption, 1924–1938*. Frankfurt am Main: S. Fischer, 1983.

————. *Franz Kafka: Kritik und Rezeption zu seinen Lebzeiten, 1912–1924*. Frankfurt am Main: S. Fischer, 1979.

————. *Kafkas Bibliothek: Ein beschreibendes Verzeichnis mit einem Index aller in Kafkas Schriften erwähnten Bücher, Zeitschriften und Zeitschriftenbeiträge*. Frankfurt am Main: S. Fischer, 1990.

Brod, Max. *Über Franz Kafka: Franz Kafka, eine Biographie: Franz Kafkas Glauben und Lehre: Verzweiflung und Erlösung im Werk Franz Kafkas*. Frankfurt am Main: Fischer Bücherei, 1974.

Brod, Max, and Franz Kafka. *Max Brod, Franz Kafka, eine Freundschaft*. Edited by Hannelore Rodlauer and Malcolm Pasley. 2 vols. Frankfurt am Main: S. Fischer, 1987.

Brookner, Anita. "A Brave Stance to Take." *The Spectator,* September 13, 2003, 63.

Buber, Martin. *Briefwechsel aus sieben Jahrzehnten*. Edited by Grete Schaeder. 3 vols. Vol. 1. Heidelberg: L. Schneider, 1972.

Buber-Neumann, Margarete. *Milena: Kafkas Freundin: Ein Lebensbild.* Frankfurt am Main: Ullstein, 1996.

Büchner, Georg. *Dichtungen.* Edited by Henri Poschmann and Rosemarie Poschmann. Bibliothek Deutscher Klassiker edition. Vol. 1 of *Georg Büchner: Sämtliche Werke, Briefe und Dokumente in zwei Bänden.* 2 vols. Frankfurt am Main: Deutscher Klassiker Verlag, 1992.

Calasso, Roberto. *K.* Translated by Geoffrey Brock. New York: Vintage International, 2005.

Canetti, Elias. *Der andere Prozeß. Kafkas Briefe an Felice.* München: Carl Hanser, 1984.

Celan, Paul. *Gedichte, Prosa, Reden.* Edited by Beda Allemann and Stefan Reichert. Vol. 3 of *Gesammelte Werke.* 3 vols. Frankfurt am Main: Suhrkamp, 2001.

Cervantes Saavedra, Miguel de. *Exemplary Stories.* Translated by Lesley Lipson. Oxford: Oxford University Press, 1998.

Coetzee, J. M. "As a Woman Grows Older." *New York Review of Books* 51, no. 1 (January 15, 2004): 11–14.

———. *Diary of a Bad Year.* London: Harvill Secker, 2007.

———. *Disgrace.* New York: Viking, 1999.

———. *Dusklands.* New York: Penguin Books, 1985.

———. *Elizabeth Costello.* New York: Viking, 2003.

———. "Elizabeth Costello and the Problem of Evil." *Salmagundi* 137–38 (2003): 49–64.

———. *Foe.* New York: Penguin Books, 1987.

———. *Giving Offense: Essays on Censorship.* Chicago: University of Chicago Press, 1996.

———. "He and His Man." 2003.

———. "Heir of a Dark History." *New York Review of Books,* October 24, 2002.

———. "Homage." *Threepenny Review,* Spring 1993, 5–7.

———. *The Humanities in Africa* (*Die Geisteswissenschaften in Afrika*). Munich: Carl Friedrich von Siemens Stiftung, 2001.

———. *In the Heart of the Country.* London: Vintage, 1999.

———. *Inner Workings: Essays 2000–2005.* London: Harvill Secker, 2007.

———. "Interview with David Attwell (Kafka)." In *Doubling the Point: Essays and Interviews,* edited by David Attwell and J. M. Coetzee, 197–209. Cambridge, Mass.: Harvard University Press, 1992.

———. "Kafka: Translators on Trial." *New York Review of Books* 45, no. 8 (May 14, 1998).

———. *The Nobel Lecture in Literature, 2003.* New York: Penguin, 2004.

———. *The Lives of Animals.* London: Profile Books, 2001.

———. "Samuel Beckett's *Lessness:* An Exercise in Decomposition." *Computers and the Humanities* 7, no. 4 (1973): 195–98.

————. *Slow Man.* New York: Viking, 2005.

————. *Stranger Shores: Literary Essays, 1986–1999.* New York: Viking, 2001.

————. "Thematizing." In *The Return of Thematic Criticism*, edited by Werner Sollors, 289. Cambridge, Mass.: Harvard University Press, 1993.

————. "Time, Tense, and Aspect in Kafka's 'The Burrow.'" In *Doubling the Point: Essays and Interviews*, edited by David Attwell and J. M. Coetzee, 210–32. Cambridge, Mass.: Harvard University Press, 1992.

————. "Translating Kafka." In *Stranger Shores: Literary Essays, 1986–1999.* New York: Viking, 2001.

————. "What Is a Classic?" In *Stranger Shores: Literary Essays, 1986–1999.* New York: Viking, 2001.

————. "What Is Realism?" *Salmagundi,* no. 114–15 (1997): 60–81.

————. "What Philip Knew." *New York Review of Books* 51, no. 18 (November 18, 2004).

————. *Youth.* London: Secker and Warburg, 2002.

Coetzee, J. M., and David Attwell. *Doubling the Point: Essays and Interviews.* Cambridge, Mass.: Harvard University Press, 1992.

Cohn, Dorrit. "Kafka's Eternal Present: Narrative Tense in 'Ein Landarzt' and Other First-Person Stories." *PMLA: Publications of the Modern Language Association of America* 83, no. 1 (1968): 144–50.

Corngold, Stanley. *Lambent Traces: Franz Kafka.* Princeton, N.J.: Princeton University Press, 2004.

Deb, Siddhartha. "Mind into Matter." *Boston Globe,* October 26, 2003, D6.

Defoe, Daniel. *Robinson Crusoe.* Edited by John Richetti. New York: Penguin, 2003.

————. *Serious Reflections During the Life and Surprising Adventures of Robinson Crusoe: With His Vision of the Angelic World.* Edited by G. H. Maynadier. Vol. 3 of *The Works of Daniel Defoe.* 16 vols. Boston: D. Nickerson, 1903.

Demetz, Peter. "Mit Franz Kafka in den Straßen von Newark." *Frankfurter Allgemeine Zeitung,* March 23, 2002.

————. *Prague in Black and Gold: The History of a City.* London: Penguin, 1997.

Denham, Scott, and Mark McCulloh, eds. *W. G. Sebald: History, Memory, Trauma.* Berlin: Walter de Gruyter, 2006.

Dickinson, Emily. *The Complete Poems of Emily Dickinson.* Edited by Thomas H. Johnson. Boston: Little, Brown, 1960.

Dodd, William J. *Kafka and Dostoyevsky: The Shaping of Influence.* London: Macmillan, 1992.

Dovey, Teresa. *The Novels of J. M. Coetzee: Lacanian Allegories.* Johannesberg: Ad. Donker, 1988.

Dyer, Geoff, Susan Sontag, Millicent Dillon, Anne M. Wagner, James Wood, T. J. Clark, Lynn Sharon Schwartz, and Arthur Lubow. "A Symposium on W. G. Sebald." *Threepenny Review,* Spring 2002.

Eysteinsson, Astradur. *The Concept of Modernism*. Ithaca, N.Y.: Cornell University Press, 1990.

Fiedler, Leslie A. *A New Fiedler Reader*. Amherst, N.Y.: Prometheus Books, 1999.

Foer, Jonathan Safran. "Jeffrey Eugenides Interviewed by Jonathan Safran Foer." *BOMB Magazine* (Fall 2002), http://www.bombsite.com/issues/81/articles/ 2519 (accessed September 9, 2008).

Franklin, Ruth. "Rings of Smoke." *New Republic* (September 23, 2002): 32.

Freud, Sigmund. *Das Unheimliche*. Edited by Anna Freud, Edward Bilbring and Ernst Kris. Vol. 12 of *Gesammelte Werke*. 18 vols. Frankfurt am Main: Fischer Taschenbuch Verlag, 1999.

———. *Der Dichter und das Phantasieren*. Edited by Anna Freud, Edward Bilbring and Ernst Kris. Vol. 7 of *Gesammelte Werke*. 18 vols. Frankfurt am Main: Fischer Taschenbuch Verlag, 1999.

———. *Der Humor*. Edited by Anna Freud, Edward Bilbring and Ernst Kris. Vol. 14 of *Gesammelte Werke*. 18 vols. Frankfurt am Main: Fischer Taschenbuch Verlag, 1999.

———. *Jenseits des Lustprinzips*. Edited by Anna Freud, Edward Bilbring and Ernst Kris. Vol. 13 of *Gesammelte Werke*. 18 vols. Frankfurt am Main: Fischer Taschenbuch Verlag, 1999.

———. *Studien über Hysterie*. Edited by Anna Freud, Edward Bilbring and Ernst Kris. Vol. 1 of *Gesammelte Werk*. 18 vols. Frankfurt am Main: Fischer Taschenbuch Verlag, 1999.

———. *Trauer und Melancholie*. Edited by Anna Freud, Edward Bilbring and Ernst Kris. Vol. 10 of *Gesammelte Werke*. 18 vols. Frankfurt am Main: Fischer Taschenbuch Verlag, 1999.

———. *Vorlesungen zur Einführung in der Psychoanalyse*. Edited by Anna Freud, Edward Bilbring and Ernst Kris. Vol. 11 of *Gesammelte Werke*. 18 vols. Frankfurt am Main: Fischer Taschenbuch Verlag, 1999.

Gallagher, Susan VanZanten. *A Story of South Africa: J. M. Coetzee's Fiction in Context*. Cambridge, Mass.: Harvard University Press, 1991.

Gay, Peter. *Freud: A Life for Our Time*. New York: Norton, 1988.

Gilman, Sander L. *Franz Kafka, the Jewish Patient*. New York: Routledge, 1995.

———. *Jewish Self-Hatred: Anti-Semitism and the Hidden Language of the Jews*. Baltimore: Johns Hopkins University Press, 1986.

Goethe, Johann Wolfgang von. *Dichtung und Wahrheit*. Edited by Klaus-Detlef Müller. Vol. 5 of *Werke*. 6 vols. Jubilee edition. Frankfurt am Main: Insel, 1998.

———. Vol. 2 of *Gedichte in zeitlicher Folge: Eine Lebensgeschichte Goethes in seinen Gedichten*. 2 vols. Frankfurt am Main: Insel, 1978.

Goethe, Johann Wolfgang von, Karl Richter, Katharina Mommsen, and Peter Ludwig. *West-Östlicher Divan*. Edited by Karl Richter, Hubert G. Göpfert,

Norbert Miller, Gerhard Saudir, and Edith Zehm. Munich edition. Vol. II of *Sämtliche Werke nach Epochen seines Schaffens.* 20 vols. Munich: Carl Hanser Verlag, 1998, 1.2.

Goffard, Christopher. "Philip Roth Unbound." *St. Petersburg Times,* July 4, 2004.

Gorky, Maksim. *Literary Portraits.* Translated by Ivy Litvinov. Moscow: Foreign Languages Publishing House (n.d.).

Green, Martin. "Half a Lemon, Half an Egg." In *Reading Philip Roth,* edited by Asher Z. Milbauer and Donald G. Watson, 73–81. New York: St. Martin's, 1988.

———. "Introduction." In *A Philip Roth Reader,* edited by Philip Roth. New York: Farrar, Straus and Giroux, 1980.

Grillparzer, Franz. "Tagebücher." In *Ausgewählte Briefe, Gespräche, Berichte.* Edited by Peter Frank and Karl Pörnbacher. Vol. 4 of, *Sämtliche Werke.* 4 vols. Munich: Carl Hanser, 1965.

Grözinger, Karl Erich, Stéphane Mosès, and Hans Dieter Zimmermann, eds. *Kafka und das Judentum.* Frankfurt am Main: Jüdischer Verlag bei Athenäum, 1987.

Guston, Philip. "Faith, Hope and Impossibility." In *Philip Guston Retrospective,* edited by Michael Auping. New York: Thames and Hudson, 2003.

Hackermüller, Rotraut. *Kafkas letzte Jahre: 1917–1924.* Munich: P. Kirchheim, 1990.

Halio, Jay L. *Philip Roth Revisited.* New York: Twayne, 1992.

Head, Dominic. *J. M. Coetzee.* Cambridge, Eng.: Cambridge University Press, 1997.

Heine, Heinrich. *Gedichte.* Edited by Hans Mayer. Vol. I of *Werke.* Frankfurt am Main: Insel, 1968.

Henel, Heinrich. "Das Ende von Kafkas 'Der Bau.'" *Germanisch-Romanische Monatsschrift,* no. 22 (1972): 3–23.

Herbert, George. *Complete English Works.* Edited by Ann Pasternak Slater. London: Everyman, 1995.

Hofmannsthal, Hugo von. *The Lord Chandos Letter.* Translated by Joel Rotenberg. New York: New York Review Books, 2005.

Hölderlin, Friedrich. *Selected Poems and Fragments.* Translated by Michael Hamburger. Edited by Jeremy Adler. London: Penguin, 1998.

Howard, Richard. "Translator's Afterword." *The Charterhouse of Parma,* by Stendhal. New York: Modern Library, 1999.

Isenschmid, Andreas. "Melancolia. W. G. Sebalds *Schwindel.Gefühle.*" In *W. G. Sebald,* Porträt 7, edited by Franz Loquai, 70–74. Eggingen, Ger.: Isele, 1997.

Iyer, Pico. "Dead Man Writing: The Strange, Haunted World of W. G. Sebald." *Harper's Magazine,* October 2000, 86–90.

Jagow, Bettina von, and Oliver Jahraus, eds. *Kafka-Handbuch.* Göttingen, Ger.: Vanderhoeck und Ruprecht.

James, Henry. *Complete Stories, 1892–1898.* New York: Library of America, 1996.

———. *Literary Criticism, Volume 2: European Writers and Prefaces to the New York Edition.* Edited by Leon Edel. 2 vols. New York: Library of America, 1984.

Jesenská, Milena, ed. *"Ich hätte zu antworten Tage- und Nächtelang": Die Briefe von*

Milena. Edited by Alena Wagnerová. Frankfurt am Main: Fischer Taschenbuch Verlag, 1999.

Kafka, Franz. *Amtliche Schriften*. Edited by Klaus Hermsdorf and Benno Wagner. Frankfurt am Main: S. Fischer, 2004.

————. *Beim Bau der chinesischen Mauer und andere Schriften aus dem Nachlaß*. Edited by Hans-Gerd Koch. Vol. 6 of *Gesammelte Werke in zwölf Bänden*. 12 vols. Frankfurt am Main: Fischer Taschenbuch Verlag, 1994.

————. *Beschreibung eines Kampfes und andere Schriften aus dem Nachlaß*. Edited by Hans-Gerd Koch. Vol. 5 of *Gesammelte Werke in zwölf Bänden*. 12 vols. Frankfurt am Main: Fischer Taschenbuch Verlag, 1994.

————. *Briefe an die Eltern aus den Jahren 1922–1924*. Edited by Josef Čermák and Martin Svatoš. Frankfurt am Main: Fischer Taschenbuch Verlag, 1993.

————. *Briefe an Felice und andere Korrespondenz aus der Verlobungszeit*. Edited by Erich Heller and Jürgen Born. Frankfurt am Main: Fischer Taschenbuch Verlag, 1976.

————. *Briefe an Milena, erweiterte und neu geordnete Ausgabe*. Edited by Jürgen Born and Michael Müller. Frankfurt am Main: Fischer Taschenbuch Verlag, 1986.

————. *Briefe an Ottla und die Familie*. Edited by Hartmut Binder and Klaus Wagenbach. Frankfurt am Main: Fischer Taschenbuch Verlag, 1981.

————. *Briefe 1902–1924*. Edited by Max Brod. Vol. 8 of *Gesammelte Werke*. 8 vols. Frankfurt am Main: Fischer Taschenbuch Verlag, 1998.

————. *Briefe 1900–1912*. Edited by Hans-Gerd Koch. Frankfurt am Main: S. Fischer, 1999.

————. *Briefe 1913–1914*. Edited by Hans-Gerd Koch. Frankfurt am Main: S. Fischer, 2001.

————. *Briefe 1914–1917*. Edited by Hans-Gerd Koch. Frankfurt am Main: S. Fischer, 2005.

————. *Das Ehepaar*. Edited by Hans-Gerd Koch. Vol. 8 of *Gesammelte Werke in zwölf Bänden*. 12 vols. Frankfurt am Main: Fischer Taschenbuch Verlag, 1994.

————. *Der Proceß*. Edited by Hans-Gerd Koch. Vol. 3 of *Gesammelte Werke in zwölf Bänden*. 12 vols. Frankfurt am Main: Fischer Taschenbuch Verlag, 1994.

————. *Das Schloß*. Edited by Hans-Gerd Koch. Vol. 4 of *Gesammelte Werke in zwölf Bänden*. 12 vols. Frankfurt am Main: Fischer Taschenbuch Verlag, 1994.

————. *Ein Landarzt und andere Drucke zu Lebzeiten*. Edited by Hans-Gerd Koch. Vol. 1 of *Gesammelte Werke in zwölf Bänden*. 12 vols. Frankfurt am Main: Fischer Taschenbuch Verlag, 1994.

————. *Hochzeitsvorbereitungen auf dem Lande*. Edited by Max Brod. Vol. 6 of *Gesammelte Werke*. 8 vols. Frankfurt am Main: Fischer Taschenbuch Verlag, 1998.

————. *Nachgelassene Schriften und Fragmente I: Apparatband*. Edited by Hans-Gerd Koch. Vol. 10 of *Kritische Ausgabe in 15 Bänden*. 15 vols. Frankfurt am Main: Fischer Taschenbuch Verlag, 2002.

———. *Nachgelassene Schriften und Fragmente II: Apparatband.* Edited by Hans-Gerd Koch. Vol. 12 of *Kritische Ausgabe in 15 Bänden.* 15 vols. Frankfurt am Main: Fischer Taschenbuch Verlag, 2002.

———. *Reisetagebücher.* Edited by Hans-Gerd Koch. Vol. 12 of *Gesammelte Werke in zwölf Bänden.* 12 vols. Frankfurt am Main: Fischer Taschenbuch Verlag, 1994.

———. *Tagebücher, Band 1: 1909–1912.* Edited by Hans-Gerd Koch. Vol. 9 of *Gesammelte Werke in zwölf Bänden.* 12 vols. Frankfurt am Main: Fischer Taschenbuch Verlag, 1994.

———. *Tagebücher, Band 2: 1912–1914.* Edited by Hans-Gerd Koch. Vol. 10 of *Gesammelte Werke in zwölf Bänden.* 12 vols. Frankfurt am Main: Fischer Taschenbuch Verlag, 1994.

———. *Tagebücher, Band 3: 1914–1923.* Edited by Hans-Gerd Koch. Vol. 11 of *Gesammelte Werke in zwölf Bänden.* 12 vols. Frankfurt am Main: Fischer Taschenbuch Verlag, 1994.

———. *Zur Frage der Gesetze und andere Schriften aus dem Nachlaß.* Edited by Hans-Gerd Koch. Vol. 7 of *Gesammelte Werke in zwölf Bänden.* 12 vols. Frankfurt am Main: Fischer Taschenbuch Verlag, 1994.

Karl, Frederick Robert. *Franz Kafka, Representative Man.* New York: Ticknor and Fields, 1991.

Keats, John. *The Letters of John Keats, Volume 1: 1814–1818.* Edited by Hyder Edward Rollins. Vol. 1 of *The Letters of John Keats, 1814–1821.* 2 vols. Cambridge, Eng.: Cambridge University Press, 1958.

———. *Poetical Works of John Keats.* Edited by H. W. Garrod. Oxford: Clarendon, 1958.

Kiely, Robert. "Roth's Writer and His Stumbling Block." *New York Times,* October 30, 1983.

Kierkegaard, Søren. *Fear and Trembling/Repetition.* Translated and edited by Edna H. Hong and Edward V. Hong. Vol. 6 of *Kierkegaard's Writings.* Princeton, N.J.: Princeton University Press, 1983.

Kieval, Hillel. *Languages of Community: The Jewish Experience in the Czech Lands.* Berkeley, Calif.: University of California Press, 2000.

———. *The Making of Czech Jewry: National Conflict and Jewish Society in Bohemia, 1870–1918.* New York: Oxford University Press, 1988.

Kilbourn, R. J. A. "Kafka, Nabokov, Sebald: Intertextuality and Narratives of Redemption in *Vertigo* and *The Emigrants.*" In *W. G. Sebald: History, Memory, Trauma,* edited by Scott Denham and Mark McCulloh, 33–64. Berlin: De Gruyter, 2006.

Kittler, Wolf, and Gerhard Neumann, eds. *Franz Kafka—Schriftverkehr.* Freiburg, Ger.: Rombach, 1990.

Koch, Hans-Gerd. *"Als Kafka mir entgegenkam": Erinnerungen an Franz Kafka.* Frankfurt am Main: Fischer Taschenbuch Verlag, 2000.

Koch, Hans-Gerd, and Klaus Wagenbach. "Kafkas Fabriken." *Marbacher Magazin*, no. 100 (2002).

Koelb, Clayton. *Kafka's Rhetoric: The Passion of Reading*. Ithaca, N.Y.: Cornell University Press, 1989.

Kraus, Karl. "Heine und die Folgen." In *Untergang der Welt durch schwarze Magie*, 185–212. Frankfurt am Main: Suhrkamp, 1989.

———. "Literatur oder Man wird doch da sehn." In *Dramen*, 9–75. Frankfurt am Main: Suhrkamp, 1989.

Kundera, Milan. "Some Notes on Roth's *My Life as a Man* and *The Professor of Desire*." In *Reading Philip Roth*, edited by Asher Z. Milbauer and Donald G. Watson, 160–67. New York: St. Martin's, 1988.

———. *Verratene Vermächtnisse*. Translated by Susanna Roth. Frankfurt am Main: Fischer Taschenbuch Verlag, 1996.

Lee, Hermione. *Philip Roth*. London: Methuen, 1982.

Lehmann-Haupt, Christopher. Review of *Life & Times of Michael K*, by J. M. Coetzee. *New York Times*, December 6, 1983, C22.

Leonard, John. "Beckett Safe from Computers." *New York Times Book Review*, August 19, 1973, 27.

Lethem, Jonathan. "The Figure in the Castle." *New York Times Book Review*, May 1, 2005, 16.

Levitt, Morton P. "Roth and Kafka: Two Jews." In *Critical Essays on Philip Roth*, edited by Sanford Pinsker, 245–54. Boston: Hall, 1982.

Lichtenberg, Georg Christoph. *Sudelbücher*. Edited by Franz H. Mautner. Frankfurt am Main: Insel, 1984.

Loquai, Franz, ed. *W. G. Sebald*, Porträt 7. Eggingen, Ger.: Isele, 1997.

Lubasch, Arnold H. "Philip Roth Shakes Weequahic High." *New York Times*, February 28, 1969.

Lubow, Arthur. "Preoccupied with Death, but Still Funny." *New York Times*, December 11, 2001.

Lukács, Georg. *Wider den missverstandenen Realismus*. Hamburg: Claasen, 1958.

Mächler, Robert. *Das Leben Robert Walsers: Eine dokumentarische Biographie*. Frankfurt am Main: Suhrkamp, 1978.

Mann, Thomas. *Der Zauberberg*. Edited by Peter de Mendelssohn. Frankfurt edition. Vol. 5 of *Gesammelte Werke in Einzelbände*. 20 vols. Frankfurt am Main: S. Fischer, 1981.

Mars-Jones, Andrew. "It's Very Novel, But Is It Actually a Novel?" *The Observer*, September 14, 2003.

Maslin, Janet. "The Mockery Can Still Sting with a Target in the Mirror." *New York Times*, October 21, 2003, E7.

Mayer, Musa. *Night Studio: A Memoir of Philip Guston*. New York: Da Capo, 1997.

McCrum, Robert. "What's the Best Novel in the Past 25 Years?" *Guardian* (1996).

http://www.guardian.co.uk/books/2006/oct/08/fiction.features1 (accessed September 9, 2008).

Meyer, Sven. "Das Fähnlein auf der Brücke." *Akzente: Zeitschrift für Literatur* 50.1, special issue, "W. G. Sebald zum Gedächtnis" (2003).

Milbauer, Asher Z., and Donald G. Watson, eds. *Reading Philip Roth*. New York: St. Martin's, 1988.

Miłosz, Czesław. *Conversations with Czesław Miłosz*. Ed. Ewa Czarnecka and Aleksander Fiut. Trans. Richard Lourie. San Diego: Harcourt, 1987.

———. *New and Collected Poems, 1931–2001*. New York: Ecco, 2003.

Müller, Michael. "Kafka und Casanova." *Freibeuter*, no. 16 (1983): 67–76.

Müller, Wilhelm. *Die Winterreise: Und andere Gedichte*, edited by Hans-Rüdiger Schwab. Frankfurt am Main.: Insel, 1986.

Musil, Robert. *Der Mann ohne Eigenschaften, Erstes und Zweites Buch*. Edited by Adolf Frisé. 2 vols. Vol. 1. Reinbek bei Hamburg: Rowohlt Taschenbuch Verlag, 1999.

Northey, Anthony. *Kafkas Mischpoche*. Berlin: Wagenbach, 1988.

Ozick, Cynthia. *Quarrel and Quandary*. New York: Knopf, 2000.

Parks, Tim. "The Hunter." *New York Review of Books* 47, no. 10 (June 15, 2000).

Parrish, Timothy, ed. *The Cambridge Companion to Philip Roth*. Cambridge, Eng.: Cambridge University Press, 2007.

Pasley, Malcolm. *"Die Schrift ist unveränderlich—": Essays zu Kafka*. Frankfurt am Main: Fischer Taschenbuch Verlag, 1995.

———. "Drei literarische Mystifikationen Kafkas." In *Kafka-Symposion,* edited by Jürgen Born, Ludwig Dietz, Malcolm Pasley, Paul Raabe, and Klaus Wagenbach, 1990.

———. "Kafka and the Theme of 'Berufung.'" *Oxford German Studies*, no. 9 (1978): 139–49.

Pasley, Malcolm, and Klaus Wagenbach. "Datierung sämtlicher Texte Franz Kafkas." In *Kafka-Symposion*. Munich: Deutscher Taschenbuch Verlag, 1969.

Paustovsky, Konstantin. *The Story of a Life: Years of Hope*. Translated by Manya Harai and Andrew Thompson. New York: Pantheon Books, 1968.

Pawel, Ernst. "Franz Kafkas Judentum. In *Kafka und das Judentum,"* edited by Karl Erich Grözinger, Stéphane Mosès and Hans Dieter Zimmermann, 253–58. Frankfurt am Main: Jüdischer Verlag, 1987.

———. *The Nightmare of Reason: A Life of Franz Kafka*. New York: Farrar, Straus, Giroux, 1984.

Penner, Dick. *Countries of the Mind: The Fiction of J. M. Coetzee*. New York: Greenwood, 1989.

Pfeiffer, Peter C. "Korrespondenz und Wahlverwandtschaft: W. G. Sebalds *Die Ringe des Saturn*." In *Gegenwartsliteratur: Ein germanistisches Jahrbuch* 2, edited by Paul Michael Lützeler and Stephan K. Schindler, 226–44. Tübingen: Stauffenburg, 2003.

Pinsker, Sanford. *The Comedy that "Hoits": An Essay on the Fiction of Philip Roth.* Columbia: University of Missouri Press, 1975.

———. *Critical Essays on Philip Roth.* Boston: G. K. Hall, 1982.

Posnock, Ross. *Philip Roth's Rude Truth: The Art of Immaturity.* Princeton, N.J.: Princeton University Press, 2006.

Remnick, David. "Into the Clear: Philip Roth." In *Reporting: Writings from the New Yorker,* 101–24. New York: Knopf, 2006.

Riemer, Andrew. "A Marriage of One." *Sydney Morning Herald,* September 13–14, 2003, 14.

Robertson, Ritchie. *Kafka: Judaism, Politics, and Literature.* Oxford: Clarendon, 1985.

Rodgers, Bernard F *Philip Roth.* Boston: Twayne, 1978.

Roth, Joseph. *Radetzkymarsch.* Munich: Deutscher Taschenbuch Verlag, 1998.

Roth, Philip. *American Pastoral.* Boston: Houghton Mifflin, 1997.

———. *The Anatomy Lesson.* New York: Vintage, 1996.

———. "The Breast." In *A Philip Roth Reader,* edited by Philip Roth. New York: Farrar, Straus and Giroux, 1980.

———. *Conversations with Philip Roth.* Edited by George J. Searles. Jackson: University Press of Mississippi, 1992.

———. *The Counterlife.* New York: Farrar, Straus, Giroux, 1986.

———. *The Facts: A Novelist's Autobiography.* New York: Penguin Books, 1989.

———. *The Ghost Writer.* New York: Vintage, 1995.

———. *The Great American Novel.* New York: Holt, 1973.

———. *The Human Stain.* Boston: Houghton Mifflin, 2000.

———. *I Married a Communist.* Boston: Houghton Mifflin, 1998.

———. "In Search of Kafka and Other Answers." *New York Times Book Review,* February 15, 1976, 6–7.

———. "Juice or Gravy? How I Met My Fate in a Cafeteria." *New York Times,* September 18, 1994, 21–22.

———. *My Life As a Man.* New York: Penguin Books, 1985.

———. "On the Air: A Long Story." *New American Review* 10 (1970): 7–49.

———. *Our Gang (Starring Tricky and His Friends).* New York: Random House, 1971.

———. *Patrimony: A True Story.* New York: Vintage, 1996.

———. *A Philip Roth Reader.* Edited by Philip Roth. New York: Farrar, Straus and Giroux, 1980.

———. *The Plot Against America.* Boston: Houghton Mifflin, 2004.

———. *Portnoy's Complaint.* London: Cape, 1969.

———. *The Prague Orgy.* New York: Vintage, 1996.

———. *Reading Myself and Others.* Revised edition. New York: Penguin, 1985.

———. *Sabbath's Theater.* Boston: Houghton Mifflin, 1995.

———. *Shop Talk: A Writer and His Colleagues and Their Work.* Boston: Houghton Mifflin, 2001.

————. "The Story Behind *The Plot Against America*." *New York Times Book Review*, September 19, 2004.

————. *Zuckerman Unbound: A Trilogy and Epilogue 1979–1985*, edited by Ross Miller. New York: Library of America, 2007.

Rothstein, Edward. "The Revenge of the Vrai." *New York Review of Books* 28, no. 11 (1981).

Sandbank, Shimon. *After Kafka: The Influence of Kafka's Fiction*. Athens: University of Georgia Press, 1989.

Santner, Eric L. *On Creaturely Life: Rilke, Benjamin, Sebald*. Chicago: University of Chicago Press, 2006.

Santner, Eric L. "W. G. Sebald and the Poetics of Exposure." *Approaching W. G. Sebald*. New Haven, Conn., 2004.

Schulevitz, Judith. "Author Tour." *New York Times,* October 26, 2003.

Sebald, W. G. *After Nature*. Translated by Michael Hamburger. New York: Random House, 2002.

————. *Austerlitz*. Frankfurt am Main: Fischer Taschenbuch Verlag, 2003.

————. *Austerlitz*. Translated by Anthea Bell. New York: Random House, 2001.

————. *Campo Santo*. Edited by Sven Meyer. Munich: Hanser, 2003.

————. *Campo Santo*. Translated by Anthea Bell. New York: Random House, 2005.

————. "Das Geheimnis des rotbraunen Fells: Annäherung an Bruce Chatwins aus Anlass von Nicolas Shakespeares Biographie." *Literaturen* (November 2000): 72–75.

————. "Das Gesetz der Schande—Macht, Messianismus und Exil in Kafkas *Schloß*." In *Unheimliche Heimat*, 87–103. Frankfurt am Main: Fischer Taschenbuch Verlag, 1995.

————. "Das unentdeckte Land: Zur Motivstruktur in Kafkas *Schloß*." In *Die Beschreibung des Unglücks*, 78–102. Frankfurt am Main: Fischer Taschenbuch Verlag, 2003.

————. *Die Beschreibung des Unglücks: Zur österreichischen Literatur von Stifter bis Handke*. Frankfurt am Main: Fischer Taschenbuch Verlag, 2003.

————. *Die Ringe des Saturn: Eine englische Wallfahrt*. Frankfurt am Main: Fischer Taschenbuch Verlag, 1997.

————. "Eine kleine Traverse: Das poetische Werk Ernst Herbecks." In *Die Beschreibung des Unglücks: Zur österreichischen Literatur von Stifter bis Handke*, 131–48. Frankfurt am Main: Fischer Taschenbuch Verlag, 2003.

————. *The Emigrants*. Translated by Michael Hulse. New York: New Directions, 1996,

————. "K.s Auswanderung—Mölkerbastei—Unerschlossen." *Das Zeitschrift für Literatur und Graphik* 10 (1975): 18–19.

————. "Kafka im Kino. Nicht nur, aber auch: Über ein Buch von Hans Zischler." *Frankfurter Rundschau*, January 18, 1997, ZB3.

———. "The Law of Ignominy—Authority, Messianism, and Exile in Kafka's *Castle.*" In *On Kafka—Semi-Centenary Prespectives,* edited by Franz Kuna, 42–59. London, 1976.

———. "*Le promeneur solitaire:* Zur Erinnerung an Robert Walser." In *Logis in einem Landhaus: Über Gottfrid Keller, Johann Peter Hebel, Robert Walser und andere.* Frankfurt am Main: Fischer Taschenbuch Verlag, 2000.

———. *Logis in einem Landhaus: Über Gottfrid Keller, Johann Peter Hebel, Robert Walser und andere.* Frankfurt am Main: Fischer Taschenbuch Verlag, 2000.

———. *Nach der Natur: Ein Elementargedicht.* Nördlingen, Ger.: Greno, 1988.

———. *Schwindel.Gefühle.* Frankfurt am Main: Fischer Taschenbuch Verlag, 1994.

———. "Summa Scientiae. System und Systemkritik bei Elias Canetti." In *Die Beschreibung des Unglücks: Zur österreichischen Literatur von Stifter bis Handke,* 93–102. Frankfurt am Main: Fischer Taschenbuch Verlag, 2003.

———. "Thanatos—Zur Motivstruktur in Kafkas *Schloß.*" *Literatur und Kritik,* no. 66/67 (1972): 399–411.

———. "The Undiscover'd Country—The Death Motif in Kafka's 'Castle.'" *Journal of European Studies,* no. 2 (1972): 22–34.

———. "Tiere, Menschen, Maschinen—Zu Kafkas Evolutionsgeschichten." *Literatur und Kritik* 205–6 (1986): 194–201.

———. *Vertigo.* Translated by Michael Hulse. New York: New Directions, 2000.

———. "Walser im Urwald." *du* 730 (October 2002): 53.

Sebald, W. G., and Michael Hulse. Sebald–Hulse Translation Manuscripts (Letters and Drafts). *2003 M-20." Houghton Library, Harvard University, Cambridge, Mass.

Seelig, Carl. *Wanderungen mit Robert Walser.* Edited by Elio Fröhlich. Frankfurt am Main: Suhrkamp, 1996.

Shakespeare, William. *The Tragedy of Macbeth.* Edited by G. Blackmore Evans. In *The Riverside Shakespeare.* Boston: Houghton Mifflin, 1974.

———. *The Tragedy of Romeo and Juliet.* Edited by G. Blackmore Evans. In *The Riverside Shakespeare.* Boston: Houghton Mifflin, 1974.

———. *The Winter's Tale.* Edited by G. Blackmore Evans. In *The Riverside Shakespeare.* Boston: Houghton Mifflin, 1974.

———. *The Winter's Tale: Texts and Contexts.* Edited by Stephen Orgel. Oxford: Oxford University Press, 1998.

Shechner, Mark. *Up Society's Ass, Copper: Rereading Philip Roth.* Madison: University of Wisconsin Press, 2003.

Shestov, Lev. *Chekhov, and Other Essays.* Edited by Sidney Monas. Ann Arbor: University of Michigan Press, 1966.

Shostak, Debra B. *Philip Roth: Countertexts, Counterlives.* Columbia: University of South Carolina Press, 2004.

Spector, Scott. *Prague Territories: National Conflict and Cultural Innovation in Franz Kafka's Fin de Siécle.* Berkeley: University of California Press, 2000.

Stach, Reiner. *Kafka: Die Jahre der Entscheidungen*. Frankfurt am Main: S. Fischer, 2002.

——. *Kafka: Die Jahre der Erkenntnis*. Frankfurt am Main: S. Fischer, 2008.

Stendhal. *The Charterhouse of Parma*. Translated by Richard Howard. New York: Modern Library, 1999.

——. *The Life of Henry Brulard*. Translated by John Sturrock. New York: Penguin, 1995.

——. *Love*. Translated by Gilbert Sale and Suzanne Sale. New York: Penguin, 1975.

Stölzl, Christoph. *Kafkas böses Böhmen: Zur Sozialgeschichte eines Prager Juden*. Munich: Edition Text + Kritik, 1975.

Szalai, Jennifer. "Harvest of a Quiet Eye: J. M. Coetzee and the Art of Identity." *Harper's Magazine* (July 2004): 85–89.

Svevo, Livia Veneziano. *Memoir of Italo Svevo*. Translated by Isabel Quigly. Marlboro, Vt.: Marlboro, 2001.

Tabbert, Reinbert. "Max in Manchester." *Akzente: Zeitschrift für Literatur* 50.1, special issue, "W. G. Sebald zum Gedächtnis" (2003): 21–30.

Treichel, Hans-Ulrich, Ilse Aichinger, and Imre Kertész. "Kafka und Seine Kinder." *Literaturen*, January/February 2003.

Twain, Mark. *The Complete Essays of Mark Twain*. Edited by Charles Neider. Garden City, N.J.: Doubleday, 1963.

——. *Mark Twain's Letters*. Edited by Albert Bigelow Paine. Vol. 2. New York: AMS, 1975.

Unseld, Joachim. *Franz Kafka: Ein Schriftstellerleben*. Frankfurt am Main: Fischer Taschenbuch Verlag, 1984.

Virgil. *The Aeneid of Virgil: A Verse Translation*. Translated by Allen Mandelbaum. Berkeley: University of California Press, 1982.

Wade, Stephen. *The Imagination in Transit: The Fiction of Philip Roth*. Sheffield: Sheffield Academic Press, 1996.

Wagenbach, Klaus. *Franz Kafka, Bilder aus seinem Leben*. 1st ed. Berlin: Wagenbach, 1983.

——. *Franz Kafka, Bilder aus seinem Leben*. 3rd ed. Berlin: Wagenbach, 2008.

——. *Franz Kafka: Eine Biographie seiner Jugend, 1883–1912*. Bern: Francke, 1958.

——. *Franz Kafka mit Selbstzeugnissen und Bilddokumenten*. Reinbek bei Hamburg: Rowohlt, 1998.

Wagnerová, Alena. *Milena Jesenská*. Frankfurt am Main: Fischer Taschenbuch Verlag, 1997.

——. "Nachwort." In *Franz Kafka: Brief an den Vater*, edited by Hans-Gerd Koch. Berlin: Wagenbach, 2004.

Walser, Robert. *Aufsätze*. Edited by Jochen Greven. Vol. 3 of *Sämtliche Werke in Einzelausgaben*. 20 vols. Frankfurt am Main: Suhrkamp, 1985.

————. *Für die Katz.* Edited by Jochen Greven. Vol. 20 of *Sämtliche Werke in Einzelausgaben.* 20 vols. Frankfurt am Main: Suhrkamp, 1985.

————. *Geschichten.* Edited by Jochen Greven. Vol. 2 of *Sämtliche Werke in Einzelausgaben.* 20 vols. Frankfurt am Main: Suhrkamp, 1985.

————. *Kleine Dichtungen.* Edited by Jochen Greven. Vol. 4, *Sämtliche Werke in Einzelausgaben.* 20 vols. Frankfurt am Main: Suhrkamp, 1985.

Wilson, Edmund. "A Dissenting Opinion on Kafka." In *Kafka: A Collection of Critical Essays,* edited by Ronald D. Gray. Englewood Cliffs, N.J.: Prentice-Hall, 1962.

Wirth-Nesher, Hana. "From Newark to Prague: Roth's Place in the American-Jewish Literary Tradition." In *Reading Philip Roth,* edited by Asher Z. Milbauer and Donald G. Watson. London: Macmillan, 1994.

Wolff, Lynn. "'Das metaphysische Unterfutter der Realität': Recent Publications and Trends in W. G. Sebald Research." Review of *Understanding W. G. Sebald* by Mark R. McCulloh; *W. G. Sebald—A Critical Companion,* ed. J. J. Long and Anne Whitehead; *W. G. Sebald. Mémoire: Transferts: Images/Erinnerung: Übertragungen: Bilder,* ed. Ruth Vogel-Klein; *W. G. Sebald: Politische Archäologie und melancholische Basteli,* ed. Michael Niehaus and Claudia Öhlschlager. *Monatschefte* 99, no. 1 (2007): 78–101.

Wood, James. *The Broken Estate: Essays on Literature and Belief.* New York: Modern Library, 2000.

————. "A Frog's Life." *London Review of Books* 25, no. 20 (2003).

Wood, Michael. "Kafka's China and the Parable of Parables." *Philosophy and Literature* 20, no. 2 (October 1996): 325–37.

Woolf, Virginia. "Robinson Crusoe." In *The Common Reader, Second Series,* 51–58. London: Hogarth, 1965.

————. *The Voyage Out.* San Diego: Harcourt Brace, 1948.

Zimmermann, Hans Dieter. *Der babylonische Dolmetscher: Zu Franz Kafka und Robert Walser.* Frankfurt am Main: Suhrkamp, 1985.

————. *Kafka für Fortgeschrittene.* Munich: C. H. Beck, 2004.

Zischler, Hanns. *Kafka geht ins Kino.* Reinbek bei Hamburg: Rowohlt, 1996.

————. "Kafkas Sätze (14): 'Im Süden ist, glaube ich, alles möglich.'" *Frankfurter Allgemeine Zeitung,* July 18, 2008.

Index

Beyle. *See* Stendhal (Marie-Henri Beyle)

Big Bang theory, 63

Binder, Hartmut, 15, 109, 121, 131, 223n166, 224n195

Bloch, Grete: Kafka's letters to, 66, 99, 225n205

Bloom, Harold, 12, 27, 36, 80–81, 145, 150, 161, 166, 235n62; and *clinamen,* 13, 191; and "creative revisionism," 82; criticizes Roth, 45, 46; quoted, 5, 9, 94, 144, 148, 189

works: *Agon,* 8, 11, 94, 189; *The Anxiety of Influence,* 7–11, 13; *The Breaking of the Vessels,* 8; *Kabbalah and Criticism,* 8; *A Map of Misreading,* 7, 8; *Poetry and Repression,* 8; *Ruin the Sacred Truths* (Charles Eliot Norton lectures), 10, 144; *Shakespeare: The Invention of the Human,* 7; *The Western Canon,* 194n11, 201n25, 235n62

Bohemia, kingdom of, 18, 19, 25, 137; Jewish community of, 24; queen of, 136. *See also* Czechoslovakia

Borges, Jorge Luis, 5, 92; "Pierre Menard, Author of the *Quixote,*" 120

Braun, Else, 132

Braun, Lily, 231n299

Brentano, Clemens, 12, 45

Brod, Max, 15, 20, 129, 159–60, 219n98, 225n203, 227n233; biography of, 41; influence of, 213n9; Kafka's letters to, 21, 28, 32–33, 36, 52, 76, 119, 125, 222n149; quoted, 27, 34, 106, 227n243; and reductive pessimism, 144

Brodkey, Harold, 148

Bruckner, Ferdinand. *See* Tagger, Theodor.

Buber, Martin, 22

Büchner, Georg: *Lenz,* 118

Byron, Lord George, 55

Calasso, Robert: *K,* 6, 220n117

Camus, Albert, 3, 5, 6

Canetti, Elias, 105, 224n189

Casanova de Seingalt, Giovanni Giacomo, 101, 105–7, 114, 115, 117; *Histoire de ma fuite des prisons de la république de Venise qu'on appelle les Plombs,* 106

Catholic League, 136

Celan, Paul, 118

Cellini, Benvenuto, 95

censorship, 37, 40

Cervantes Saavedra, Miguel de, 38, 69, 148, 219n96, 235n64; *Don Quixote,* 128

Chateaubriand, François-Auguste-René, 92

Chatwin, Bruce, 92–93

Chekhov, Anton, 43, 64, 78

Chopin, Frederic, 55

Christianity: conversion to, 21; eschatology, 145; Kafka's "German-Christian General" anecdote, 17; Roth's "Christian friends," 49; Roth's representation of, 38; Twain's letter about, 19

classic, test of, 4, 37

clinamen, concept of, 13, 191

Coetzee, J. M., 4, 6, 14, 35, 37, 132–33; interviews with David Attwell, *see* Attwell, David

works: "Apartheid Thinking," 187; "At the Gate," 63, 147, 148, 176–85, 189; *Disgrace,* 147; dissertation on Samuel Beckett, 12; *Doubling the Point* (co-editor of), 147, 149, 181; *Dusklands,* 147; *Elizabeth Costello,* 7, 12, 146–92; "Eros," 177; essay on *Robinson Crusoe,* 166; *Foe,* 147, 148;

name in, 27; Kafka's study of, 42–43. *See also* Yiddish language and literature

Heilbut, Anthony, 228n251

Heine, Heinrich, 21; *Deutschland: Ein Wintermärchen,* 136, 137

Henel, Heinrich, 150–51; "The End of Kafka's 'The Burrow,'" 155–56

Herbeck, Ernst, 100–104, 119, 130, 134

Herbert, George: "The Collar," 67–68, 72

Herbert, Zbigniew, 180

Herzl, Theodor: "Vanished Times," 19

Herz-Sommer, Alice, 22

High Romantic model. *See* Romanticism

Hilsner, Leopold, 23–24

Hitler, Adolf, 203n64, 224n189

Hofmannsthal, Hugo von, 174, 232n7

Hölderlin, Friedrich: "Bread and Wine," 177; *Hyperion,* 177; "The Titans," 177

Holocaust, the, 5, 49, 50, 141; post-Holocaust views of life, 51, 207n117

Homer: *The Odyssey,* 168, 178

homosexuality, 132–33

Hong, Howard and Edna, 214n18

Horace, 186

"hovering trope," 15–18, 25–26, 32, 33, 34, 70, 89, 196n25

Howard, Richard, 95

Howe, Irving: "Philip Roth Reconsidered," 73

Hrůsová, Anežka, 23–24

Hulse, Michael, 96, 110, 127, 228n254, 230n283, 231n301; Sebald's letter to, 120

Hungary, 5, 23. *See also* Austria-Hungary

Hunter, the. *See* Gracchus (Hunter) figure

Hušek, Jaromír, 23

Iggers, Wilma, 24

Isenschmid, Andreas, 81

Ishiguro, Kazuo, 5

Iyer, Pico, 221n131

James, Henry, 38, 52, 61, 78, 217n66 works: "The Aspern Papers," 47; "The Middle Years," 55, 56, 57, 210n162

James I, king of England, 136

Jesenská, Milena, 201n27; Kafka's letters to, 22–23, 25, 28, 31–32, 37, 106, 197n36

Jews. *See* Judaism

Jonson, Ben, 229n273

Joyce, James, 3, 48, 177, 189, 237n92; *Ulysses,* 4, 166–68, 178

Judaism: ambivalence toward, 32, 36, 58, 76; essays on, 18; Jewish-American identity, 78–79; Jewish upbringing, 52; Jews in Czechoslovakia, 18–20, 23–24; Kafka and, *see* Kafka, Franz (as Jew). *See also* anti-Semitism; Zionism

Jude, Der (periodical), 22

Kafka, Franz, 73, 86; arrives at Riva, 95, 97, 112, 120, 130, (visits Verona en route) 108, 110–11, 115–16, 126–27; audience of, 37; biographies of, 147; as comic, 46, 88–89; criticism of, 3–6, 34; employment of, 25–26; and fictional "K," 15, 30, 70–72, 83–92, 95, 106, 113, 121–22, 135–36, ("Dr. K") 80, 91, 110, 111, 114, 120–33; hovering trope of, 15–18, 25–26, 70, 89, 196n25; illness of, 15, 17, 119, 124, 234n47, 235n53, (death) 119–20; influence of, 11–15, 60, 78, 147, 178–81, 240n149, (on Roth) 6–7, 15, 38–45, 73, 135, 161; influences on, 12–13, 27–29, 147, 215n26; as

Jew, 22–23, 31–34, 35–37, 39, 42, 49, (and anti-Semitism) 18, 20, 25, 28; journals/diaries/notebooks of, 15, 123, 159–60, 222n146, (quoted) 26, 28, 33–34, 38, 42, 129; language/ style of, 16, 20–21, 89, 99, 150–54, 158, 171–72, 180–81, (slaughterhouse imagery) 28; liaison with G. W., 129–30; photographs of, 35, 39, 82, 124, 128, (photograph resembling) 112, 113, 124; postwar fascination with, 3, 39; second fiancée of, 129; and the supernatural, 121; and thoughts of suicide, 199n52; and time relations, 156–59; universalism of, 5; as vegetarian, 28–29; wedding plans, 111, 120, 201n27, (second fiancée) 129

letters, 211n165; to Felice, *see* Bauer, Felice; to Felix Weltsch, 103–4; to Grete Bloch, 66, 99, 225n205; to Max Brod, *see* Brod, Max; to Milena Jesenská, see *Letters to Milena,* below; to Oskar Pollak, 207n116

works: "Advocates," 158; *Aphorisms,* 82, 159, 160, 161, 235nn53,62; "Before the Law," 12, 178–82, 184, 188, 200n77; "The Burrow," 42, 147, (Coetzee on) 149–61, 170, 181, 187; "The Cares of a Family Man," 119, 145, 167; *The Castle,* 15, 37, (Coetzee and) 146, 147, 171, 180, 182–83, 187, (criticized) 4, 6, (death motif in) 81, 85–86, 89, (Sebald's reading of) 80–92, 104, 106, 113, 121–22, 125, 130–31, 134–35, 138, 145, 222n146; *The Collected Stories,* 157; *A Country Doctor: Little Stories,* 59, 134, 138–40, 188; *Description of a Struggle,* 127–28; "Eleven Sons," vii; "Excursion into the Mountains, " 67, 89,

228n255; "First Sorrow," 33; "The Great Wall of China," 158, 183, 188, 232n4; *The Great Wall of China: Unpublished Stories and Prose from the Posthumous Papers,* 161; "He," 15–17, 26, 32; "A Hunger Artist," 33, 190; "The Hunter Gracchus," 67, 91, 109–10, 119, 121, 140, 143, 145, 225n205 (*see also* Gracchus [Hunter] figure); "An Imperial Message," 183, 188, 232n4; "In the Attic," 121, 141–42; "In the Penal Colony," 18, 28, 37, 69, 70, 147, 182; *The Investigations of a Dog,* 33; "Josephine the Singer," 33; "The Judgment," 29–30, 32, 37, 50, 59–60, 62, 64, 70, 182; *Letters to Milena,* 22–23, 25, 28, 31–32, 37, 106; *Letter to His Father,* 15, 29–33, 77, 78, 79; *The Man Who Disappeared,* 223n162; *Meditation,* 228n255; "The Metamorphosis," 5, 32, 34, 37, 50, 70, 113, 221n131; "The Next Village," 158; *Nichts von Judentum,* 32; "Olga's Plans," 90; "On Parables," 163, 170; *Posthumous Writings and Fragments,* 160; "The Problem of Our Laws," 105; *Punishments,* 59, 70, 79; "Reflections on Sin, Suffering, Hope, and the True Way," 159; "A Report to an Academy," 12, 20, 33, 60, 67, 147, 170, 172–77, 242n183; *The Sons,* 59, 70, 79; "The Stoker," 22, 211n181; "To Elsa," 71; "The Trees," 89, 196n25; *The Trial,* 58, 59, 70–72, 84, 89, 113, 126, (audience for) 37, (Coetzee on) 147, 178, 182, 184, 232n6, (criticized) 4–6, (execution scene) 15, 18, 30–31, 105–7, 232n5; "Unmasking of a Confidence Trickster," 127; "Up in the Gallery," 33, 89;

Austerlitz, 12, 92, 96, 218n74, 230n281; author's translations of, 218n74; "Beyle, or Love Is a Madness Most Discreet," 93, 99–100, 111, 113, 121, 128–29; *Campo Santo*, 12, 148; *Describing Misfortune*, 81, 148, 216n46; "Dr. K. Takes the Waters at Riva," 120, 121–22, 133; *The Emigrants (Die Ausgewanderten)*, 12, 81, 89, 92, 96, 119, 218n74, 230n281; *Huntsman Gracchus*, 91–92, 120; "Kafka Goes to the Movies," 127; *Le promeneur solitaire: Zur Erinnerung an Robert Walser*, 102, 130; *Lodgings in a Country House*, 148, 195n32, 216n52, 219n91; *The Rings of Saturn*, 92, 96, 122, 218n74, 221n131; "Il Ritorno in Patria," 99, 121, 134, 138–40, 144, 231n311; *Schwindel. Gefühle/Vertigo*, 7, 12, 80–81, 82–145, 146, 149, 166, (translation of) 96–97, 110, 218n74; "Thanatos," 35, 85, 112, 214n14; *Uncanny Homeland*, 148; "The Undiscover'd Country," 35, 81–91, 93, 97, 104, 108, 112–13, 123, 144, 148, 151, (epigraph for) 214n21, (and Kafka's *Castle*) 130, 134–35, 138, 222n146, (publication of) 121

Seelig, Carl, 219n91; *Wandering with Robert Walser*, 102, 103, 104

Seidel, Walter Müller, 224n195

Selbstwehr (Zionist newspaper), 24

Shakespeare, Nicholas, 92

Shakespeare, William, 3, 7, 12, 37; misreading of, 201n25

works: *As You Like It*, 230n293; *Hamlet*, 214n14; *Macbeth*, 169, 237n93; *Romeo and Juliet*, 93, 144; *The Tempest*, 136; *Venus and Adonis*, 230n293; *The Winter's Tale*, 134, 136, 137–38

Shechner, Mark, 74

Shestov, Lev, 169

Shostak, Debra, 49, 58, 72

Simic, Charles, 218n73

Singer, Isaac Bashevis, 35, 52, 202n52, 204n77

Singer, Israel Joshua, 207n113

Smith, Zadie, 194n12

Solotaroff, Ted, 148

Sontag, Susan, 218n73

Soviet Union: occupies Czechoslovakia, 4; purges in, 54. *See also* Russia

Spector, Scott, 196n24

Stach, Reiner, 125, 129, 199n63

Stade, George, 206n109

Stauffenberg plotters, 186

Steller, Georg Wilhelm, 231n299

Stendhal (Marie-Henri Beyle), 12, 81, 92–99, 103, 114, 128, 133; death of, 98, 119

works: *The Charterhouse of Parma*, 95; *The Life of Henry Brulard*, 93, 95, 98; *Love*, 92, 93–94, 97, 98, 129; "The Salzburg Bough," 95

Stern, James, 132

Štern, Mila: *The Bohemian Sea*, 137

Stevens, Wallace, 8

Stiller, Georg Wilhelm, 219n84

Stölzl, Christoph, 23, 224n195

Streicher, Julius, 50

structuralism and post-structuralism, 150

Süddeutsche Zeitung (newspaper), 22

Suez Canal, 118

surrealism, 36

Svevo, Italo, 232n7

Svevo, Livia Veneziano, 198n51

Swainson, Bill, 110

Syrkin, Marie, 203n64
Szalai, Jennifer, 172

Tabbert, Reinert, 100–101, 217n57
Tagger, Theodor (Ferdinand Bruckner), 120, 223n166; *Die Verbrecher,* 115
Talmud, the, 23, 42
terrorist organization. *See* Organizzazione Ludwig
Tiepolo, Giovanni Battista, 117; *Saint Tecla Liberating the City of Este from the Plague,* 104–5
Tiszaeszlar trial, 23
Tolstoy, Leo, 74, 79
Treichel, Hans-Ulrich, 5
Twain, Mark, 18–19
works: "Concerning the Jews," 23; "Stirring Times in Vienna," 23
Twichell, Joe, 19
twins. *See* double motif

Unseld, Joachim, 41, 223n166

vegetarianism, 28–29
Verdi, Giuseppe: *Aida,* 118–19, 127, 144
Verlaine, Paul, 11
Vietnam war, 61
Virgil, 86; *The Aeneid,* 85, 213n11
Viscontini, Métilde Dembrowski, 95
von Regensburg, Berthold, 86

Wagenbach, Klaus, 16, 147, 221n137, 224n195; *Pictures of a Life,* 112, 128, 140
Wagner, Richard, 65
Wagnerová, Alena, 199n71
Waiblinger, Wilhelm, 219n91
Walser, Robert, 11–12, 16, 45, 232n7; Sebald and, 36, 81, 101–4, 130, 134, 219n91

works: "Brentano: A Phantasy," 45; "From Stendhal," 129; *Jakob von Gunten,* 99; "Kleist in Thun," 129
Wasner, Gerti "G. W.," 128–29, 130
Weich, Martin, 209n139
Weltsch, Felix, 24; Kafka's letter to, 103–4
Werfel, Franz, 32, 123
works: *The Mirror Man,* 21; *Verdi,* 119
West, Paul, 186–87
Whitman, Walt, 8
Wilson, Edmund: "A Dissenting Opinion on Kafka," 3–4, 6
"Winter Queen," 136–37
Wirth-Nesher, Hana, 207n117
Wittgenstein, Ludwig, 92
Wohryzek, Julie, 15, 129
Wood, James, 7, 65, 91, 181, 218n73
Woolf, Virginia, 189, 237n92, 240n148; *The Voyage Out,* 165
Wordsworth, William, 8
Workmen's Accident Insurance Institute, 25
World War I, 18, 25, 59, 114
World War II, 3, 135–36; aerial warfare, 141

Yiddish language and literature, 21, 42, 43, 74–75, 90; Yiddish theater, 24, 215n40

Zaunert, Paul, 121; *Of Mermaids and Goblins and Other Spirits,* 109
Zeno's paradox, 158
Zimmermann, Hans Dieter, 18, 32
Zionism, 19, 22–24, 42, 54, 203n64. *See also* Judaism
Zischler, Hanns, 121, 127, 224n195
Zweig, Arnold, 24; *Ritual Murder in Hungary,* 23

About the Author

Daniel L. Medin is an assistant professor of comparative literature and English at the American University of Paris.